A Decided Novelty

-

The Essential Guide
to
Black Pro Wrestling
History
1880 to 1950

A Decided Novelty

-

The Essential Guide to Black Pro Wrestling History 1880 to 1950

By Ian Douglass

Edited by Oliver Lee Bateman

Copyright Ian Douglass 2025. All Rights Reserved.

Published by:
Darkstream Press

www.darkstreampress.com

All rights reserved. This book may not be reproduced in whole or in part in any form without written permission from the author.

This book is set in Garamond.

10 9 8 7 6 5 4 3 2 1

ISBN 979-8-218-71462-8

This book is dedicated to the memory of

Brian Jean-Joseph

April 30, 1979 — June 23, 2002

Watching wrestling hasn't been nearly as much fun since you left us.

Table of Contents

Foreword 1		2
1	The Cuban Wonder	5
2	Thirty Pounds More	27
3	An Impudent Prosecution	49
4	Smoked German	69
5	The Black Dutchman	95
6	Among the Darker Races	116
7	So Few Negro Wrestlers	139
8	Boss of the Colored Middleweights	162
9	The Kansas City Negro	185
10	Eightball Can't Take It	207
11	The Black Demon	231
12	Color for a Show	254
13	An Unethical Wrestler	276
14	Gentleman Jack	299
15	The Dark Angel	320
16	Luck and Godspeed	341
17	A Large Negro Audience	366
18	Plenty of Color	389
19	The Gold Dust Twins	409
20	For Goodness' Sake	432
21	The So-Called Hero	454
22	Bad for the Box Office	476
23	Mildred, I…	499
24	Unexpected Ability	524
25	Oldest Negro in the Business	545
Epilogue		567
Afterword		572
Editor's Note		576
Acknowledgements		580
Credits		581
About the Author		582

A Decided Novelty

FOREWORD

There's a funny thing about history: Most people take it for granted.

We learn the broad strokes—dates, names, events—and accept them as complete. Rarely do we pause to consider not only how history is made, but how it's recorded, who records it, and what gets left out.

We've all heard the well worn phrase, "history is written by the victors," but the truth is more complicated. Even with the best of intentions, history can be obscured. The person retelling the story may only know fragments of the truth—or may choose to pass along a version that flatters their own legacy. Sometimes, unspoken rivalries, buried resentment, or personal bias silently shape what survives the passage of time. And sometimes, it's just the erosion of time itself. Paper fades. Archives vanish. Websites go offline. Newspapers close. Entire eras can be lost to disaster, neglect, or plain bad luck.

This is true across all facets of history—political, cultural, artistic.

Now consider how chaotic the history of professional wrestling must be—a world built on illusion, where truth and fiction are often indistinguishable by design. Wrestling is a performance sport driven by hype and spectacle, its legacy crafted as much in locker rooms as in the ring. It's an industry where oversight has always been scarce, and where the most elaborate con jobs weren't necessarily aimed at fans, but sometimes came from the wrestlers themselves—battling each other, promoters, and their own physical limits in pursuit of glory before Father Time forced them to pass the torch.

Real-life feuds often outlast the scripted ones. Backstage politics, personal betrayals, and societal shifts crash against the already-blurred lines between kayfabe and reality. The result? A messy, often incomplete archive of what really happened—and who truly mattered.

That is, unless someone comes along with the skill, passion, and relentless dedication to set the record straight. Someone like Ian Douglass.

In recent years, Ian has carved out an impressive legacy of his own. With one acclaimed book after another, he's spotlighted overlooked chapters of wrestling history, uplifted underappreciated figures, and reminded us of just how layered and rich this world truly is. From biographies of beloved wrestling figures to deep dives into regions like The Bahamas, his work doesn't just preserve history—it elevates it.

The book you're holding—*A Decided Novelty*—is the latest, and perhaps most powerful, example of Ian's gift. In these pages, he doesn't just tell forgotten stories. He rewrites the accepted narrative, challenging long-held assumptions about the history of Black professional wrestlers in particular.

Yes, we know the names that are usually celebrated: Bobo Brazil, often likened to Jackie Robinson for breaking barriers. Rocky Johnson and Tony Atlas, the first Black WWF Tag Team Champions. The Junkyard Dog, a larger-than-life presence in Mid-South. Ron Simmons, the first Black World Heavyweight Champion in WCW. All icons.

But what if they weren't the first?

What if the groundwork for their triumphs was laid decades earlier, by men who performed in obscurity, who endured greater challenges in even more unforgiving times, and who were all but erased from the mainstream retelling of wrestling's past?

In *A Decided Novelty*, Ian Douglass takes you on a journey across the United States and beyond, uncovering the lives and legacies of extraordinary athletes—Joe Walcott, Jim Wango, Reginald Siki, and many more—who helped shape the wrestling world long before the spotlight was ready to recognize them.

A Decided Novelty

Like the opening crawl of a *Star Wars* film, this book gives context to a saga already in motion—one too few people realized was even happening. These pioneers weren't just part of wrestling history. They *are* wrestling history. They opened the door for the likes of Booker T, Swerve Strickland, 2 Cold Scorpio, Shelton Benjamin, Bobby Lashley, and countless others who followed.

Their stories might have stayed buried—forgotten by time or ignored by design—if not for Ian Douglass. With rigorous research and compassionate storytelling, he restores their rightful place in the wrestling pantheon. More than that, he reveals the tapestry they helped weave; a fraternity of trailblazers whose impact can still be felt, even if their names were once lost to history.

The lives chronicled in this book are worthy of recognition—and honestly, worthy of adaptation. If *A Decided Novelty* doesn't eventually inspire a streaming series, it would be a cultural oversight.

So as you turn the pages, prepare to be inspired, heartbroken, and enlightened. These men faced adversity not just in the ring but in the world beyond it. And through each match, each journey, each sacrifice, they helped change both professional wrestling and the cultural fabric of America.

After reading this book, you'll be among the fortunate few who understand that wrestling's forgotten history is no less vital than its most celebrated moments.

Thanks to Ian Douglass, this history won't be forgotten again.

Mike Johnson
PWInsider.com and MikeJohnsonWrites.com

A Decided Novelty

1 – The Cuban Wonder

During the presidency of Theodore Roosevelt, and the related push for Americans to immerse themselves in a culture that embraced sports and the pursuit of physical health through painstaking effort, a syndicated news piece from June 1903 made its rounds throughout the Northeastern United States.

In an editorial that was included in the pages of news publications like *The Rochester Democrat and Chronicle*, a sportswriter editorialized about what he perceived to be the disappointing shortage — bordering on total absence — of Black wrestlers in American wrestling rings

"One of the surprising things in the present revival of wrestling is that there are no representative colored champions or clever grapplers," he wrote. "A well-known New York promoter, in speaking of the subject the other night, said: 'Joe Walcott is probably the only negro now before the public who knows anything about the game. He was an expert at wrestling before he became a pugilist, but he took up fighting because there is more money in it.'

"White wrestlers, if there were any negroes in the game, would naturally refuse to meet them. This is one of the reasons, probably, why colored men do not get the opportunity to get into the business. In several of the colored clubs around the country there are plenty of clever negro wrestlers, but they never get a chance to appear in public. I think a carnival between really clever colored wrestlers would be a decided novelty."

The reference to Joe Walcott alludes to one of the clearest instances of boxing's financial allure siphoning promising Black athletes away from organized wrestling. Often referred to as "Barbados Joe" in later years to differentiate him from the future world heavyweight champion "Jersey" Joe Walcott — whose real name was Arnold Cream — Joe Walcott first emerged on the New England combat sports scene in the early 1890s.

Walcott was a member of the Trimount Athletic Club of Boston, a group of athletes who collectively specialized in boxing, wrestling, weightlifting, and general exercise. Through his participation with this club, Walcott was educated in all the athletic elements that the organization prioritized, meaning that he simultaneously trained as both a boxer and wrestler, while developing a standout physique in the process.

Joe Walcott

This also meant that Walcott would alternate between boxing and wrestling depending upon what events were being held on any given day. In February 1892, *The Boston Globe* described Walcott as "the colored boxer and wrestler," as he was equally likely to participate in both forms of combat.

A Decided Novelty

The level of competitive flexibility necessitated by that environment is excellently exemplified by the description of one of Walcott's wrestling matches. At the Union Hall of Cambridge, Walcott participated in the standout event of the evening, which was a grappling contest that pitted him against Patrick Fitzgerald of the Riverside Boat Club.

"Walcott secured his favorite breast lock, brought Fitz on his knees, and forced his man over and square on his back in 1m.54s.," reported *The Globe*. "The matting was then removed, and the fun began with the gloves."

Once Walcott had finished mopping the mat with Fitzgerald in pure wrestling, seven officiated fights took place that evening, none of which featured Walcott, who was easily the club's standout fighter.

Walcott's rise through the local boxing scene would be meteoric, and he turned pro by the end of the year. With that level of pugilistic success, it made no sense for Joe not to specialize exclusively in boxing, and in 1901 he became the first Black fighter to capture the world welterweight championship.

While Walcott's all-around skill on the mat with both holds and fists made him a standout in general, let alone among representatives of his racial group, he wasn't even close to being the first Black wrestler in the Northeast to capture public attention. That distinction is normally laid at the feet of Viro Small, who is frequently credited as the first Black professional wrestler to achieve any semblance of notoriety or fame.

Small was reportedly born into slavery in Buford, South Carolina in 1854, but he was a long way from America's Mid-Atlantic region the first time any notoriety fell his way. That occurred while Small was a member of a Vermont prison work crew and took steps to remove himself from the unfortunate circumstances of his detention.

On December 23, 1878, *The Burlington Free Press* identified Small as one of "four prisoners of the House of Corrections at Rutland" who "took to the woods" after seeing

A Decided Novelty

an opportunity to flee from the barn they had been assigned to work in.

Small is listed in the article as "Viro Small (colored) of St. Albans," and was the only one of the escapees identified as Black. This also would have made him one of a paltry few Black residents of St. Albans, which had just over 7,000 total residents at the time.

Quickly recaptured, Small and his fellow convicts were reprocessed, and news coverage of the incident included each of the felons' nicknames. In this case of the soon-to-be pro wrestling legend, Small was listed in the December 28 edition of *The Free Press* as "Viro Small, *alias* 'Black Sam, hostler, aged 22 years.'"

It wasn't until May 1879 that Small was reported as being legally released from the House of Corrections after completing a five-month sentence for larceny.

If Small's well-rounded athleticism was not properly displayed during his escape attempt, he soon found more socially acceptable ways to demonstrate it. In March 1881 at the Armory in St. Albans, Small finished fourth in a half-mile race over 56 hurdles and then came in third in a one-and-a-half mile run contested during that same afternoon.

Sadly, it seemed like Small could never outrun trouble. Just days after the races, Small and two of his friends were hauled before a judge for their role in the beating of Daniel Prince. According to a story in *The St. Albans Daily Messenger*, Small and his associates somehow lured Prince away from the security of his residence on "The Block," and then "proceeded to kick and beat him as a result of a little rivalry concerning who should be considered the best man of the four."

Apparently, proving that he was the best man in all areas of physical competency was Small's foremost priority. After concluding his business with the St. Albans court, Small returned to his pursuit of competition. That September, he competed in the 220-yard footrace in St. Albans for a $10 prize and finished second.

A Decided Novelty

Then, in November 1881, just two months after the assassination of President James Garfield, *The Fall River Daily Herald* printed word of Small's arrival in New York City. The publication also relayed valuable descriptive information about the physical characteristics of Black Sam.

"Black Sam, who claims to be the champion collar-and-elbow wrestler of Vermont, has arrived in New York, where he is engaged by Owney Geoghegan," declared *The Daily Herald*. "On Monday night, Nov. 21, Black Sam will be ready to enter the arena and wrestle any man in New York, collar-and-elbow, for $25 to $100 a side. He is 24 years of age, stands 5 feet 9 inches, and weighs 190 pounds."

The match that effectively spread the word of Viro Small's advanced wrestling ability well outside of New York took place in April 1882. That was when William Johnson, of Rutland, Vermont, who was regarded as the legitimate middleweight champion of the United States, traveled to New York and wrestled Black Sam, who was being heralded as the colored heavyweight champion of the world. The event took place at a prizefighting establishment owned by Harry Hill, and as Small was classified as a heavyweight, he enjoyed a considerable size advantage over Johnson.

"The first and only bout lasted fifteen minutes, and ended by Black Sam fairly lifting Johnson from his feet and throwing him squarely over the right hip," recounted *The New York Star*, in an article carried as least as far from the city as Cincinnati, Ohio. "As time was due on the next bout, Mr. Hill explained that Johnson, in consideration of the fact that Sam was thirty pounds heavier than himself and was so powerful and tall that he could not keep hold of him, was willing to allow a defeat, and that the stakes should go to Black Sam. This rather impotent conclusion was regretted by many who concurred, however, in the wisdom of Johnson's proposition."

The St. Alban's Daily Messenger would add, "Sam carried off the stakes, and fifty dollars, and a purse of forty dollars made up for him by the spectators."

A Decided Novelty

Black Sam remained quite active in his profession as a wrestler who seemed prepared to take on all comers at the drop of a hat. A report from *The St. Albans Daily Messenger* in May 1882 stated, "A New York Dispatch to the Boston Sunday Times, dated the 13th, says 'Viro Small, better known as Black Sam, of St. Albans, Vt. was matched today to wrestle collar-and-elbow, May 25, with William Kennedy of this city.'"

As well as things seemed to be going for Small, his penchant for associating with violent characters outside of sanctioned wrestling events remained embedded in his personality. In September of the same year, Small was shot in the throat at a local bar by boxer William McCullum and hastily rushed to New York Street Hospital.

"His wound, which is on the left side of the throat, just under the chin, was considered dangerous, but not necessarily fatal," reported *The Sun* of New York City.

The original name attributed to the shooting victim was Samuel Hackett, but this was seemingly a ruse to hide the true identity of the famous wounded party, as "Hackett's name was given at Chambers Street Hospital as Viro Small. He is 29 years old and was known as 'Black Sam, the Wrestler,' and 'the Champion of Vermont.'"

According to eyewitnesses, Small and McCullum got into an altercation, which Small ended by striking McCullum in the face. When McCullum left the bar to regroup, Sam dozed off at a table behind the ice box and remained there well into the morning. At 9:00 a.m., while Small was still sleeping, McCullum returned to the bar with a friend and a revolver.

"A minute after, I heard a shot and saw McCullum standing about four feet from Sam with the revolver in his hand," described Robert Kennedy, a witness to the event. "Then he walked over and struck Sam in the face with the butt end of his revolver... About five minutes after, Sam woke up. He had slept while he was being shot and struck. When he woke, he tried to speak, but he could scarcely use his lower jaw. He finally stuttered out: 'Pick me up and walk me around.' We sent for a policeman."

Later that day, as McCullum sat in custody at the courthouse, a certificate from house surgeon Vanderpool of New York Hospital was presented to Justice Smith stating that Small was in good condition. However, Vanderpool noted that "the bullet, which entered at the neck, cannot be reached."

Viro "Black Sam" Small

Somehow surviving the ordeal, Small continued competing in regular professional wrestling contests with a bullet permanently lodged in his neck, and news of Small eventually wrestling in no less of a venue as Madison Square Garden made its way at least as far as Chicago, Illinois. In February 1883, Small faced Joe Ryan in a collar-and-elbow-style contest at MSG, and *The Chicago Tribune* reported that "the first and third falls were won by 'Black Sam,' Ryan having to content himself with the second."

Two months later, at Clark's Olympic at Eighth & Vine in Philadelphia, Pennsylvania, Small was part of a collection of combat athletes who were advertised to appear, and he was the foremost among the listed athletes based on the placement of his name. The promotional materials proudly declared it to be the "first appearance of Viro Small, better known as Black Sam, champion boxer and wrestler of the world."

It's worth noting that no racial qualifier was added to the proclamation that Small was recognized as a world champion. Granted, the advertisement must be appraised as a piece of pure marketing fantasy, as Small's claim to status as a world wrestling champion was nearly as tenuous as his claim to being a world boxing titleholder. Still, the fact that a Black wrestler in the 19th century was having professions of world title status made on his behalf by a promoter of any sort is extraordinary in and of itself, and the fact that he was competing with a bullet still nestled snugly in his neck only adds to his legend.

Black Sam continued to be advertised as the world champion of all colored wrestlers until at least 1887, although it's quite possible that no other Black wrestlers capable of offering a respectable challenge to his claim on that particular title ever emerged to spar with him. In the meantime, reports indicate that Small was still regularly competing against the best White wrestlers in the nation.

In early March 1887, Small penned a letter to the editor of *The Passaic Daily News* of New Jersey, apparently annoyed that Passaic resident Bill Finnigan had dared to suggest that he could defeat him.

"I hear that Mr. William Finnigan of Passaic thinks he can defeat me in a wrestling match," wrote Small. "Now, I challenge the said Finnigan to wrestle me collar-and-elbow style, best two in three falls, for $100 a side. Time and place of match to be named when money is put up. Viro Small (Black Sam)"

A Decided Novelty

Sam's challenge was the epitome of someone putting their money where their mouth was, as Finnigan was no slouch. At the time, he was recognized as the U.S. middleweight wrestling champion.

Finnigan accepted Small's offer, and each man was required to deposit $100 to guarantee his appearance for the contest, with former world champion Jim Gibbons serving as the referee. With intermissions every half hour, the match between Small and Finnigan lasted one-and-a-half hours until it was ruled a draw.

"The spectators were highly pleased with the exhibition, and all of them were of the opinion that neither was the other's superior," added *The Daily News*. "It is believed that another match will be made between Finnegan and Black Sam at some early date."

The legend of Black Sam died out as professional wrestling became more organized and codified as the 20th century dawned. Appearances by Black wrestlers became rarer, especially amongst those with proven skills, and Black wrestlers who achieved some semblance of notoriety — like Joe Walcott — usually exhibited their wrestling prowess alongside one or two other forms of physical might or mastery.

Such was the case with the curious emergence of Billy A. Clarke in 1900. Commonly referred to by his stage names "The Professor" and "The Colored Hercules," Clarke marketed himself as an all-purpose combatant and strongman. During the summer of 1900, Clarke appeared at several venues in El Paso as "champion prize fighter and all-round wrestler in Mexico."

Although he was hailed as a skilled wrestler of men, the only opponent Clarke reportedly faced during his Texas shows — aside from the four horses he trotted out to engage in coordinated tugs of war with — was a wild bull.

Clarke's first performances were apparently compelling enough to receive positive reviews. *The El Paso Daily Herald* said that Clarke "gave a good exhibition of strength before a small audience," and that he "had succeeded in throwing a

A Decided Novelty

strong and aggressive bull, according to his promise, and the crowd was enthusiastic."

However, working with animals is an unpredictable business, and subsequent reports suggest that events did not always unfold smoothly, or in Clarke's favor. *The Davenport Democrat* carried the story from El Paso all the way to its Iowa readership that Clarke's bovine opponent "managed to get the black athlete on the ground and trample upon him." Clarke was then said to have been carried out of the arena "in a precarious position."

Clarke seems to have departed from Texas under fraught circumstances. As he made his exit from El Paso, Clarke was allegedly asked about his success in the city by a representative of *The Daily Herald*, to whom Clarke is reported to have replied, "I didn't do nothin' at all; there ain't nothin' here for me. El Paso ain't got no use for a nigger nohow."

As the summer drew to a close, Clarke was advertised for a series of shows in Little Rock, Arkansas, and *The Arkansas Democrat* provided interested parties with a description of Clarke and what they should expect to see from the "champion bull wrestler of Mexico and South America" during his act.

"Clarke is a powerful-looking man, with a frame as solid as a mountainside and his limbs and muscles are as hard as iron girders," gushed *The Democrat*. "He conquered Romulus in the city of Mexico recently, and is now traveling the United States looking for contests with pugilists, horses, or oxen. He wrestles bulls, or engages in juggling cannon balls, pulling against four horses, or licking prize fighters. He has traveled extensively throughout South America and Mexico, and his exhibitions have been liberally attended everywhere."

Coincidental to Clarke's arrival in Arkansas, a stern warning reached *The Pine Bluff Daily Graphic* advising fans to be wary of the strongman's authenticity, and calling his credibility into question.

"Last month this so-called 'bull wrestler' gave a fake performance in Fort Worth, Texas, and came near being mobbed by an outraged audience, who had been separated from their money by false promises," contended *The Daily Graphic*. "Let the Little Rock public beware."

Apparently, Clarke failed to attract an audience of spectators to his Little Rock shows that was sufficient to pay off his mounting debts. In late September, *The Arkansas Gazette* notified Little Rock residents that Clarke had been accused of forgery and had abruptly absconded to Pine Bluff once a warrant had been issued for his arrest.

"It seems that the 'Professor' had been giving some exhibitions at Hot Springs, but had failed to attract enough shekels to his money box with which to pay his board bill to Mose Broglin, with whom he was stopping," reported *The Gazette*. "Mose therefore retained a large part of the 'Professor's' paraphernalia as security pending the payment of the $30 board bill."

Clarke was then accused of forging a telegram to Broglin in the name of Ed Moore, a man known by both himself and Broglin, explaining that Broglin should send Clarke's things over, and that Moore would then pay off Clarke's debt. Broglin promptly sent Clarke's items over, but when he approached Moore for payment, Moore said he was "entirely ignorant of the message being sent."

It seems plainly evident that by spring 1901, Clarke had fully transitioned to professional wrestling. In Chicago, Clarke acquired Tom Diggens as his manager, and Diggens called the office of *The Inter Ocean* to complain that he had been attempting to line up a wrestling match between Clarke and Jack Rooney, who was promoted as the world heavyweight champion of Greco-Roman wrestlers in the area. According to Diggens, Rooney's manager Charles Essig replied that Rooney "draws the color line" and refused to compete against Black competitors.

Clarke received his public showcase in September 1901, when he was scheduled to wrestle against Charles Moth of Reedsburg, Wisconsin at the city's armory. *The Reedsburg Times* introduced Clarke as a 210-pound man who had "defeated every Greco-Roman wrestler in the country except Moth and

A Decided Novelty

Whittenore," even though it is difficult to locate a single confirmed report of Clarke climbing into the ring and wrestling against any competitors who lacked prominent horns on their heads.

The bout between Clarke and Moth was promoted as being for the heavyweight championship of America, with Moth as the defending champion. Evidently, Clarke managed to display some competent wrestling ability during their contest, as *The Reedsburg Free Press* stated that it was evident from the outset "that two skillful wrestlers had met."

Illustration of Prof. Billy Clarke

"Every advantage was quickly taken by each until Moth secured a combination hammerlock and half nelson and won the first fall in nine minutes, eight seconds," reported *The Free Press*. "In the second round, Clarke had evidently made up his mind to win, and he set a rapid pace, but again Moth proved too clever and won the second fall in seventeen minutes, this also with a combination hammerlock and half nelson."

A Decided Novelty

Clarke quickly disappeared from the professional wrestling landscape just as suddenly as he had arrived, and it's debatable whether he would have achieved even half the notoriety that came his way had he not been a strongman first, and a wrestler second. More often than not, Black wrestlers of the era who focused their efforts in only one field failed to sustain much attention.

A clear example of this occurred in April 1900, when Black heavyweight wrestler Eugene Stone of Fort Wayne, Indiana was reported by *The South Bend Tribune* as being active in Rhinelander, Wisconsin, and searching for men of a similar size to wrestle against.

The Tribune identified Stone as a curiosity inasmuch as he "carries a Bible with him constantly and is never profane" while abhorring the use of liquor and tobacco.

Apparently, Stone's Midwestern origin and abstemious lifestyle weren't sensational enough to attract eyes. By June, *The New North* of Rhinelander was advertising Stone as the "champion colored wrestler of Texas," while also revealing that arrangements were being made to have him step into the ring for a boxing match.

Nothing much appears to have been made of Stone's wrestling career outside of these few months of activity. However, on the eastern edge of the American Midwestern states, a Black wrestler was just embarking on a career that would bring him unimaginable success, and throughout its duration, no one would even realize he was Black.

Of all the cases of retroactively evaluating the significance of a professional wrestler's career accomplishments, the case of Clarence Eugene Bouldin is perhaps the most complex. Plainly stated, the source of the complication is rooted in the obfuscation — either by choice or compulsion — of his racial identity, and what the revelation of his true racial identity means within the broader context of wrestling history is unlikely to ever be a settled matter.

Bouldin's story is far more comprehensible when told in a straightforward fashion, and it begins in 1873 in

A Decided Novelty

Albuquerque, New Mexico. That's where Bouldin was born on October 7 to Charles Bouldin and Maria Butler. While photographic evidence has confirmed that Maria Butler was of clear Black ancestry, and Clarence Bouldin's facial features display a clear resemblance to his mother, it is equally evident from both anecdotal accounts and visual proof that Clarence Bouldin was light skinned enough to pass for White.

Further, because of the multitude of evasive measures taken by Bouldin over the course of his life with respect to concealing identities and personal information, it is difficult to take many of the supposed facts of his life at face value.

Based on the birth location of Bouldin's brother Harvey, it is believed that Bouldin's family relocated to Missouri early in his childhood. Bouldin then lied about his age and got married to 18-year-old Mamie Vaughn when he was also 18, with the lie being necessary to complete the wedding since the state of Missouri required all prospective husbands to be at least 21-years-of-age during the exchange of nuptials.

It's unknown whether or not Charles and Harvey were already in trouble with the law by the conclusion of their teenage years, but they certainly captured their fair share of negative attention in their 20s. The fact that both brothers had at least partial Black ancestry — but were evidently pale enough to pass as White upon a cursory evaluation — is something that flummoxed the local authorities and resulted in at least one clear case of mistaken identity.

On April 12, 1898, *The Kansas City Journal* reported how Harvey Bouldin, "a negro of very light complexion," had been arrested "on the suspicion of being the 'white' man who assisted Robert Butler, a negro, in holding up W.G. Ennis, a clerk at the Armour Packing Company." That's when Harvey's older sibling Clarence dutifully attempted to spring him from jail.

"His brother, Clarence E. Bouldin, followed the officers to Central police station to furnish bond for Harvey, and Ennis said that if it were not for his brother, he would positively identify Clarence as the man wanted," reported *The*

A Decided Novelty

Journal. "Both were locked up for investigation. Clarence Bouldin is known to have been an associate of Butler, who was arrested the night of the holdup and identified by Enis."

The Kansas City Times focused all of its reporting on the elder Bouldin brother, and disclosed that "Clarence E. Bouldin, a negro," had been arrested, and was in jail as the presumed accomplice of Robert Butler in the holdup of "the Armour packing house, at Ninth street and Michigan avenue."

In 1900, a U.S. Federal census taker visited the Bouldin residence at 1319 Walnut Street in Kansas City, Missouri. Recorded as living at the residence at the time were Clarence Bouldin and his wife Mamie, along with Mamie's mother Mary, her brother Harry, and two additional boarders.

Unsurprisingly, all six residents of the house were listed on the census as Black. In fact, thanks to the passage of an 1835 anti-miscegenation law, it would have been *illegal* for Bouldin and Vaughn to have been married if both of them weren't Black according to the rigid laws of the state. In 1879, another Missouri statute clarified the matter of who was legally Black, and made it illegal for anyone believed to be one-eighth or more Black to wed a White person.

In short, Bouldin had been repeatedly identified as traceably Black in the press, and was also listed as Black in the 1900 U.S. Federal Census. This only becomes a matter of historical interest because of what Bouldin did next… or what he was already in the process of doing.

The fact of the matter is that Bouldin may have already departed from Missouri by the time the census taker reached his legal residence in 1900. Approximately 800 miles away in Cleveland, Ohio, a "Clarence Boldin" claiming to have been a waiter born in Kansas in 1875 was found boarding with nine other residents at 57 Prospect Street. He also identified himself as "White."

If the Clarence Boldin of Prospect Street was identical to the Clarence Bouldin of Kansas City, it would merely be the first in a long series of instances in which Clarence Eugene Bouldin recast himself as unapologetically White once he had

A Decided Novelty

departed from a state that enforced racist Jim Crow laws, and had migrated to a state where it was far easier to live everyday life as a White than as a Black man.

However, before any further legal documents would be signed through which Bouldin could affirm his new White identity, he would undergo a career change so extraordinary that it was worthy of coverage by *The Cleveland Plain Dealer* in June 1901. That's when wrestling trainer Mark Lamb announced that he had identified a pupil in the form of Clarence Bouldin that was prepared to compete against local regular Doc Payne.

Two months later, Walter C. Kelly of *The Buffalo Courier* formally introduced Bouldin to the public as "The Terrible Cuban," the latest and most promising protege of veteran wrestler Prof. Mark Lamb.

"Having known Mark Lamb for years, and being familiar with his judgement related to wrestlers, the writer is inclined to the belief that this Cuban must be of great timber, and a wrestler of more than ordinary ability," noted Kelly.

Now fully cloaked in a phony Cuban identity, Bouldin made a huge splash on the local wrestling scene when he technically bested former world middleweight champion Ed Atherton according to the preconditions of the bout. Atherton was required to subdue Bouldin twice in 60 minutes to declare victory; he barely managed to pin the newcomer one time, with that pinfall coming just before time expired to conclude the match.

"It was a fierce contest, both trying desperately for the mastery," reported *The Buffalo Courier*. "The Cuban was very aggressive, and several times had Atherton in danger. Once the men tumbled from the platform to the floor, both getting bruised arms. The Cuban was behind Atherton at the fifty-ninth minute trying desperately for a throw when Atherton secured an elbow hold and by a sudden roll brought Bouldin to his back. The Cuban, who scaled 149 pounds to Atherton's 160, caused a sensation by his great work. Experts declare that in him Mark Lamb has another champion."

A Decided Novelty

Following the abating of his nickname into the more respectable "Cuban Wonder," Bouldin had a match in October with Cleveland mainstay Doc Payne, and was so aggressive with his tactics right from the opening bell that he threw Payne twice in 30 seconds and left the experienced matman dazed. Bouldin was unrelenting throughout the bout, gaining the support of the fans, and setting the stage for a finish that was frenetic, and also somewhat confusing.

"Bouldin forced one shoulder (to the mat) and then the other, but the referee would not allow the fall, declaring that it was a rolling one," noted *The Cleveland Leader*. "As soon as Payne learned this, he rushed at Bouldin like a demon, making a vicious swing at 'The Cuban Wonder,' but the latter ducked it cleverly. Bouldin rushed Payne to the ropes and tried to throw him into the chairs. Here the police took a hand and separated the contestants, while the large crowd was in an uproar and pandemonium reigned. Bouldin tried to hit Payne, but he was forced to his corner by the police. The people were under the impression that the 'Cuban Wonder' had won, and while Payne was hissed when leaving the mat, Bouldin was given an ovation seldom seen in Cleveland."

The ensuing announcement that referee James Ambrose had ruled the bout a no-contest nearly caused a riot, and the crowd "would not listen to Announcer George Touhey for fully five minutes" after the disappointing declaration had been uttered.

Bouldin immediately began to stalk Ed Atherton through the press, claiming that he could defeat the former world champion in a match that continued until a conclusive finish was reached. In February 1902, the two wrestled at the Monroe Athletic Club in Rochester in an affair that lasted well over an hour. Just as in their first bout, Bouldin surrendered a fall to Atherton just after the 59-minute mark, falling prey to a hammerlock and half nelson.

"The second fall went to Bouldin in 7 minutes on a front lock, which Atherton tried to bridge but found his opponent too strong," continued *The Plain Dealer*. "Atherton

A Decided Novelty

won the final bout with a half Nelson and crotch hold, which he shifted suddenly into a back hammer and crotch. The Cuban was practically put out when he went down for the last time."

The report of the match added that the affair was "probably the best wrestling match ever held in the city of Rochester," but that was likely of little solace to Bouldin.

Pro wrestling's invisible Black star spent the remainder of 1902 in pursuit of a bout with Butch Saar, a Canadian wrestler who had defeated him soundly during the faux Cuban's earliest months of activity. However, when he was unable to secure Saar as an opponent, Bouldin contented himself with a handicap match at Cleveland's League Park, defeating Fred Kalmbach with a half nelson in 11 minutes, and P.F. Beeman with a full nelson in 12 minutes.

As 1903 opened, Bouldin made his debut in New York City and trounced Frank Herrick, the assistant wrestling coach of the New York Athletic Club, in straight falls in front of 1,000 spectators at the New Polo Athletic Club at the corner of 129th Street and Park Avenue.

"After the men had been wrestling more than fifteen minutes, Bouldin, while trying for a long hold, accidentally kicked Herrick in the face and broke his nose," reported *The Sun*. "At the end of the thirty-second minute, Bouldin secured a leg hold with a half Nelson and put the A.C. man down. The match was resumed after fifteen minute's intermission. Herrick's mutilated nose began to bother him at the fortieth minute and the Cuban threw him with a barlock. The time was 48 minutes."

In the aftermath of this exhibition, multi-time American heavyweight champion Tom Jenkins, who was in the midst of training for a match against star heavyweight Frank Gotch, opined to *The Plain Dealer* that Bouldin was the best wrestler in the world in the middleweight division. The next few bouts of Bouldin's would seemingly be wrestled with the intent of proving Jenkins right.

Making his return to Cleveland after several months away, Bouldin "easily disposed of two local wrestlers, Paul Beeman and Widmeyer" at the end of February, downing them in 14 minutes and 13 minutes respectively.

"The bouts served to show that Bouldin has improved wonderfully since he last appeared in public here," added *The Plain Dealer*. "Without a doubt, he is clever and strong enough to give any man of his weight in the business a good battle."

"The Cuban Wonder" Clarence Bouldin

Next up for the Cuban Wonder would be a May match against Butch Saar, against whom Bouldin had been aching for a return bout for nearly two years. The brash Bouldin was quite

A Decided Novelty

vocal in the press, insisting that the outcome this time around would be very different.

"He will catch no greenhorn this time," Bouldin assured *The Plain Dealer*. "When we met before, I hardly knew a thing about the game, and was too easy for him. Now I think I know as much about wrestling as Saar. I know I am stronger, and I tell you that my time in meeting all comers during the last year has not been wasted. If I do not win, I shall be greatly surprised."

The only surprise yielded by the outcome of their match was just how dramatically the tables had turned in two short years, and how thoroughly Bouldin had mastered the intricacies of wrestling. During their first meeting, Saar took two falls from the woefully inexperienced Bouldin in six minutes. The rematch saw Bouldin defeating the elite champion of Canada twice in only nine minutes.

"When the pair stepped into the ring, it was seen that Bouldin was in the pink of condition, while Saar was certainly overweight," observed *The Plain Dealer*. "Although he claimed to weigh only 157 pounds, he looked ten pounds heavier. Bouldin soon assumed the offensive, and at the end of the seven minutes secured a fall with a scissors hold, in which he employed his feet to great advantage. The second fall was too easy, Bouldin soon gaining a double hammer lock, a hold seldom acquired, and pinning the Canadian to the mat, the time being two minutes."

With the most glaring loss on Bouldin's record emphatically avenged, his management team transformed their client's workouts into public exhibitions, offering $25 to any man who could stay in the ring with him for 15 minutes while sparring with him at Cleveland's Star Theater. So great was Bouldin's confidence that he imposed no weight restrictions on his opponents, allowing men who outweighed him by upwards of 20 percent of his body weight to submit their names to the Star Theater's box office and be approved as competitors.

In the early stages of these public exhibitions, Bouldin displayed his ability to "carry" his opponents in the classic sense of the term, allowing bouts to extend past the 10-minute mark before finally defeating his rivals and proving that the outcomes were never truly in doubt.

"Owing to the inability to get a heavy man to meet [Bouldin] yesterday afternoon, 'Kid' Russell was given a chance, and he was on the mat nine minutes and twenty seconds before being downed with a bar and half-nelson," printed *The Leader*. "In the evening, Bouldin met Sam Davis, and this was a clever match in which Bouldin had a chance to show some of his skill and new holds, which surprised even his many friends. He never tried to throw Davis until after the ten minutes were up, being satisfied with trying new holds and experimenting on others. He finally threw Davis in eleven minutes. The crowd appreciated this match."

In early June, experienced wrestler Billy Kurfist just barely managed to last the full 15 minutes against Bouldin. *The Leader* reported that Bouldin had Kurfist in serious danger of being pinned several times, but Kurfist, "cheered on by his many friends in the audience," managed to wriggle free each time, and walked away with $25. Seemingly annoyed at having to part with money, Bouldin and his team quickly arranged a rematch with Kurfist for later that week.

Even before that rematch could materialize, an even worse outcome befell Bouldin during his public exhibitions. This time, his opponent was trained professional wrestler F.W. Kalmbach, whom Bouldin has previously defeated during these same public workouts, and Bouldin apparently paid the price for taking Kalmbach too lightly.

"For the first ten minutes, both men worked hard, Kalmbach taking many chances to gain a fall on the Cuban," explained *The Leader*. "In fact, it was one of the best matches ever seen at the Star Theater, and the crowd went wild. In eleven minutes, Kalmbach had gained a fall on the Cuban, but it was not allowed. This woke up Bouldin, who never showed to better advantage, and after desperate and rough work he was able to down Kalmbach in under two minutes. Many who witnessed the match claimed that Kalmbach ought to have been given the match owing to his gaining the fall on Bouldin, but the terms do not read that way."

In essence, the official terms of the pre-match agreement did not honor pinfalls scored against Bouldin by his opponents; the opponents were required to *prevent* Bouldin from pinning them within 15 minutes. In short, according to the rules, Kalmbach gained no advantage — and therefore no money — from pinning Bouldin, and lost the challenge on that technicality.

Now motivated to restore his reputation, Bouldin defeated Billy Kurfist later that week with a half nelson, preventing the loss of a further $25. The same stunt of issuing open challenges to the public was then duplicated at the Dewey Theater in New York City with $100 on the line. This time, occasional professional wrestler and former U.S. Army 5th Cavalry soldier Frank Idone answered Bouldin's challenge, and the Cuban Wonder wasted no time in defeating Idone in just four minutes and 30 seconds with a half nelson, according to *The Waterbury Democrat*.

With momentum squarely behind him, it would remain to be seen whether or not Bouldin could strengthen his unproven claim to being the best middleweight wrestler in the world. He would receive his opportunity soon enough when presented with a challenge from the most popular wrestler of his generation.

2 – **Thirty Pounds More**

Clarence Bouldin set out to make 1904 an even more successful year for him than 1903 had been. In his first major match of the year, Bouldin looked impressive against Gus "Americus" Schoenlein at Baltimore's Maennerchor Hall in January, but failed to win per the terms of the contest.

Bouldin had promised to record three falls against Americus in an hour, and appeared to be well on his way to doing so when he submitted his opponent with a combination arm-and-leg hold at the 45-minute mark. At that point, Bouldin immediately halted the bout, citing a broken rib that he had suffered during an awkward side roll earlier in the action.

A similar scenario played out at the Lenox Lyceum of New York City when Bouldin faced George Bothner in February. Promising to defeat Bothner twice in an hour, Bouldin forced Bothner to submit to an arm-and-leg hold in just under 48 minutes, but was unable to secure the second fall before the time limit expired.

Although he had suffered what had technically been losses in these latter two matches according to the terms of engagement, Bouldin had still been the most masterful grappler in these bouts, and he made a debatable sort of history with the designation bestowed to him when he visited Minnesota the following month.

Before describing Bouldin's hard training at the St. Paul YMCA under Professor Fred Burns in preparation for his bout with Jim McAuley, *The St. Paul Globe* identified Bouldin as "world's middleweight champion."

This label would probably have made Bouldin the first Black pro wrestling world champion in the U.S., given his significant Black ancestry, if it had been linked to an authentic match. Instead, the newspaper traced Bouldin's title claim to "when he met Americus at Baltimore and won the world's title." Since no title had been advertised as being attainable during the Bouldin-Schoenlein match in Baltimore, and since

Bouldin had technically *lost* the match by failing to defeat Schoenlein three times in an hour, it was an odd contest to use to validate a title claim.

Speaking from a regional perspective, conferring a "world title" to Bouldin may *have* been a way of justifying why a true middleweight like Bouldin was so heavily favored to defeat St. Paul's top heavyweight, who weighed approximately 30 pounds more than the 154-pound Bouldin.

Even if Bouldin's claim to world title status was unjustified, he looked the part of a world champion against McAuley. *The Globe* detailed how "the boy with the yellow skin" fell behind one fall to nothing, then rallied to win the final two decisions.

"McAuley started again on the offensive, and was behind the Cuban continually for the first fifteen minutes, but then he made a fatal mistake, and before he knew it, Bouldin had moved behind and had the local man wrapped up in a full nelson that McAuley could not break," said *The Globe*. "Slowly but surely the Cuban pushed and McAuley's shoulders moved toward the mat. The local man used every ounce of strength, but could not save himself, and went down with both shoulders in the nineteenth minute."

The match's third fall ended similarly, with Bouldin applying a full nelson that McAuley slipped free from, but Bouldin quickly recovered to ensnare McAuley in a half nelson before carefully forcing him into position for a pinfall.

Next up for Bouldin during his tour of Minnesota would be a match with leading Greco-Roman-style heavyweight Charley Moth in Minneapolis. *The Minneapolis Journal* supplied its readers with insight into precisely what characteristics of Bouldin made him such a nightmare on the mat for men who outweighed him by a full 20 percent of his body weight.

"Bouldin is a freak in physical make-up," explained *The Journal*. "Nearly all his weight lies in his shoulders and torso, his legs being ridiculously small as compared with his upper works. His head sets low between his shoulders, and he has practically no neck. This build has proven a great advantage to him in wrestling."

Opting to use slightly different words to describe Bouldin's physique just a few days later, *The Journal* added that Bouldin's "arms, shoulders, and torso are those of a 200-pound man," and that his legs would fit a featherweight. To put it another way, Bouldin had upper-body musculature that was more prodigious than that possessed by most of the heavyweights he faced in what were usually presented as mismatches that disadvantaged him.

The bout between Bouldin and Moth at the small hall on Washington Avenue began with a coin flip, which was won by Bouldin. This meant that the first and third fall — if a third fall was required — would be contested in Bouldin's preferred catch-as-catch-can style. The second fall would be held under Greco-Roman rules, permitting no holding below the waist, and no use of the legs for either offense or defense.

The first two falls went according to logical predictions, with each man winning the fall that matched his preferred wrestling style. The pattern also held for the final fall, which Bouldin won by tying up Moth with his powerful arms.

"Moth made another game fight in the final bout, but he was outclassed by the Cuban's style of wrestling and could only work on the defensive," stated *The Globe*. "For fifteen minutes he broke away from holds in a way that won him the applause of the crowd, but the Cuban continued after him, and at last slipped from a combination hold to a half-nelson and won the match."

The Globe again described Bouldin as "the yellow-skinned boy" in its match coverage. The newspaper would later illustrate this physical trait in promotional materials for "the Cuban's" bout against German wrestler Max Luttbeg. In a detailed drawing depicting Bouldin sparring with a partner, *The Globe* differentiated between the two by sketching Bouldin with dramatically darker skin than his fellow middleweight opponent.

A Decided Novelty

The bout between Luttbeg and Bouldin was advertised as a contest with different championships at stake depending on the region it received media coverage in. As far away as Virginia, it was stated to have been for the U.S. middleweight championship, while in multiple Midwestern states it was advertised as a world title match. Regardless, Bouldin lost the first fall in Luttbeg in 21 minutes before coming back to take the next two in a total of 17 minutes, strengthening his claim to national-championship status at a minimum in several regions of the country.

Illustration of Clarence Bouldin in action

Apparently, *Police Gazette Magazine* agreed with the consensus, as *The Buffalo Enquirer* introduced Bouldin to Buffalonians in late May by stating, "He is a middleweight, and according to the Police Gazette, is the best man at that weight who has been seen in America in many years."

Bouldin's skills were about to be put to their most severe test. Before the month reached its end, he was signed to face Frank Gotch in a handicap match, with the much heavier Gotch required to record two falls against Bouldin inside of an hour in order to claim victory.

Gotch had successfully captured the American heavyweight championship earlier in the year, and while his sights were set on eventually securing an official world title match, he was already being recognized as the world heavyweight champion in some sectors of North America. In the meantime, Gotch would attempt to accomplish the seemingly simple task of dominating a wrestler two full weight divisions below him.

Even though he was facing a serious weight disadvantage against a younger wrestler who also had the edge of several more years of training and competitive experience working in his favor, Bouldin was undaunted, and displayed an overconfidence that bordered on arrogance in his interviews leading up to the June 15 showdown with Gotch.

"I cannot see how Gotch can throw me twice in an hour," Bouldin told *The Plain Dealer*. "I know he is strong, skillful, and the fastest big man on the mat, but I consider myself the strongest man of my size on the mat, and Gotch will have to work very hard to throw me twice in sixty minutes. In fact, I am as strong in my arms and shoulders as any heavyweight, and my speed will enable me to get away from him more than once."

Questioned about Bouldin's remarks by *The Plain Dealer* as soon as he arrived in Cleveland, Gotch appeared to shrug them off, saying, "I have never seen Bouldin but once and have never seen him wrestle, but I think he will have to be an unusually good man for his weight to keep me from throwing him twice in an hour."

After actually trading holds with Bouldin, Gotch minced no words in opining "He's the best man of his weight

A Decided Novelty

in the United States." The remark by Gotch was uttered after a bout in which Bouldin was said to be of equal strength to Gotch, with superior speed, and surrendered only an advantage in size. The result was that Gotch was only able to secure a single fall on Bouldin very late in the match, making Bouldin the technical winner of a bout against the man who was almost universally regarded as the best heavyweight wrestler in America.

"One thing was in Bouldin's favor: That was the temperature," elaborated *The Plain Dealer*. "The weather was so warm that both wrestlers were dripping with perspiration soon after the bout started, making it difficult for Gotch to retain some of his holds. When it came to speed there was nothing to it but Bouldin. Many a time Gotch fell flat on his face or his hands and knees in trying to grab the little fellow effectively. In fact, it was in weight only that Gotch had any advantage."

Apparently believing Bouldin's technical victory over Gotch was a fluke, Swedish heavyweight Hjalmar Lundin met Bouldin in Worcester, Massachusetts. Lundin agreed to the same stipulation: he would need to defeat Bouldin twice in an hour to claim victory. Bouldin sent Lundin home without any falls successfully recorded.

"The match was rough in the extreme," printed *The Plain Dealer*. "Lundin worked hard and showed great strength. He weighed forty pounds more than Bouldin, who looked like a child against the Swedish giant, but Bouldin showed wonderful quickness, and that, coupled with his science, made it easy for him to stall off the gigantic Lundin."

Bouldin then returned to the Star Theater in Cleveland to defeat Jack Munroe in straight falls. The adopted Clevelander turned Munroe's 60-pound weight advantage against him by outmaneuvering him, and then downing him in two straight falls that took less than 25 minutes.

All of this was merely a prelude for Bouldin's title opportunity against Frank Gotch. Even though Bouldin had won his initial match with Gotch according to the stipulations set forth by their management teams, he would now be required to attempt to pin Gotch in a bout that was advertised as a world heavyweight title defense by Gotch against a man whom he outweighed by approximately 30 pounds.

Once again, Bouldin was interviewed by the Cleveland press, and presented himself as someone who was unimpressed by an American heavyweight champion who was now more directly and openly claiming world championship status.

"He's big, but I don't think he is any stronger than I am, and I know he is not as fast, nor does he know as much about the game in spite of the fact that he is champion," proclaimed Bouldin to *The Plain Dealer*.

Meanwhile, Gotch was uncharacteristically confident for a man who had failed to register a fall against Bouldin until 50 minutes had elapsed during their first struggle.

"I feel confident of victory, and think that it is only a question of time when I will have disposed of the 'Cuban Wonder,' though I realize that he is a plucky man," Gotch boasted to *The Leader*. "I believe that I will win this match as I have my others, in straight falls. I confidently expect to win in less than an hour and a half."

In the meantime, the attention Bouldin was receiving in the build-up to his title encounter with Gotch was elevating the level of his celebrity both inside and outside of Cleveland. One week before Bouldin's mid-December match with Gotch, *The Rochester Democrat and Chronicle* tracked him down at his Bible study at the Cleveland YMCA to ask him about the guiding philosophy of his life, as well as how he spent his pro wrestling earnings.

"The money earned by him is spent in the quest of education and culture," reported *The Democrat and Chronicle*. "When he first took up wrestling a few years ago, he did not know how to write or read his own name, and was employed as a laborer on the railroad. His efforts have made him fairly well read and able to discuss intelligently all current topics, and some historical matters."

The interviewer also asked Bouldin if he perceived there to be any incongruity between his identity as a fighter, and his choice to identify as a Christian, noting that Bouldin's regular attendance at the YMCA's Bible study was one of the reasons for its outsized popularity. This religious dimension clearly reflected the broader "muscular Christianity" movement of the era, which sought to reconcile physical prowess with moral virtue — though it was typically evoked by (and reserved for) White Protestant men.

"If a man wants to be square, he can do it just as well in the wrestling world as in the church," replied Bouldin. "I have found that gamblers, saloonkeepers and others who are sometimes considered as questionable characters have as much respect for a square, Christian man as any other man has. It's all a question of what the man is inside, not the atmosphere in which he moves, that decides whether a man can be a Christian or not. I believe the prize fighter could be as good a Christian man as one in any other profession or business."

Perhaps seizing upon the opportunity to press Bouldin more about his past, the article added that Bouldin "was born in St. Louis and has never seen Cuba, in spite of his nickname, 'The Cuban Wonder.'" Bouldin was *not* born in St. Louis as the report stated, but he had provided the first public acknowledgement of his prior life in Missouri, and the fact that he was not of Cuban extraction.

Had the nation known Bouldin's true racial identity — that he qualified to be legally classified as Black in all states with hypodescent laws — the outcome of his match with Gotch would have been even more remarkable. At the very opening of the bout, the 165-pound Bouldin stunned his heavyweight opponent, the referee, and everyone in attendance at Gray's Armory by pinning the world heavyweight title claimant who had not been pinned once since attaining the American heavyweight championship.

"Bouldin gained the first fall in thirteen minutes and forty-five seconds of wrestling when Gotch, in trying to get a cross buttock on him, fell into the hold that Bouldin was after, a half-nelson and crotch hold, and in a second was forced to the mat," illustrated *The Leader*. "It came so suddenly and quickly that Referee Edwards at first appeared to be in a daze, but woke up soon enough to give the Clevelander the fall."

Gotch leaned on Bouldin with all of his weight to force the Cuban's shoulders to the mat 48 minutes into a second fall that left both men the worse for wear. In the third fall, Bouldin appeared to have Gotch in serious danger of losing his championship on two occasions, but Gotch managed to break free both times, and scored a disputed fall at the 19-minute mark.

The Cleveland fans had been under the impression that a wrestler's entire body needed to be down in order for a fall to be counted, but only Bouldin's shoulders were on the mat at the time. *The Leader* noted that Bouldin's friends in the crowd "were angry and hissed the decision."

"This match proved that Bouldin, with a little more weight, say about fifteen pounds, would be in a class by himself," surmised *The Leader*. "In cleverness he showed up far better than Gotch, and it was the latter's weight and long reach that told in the long run. Bouldin's showing was a grand one, and he has made hosts of friends by the manner in which he handled the champion."

For what it's worth, Gotch agreed, and unequivocally stated, "Clarence Bouldin is the best wrestler in the world at his weight, and I stand ready to back him against any man in the country at 165 pounds… if he weighed 30 pounds more he would be holding the world's championship today."

This concession by Frank Gotch that he would have lost to Bouldin if they had met at the same weight was tantamount to an admission that Bouldin should have ranked as the best wrestler in the world pound-for-pound, if such a ranking system existed at the time. At a time when the only Black American to have won a world championship in boxing had been lightweight Joe Gans, the news that arguably the best wrestler in the world was Black would have been a shocking revelation.

Given a night to sleep on his opinion, Gotch even doubled down on it, informing *The Plain Dealer* that the only

A Decided Novelty

two men in the country that Bouldin couldn't defeat, regardless of weight differences, were Gotch and Tom Jenkins, the heavyweight whom Gotch had defeated earlier in the year to become the American heavyweight champion.

"To tell the truth, I would rather wrestle Jenkins than Bouldin," added Gotch. "With Tom, he works cautiously, and you are not kept on the anxious seat as you are with the Cuban. The latter is full of tricks and is so fast that you are afraid to go ahead and take any chances yourself."

At no point were Bouldin's skills displayed more inspiringly than in his bout with Two Feathers, a Native American Indian prodigy who traveled to Cleveland to compete with Bouldin during the opening week of 1905. Standing 6'4" and weighing 227 pounds, Two Feathers absolutely dwarfed the 5'4", 160-pound Bouldin.

Even though the glaring size difference caused the bout to be classified — at least on paper — as an extreme handicap match, it was Bouldin who exposed the vast skill differential between himself and his giant opponent, and revealed that any handicap present in the contest was decidedly in his favor.

In fact, *The Plain Dealer* described how Bouldin "sized up his adversary properly" in five minutes, and then allowed his Native American opponent "to escape hold after hold that looked sufficient to place the Indian square upon his shoulders, being of the apparent belief that it would hardly do to send the crowd home without more than ten or fifteen minutes of wrestling."

"When they had been at it for twenty minutes the Cuban gained a generous round of applause by picking the human toothpick up bodily and twirling him about several times, thus displaying his great strength," proceeded *The Plain Dealer*. "After that, there was nothing to it but the Cuban, and he finally won in forty-eight minutes, throwing Two Feathers bodily to his shoulders and holding him there long enough to gain a fall."

In the aftermath of the decimation of Two Feathers at Bouldin's hands, *The Plain Dealer* informed its readers that the world's best middleweight was being besieged by challenges from all corners of the world, and he intended to only accept the offers that would finally result in some money finding its way into his pockets.

This sentiment followed statements from a clearly frustrated Bouldin who lamented that while he had received his share of glory from pinning Gotch, the heavyweight champion "got the coin" at the end of the night. Bouldin also revealed that Two Feathers would be departing from Cleveland with all of the money from their bout due to the large guarantee he had been promised, even though he had ultimately been "easy meat" for Bouldin.

"I got the decision and the Indian got the money, my share being about as much as was received by those who took part in the preliminaries," Bouldin complained. "Henceforth, I am going to insist on wrestling for a percentage of the gate receipts. This taking what's left after the 'attraction' gets his and the expenses are paid does not pay, especially when I have a good thing with a theatrical company, meeting all comers."

Bouldin's habit of regularly facing any opponent who dared to present him with a challenge at the Star Theater throughout the week had prepared him to contend with challengers of any size, speed, and dimension. Unlike the severe hassle he presented to opponents who were 30 or more pounds heavier than himself, the same was not true when the situation was reversed and Bouldin had his opposition outweighed by a similar margin.

Such was the case when he dealt with lightweight wrestler Joe Gilbert of New York during a mid-April matchup in front of 1,000 spectators at the Star Theater. The observer from *The Cleveland Leader* saw it as "a game fight" in which Gilbert "broke several bad holds" before finally succumbing to Bouldin twice within 20 minutes. The reporter from *The Plain Dealer* saw things differently.

Declaring that the person who paired Bouldin and Gilbert together "had a lot of nerve or was most woefully

A Decided Novelty

gulled," *The Plain Dealer*'s account of the contest saw the bout as a farce that Bouldin could have halted any time he wished.

"In the first place, Bouldin had considerable advantage in weight. That, added to his experience and remarkable strength made it perfectly simple for him to win when he pleased," said *The Plain Dealer*'s report. "But as he did not want to send the crowd home without having provided them with any amusement whatsoever, he let Gilbert stay for sixteen minutes for the first fall. Then to show what he really could do, he downed him in forty-two seconds in the second fall. There is no doubt of Gilbert being a good man for his weight, but he had no business whatsoever against a man like Bouldin."

A wrestler who had serious business to conduct in the ring with a man like Bouldin was Jim Parr of England, who had been accused of ducking Bouldin for two years while alleging that the Cuban Wonder "lacked science and knowledge of the sport." Now that there was attractive money being offered to compete against Bouldin — even if it was a losing proposition — it was now apparently worth absorbing a loss. It was especially true in this case, as the match was contested with the light heavyweight championship of the world on the line.

Just days before the bout between Bouldin and Parr was set to take place, *The Sun* of New York City published what was ostensibly an anodyne article about the scarcity of Black wrestlers in the United States, even in comparison with the number of Black wrestlers that participated in matches in select European venues. Then things took a bizarre turn when Bouldin's name was inserted into the article without any warning or buildup.

"In this country there are very few clever negro grapplers," added *The Sun*. "In fact, there have not been any colored grapplers in America during the past 20 years who have amounted to anything except Claren(ce) Bouldin, who is known as the 'Cuban Wonder,' although he is a pure-blooded negro. Bouldin is a pupil of Tom Jenkins and an exceptionally clever man. He knows a lot about wrestling, but finds it difficult to secure matches on account of his color and skill."

A Decided Novelty

Most allusions to the supposedly competent Black wrestlers in Europe had been akin to the story from that same year of Prince Decco of Dahomey, who faced Gus Rennart in a British wrestling tournament and was easily dispatched by the Englishman on Rennart's way to a showdown with dominant Estonian heavyweight George Hackenschmidt.

Clarence Bouldin flexing for the camera

Aside from the problematic comparison, the bizarre allusion to Bouldin's Blackness was also fraught with either outright errors or era-specific misunderstandings. First of all, the fact that Bouldin was legitimately of significant Sub-Saharan African descent hadn't even been hinted at by the press since the beginning of his wrestling career.

Second, Bouldin had received so many requests to wrestle during the prior two years that it hardly seemed like willing challengers were in short supply to any measurable degree, let alone because of any rumors circulating about his Blackness.

Finally, the idea that Bouldin — a man who had become infamous in Kansas City for his ability to pass as White — could ever have been labeled as a "pure-blooded negro" is laughable. The only explanation would be that the person wielding the term was so steeped in theories of hypodescent that they believed one strand of Black DNA was sufficient to contaminate the genes so thoroughly that the result was a "pure-blooded negro" regardless of the preponderance of other genetic input.

A Decided Novelty

Regardless as to the purity of his Blackness, the surreptitiously Black wrestler would very soon have an unquestioned claim to world title status. On June 13, 1905, Bouldin lost two teeth when he was kicked in the mouth by Jim Parr, but still left the Gray's Armory ring as the light heavyweight champion of the world. The bout was a straight-falls manhandling, in which Bouldin took the first round in just over 31 minutes with a "back hammer," and the second with a scissors hold.

"Bouldin was the aggressor most of the way, and while Parr showed great cleverness he certainly was not Bouldin's match at the weight at which they weighed in, which was 162 1/2 pounds," reported *The Plain Dealer*. "Perhaps at a heavier weight or at catch weights Parr could win, but last night he seemed to have scarcely a chance. Bouldin was fully as clever as his older antagonist and as he was much the stronger it is no surprise that he won."

Immediately following Bouldin's world title win, one of his prior critics, the former editor of *The Buffalo Enquirer* Walter C. Kelley, admitted that Bouldin had indeed ascended to the ranks of the world's most elite wrestlers.

"In justice to the Cuban the writer must admit that he has developed into a wrestler of wonderful ability," conceded Kelley. "He has improved greatly in four years, and is now without question one of the foremost catch-as-catch-can wrestlers of this world. The man that beats this fellow Bouldin at any weight must wrestle at a frightful clip."

Now operating from a position of power as a man recognized in some jurisdictions as both the middleweight and light heavyweight champion of the world, Bouldin was conspicuously inactive for the remainder of 1905, and demonstrated an open and surprising reluctance to engage with any of the top contenders to his championships.

In particular, Bouldin was repeatedly dogged by accusations that he was ducking the challenge of "The Wisconsin Whirlwind" Fred Beell, and in January 1906, *The Marshfield News* of Wisconsin alleged that Bouldin had "persistently dodged making a match with Beell for the last year and a half."

Bouldin effectively admitted as much the following month, but attributed his inactivity to the business opportunities that had become available to him since winning the world title. He informed his hometown newspaper that he had just returned from "piloting a vaudeville show around the one-night stands of the sunny south," and that he would have to resume his training in order to provide an adequate showing against Beell.

"I mean business when I say I will wrestle Beell," insisted Bouldin. "I don't want my Cleveland friends to think I am afraid of him, for I am not. Perhaps he can throw me, but he will have to go some. As I know he is a very good man on the mat, I do not intend to act hastily, as I must be in the best of condition to win. Consequently, I shall take my time."

Bouldin's spell of inactivity extended to April, at which point he returned to accepting open challenges at Cleveland's Empire Theater, with *The Plain Dealer* reminding the public that the world's light heavyweight champion "has been in the theatrical business and has not wrestled for nearly a year," but had several quality wrestlers lining up to challenge him during his open workouts.

In fairness, Bouldin still appeared to be a dominant wrestler even after such a lengthy respite. He made quick work of his two official challengers during his open workouts, downing two 160-pounders — Nitzel and Klima — in 50 seconds and 12 minutes and 25 seconds respectively.

Notwithstanding these frequent public demonstrations of his prowess, Bouldin still refrained from placing either of his championships on the line against any major challengers; in several states, including Tennessee, he was still recognized as the reigning world's middleweight champion when he toured Nashville in November.

"Clarence Bouldin, who gave two moving-picture exhibitions in this city this week, is a prominent personage in the sporting world, being the champion wrestler of the world in the middleweight class," stated *The Nashville News*. "While here, Mr. Bouldin received an offer from the management of an amusement company in Cleveland of $300 for a week's exhibition in wrestling, but he declined the offer."

It's conceivable that Bouldin's absence from the ring, which was perceived by some sports publications as him holding the championships of two weight divisions as hostages, was due to a legitimate illness. Upon his reappearance for public workouts at the Star Theater in February 1907, *The Plain Dealer* attributed his disappearance from serious wrestling as a consequence of the Cuban being "taken with malaria a year ago."

"The Cuban is in his best condition and is training for his match with Fred Beell in the near future," added the article. "He will meet as many as four or five men at every performance and will forfeit $25 for anyone he fails to throw in fifteen minutes."

Bouldin returned to offering public displays of his talents in his adopted hometown, and *The Plain Dealer* reaffirmed that he was the reigning world middleweight champion without mentioning his acquisition of the world light heavyweight championship almost two years earlier. In the first demonstration of his physical capabilities in a year, Bouldin defeated three men in succession at the Star Theater, and provided onlookers with a fair dose of comedy in the process.

"In the afternoon [Bouldin] took on Charles Marotto, a featherweight, and the most amusing match ever witnessed at the Star took place," observed *The Plain Dealer*. "Marotto was as quick as a flash and treated Bouldin to a foot race that lasted nearly five minutes. Finally, the Cuban grabbed a piece of rope and lassoed his man and then tried to tie his feet together so as to prevent his running away. The bout lasted about six minutes and the spectators shrieked with laughter as long as it went. In the evening, the Cuban defeated Otto Suter in eight minutes and Claugh in five minutes."

The event that would serve as the first serious test of Bouldin's abilities since 1905 would be a match pitting the

A Decided Novelty

Cuban Wonder against Greek wrestler William Demetral, and the local newspapers were curious to see how Bouldin would fare against a man 20 pounds heavier than him, and who was "as rough as Gotch." Apparently, the layoff had done little to erode Bouldin's core skills, and he defeated "the Demon Greek" two falls to one in a little over an hour's worth of activity.

"Although the Cuban was outweighed by nearly twenty pounds, he displayed great form, and should he remain in the condition he is in at present, he should be able to hold his own against any of the best in the country," printed *The Plain Dealer*. "After the bout the victor stated that he was ready to meet anyone, but preferred to take Fred Beell on first."

Bouldin may have expressed his desire to face Beell soon after defeating Demetral, but he would have at least two more tune-up matches before the fans would get a chance to see the clash they had awaited for two years. The first match would be against heavyweight Carl Pons — real name Antoine Gonthier of Quebec — who had been exposed four years earlier for attempting to capitalize on the reputation of Paul Pons, the legendary French Greco-Roman wrestling champion.

In front of a disappointing Grays Armory crowd of only 400 fans who had dared to brave a raging thunderstorm to attend the show, Bouldin so thoroughly annihilated Pons that *The Plain Dealer* questioned what business the French-Canadian still had participating in wrestling matches.

"Perhaps, when he was a younger man, Carl Pons, the Frenchman, knew something about wrestling," posited *The Plain Dealer*. "If so, he demonstrated last night at the Grays Armory that he had forgotten a large part of the fundamental principles, for Clarence Bouldin, the Cuban, went around him like a cooper making a barrel and played with him like a cat with a mouse."

The writer heaped on more insults, saying that Pons made a habit of "almost throwing himself a dozen times," and "left openings which even an amateur could take advantage of." But for the fact that Pons outweighed Bouldin by more than 20 pounds and was an expert only at bridging his way out of pinfall attempts, *The Plain Dealer* maintained that Bouldin would have conquered him in far less time than the one hour and eight minutes that it took him, since he was the aggressor the entire time.

Bouldin's next bout — a mid-October match against former lightweight world champion Al Ackerman — was one of the first indications that his career might have finally been on a downward trajectory. For whatever reason, Bouldin weighed in at the bottommost boundary of the heavyweight division at the time, which was 175 pounds, and was significantly heavier than the 158 to 162 pounds that he usually competed at.

It had been hypothesized by no less of an expert as Frank Gotch that a heavier Bouldin would be the most unbeatable wrestler in the world, but the 150-pound Ackerman posed a surprising challenge to him. All the same, Bouldin won the bout at Akron's Perkins Park Rink in straight falls that took a little more than 50 minutes, and *The Akron Beacon Journal* credited Bouldin with attracting the presence of a surprising number of female wrestling fans.

"Sprinkled through the audience were no less than a half hundred ladies, it being one of the largest turnouts of the fair sex ever seen here at a wrestling match," noted *The Beacon Journal*. "The beautiful symmetry of the Cuban's body — his wonderfully developed neck, shoulders, and back — caught their eye, and Bouldin had a host of feminine rooters."

It's unlikely that a sportswriter from *The Beacon Journal*'s staff during the early aughts would have called so much attention to the female admiration being directed toward an athlete's physique if he knew that they were essentially eyeing and sizing up a Black man in public. Indeed, that same revelation made in a Southern state might have been sufficient to get Bouldin lynched.

At long last, the date was finally set for a world championship match between Clarence Bouldin and Fred Beell, and the Wisconsin newspapers exaggerated the extent to

A Decided Novelty

which the long-sought-after bout had been delayed. *The Grand Rapids Tribune* went so far as to brand Bouldin as a coward who had been ducking a showdown with Beell for five full years. While the event had certainly been delayed for an unforgivable length of time, it had been three years rather than five.

Meanwhile, the aggressive promotional efforts in Cleveland for the bout between Bouldin and Beell resulted in an unprecedented level of pre-match publicity in the region. *The Plain Dealer* inserted a massive photo spread of Bouldin into its coverage, informing the public that Bouldin was engaging in everyday farm chores at the home of promoter Mark Lamb, like plowing the soil, sawing wood, swinging a sledgehammer, and hurling bags of wheat as conditioning tactics.

"The bag of wheat weighs 200 pounds, and is suspended from the ceiling by a strong rope," described *Plain Dealer* reporter Harry Neily. "Bouldin takes a position directly behind it, and as the bag swings toward him, he pushes it the other way. He throws it forward with one hand and shoves it back with the other. For the benefit of the neck and upper shoulders, the bag is balanced on the head and worked back and forth. This is good exercise. The luckless newspaperman was inveigled into trying it and knows. Bouldin, though, juggles the sack of wheat as if it was a plaything."

Making note of the fact that Bouldin might have been in the best shape of his life, *The Plain Dealer* also reported that Beell was a 10-to-8 betting favorite. Writer Henry P. Edwards added what would turn out to be an ironic statement that there was "no reason to believe that the match will not be strictly on the level." He also added the ominous observation that if the events were fishy, there would be "no room for the participants in Cleveland," because the local wrestling fans "are wise enough to know a fake when they see it."

The result of the Bouldin-Beell title match was conclusive, but how the finish was achieved and what it ultimately meant to the sport of wrestling would be the subject of much media speculation. The fact of the matter is that

A Decided Novelty

Bouldin lost both the match and his claim to a world wrestling championship following 59 minutes of activity, and the conclusion was steeped in scandal derived from disagreement as to whether the outcome was authentic or fake.

Following 48 minutes of tussling, Bouldin was thrown through the ropes and fell awkwardly on the floor outside of the ring. Claiming that he had been injured by the impact — which he also believed to have been a deliberate infraction of the rules committed by Beell — Bouldin refused to return to the mat to complete the fall, prompting referee Will McKay to disqualify Bouldin and award the first fall to Beell.

"After Beell had been awarded the first fall, Bouldin started for his dressing room but was forced to go back and finish the contest," reported *The Akron Beacon Journal*. "He claimed he had been injured when thrown from the mat by his head and right arm, striking the hard floor, but when told that he would have to finish to get the short end of the purse, he returned to the mat."

Visibly upset by the decision, but apparently desiring to ensure that he would be paid for the match, Bouldin sparred with Beell for 11 more minutes and then "allowed Beell to roll him over without a struggle," which caused the crowd of 4,000 fans who paid between $1 and $3 to watch the bout live to protest loudly that they had been ripped off, according to *The Lincoln Journal Star*.

The Buffalo Enquirer piled on, claiming that Bouldin's act of deliberately lying down for Beell had "probably obliterated him from the mat game, not only in Cleveland for some time to come, but from the game all over the country." *The Journal Star* took things one step further, claiming that the fiasco had altogether "killed the wrestling game in Cleveland."

One day after losing his title in disgrace, Bouldin tracked down a reporter from *The Plain Dealer* to squelch accusations that the entire match had been faked. He proposed a rematch where all Clevelanders would be admitted for free, where there would be "no undue roughness," and for which the mat would be level with the floor so that the potential for injury would be dramatically reduced.

"Bouldin expressed great regret at the unfortunate termination of Tuesday's match, saying that Beell violated previous agreements regarding shoving and work at the edge of the mat, and in so doing put both contestants in danger of serious injury," stated *The Plain Dealer*. "Bouldin says when the referee seemed powerless to prevent the roughness and deviation from scientific wrestling, he was convinced there was no use of prolonging the bout and taking chances of both receiving hurts. Bouldin seemed very sincere in his desires for another match and made the usual proposition, binding it with a forfeit which Beell can cover by calling at this office."

No rematch with Beell was ever granted to Bouldin, who seemingly sought the next best path to redemption. Bouldin issued a challenge to heavyweight champion Frank Gotch that the American heavyweight champion and top contender to what had emerged as the true world heavyweight championship — held at that moment by George Hackenschmidt — would be unable to gain a fall against him in under 15 minutes.

Taking the bait, Gotch arrived in Cleveland one-week later while on his theatrical tour to wrestle Bouldin in one of the faux Cuban's open-challenge sessions at the Star Theater. The event was not without controversy, as promoter Doc Payne announced that 15 minutes had already elapsed while the timekeeper insisted that the pair had only wrestled for 14 minutes. Not wanting to lose the challenge, Gotch pressed onward.

"When Gotch refused to cease wrestling, Doc got a strangle hold on the big fellow and tore him loose," recounted *The Plain Dealer*. "Then Gotch landed on Payne's shoulder and Doc collided with Bouldin with the result that both went to the mat. Great excitement. Great excitement. Excited stagehand lets the curtain down. This angers the boss of the show and he orders it up. Gotch makes a speech and another fifteen-minute bout with Bouldin is arranged."

A Decided Novelty

During the 15-minute rematch, Bouldin avoided Gotch's famed toehold, and worked himself out of a near-pinning predicament when Gotch placed a hammerlock on him. At the conclusion of the 15-minute session, Gotch grudgingly handed $100 over to Bouldin, and then offered an incredulous interview to *The Buffalo Enquirer* while claiming that his travel schedule had left him unfit to take full advantage of the challenge.

"I think I can just about throw the Cuban five times inside of an hour," professed Gotch, after failing to defeat Bouldin even one time in 15 minutes. "I took his measure in those fifteen-minute bouts, and I am dead willing now to take a chance with him for all the gate receipts on the five-falls-an-hour proposition. Of course, you can't go by what happens in these theatrical bouts. A fellow traveling with a theatrical company gets no time for real training, and as a result he has not half the speed that he would have after a regular course of training such as he would take for a real match."

This analysis from Gotch was a far cry from the glowing review that he had offered Bouldin after the most accomplished yet undetected Black wrestler in the world had pinned him as an undersized underdog. Either this was hubris on the part of Gotch, or confidence stemming from the belief that Bouldin had assuredly lost a step in the ring.

Still, scoring something of a victory against America's top heavyweight had enabled Bouldin to salvage a measure of his honor, but the good times would be short-lived. Bouldin's wrestling career would soon be threatened to an even greater extent than his reputation, setting the stage for new Black wrestlers whose heritage was far more obvious to stake their claim to wrestling supremacy.

3 – An Impudent Prosecution

To Clarence Bouldin's great relief, his personal brand had received a boost thanks to his small-scale triumph over heavyweight champion Frank Gotch. Still, he was clearly haunted by accusations that his match with Fred Beell had been fixed, and that he could no longer be trusted to participate in an authentic wrestling bout in front of a paying audience.

By answering former world middleweight champion Walter Willoughby's challenge, Bouldin hoped to regain Cleveland wrestling fans' hearts.

"I want to show the public that I am on the level, and a bout in private where the real money is posted by each wrestler will go some ways to prove it," he told *The Plain Dealer*. "I never have faked, but the public wants to be shown, and I am willing to do it."

A confrontation with Willoughby would take some time to materialize. During that intervening period, Bouldin traveled to Chicago so that he could be a firsthand witness to the official world heavyweight championship match between George Hackenschmidt and Frank Gotch. The title contest was ultimately won by Gotch when Hackenschmidt quit after a two-hour first fall and refused to return for another round.

"Hackenschmidt is one of the cleanest wrestlers I ever saw, and in spite of the fact that Gotch roughed it as much as possible, he did not resort to anything that could possibly be taken as rough work," Bouldin reported to *The Plain Dealer*. "He went fair and square all the way, and his tribute to Gotch's ability after the bout was a straightforward acknowledgement of his superiority."

The remainder of 1908 proved strange for Bouldin. In September, Bouldin won a straight-falls victory over Max Muller, a top German middleweight and training partner of George Hackenschmidt, in East Liverpool, Ohio. The bout appeared to be a decisive win for Bouldin, but *The Plain Dealer* referred to the match as the hardest of Bouldin's career due to the fact that it took nearly one hour and 15 minutes of work for the Cuban to collect the two falls.

One month later, Bouldin informed *The Plain Dealer* that he would be taking some time off from wrestling, stating that it "doesn't pay to do any wrestling until the weather gets cold and the football season is over."

In the middle of his self-imposed wrestling hiatus, Bouldin wandered into one of Walter Willoughby's training sessions shortly before Thanksgiving. It was a pivotal decision, and its fallout would signal the end of Bouldin's time as a serious wrestler.

Willoughby was hard at work inside of the Public Square gymnasium training for a match against John Perelli when Bouldin made a sudden and bizarre overture to hop into the ring and spar with Willoughby "just to keep in condition."

The Plain Dealer explained how surprising this overture from Bouldin had been given the rather acrimonious relationship between the two men. Both men were still regarded as top contenders for the middleweight championship who might very well have been set against one another at a later date to establish who the top contender to the title was early in 1909.

Willoughby accepted Bouldin's offer, and the sparring session between the two quickly devolved into a brutal scrimmage. The impromptu skirmish came to its conclusion when Willoughby "gave the Cuban an extra twist and slam, and Bouldin yelled in pain."

The Buffalo Commercial reported the following day that Bouldin had been diagnosed with a dislocated shoulder accompanied by torn ligaments, while *The Plain Dealer* further disclosed that Bouldin had been forced to cease his training efforts while his arm recovered in a sling.

With that, Bouldin seemed to lose most of his interest in grappling as a competitor, and his only major appearances inside of a wrestling ring during 1909 saw him cast in the role of event promoter. He made a successful return in 1910 to down local wrestler Alex Thomas, but that was just a tune-up bout prior to a far more serious rematch with Gus "Americus" Schoenlein, who was now recognized as the world light heavyweight champion in parts of the Northeastern United States.

Bouldin had manhandled Schoenlein in Baltimore six years earlier, but he revealed to *The Baltimore Sun* that he was now far more engrossed in his career as a road inspector in Cuyahoga County, and therefore was no longer engaged in the same intense training regimen that he had once followed.

Further, *The Sun*'s description of Bouldin seemed to reveal a wrestler who had been resting on his laurels and enjoying the good life, as the reporter took note of the "large diamond horseshoe pin" in Bouldin's tie, the "air of prosperity" that he wore, and the observation that he was seemingly "enjoying a few of the luxuries of the land."

The uncharacteristically heavy Bouldin fell easily to Schoenlein in straight falls, ending his competitive career. Subsequent appearances from Bouldin would see him in the role of wrestling promoter, although he would occasionally turn aside the challenges of less skilled opposition at Cleveland's Empire Theater from time to time.

Bouldin's announcement through *The Plain Dealer* in December of 1910 that he would make a comeback and reclaim his position as one of wrestling's top stars never materialized in a match of significance. For all intents and purposes his wrestling career had reached its end 10 years after his relocation to Cleveland.

The final major references to Bouldin in a wrestling context while he was still alive border on irony. In April of 1913, the arrival of the dark-skinned Black wrestler from Germany — "The Black Panther" Illa Mora Vincent — sparked considerable media attention when the visiting grappler publicly spoke German to the surprise of many American reporters who had never before heard a Black man speaking German.

In several markets, Vincent was quickly relabeled as "Cuban," seemingly because the idea of a Black Cuban was more marketable, palatable, and relatable than that of a Black German. This prompted *The Springfield Union* to make a direct comparison between Vincent and Bouldin on the basis of their shared Cuban heritage, even though neither was Cuban, but *both* were Black.

Decades later, in February 1932, *The Minneapolis Sunday Tribune* very casually reported that Clarence Bouldin, "a Cleveland Negro who wrestled under the monicker 'The Cuban Wonder,'" had joined the Cleveland police department. The paper credited Bouldin with being "exceedingly fast and clever, assets, which with his great strength, made him a match for most of the heavyweights of his time."

This remarkably true revelation remained isolated to the Minneapolis region. Moreover, since Bouldin had been inactive for decades at this point, it was an exposé that could have been easily brushed aside, as none of the accusations of African ancestry that had been leveled against Bouldin during his heyday had ever stuck. Realistically, it's unlikely that the Cleveland police department had any idea that it had delegated a "Cleveland Negro" — who had established a criminal reputation during his former life as a Black man in Missouri — with police powers.

With his wrestling career now conclusively over, Clarence Eugene Bouldin returned to civilian life. His 1917 World War I draft registration card revealed that he had accepted employment as a shipbuilder with the Ohio Shipbuilding Company. Moreover, the card granted Bouldin the opportunity to confirm by his own hand that he was not a Cuban national, as he checked the box indicating that he was a native-born, non-alien citizen of the United States of America.

Most significantly, it confirmed that Bouldin now identified as unapologetically White, checking that box instead of "Negro."

The census also revealed that Bouldin's brother Harvey had relocated to Oklahoma, although he didn't provide Harvey's address. Harvey had gotten married to Izetta M. Baldridge — an acknowledged member of the Oklahoma

A Decided Novelty

Cherokee tribe — in 1912. This meant that Harvey Bouldin was clearly hiding his true racial identity as well, since the laws of Oklahoma prohibited "marriage between Indians and Negroes" at the time.

By 1920, Clarence Bouldin was working as an excavating contractor, and was now in the habit of publicly presenting himself as a younger man along with declaring himself to be White. On the 1920 U.S. Census, in addition to misrepresenting his birth state — and that of both of his parents — as Nebraska, Bouldin informed the census taker that he was born in 1876, and was 44 rather than 47.

Five years later, the 52-year-old Bouldin again lied about his age on his marriage record, representing himself as five years younger. This possibly made the three-decade age gap between himself and his new 22-year-old White wife, Lucy Lamotke, seem less problematic.

While apparently struggling to recall his true age, Bouldin had no difficulty remembering that he was born in New Mexico, or that he had once been previously married, as a note that he was divorced from his first wife was included on his Ohio marriage certificate.

Bouldin lived to the ripe old age of 93 years and 11 months, having listed himself as White on all subsequent census records, and with the physician even certifying him as White on his death certificate. When Bouldin ultimately passed away in September 1967, the Associated Press acknowledged his death, and word of his passing was carried in several North American publications.

Whomever it was that summarized Bouldin's wrestling career to the AP was very generous when it came to conferring laurels upon him. The AP declared that Bouldin had been "middleweight wrestling champion of the world from 1900 to 1912." The article also stated that he had "traveled all over the United States in vaudeville as an Irish tenor and musician."

The death reports omitted two of Bouldin's most remarkable accomplishments. First, that he had lived the first 27 years of his life as Black, only to live the remaining 67 as

A Decided Novelty

White. Second, that Bouldin had, according to the principles of hypodescent inherent in the race laws of his era, quite possibly been the first legitimate Black world wrestling champion in the entirety of the pro wrestling world, and almost certainly the first in North America… and he *knew* it.

Instead of going public with these facts, Bouldin went to the grave with his false public identity as a Cuban intact. Perhaps he believed that it was better to be the symbolic hero of a group to which he had no authentic attachment than to acknowledge his descent from a race of American citizens who had been legally relegated to second-class status, and suffer the consequences of that choice, for better or worse.

An amusing bookend to the Bouldin tale occurred in January 1913, when *The Springfield Daily Courant* published an article about the supposed popularity of Black wrestlers in Europe, and particularly in Sweden. *The Daily Courant* printed the account of Hjalmar Lundin, who had recently competed in a wrestling tournament in Gothenburg, Sweden, and claimed to have met with wrestler George Hackenschmidt and trainer Mike Murphy while he was there.

Lundin listed a series of "queer ideas" the Swedish had with respect to wrestling, starting with their preference for the classic Greco-Roman style of wrestling, and then landing upon what he perceived to be the Scandinavian nation's odd fascination with Black American wrestlers.

"Another queer thing was the popularity of the American negro over there," continued Lundin. "When I found that there was a negro entered in the tournament, I said I would not wrestle with him as I had never wrestled with one in America, and did not intend to there. The managers of the tournament said I would have to or else forfeit a fall. When we went on the mat, I had one hand full of powdered chalk, and when we came together, I plastered the chalk all over the black man's face and it was a funny sight.

"'That's a dirty American trick,' shouted one of the spectators. 'You seem to be fond of black men over here,' I replied, 'and the next time I come over to Sweden I guess I will use burnt cork and make myself popular, as I will have to black up to get a show.' It took me about 20 minutes to get a fall from the negro."

The obvious irony here is that unbeknownst to Lundin — who was apparently an unabashed racist — he had not only wrestled against a much smaller Black man in Bouldin, but had *lost* to him by the stipulations of the match. As such, Bouldin's failure to reveal the entirety of his heritage allowed Lundin to pass away in 1941 without the knowledge that he had been humbled by a Black wrestler while competing in his own athletic prime.

Coincidental with the reign of Bouldin, between 1906 and 1909, Tom Pemberton, a local Medford, Wisconsin boxer involved himself in a handful of wrestling matches, and *The Eau Claire Leader* labeled him as "the champion colored wrestler of the world" even though it doesn't appear that he had many matches to speak of, and none outside of Wisconsin. Such a title would have been entirely superfluous if the public would have known that the simultaneous holder of race-neutral world titles in two separate weight divisions possessed Black heritage.

While Bouldin was capable of concealing his Black heritage from the public, and therefore hid the historic significance of his accomplishments, a Black wrestler whose physical features did not grant him the privilege of secrecy achieved a similar level of success in the United Kingdom during the heart of the reign of King Edward VII, just as Bouldin's career was winding down.

By summer 1907, 25-year-old Frank Crozier was already making waves as a "coloured wrestler" within his home country of Scotland. He was the only wrestler highlighted by *The Wishaw Press and Advertiser* for his participation in a July Highland gathering in Belhaven, East Lothian.

Crozier's later listing in a catch-as-catch-can wrestling tournament in August shows that he represented the Partick region of Glasgow north of the River Clyde, indicating that this is the area where he is mostly likely to have lived and trained.

A Decided Novelty

One year later, *The Evening Standard and St. James Gazette* of London discovered Crozier wrestling as a middleweight representative of Scotland in Hengler's 1908 international catch-as-catch-can wrestling tournament. Crozier made it through two rounds of the semi-final tournament, defeating representatives of Russia and Austria before losing a nearly 50-minute match to American wrestler Sam Anderson in the finals.

Crozier and Anderson had split the first two falls before Anderson grabbed his foot and attempted a toe hold. This was a maneuver that Crozier took clear exception to.

"Crozier came forward and addressed the audience. The toe hold, he said, was not wrestling, and he was confident of beating Anderson if it were left out," illustrated *The Courier*. "Anderson at once took up Crozier's challenge, and a match was agreed on. The business ended in Crozier fastening the championship belt around Anderson's waist."

Crozier lost this title opportunity, but continued his career undaunted. *The Manchester Courier* reported that Crozier was back at it in a July wrestling tournament being held at the Palace of Varieties in Manchester. The paper declared that Crozier and Anderson were likely to be found "battling for possession of the middle-weight championship belt" when all was said and done.

Crozier's first bout with Bob Berry of Wigan was apparently halted by the referee after 55 minutes when fisticuffs were introduced into what was supposed to have been a strict grappling affair. The bout continued the next day after the two combatants had an opportunity to cool off, at which point Crozier secured the win in a total time that exceeded 80 minutes.

After the bout with Berry, Crozier had a far easier time with Ernest Delaloye of Switzerland, besting him in a 24-minute match that *The Courier* described as being well-fought. With that victory, Crozier advanced to the finals and a rematch against his rival Anderson, just as *The Courier* had originally predicted.

A Decided Novelty

For some reason, but potentially because they preferred to only acknowledge those of White Scottish descent as true products of Scotland, *The Manchester Evening News* opted to identify Crozier as Jamaican rather than Scottish. Regardless, it was at this point that Crozier's background was deemed worthy of further exploration by all of the English publications, with *The Courier* identifying Anderson as the middleweight champion of the world, and Crozier as the champion of Great Britain.

"Anderson is being trained by Ernest Delaloye, of Switzerland, and the Jamaican negro is being got into condition by Henry Irslinger, of Austria. It is a genuine money match, and the struggle of mastery is likely to prove a very stiff tussle," stated *The Courier*. "The Swedish American is a demon on the attack, and the black is a past master of the art of defence. The brutal toe hold is barred."

Crozier turned in a much better performance than he had in the prior encounter between the two, although he apparently stayed true to form and remained on the defensive. The result, according to *The Courier*, was that Anderson "did the bulk of the wrestling... however, the American could do anything but pin Crozier, and the result was a draw." The referee called a halt to the action after nearly two hours had elapsed.

As winter rolled around, Crozier entered himself into a wrestling tournament at the Co-operative Hall in the town of Bury just outside of Manchester. He got things started by defeating Edgar Hayes of Prestwich, and then found himself once again engaged in a brutal war with Bob Berry of Wigan.

"When the contest between Berry, of Wigan, and Frank Crozier, of Jamaica, had been in progress fourteen minutes, the Wigan man resorted to a formidable swinging crotch hold and at the same time broke the proscenium rails and fell among the audience," reported *The Courier*. "When the pair gathered themselves together, it was found that Berry had injured his hip bone, and the contest was postponed till today."

Now wrestling into the new year, the two reunited on January 1, 1909, at which point Berry outpointed Crozier in 30

A Decided Novelty

minutes to advance to the tournament finals, which Berry ultimately won.

Having come up just short in either the finals or semi-finals of three consecutive tournaments, Crozier entered the Alhambra Theatre's world championship wrestling tournament in London intent on finally emerging as the clear victor, and a recognized claim to world championship status.

On day one of the tournament, which featured 58 entrants into the middleweight division, Crozier seemed to take exception to the speed with which pinfalls were being counted. *The Daily Mail* recorded that Crozier "lodged an informal protest against the swiftness of the decisions."

From there, Crozier technically defeated Joseph Topping of Bolton twice, when his first fall victory in seven minutes and 50 seconds was disallowed owing to the fact that Crozier had dragged Topping across the press table, and had been cautioned for using "a half-strangle hold." When the action resumed, Crozier bested Topping in just under three minutes.

Then, in what was apparently a common practice, Crozier simultaneously entered the heavyweight bracket, and he beat Celestin Moret of France in less than 10 minutes in the opening round of that weight class. He then dropped back to the middleweight division and crushed Joe Hambley of West Houghton in nearly six minutes.

Apparently, Crozier had bitten off a little bit more than he could chew in competing against the heavyweights; he was ousted from the heavyweight bracket in only two minutes and 35 seconds in the second round thanks to a rapid drubbing by Pat Connolly of Galway, Ireland.

Back in his natural weight division, Crozier recovered to defeat James Foster in 33 minutes with a scissors hold. Then, in more than an hour of action that stretched across two days, Crozier beat Joe Carroll of Hindley, the defending world middleweight champion of the tournament. The ending to the fray was a controversial one, as Crozier won the first fall and Carroll won the second, only to immediately retire due to an injured shoulder. As a result, Crozier advanced to the finals of the world title tournament to face his frequent foe, Bob Berry of Wigan.

On February 8, the Jamaican-Scot Crozier won the Alhambra's wrestling tournament and a claim to world title status by besting Bob Berry in a final bout that once again stretched across two days. Their initial encounter on February 7 lasted a full hour and was ruled a draw, at which point both wrestlers were summoned back to the Alhambra Theatre a day later to determine a conclusive winner.

"When the men took the mat for the resumption of their overnight tussle, both were well received," reported *The Evening Standard and St. James Gazette*. "They opened very cautiously, neither throwing the slightest chance away, and at the expiration of 1 hour and 30 min. no fall had been obtained. Very even exchanges continued, and a few minutes afterwards a rest was ordered for the men to be rubbed down. On resuming, Berry did the major portion of the work, but the black, who was very strong, gained the first fall by the aid of a scissors hold in 1 hr. 45 min.

"After about ten minutes' interval, the second fall was entered upon. This was of short duration, the black again applying the scissors hold, and pinning his opponent, but the fall was disallowed, after a consultation, as Crozier had used a double nelson. At the end of 3 min. 23 sec., however, Berry was beaten, and Crozier secured the second fall and the championship."

The details provided by *The Grimsby Telegraph* indicate that the opening round of the bout was less dull than its duration would suggest, as the action spilled outside of its assigned space on multiple occasions, primarily due to the aggression of Berry.

"It was expected that [Crozier] would win with ease, but the Wigan man did all the forcing, and once in his excitement he rushed his man to the Press seats and pressed him down with such force that the table was smashed to pieces," recounted *The Telegraph*. "On another occasion, Berry rushed Crozier to the footlights, and the tall black disappeared into the orchestra with a crash, while Berry saved himself at the expense of about a dozen incandescent lights. The nigger appeared like a jack-in-the-box a few moments later, little the worse for his startling fall, and at it they went again in the most furious fashion. A second charge at the Press table did Crozier no good, but after indulging in a by no means pleasant bout for an hour, a halt was called, and the contest was postponed until this afternoon."

World middleweight champion Frank Crozier

At the conclusion of the Alhambra wrestling tournament, London's *Sunday Dispatch* assessed the winners of each weight class, and seemed somewhat reluctant to credit the newly crowned world middleweight champion, declaring that Crozier "must be accounted fairly lucky."

"He had to meet Joe Caroll, the holder, after the latter had been badly knocked about by Lomm in the heavies, while he certainly earned disqualification in his final bout with Bob Berry," continued *The Dispatch*. "That apart, however, he is a particularly punishing wrestler, and one who, once on top, is extremely hard to dislodge. His favourite grip is the scissors, and it was chiefly by means of this deadly hold that he won the championship belt."

Conversely, wrestling manager Jack Neill took no exceptions to the manner in which "the all-conquering negro" collected his world championship, and stated as much in an open letter he sent to the sports editor of *The South Wales Argus*.

"The middleweight championship was won right out by one man, Frank Crozier, beating such men as Joe Carroll, Lanritz Neilson, E. Topping, Jack Foster, Job Shambley, Bob Berry, Harry Irslinger, and H. Mills," Neill was quoted. "These men were absolutely the pick of the work in the catch-as-catch-can style, and Crozier won the middleweight championship open to the world by the same hold that Peter Wright beat Bain — the scissors. For Peter Wright and Frank Crozier to meet, it would be worth going a long way to see, for it would be when Greek meets Greek, as both would be at their own game."

Soon thereafter, Crozier entered the offices of *The Argus* in the company of Neill, providing the sportswriters with an opportunity to size up the winner of the Alhambra world's wrestling tournament.

"Crozier, who is a man of colour, is a splendidly developed athlete, 5 ft. 11 in. in height, and wrestles at 11 st. 7 lb.," described *The Argus*. "He is anxious to get on a match with Peter Wright, but is open to meet any man in the world at 11 st. 7 lb."

Several letters were received by *The Argus* from wrestlers issuing challenges to Crozier; the most important of these letters came from Peter Wright — the popular champion at 12 stone, or 168 pounds — who had been called out by both Neill and Crozier.

"In reply to Frank Crozier, whose merits no one can dispute, I am willing to wrestle him for the championship, and I may put forward a splendid opportunity," wrote Wright. "Several gentlemen have offered a purse of £25, to be wrestled for at the Tredegar Hall on May 29, in aid of the Nursing Institute. I am willing to wrestle Crozier on that occasion if he thinks fit; if he will not consent to that, I dare say we can fix up a match under other conditions, either in public or private."

The next day, *The Argus* published Crozier's acceptance of Wright's offer to wrestle at Tredegar Hall through Crozier's now backer and manager, Neill, along with Crozier's agreement to place his world championship belt on the line. Neill wrote that he "shall be only too pleased to hand over the championship belt as a guarantee to those who may be appointed to deal with the match that Frank Crozier shall wrestle Councillor Peter Wright."

Before Crozier would face Wright in an official match with his title belt up for grabs, he would be stalked incessantly by Wright, who decided to crash several of Crozier's open challenges, where the champion had agreed to pay £5 to any man he couldn't pin in less than 15 minutes.

When Crozier advertised that he would be appearing at the Tredegar Hippodrome for three consecutive nights, Wright showed up on two of those nights, and since the two men were essentially equal in their size and skill, Wright was able to effortlessly extend Crozier past the 15-minute mark each time. According to *The Argus*, Wright then donated the £10 he received to the Cottage Hospital.

These two exhibitions served as a prelude to the match between the two, and although Crozier's official title as world middleweight champion would not be on the line, his title belt would be up for grabs if Wright was able to successfully weigh in at 11 stone 7 pounds, or 161 pounds. The winner of the bout was also set to receive a financial prize to the tune of £25.

A Decided Novelty

Given the great anticipation for the unofficial world title match between Crozier and Wright, and with Tredegar Hall "packed from floor to ceiling" with wrestling fans, what ultimately occurred can only be described as an unadulterated fiasco. *The Argus* described how Crozier suddenly burst onto the center platform in the middle of the evening with his coat off and shouted, "I am a British subject, and this is how I am treated!"

"Mr. Joseph, the referee, immediately jumped down from the platform and told Crozier to retire, which he did," continued *The Argus*. "Later, Mr. Joseph said an explanation of the scene was necessary. Mr. Crozier went into the dressing room, and for some reason insulted Councillor Wright and other artistes, including those who had come down from London, as they did last year, in order to assist in the cause of charity. It went so far that he attempted to strike one of the London brigade. The Englishman struck back, and there was a rough-and-tumble for a few minutes, in which Crozier got the worst of it. Crozier put on his coat, and left the building."

Crozier returned to the building, apparently still quite flustered, and when he learned that no holds would be barred during the match, he refused to walk out to the mat to wrestle against Wright. With Crozier absent, Wright then wrestled Alf Hewitt under no-holds-barred rules, and the match proceeded to the time limit without any falls occurring.

In June, Crozier agreed to appear as the referee for a Tredegar Hall event, and while making that appearance, he insisted to a reporter from *The Argus* that he was still willing to wrestle Wright as long as the traditional grappling rules were upheld. Before that could happen, Crozier had a falling out with his manager Jack Neill that was sparked by a rather ridiculous incident.

On the evening of June 19, Neill had Crozier arrested for stealing a promotional photo of himself. *The Argus* reported how Neill "alleged that Crozier took the photo from outside the New Hall, Bargoed" and then he realized it was missing at 6:00 p.m. and assumed that Crozier was the culprit. The photo was later found in the cloak room of the Rhymney Railway Station. Crozier was arrested for the theft while waiting for the train to take him home to Newport, and after he was shuttled to the police station, he insisted that the photo had been his property to begin with.

"I brought the picture from Aberaman to Newport on May 31st," said Crozier. "I saw it this evening outside the hall, and I took it."

That same day, Wright informed *The Argus* that he had no intentions of ever entering into an agreement to wrestle Crozier again after the Tredegar Hall debacle that transpired the last time he agreed to do so.

In the meantime, Crozier had bigger fish to fry, as he was ultimately summoned to court for a hearing related to the alleged theft of his promotional photo. In front of the presiding judge, Jack Neill admitted that three of the photos that were taken indeed belonged to Crozier, but argued that he and Crozier had worked together on equal shares, and that he was therefore entitled to be recompensed for whatever investment he had made in the photos. The judge agreed with Crozier's attorney that the case was "an imprudent prosecution," and quickly dismissed it.

Now freed of Neill's management, Crozier returned to hosting his own open challenges, and seemed to wrestle more aggressively. When wrestler William Klein endeavored to hold off Crozier before the 15-minute time limit during his July 7 exhibition at Tredegar Hall, Crozier managed to secure three falls against him during three separate attempts made later in the same evening.

"All through the encounter, the coloured man was on the aggressive," observed *The Argus*. "He was the more alert, more cool, and in better condition, and although he had by no means an easy task, for he was obviously fatigued at the end, he wrestled scientifically, and Klein could not get out of the deadly scissors holds which he applied. Twice Crozier got the

A Decided Novelty

scissors on, and twice Klein had to give way, the other fall being secured through the application of a half-nelson."

The total time it took Crozier to defeat his opponent three times was just over 25 minutes, which is impressive considering Klein had not been obligated to engage with Crozier, nor to attempt to pin or submit him in order to win the challenge.

Crozier remained active and impressive right up until January 1910, when he re-entered the Alhambra catch-as-catch-can tournament eager to defend his title. *The Weekly Dispatch* stated that "the black is a force to be reckoned with," and added that it was certain that Crozier would "strain every nerve to keep the title he won last year."

Interestingly, *The Dispatch* also seemed to lump Crozier into the same pile as "another dark-skin," the Indian middleweight wrestler Buttan Singh. This was apparently an indication that at least some English citizens of the early 20th century didn't differentiate strongly between their colonial subjects on a continental basis, and seemed to classify them primarily on the basis of skin shade.

In addition to Crozier and Singh, there were 47 other wrestlers competing in the middleweight field, and *The South Wales Argus* regarded it as potentially the strongest division of wrestlers in any of the weight classes, with champions of several nationalities represented, along with former world champions Joe Carroll and Lauritz Neilsen. Still, *The Argus* tabbed Crozier as the clear favorite based on his victory in the prior tournament, and recent match quality.

"Crozier seems to stand out alone, and the fine practice he has had in Parisian tournaments recently fits him for the fray next week," added *The Argus*. "Crozier is a man of colour, with magnificent physique, and should repeat last year's victory."

In his first-round matchup, Crozier looked every bit like a man destined to duplicate his feat of the previous year. He obliterated P.R. Teale in just one minute and 44 seconds, and *The Manchester Courier* said that Crozier "showed all the cleverness that enabled him to win last January, and with his long, strong legs will be a difficult man to beat."

Crozier had a similarly easy time in the second round, eliminating Joseph Topping from the tournament in just two minutes and 15 seconds. Then he squared off with the man who he had displaced as champion the previous year, Joe Carroll.

The most exciting moment of the match occurred when Carroll dove at Crozier's legs and then lifted him onto the press table in the corner, knocking over the water jug in the process, and then turned and heaved him back onto the mat. Despite all of the turmoil, Carroll's tactic still wasn't enough to secure a fall.

When extra time was added to the match, Crozier struck with a half nelson and scored the decisive fall, granting him the satisfaction of silencing the critics who complained that his victory over Carroll the previous year had not been convincing enough.

In the semifinal round, Crozier ran into the other wrestler who the British publications had been describing as "coloured," Buttan Singh. The two men were both sent home to rest after exerting themselves for a full hour and 20 minutes during their February 1 match, with neither of them scoring a fall.

When the action resumed the following day, Singh upset Crozier by defeating him in controversial fashion. The writer from *The Argus* also seemed stunned, explaining to the readers that everyone was under the impression that falls could only be scored via pinfall during the best-of-three-falls match, but the scoring of the match did not reflect that understanding.

"To the general surprise, however, after the men had been together a total time of 2 hr. 12 min. 45 sec. Singh pulled Crozier over and hauled him down," stated *The Argus*. "It was a beautiful effort, but Crozier was out of it like a flash, only to find that a fall had been given against him. Crozier protested rather vigorously, without, of course, producing any effect, and the men were ordered to take the mat again after the customary rest.

"As an exhibition of the art of wrestling it was too one sided to be good. Crozier, although nearly a stone heavier than his rival, was underneath all the time. He was out-generalled at all points, but he was sufficiently strong to defy the Indian to turn him over."

After the wrestlers had competed for an additional one hour and 11 minutes on that second day, the referee turned to Crozier and told him that he would be disqualified if he did not put forth a more aggressive showing and give the impression that he was actually attempting to win.

"The nigger being underneath was afraid to do much, as Singh had fastened his wrists and was trying to put an arm up the back, and at the end of 15 minutes, being spoken to by the referee, the wrestling was stopped, and it was announced that Crozier was disqualified and the verdict given to Singh," concluded *The Argus*. "The decision was popular with the crowd who wanted to see some of the other wrestlers, but seemed to be in opposition to the rules governing the tournament, and in consequence caused not a little hostile criticism."

To summarize what happened, defending champion Crozier entered the best-of-two-falls match expecting only pinfalls would count, yet was eliminated without a single clear pinfall being recorded against him.

Before the month was out, Crozier's former manager Jack Neill rematerialized as the public face of Buttan Singh, the man who had dethroned Crozier. Amusingly, when Singh made his first public appearance alongside Neill — who was set to perform a heavy-club-swinging exhibition — *The Argus* described the Indian middleweight as "a dusky negro."

Following what some people probably considered an unjust loss and the surrendering of his claim to world-title status, Crozier faded into obscurity in wrestling circles. Although he had never competed in the United States, his name was still brought up for at least three years as the

A Decided Novelty

"champion of Africa" that several wrestlers visiting from Europe claimed to have defeated to earn their stripes.

Perhaps to avoid drawing attention to the paucity of active Black American wrestlers at the time — let alone the absence of success achieved by the Black wrestlers who did appear — the fact that Crozier spent a full year recognized as a world champion in Europe was never mentioned in the American press.

Regrettably, there were no overtly Black Americans of comparable status whose primes overlapped with that of Crozier, but that doesn't mean that none of them made respectable attempts to showcase their competence as grapplers. In fact, even while Crozier was reigning at the top of the European mat game, an ambitious wrestler in the central United States had been doing everything he could to make a name for himself and gain respect as "the Black king of Kansas."

4 – Smoked German

Arthur "A.W." Gates was born in Nebraska in 1885, and eventually found his way to Chanute, Kansas. According to interviews he would provide later, Gates began wrestling in 1906, and by 1908, he had developed a reputation as being one of the finest collar-and-elbow wrestlers in the Midwest, and was certainly among the premier wrestlers of Kansas.

Gates arrived in Chanute, Kansas — a town with fewer than 10,000 residents — in August 1908, already possessing tremendous wrestling skills. *The Sun* newspaper of Chanute announced the arrival of Gates and his particular brand of wrestling on August 10 under the headline "Colored Men Will Wrestle."

"Something entirely new to Chanute will be pulled off next Friday evening," promised *The Sun*. "The affair will be a wrestling match between A.W. Gates, from Nebraska, and George Preston, from Parsons, both of whom are negroes. Both contestants claim to have had experience, and the match should be interesting."

After defeating Preston, Gates looked for tougher competition. *The Nowata Times*, an Oklahoma publication, carried word of his victory over another Black wrestler — D.R. Hull of Rochester, New York — during a match that took place in the Sooner State. By the time the ink dried on that article, Gates was already back in Chanute for a bout against F.B. Franks at the local Star Skating Rink.

Word of Gates' wrestling acumen spread, and as he took up residence in Chanute, wrestlers from all areas began to descend upon Chanute to challenge a wrestler who was soon going to be regarded as the best Black wrestler in the United States.

One of the earliest such bouts was a rematch against Hull, now labeled as a Kansas City resident and the colored champion of Missouri. It proved a rare loss for Gates at this career stage. The best-of-two-falls encounter lasted nearly two full hours. Hull won in straight falls, but it took him a full hour to capture the first fall, and another 59 minutes to secure the second. *The Chanute Daily Tribune* reported that Hull won both of the falls with "bar locks."

In April 1909, apparently hoping to capitalize on attention from a Kansas City bout between world champion Frank Gotch and French champion Raoul De Rouen, Gates staged a match in Chanute against Will Allen of St. Joseph, Missouri. The advertisement for the match noted that Gates was now training regularly under D.R. Hull, the Black wrestler who had bested him a few months prior.

Weeks later, Gates competed against Billy Rush of Oklahoma at Booker's Hall in Iola, another small town roughly 20 miles from Chanute. The writer from *The Iola Daily Register* made it abundantly clear that the complexions of the match participants were a contributing factor to the allure of the contest.

"This will be an interesting event, as Gates is the colored champion of Kansas, while Rush is the best white wrestler in Oklahoma," stated *The Daily Register*.

The following day, *The Register* reported that a lot of out-of-towners had descended upon Iola in anticipation of the match between Gates and Rush. The publication also carried the additional news that a match had been added to the undercard of the show, so to speak. There would be an exhibition of wrestling between the referee of the Gates-Rush encounter, and Charles Coffey, "a porter at a local barber shop."

When the appointed hour of the Gates-Rush match arrived, it brought great disappointment to the gatherers who had packed Groomer's Hall to see first-class wrestling action.

"About 9 o'clock, an ADT boy walked into the hall with a message from Rush to the effect that he had sustained a broken leg in a match at Chickasha, Oklahoma, and would be unable to fulfill his engagement in this city," reported *The Register*.

A Decided Novelty

Unwilling to disappoint anyone who had gathered to watch wrestling, Gates stood in front of the crowd and volunteered to take on any challengers who were present that evening, one at a time. Three different would-be wrestlers stepped forward to see how they would fare against the local hero.

"Charles Coffey was the first offender, and he was thrown in 4 minutes and 36 seconds with a toe hold and hammer lock," continued *The Register*. "Referee Shaw was the next victim, and stood the punishment for 4 minutes and 30 seconds. He bumped the mat through the hammer lock and crotch route. Arthur Johnson, the last of the local lights, succeeded in making things lively for Gates for 12 minutes and 12 seconds. His Waterloo was a half nelson and scissor hold."

In August 1909, Gates welcomed Harley Claiborne to the Star Skating Rink of Chanute for a bout that was intended to determine who the wrestling champion of Southern Kansas truly was. Gates pinned Claiborne with a scissor hold and armlock for the first fall, only to lose the second fall via crotch hold. The final 30-minute round elapsed without a clear victor, and the match was declared an inconclusive draw.

The rematch between Gates and Claiborne was held at the Beldorf of Independence, Kansas in February 1910. *The Evening Star* of Independence noted that "nearly half of the audience was composed of colored persons," and the odds are favorable that they went home happy when Gates won his showdown with Claiborne in two consecutive falls.

"The first fall was won by a half nelson and scissor, with left arm hook," noted *The Star*. "The second was won by a rolling fall, and Gates, in his eagerness to hold his man, jammed him in the abdomen with his knee in a way to knock the wind out of him."

After the bout, Claiborne pitched the excuse for his loss that he was "short-winded" because he had been "working in the oil fields of Arizona" for several months. In the meantime, Gates dismissed accusations that the match had been fixed, adding that he "always wrestles on the square." In the meantime, he expressed his desire for a match with Charles Delivuk of Wichita, the recognized champion of Kansas, or his own mentor D.R. Hull, who was still being called the colored champion of Missouri.

In the background of all of this, Gates was forced to contend with the ridicule of wrestler Tim Hurley of Joplin, Missouri. That January, Hurley had taunted Gates in the press, claiming that he could easily take a fall from Gates in under 20 minutes.

Arthur Gates outwrestles an adversary

Gates had a tendency to make haughty foes eat their words. When Gates rolled into Kansas City to face Ed Smith, he was told that the only condition required for him to declare victory was for him to prevent Smith from capturing two falls from him in an hour. Ostensibly, this had something to do with the significant weight advantage Smith had over Gates. Instead, it was Gates who pinned the heavier Smith in 33 minutes with a hammerlock and leg nelson.

Hurley continued to hound Gates into March. He even submitted a letter to the editor of *The Evening Star*, requesting that they put an advertisement in the newspaper to promote him in his efforts to wrestle against Gates.

"I can wrestle Arthur Gates at your town, and I wish to say that I be in shape for the match, for I am training every day 2 hours in the gymnasium good and hard," stated Hurley. "And if Gates trims me, I won't have no kick coming, but that word *if* is a big word sometimes — so I say put a little bet down on me and you won't forget it."

The smart money was *not* on Hurley that night; Gates put him down twice in 44 minutes, in front of another crowd that was very racially mixed.

"Hurley was easy picking for his opponent, who put him to the mat the first time in 26 minutes with a toe hold," reported *The Evening Star*. "Hurley was gritty and went over only after showing remarkable endurance. The second fall came in 18 minutes with a hammer lock."

With the challenge from Hurley now behind him, Gates formalized a match with Charles Delivuk, better known as Karl Von Delivuk. Gates would be a heavy underdog in the match; Delivuk had won wrestling championships in Kansas, Canada, and Austria, in addition to winning the Northwestern championship of the United States in Spokane, Washington three years prior. He also finished third in the catch-as-catch-can tournament held in Buffalo, New York in 1906, where he was defeated by world heavyweight champion Frank Gotch in one hour and six minutes.

Delivuk was clearly irritated by Gates' claim that he was now the rightful wrestling champion of Kansas. He made a public declaration that Gates needed to either meet him for a match, or disavow that he had ever been the champion of Kansas.

A Decided Novelty

The Chanute Daily Tribune received a letter from Delivuk stating that he agreed to face Gates under the terms of a handicap, meaning that Delivuk would technically lose the match and forfeit $25 if he failed to defeat Gates twice in one hour. *The Daily Tribune* also noted that Delivuk was the man responsible for staging the first wrestling match ever held in Chanute.

When Delivuk arrived to face Gates, he told the press, "I am feeling fine. I think I will show them the toe-hold," the move that had become even more synonymous with Frank Gotch since his ascendance to the status of undisputed world heavyweight champion. When informed of Delivuk's bold statement that he had preselected the method by which he would achieve victory, Gates supposedly answered with, "Well, he looks as if he could use it, if any man can."

In the words of the March 19 edition of *The Chanute Daily Tribune*, it turned out that Delivuk "bit off more than he could chew." Yes, the world-class grappler secured a pinfall victory over Gates, but it took him a full 46 minutes to do so, and he failed to achieve a second fall. By the terms of the match, Delivuk had technically lost, and he forfeited $25 directly to his opponent.

"I tried my best to win tonight," Delivuk declared to the fans in attendance. "I couldn't because your home man is a better man than I thought he was. He is a good one. If any of you don't believe it, just go out on that mat with him and try."

Delivuk promptly invited Gates to challenge him for the Kansas state championship on the next convenient evening, but Gates seemed to acknowledge the gaps in skill and experience that existed between them at that point, and essentially disavowed any title claims of his own in the process.

"He gave me the hardest hour's work I ever did in my life," Gates conceded. "I don't think I'm ready to battle for the state championship yet. Three or four weeks from now, I may try it. I have about four matches in sight. This will give me the seasoning that I would need to grapple Delivuk to a finish."

A Decided Novelty

Gates had effectively rejected any notion that he was the true wrestling champion of Kansas, but by holding his own with the Austrian champion who had tussled with the famous Frank Gotch for more than an hour before meeting defeat, Gates began claiming the title of "champion colored wrestler of the United States," and the newspapers began to acknowledge him as such. This added intrigue to his subsequent bouts with Delivuk.

The rematch was on July 4, and was fittingly held in Independence, Kansas. Delivuk scored the first fall on Gates in 18 minutes, only to have Gates turn the tables on the Austrian and capture a fall of his own after a further 19 minutes had elapsed. During the final fall, Delivuk escaped from a pinning predicament and managed to pin Gates at the 20-minute mark to officially retain his title as the recognized champion of Kansas.

Unfortunately for Gates, that would be the closest he would ever get to defeating Delivuk, and he was soundly defeated during the next two bouts between the two. However, even in defeat, Gates managed to make history. When the final bout between the two took place in Wichita in November, *The Wichita Eagle* declared it to be "the first match with a colored man as principal ever staged in this city."

As laudatory as that accomplishment would be, there is some debate as to whether or not it was truly Gates participating in that final match with Delivuk. *The Independence Daily Reporter* alerted its readers in March that there was allegedly another Black wrestler masquerading as Gates in neighboring states, as well as areas of Kansas where Gates had never set foot.

"Gates was seen this morning at his training quarters, and when asked about the Gates in Oklahoma, said he understood there was a colored wrestler in Oklahoma posing as himself for the past year or two, and very frequently he has heard about himself losing or winning matches in Oklahoma, Arkansas, Texas, Kansas, or Missouri, when he would never be any further away than the Brunswick Pool Hall on West Main Street," stated *The Daily Reporter*.

In other words, it's possible that the final bout of note in which fans were treated to an appearance by the true Arthur Gates had been his near miss against Delivuk in the first official state title bout between the two.

Gates had gotten married to Cora Jones of Independence on January 7 of that year, and the pair would become newsworthy three years later for a reason that unfortunately had little to do with wrestling. On April 29, 1914, *The Topeka Daily Capital* would detail how Gates had been shot by his wife, with the bullet entering at Gates' left hip, traveling through his body, and exiting on his right side.

"It is believed [Gates] will recover," stated *The Capital*. "The officers say jealousy was the cause. Gates refuses to prosecute."

While Gates seldom wrestled after the shooting, he had proven to at least some rural American audiences that an identifiably Black wrestler could compete on a level playing field with some of the most accomplished and legitimate catch-as-catch-can wrestlers in the world, even if he lacked years of formal training. Just a few years later, a Black wrestler of foreign extraction would send a similar message while grappling in front of much larger audiences.

It's likely that the man known as Illa Vincent received his start in wrestling around 1906 under the name Illa Kuba, but the first time the name of Illa Vincent was exposed to the English-speaking part of the world was in July 1910 when *The Daily Mirror* of London, England reported on the results of matches that had recently taken place in Switzerland.

"Armand Cherpillod, who claims the world's heavyweight wrestling championship, yesterday failed to throw Illa Vincent, a negro, in four bouts at Chaux de Fonds, and was declared the loser by a referee," reported *The Mirror*.

That a Black wrestler other than Frank Crozier would score any victory over a world heavyweight title claimant was remarkable. Vincent's presence in Switzerland made it even more extraordinary. *The Evening Standard* affirmed as much with its own report of the incident.

"Another negro athlete scored a victory over a white opponent (says our Geneva correspondent) when Illa Vincent, a wrestler, defeated Armand Cherpillod, who claims to be the heavyweight champion of the world," stated *The Standard*. "Cherpillod, who recently won a competition in London, was declared beaten after three and a half rounds. He disputes the decision."

Partially due to the wholesale transformation of pro wrestling into a business that relied on cooperation between opponents and predetermined finishes, the idea that a Black wrestler would be given the visual benefit of a clean win over a world wrestling champion would have been unthinkable, especially in the United States. Making the matter all the more intriguing were the reports from the British papers implying that the only reason Cherpillod emerged from his bout with Vincent still in possession of his championship is because that title had not been on the line during the outing.

It wouldn't be too long after that before Vincent's name would be uttered in the professional wrestling circles of North America. *The Western Laborer* of Omaha, Nebraska made a casual reference to Vincent, declaring that Vincent's manager had been chasing George Hackenschmidt all over England, presumably attempting to secure a match between Vincent and one of the most famous wrestlers in the world.

Early in 1911, during William Howard Taft's presidency, Vincent reached the United States and settled in Chicago alongside several other world-class wrestlers. When reporting on the activities of the elite grapplers that had overrun the Windy City, *The Cincinnati Enquirer* introduced Vincent to its readers as a "smoked German."

It was a colorful allusion to the fact that Vincent's dark skin color was a rare feature among speakers of the German language, at least outside of modern Namibia, which had just concluded three decades as a German colonial possession, along with portions of modern Tanzania, Burundi, and

A Decided Novelty

Botswana. Several of these are also countries where at least one variation of Vincent's originally provided surname — Kuba — is relatively common.

"Illa claims a great variety of habitats, beginning with the East Indies and winding up with the interior of East India," printed *The Enquirer*. "It is a case of 'Illa, wo wohnst du?' The only matches Illa can get are staged at Motts' Pekin Theater, where the ebony gang hangs out, and where dusky championships are decided. The plantation kid can talk only in the language of the Kaiser, and suspicion speaks to the fact that he may have come from Milwaukee."

Unpacking this commentary, it's evident that its writer lacked sufficient understanding of human migration and linguistics to understand the confluence of elements that likely went into the creation of Illa Vincent. The answer to the question "Wo wohnst du?" — or "Where do you live?" — didn't need to be particularly complicated, even if the description of Vincent as being of partial East Indian descent also happened to be true.

Based upon events that were to follow, it's likely that the writer intended to say "beginning with the *West* Indies" when describing Vincent's point of origin. The forename Illa and surname Vincent are both very common in territories of Africa and the Caribbean that were colonized by France, and especially in Haiti.

Moreover, Indian indentured servitude in the aftermath of the abolition of slavery contributed to the mass migration of India natives to several areas of the Caribbean. Intermarriage between Blacks and Indians in the Caribbean became quite common, resulting in the creation of the term "dougla" to describe the offspring of such unions in multiple locales within the Anglophone Caribbean.

On the other hand, as it is perhaps even more likely that Vincent was from German East Africa (modern-day Tanzania, Rwanda, and Burundi) — which had been one of the recipients of the nearly 800,000 Indian migrants who had been shipped to South and East Africa beginning in the late 1800s

A Decided Novelty

— it was also entirely possible for the same intermarriage scenario to have occurred outside of a New World environment.

Illa Vincent

In short, for a dark-skinned Black man with a French-sounding (albeit likely false) surname to have claimed both Afro-Caribbean and East Indian identities would not have taken a huge leap in logic for anyone who had spent more than a couple of minutes contemplating the history and demographics of the Caribbean. All the same, this ignores the most likely scenario of Vincent having roots in one of Germany's colonial possessions in Africa on the basis of his mastery of German, and his original surname's frequency in that region.

Regardless as to his point of origin, it *is* true that Vincent's complexion made him an attraction at the Pekin Theater, often cited as the first Black-owned theater in Chicago, which was situated at 2700 S. State Street. Bob Motts, the proprietor of the venue, promoted Vincent as a wrestler capable of turning back Youssif Mahmout following the Turkish wrestling champion's boast that he could defeat any wrestler under circumstances in which he faced a severe handicap.

"Motts also has a grievance because the managers of Mahmout, who have been saying their man could throw all the wrestlers in the country many times an hour, have turned down his offer to bet $1,000 that Mahmout cannot throw Vincent three times in thirty minutes," reported *The Inter Ocean* of Chicago. "He said last night that they had offered to take on Vincent, but when he went to them with the money they drew the color line. Bob fails to see where the Turk has any call to draw the color line against the West Indian negro."

By the end of March, the writer from *The Cincinnati Enquirer*, apparently now convinced at least of Illa Vincent's provable experience as a European wrestler, had included Vincent — who he insisted on dubbing "The German Smoke" — on his list of German wrestlers who had "met with more or less indifferent success" since arriving in the United States.

Vincent also competed in events beyond wrestling to earn a living. Very early in May, *Chicago Tribune* writer Walter H. Eckersall mentioned how a large crowd at O'Connell's Gymnasium was given a treat when Navy champion Phil Schlossberg squared off against Vincent in an impromptu boxing match.

"The sailor was too much for the wrestler with pugilistic aspirations, and Vincent was compelled to quit in the second round," noted Eckersall. "The colored man would have called 'quits' earlier in the fray if he had been able to speak English."

In late September, Vincent emerged from a seasonal absence, and was labeled "The Black Panther" for a match at Schorling's Park against "The Danish Demon" Jack Peterson. The bout was advertised as the chief entertainment of a Columbus Day event that included "broad and high jumping, fungo ball hitting, base running, pole vaulting, and foot races." The fact that tickets for the show were available at the Pekin Theater suggests that Bob Motts was directly involved in the promotion of the show.

"Illa Vincent, the Black Panther, who has easily floored every giant who has attempted to stand up before him on the stage of the Pekin Theater, and Jack Peterson, the Danish Demon, will engage in a fair and square wrestling bout for the benefit of the Dearborn Center Day Nursery, which is run in connection with the Institutional Church, 3825 Dearborn st., and the affair promises to be the greatest sporting event of the season and no fake," insisted *The Broad Ax*.

One week later, *The Broad Ax* further reported that Jack Peterson had "shown the white feather" — meaning that he had decided to act in a cowardly fashion — and withdrawn from his scheduled bout with Vincent. "The German Thunderbolt" Frank Ehler was quickly offered as a substitute for Peterson, ensuring that the fans who gathered at Schorling's Park would still get to watch some wrestling action.

When it was all over, Vincent was declared the winner of the bout, "having laid Frank Ehler low on his broad back, catch-as-catch-can, in the best two out of three falls in 20 minutes time."

"At the end of the bouts, Vincent was carried to his quarters on the shoulders of some of his friends amidst the shouts of those who are always willing to lay down a little something on his ability to wrestle and toss over his head all-comers," reported *The Broad Ax*. "It can be said to the great

A Decided Novelty

credit of the promoters of the whole affair, namely, that the wrestling match was on the square."

The extent to which Illa had carved out a fanbase amongst the Black residents of the Windy City is evidenced by the reports of how his bouts at the Pekin Theater were received. In November, *The Broad Ax* described how one of Vincent's wrestling bouts capped a full day of acts ranging from vaudeville to performances from organized acting companies. Then, when it was time for Vincent to make an appearance, "the mat lovers began to flock in."

"When the first bout began not a vacant seat was to be had," stated *The Broad Ax*. "Many ladies were unable to get seats. Quite a number were disappointed. Two very exciting bouts took place, both being won by the Colored champion and the Douglas Club champion. Tuesday night, Vincent was returned the winner of a 30 minute's handicap."

Outside of the confines of the Pekin Theater is where Illa Vincent first began getting referred to as Cuban; *The Inter Ocean* specifically labeled him as such when he was announced as a competitor at a Riverview Rink show featuring several European performers. From then on, it became a label that was consistently applied to Vincent despite the fact that the only clues to Vincent's background that had ever been displayed were his German-language mastery, his dark skin, and his fully French ring name — including a forename that literally means "from the island."

Even outside of the buildings in which he held a theoretical home-venue advantage of a racial sort, Vincent could still expect to be booked to be victorious, such as when he beat German wrestler Carl Schultz in straight falls at the Riverview event, and defeated Joe Wallace at the next event held there in early December.

From there, the action moved back inside of the Pekin Theater, where Motts managed to book a headlining bout between Illa Vincent and Sampson, the German strong man. As Sampson reportedly weighed 265 pounds against Vincent's 195 pounds, the stipulations of the match required Sampson to

A Decided Novelty

defeat Vincent twice within 30 minutes in order to be declared the winner.

"All who are fortunate enough to see these great athletes in a grueling contest will see the wonderful Black struggling to sustain his unbroken record and defend his reputation, justly styled the 'Black Panther,'" stated *The Broad Ax*.

Not only did Sampson fail to defeat Vincent twice in 30 minutes, he failed to register a single victory during a bout in which he was constantly forced into a defensive position. This led *The Broad Ax* to report that many of the spectators who viewed Vincent's bout with Sampson "were more than satisfied that had it been a finished match that Vincent would have been the victor." This prompted Leon Motts to immediately advertise a bout between Vincent and American wrestling champion Dr. Roller at the same venue.

"So in meeting Roller, Vincent's class will be demonstrated to his admirers, as today Roller is the champion of American wrestlers, and no one has thrown Vincent, and for him to be pitted against a champion means much for his future standing among the best grapplers, and will surely pave the way for him to be able to get matches with the best of them," continued *The Broad Ax*.

Vincent was also booked for a match with Mehmet Bux as the semifinal bout of an event held at the Chicago Coliseum. It was stated in the sports page of *The Inter Ocean* that those who watched the training routines of "the West Indian negro" and his East Indian opponent "expect that the latter match will overshadow the wind-up contest in the matter of interest."

"Vincent claims that not until this match was made for him has he ever had a chance in Chicago to show his wrestling prowess against a clever rival," added *The Inter Ocean*. "The negro population evidently has coincided with the West Indian athlete and he will not lack for encouragement from members of his race."

A Decided Novelty

Vincent was able to appeal to more than just the rank-and-file Black Chicagoans. As far away as Minneapolis, it was reported that heavyweight boxer Jack Johnson — who was in the middle of a six-year reign as the world heavyweight boxing champion — was also more than just a passive fan of the latest Black wrestling phenom.

"Jack Johnson, the pugilistic champion, will be at the Coliseum wrestling show New Year's night as a rooter for Illa Vincent, the West Indian light-heavy-weight wrestler," reported *The Evening Tribune* of Albert Lea, Minnesota.

As expected, the contest between Bux and Vincent was indeed the match of the night, as the two wrestled for two hours and 45 minutes without a clear winner being decided. In the aftermath, when Vincent was advertised for a bout with Gus Pedersen, his famous friend decided that his showing against Bux made him a safe bet to wager money on.

"Impressed by Illa Vincent's showing against Bux, the East Indian wrestler, and urged by the confidence of the colored grappler, Jack Johnson today took the $200 bet offered by Moje, the manager of Pedersen," printed *The Inter Ocean*. "Mr. Pedersen has agreed to throw Vincent in twenty minutes of actual wrestling time, a feat which Bux could not accomplish in almost three hours."

In the midst of this, word of Vincent's success caught the attention of the colorful writer Lloyd Kenyon Jones, who continued pulling on the thread of Vincent being a "Smoked German."

"He styles himself Illa Vincent, and is proficient in German and French," wrote Jones. "In fact, he comes from Germany, and handles the tongue of the Fatherland with fine abandon, mixing with it the rich southern accent of the negro."

As there is no evidence whatsoever that Vincent was a Black American of Southern descent, it's equally likely that Jones — or whomever relayed this story to him — simply made an assumption about Vincent's origin when he heard German and French being spoken by a Black man with a pronounced accent, with it being a common occurrence to hear

A Decided Novelty

both Caribbean and African natives speaking the latter language in said manner.

From there, Jones takes an almost sympathetic approach to Vincent, complimenting his desire to take on all comers, and acknowledging how "the color line prevents long chances when it comes to the reputations of Caucasians." It was a rhetorical way of acknowledging that the perceived inherent inferiority of Black wrestlers resulted in damage being done to the drawing power of White wrestlers who lost to them, leading to few being willing to accept that risk.

Jones then spoke of two Irishmen who entered the building and stood at the fringes of the crowd as Vincent made use of the German language in front of several of the people who had gathered there. According to Jones, one of the Irish onlookers said, "It's either a Dutchman dying the black death, or it's a fitting punishment for letting Tom Malone talk us into drinking that kümmel!"

As kümmel is a popular German liqueur, Jones was attempting for his anecdote to convey the discomfort and alarm that was felt by many of the White Chicagoans in attendance — potentially even including himself — at the notion that a multilingual Black wrestler could handle multiple European languages with such aplomb.

With respect to Jack Johnson's money, Vincent truly did emerge as a safe bet. Even with the length of the bout extended to 30 minutes, Gus Pedersen was incapable of scoring a fall on Vincent, and their match was declared a draw.

To whatever extent Vincent had been on a winning streak, that run of good fortune was snapped when he met Charles Cutler on the first of March. After more than 28 minutes of wrestling, Cutler caught Vincent with what *The Chicago Tribune* termed "a vicious toe hold," prompting Vincent to submit. *The Tribune* suggested that Vincent's heroic performance in defeat showed that he was "a good trial horse" for any of the top-tier wrestlers.

After the bout, assistant Chicago police chief Herman Schuettler, an avowed wrestling fan, cited the use of a toe hold

A Decided Novelty

in the Vincent-Cutler bout as further evidence that the favorite hold of world heavyweight champion Frank Gotch should be categorically banned from use in sanctioned wrestling.

"Schuettler said Cutler, with all his knowledge and experience, could not do anything with the colored grappler until he secured the toe hold, and it simply was a case of Vincent giving up or having his foot broken," reported *The Tribune*.

Schuettler added that there were several other holds that would have yielded the same result without imperiling a wrestler's foot, which is why he saw a ban on the toe hold as justified. A druggist named W.L. Sergeant of Ottumwa, Iowa was of the same opinion. Sergeant traveled from Iowa to Chicago for the event and insisted Cutler's use of the toe hold to defeat Vincent "ruined the match."

Some commentators found the idea of a Black wrestler competing against Whites on such a prominent stage humorous. Sandy Griswold, who authored the "Sandy's Dope" editorial section of *The Evening World-Herald* of Omaha, Nebraska, went so far as to disparage Vincent by calling him "Jack Johnson's saddle-colored valet," apparently assuming that someone of the Black wrestler's shade would have been relegated to a menial day job, and that he possessed no credible wrestling ability.

As the fall neared its end, Vincent began a feud with William Demetral that would come to define his career in several respects. On December 3, the two waged war inside of the Globe Theater's ring for two hours and 18 minutes before Vincent finally managed to pin Demetral's shoulders to the mat. However, since it was a multi-fall match, the bout continued, and Vincent submitted to a controversial toe hold 15 minutes later.

"The men wrestled 2:04:00 in the final bout before the referee awarded Demetral the match because of his aggressiveness," reported *The Chicago Tribune*. "Demetral wrenched the muscles of the back of his neck and will be out of training at least a week."

A Decided Novelty

Unaware of the historic significance, *The Chicago Tribune* simply reported on the four-plus-hour Vincent-Demetral bout declaring it "one of the longest wrestling matches ever held in this country," with other publications, like *The Battle Creek Enquirer*, calling it "the longest match on record."

In the aftermath of his decision victory, Demetral was "unable to accept the offer of the Wabash Athletic Club to be one of the stars in the windup at the same place Monday night," according to *The Inter Ocean*. In the meantime, *The Battle Creek Enquirer* noted that "a few good rubs got all the kinks out of the powerful Cuban, and he says he feels no ill effects from the long match," despite Vincent being logged as the official loser of the torturous affair.

As *The Enquirer* rounded the length of the battle up to five hours in subsequent reports, it also added that Vincent complained that the official result should have been recorded as a draw.

Following his marathon effort against Demetral, Vincent leapt straight into a match with Charley Cutler, and multiple publications predicted that Cutler's 20-pound weight advantage over Vincent, "admittedly one of the greatest of the smaller heavyweights," would be too much for "the Cuban Wonder" to overcome.

"Vincent is an out-and-out contender for the light-heavyweight title, and if beaten by Cutler intends to stick in the game for matches with men more evenly matched with him as far as weight is concerned," added *The Inter Ocean*.

As predicted, Cutler won the bout, and became "the first man to pin the shoulders of Illa Vincent, the Cuban, to the mat." Despite the loss, Vincent added to his reputation for durability, wrestling for a total of two hours and 38 minutes before surrendering two falls to his heavier opponent.

"Cutler won the first fall in their last night's match after fifty-eight minutes and twenty-two seconds of hard wrestling. A toe hold did the work," reported *The Lincoln Star Journal*. "Vincent said that his leg was injured and he refused to continue the bout. A doctor was called, and after examining the

Cuban's leg, said he found nothing wrong. Cutler obtained his second fall in one hour and forty minutes with a body lock."

In the aftermath of this second consecutive grueling contest, Vincent stated that it was his failure to adequately rest after his four-hour-plus effort against Demetral that caused his loss to Cutler.

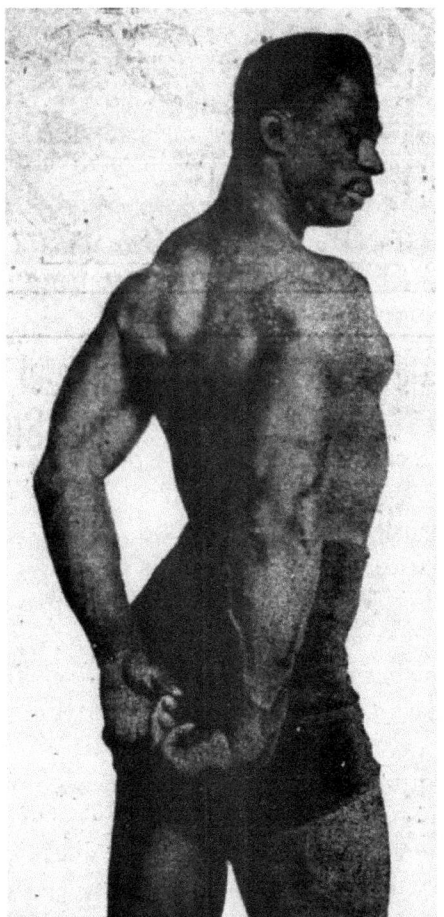

Illa Vincent shows off his muscularity

"I have recovered the full use of my muscles, and I am positive that I am the master of Cutler," insisted Vincent to the Associated Press. "Had I not had my grueling battle with

Demetral, I certainly would have won. If Cutler cares to meet me, I am willing to go on a winner-take-all basis or divide the best obtainable purse as Cutler dictates."

In response, Cutler said he might give Vincent another opportunity, conceding that the West Indian "gave me a grand battle," but then adding "I can defeat him again, in spite of his belief to the contrary."

Other coverage of the bout between Cutler and Vincent maintained an obsession with Vincent's skin color. *The Daily Book* of Chicago remarked that Vincent "claims he is Cuban" and added with an air of suspicion that he "is a mighty dark Cuban."

Apparently, the Chicago sportswriters had never actually visited Cuba, or they would have been familiar with the fact that Afro-Cubans constituted approximately 12 percent of Cuba's population in 1912.

Questions about Vincent's nationality and skin color continued to follow him. When Vincent made his debut in Ottawa late in March 1913 for a bout that *The Ottawa Evening Journal* declared to be "the first time wrestling fans will see a negro in the wrestling ring," they called immediate attention to Vincent's unusually exotic background.

"Illa Vincent is a Cuban, but is a Cuban negro, and is as black as the ace of spades," noted *The Evening Journal*. "It will be a lot like witnessing 'Lil Artha' Johnson to see Vincent mix it up with Constant LeMarin. The Cuban is one of the shiftiest men on the mat from his showing since arriving in this country."

Vincent was shuffled into matches with other opponents after suffering back-to-back losses to LeMarin. Along the way, Vincent's conspicuously French surname likely made passing as Cuban difficult in a country where one in five residents spoke both English and French. From then on, he was called either "Isla Mora Vincent" or simply "Mora Vincent" — with "mora" being the Spanish word for "blackberry."

A Decided Novelty

Before Vincent wrestled Frenchman Raymond Cazeaux at Rideau Rink, a rather crude racial epithet was lobbed in his direction by Cazeaux, who was quoted as saying "no coon from Africa to Yucatan can beat him," before tacking on "Non, parbleu, c'est impossible!"

Vincent retained his new middle name of "Mora" and his identity as a Cuban when he finally traveled to Springfield, Massachusetts to wrestle Dr. Ben Roller. *The Springfield Union* announced that Vincent had been "beating up all the good ones in the Middle West," and he was considered "practically unbeatable in a match to the finish."

"Vincent weighs 205 pounds and his pictures proclaim him to be an athlete trained to the minute and without an ounce of superfluous flesh on his bones," added *The Union*. "He stands slightly over the six-feet mark and is said to be the acme of toughness, a wrestler who can give and take plenty of punishment and go at top speed all the time."

The Republican got in on the act of revealing details about Vincent's background, explaining that he was supposedly born in Cuba, and had then traveled to Switzerland where he was taught to wrestle. Vincent had then purportedly competed in tournaments held in Berlin, Paris, Vienna, and Budapest.

"He wrestled Cutler to a draw in two hours and one-half, and also had a three-hour draw with Immin Bux," cautioned *The Republican*. "He beat Demetral, the Greek."

While these reported results were not entirely accurate, the spirit of them is correct, inasmuch as Vincent had multi-hour matches against all three main-event wrestlers, and even the bouts he lost concluded with contested finishes that often made him appear to be the more capable combatant.

Like some other publications, *The Springfield Sunday Union* seemed uncertain as to who was qualified to be classed as Black, stating that Vincent, who had been "styled the Jack Johnson of the mat," was "not a negro," yet was somehow still "as black as one."

"The early arrival of the Cuban is due partly to his desire to put the finishing touches to his training right in the city where he is to contest," said *The Sunday Union*. "He has learned by experience that even such a simple thing as a change of drinking water can put an athlete to the bad, and he doesn't want to take any chances of not being absolutely fit for a finish fight when he tackles Roller. Moreover, he wanted to be on hand to see Roller work in his Chicopee match last night, believing he could collect some valuable pointers as to just how the doctor's attack should be met."

While perhaps not as overtly racist as Hjalmar Lundin, Roller apparently enjoyed telling tales to the press where he referred to Black wrestlers in unflattering terms. In June 1910, Roller treated *The Winnipeg Tribune* to a story of his supposed manhandling of "a heavyweight negro wrestler that once flourished on the coast." The paper added that "as everyone is aware, wrestling is one sport which the Ethiopians shun."

"This big negro," observed Roller, "had made for himself a reputation on the coast, and his friends were heralding him as the best in the business. This was at a time when Tom Jenkins was good and the latter was brought out to meet the dusky skinned artist. Well it was a shame what Jenkins did to his opponent. For two hours he mauled him and made that negro think he was in the midst of a stable of bucking mules. Before the match was over, the eyes of Mr. Darkey stuck out like the beacons on a gasoline gig. When it was all over the negro just said: 'I'm gone.' And do you know that Ethiopian ran from the arena and disappeared as completely as if the earth had swallowed him."

Curiously, ahead of his bout with Vincent, Roller dispensed an entire article's worth of interview content to *The Springfield Union* railing against the toe hold and its pervasive use in the wrestling of that era.

"I firmly believe that the wrestling fraternity throughout the United States should cooperate in an attempt to abolish the toe hold for all time," declared Roller. "Practically every wrestler in the country would be glad enough to have it legislated out of the book if it were possible, but since Frank Gotch is champion and a champion can do

A Decided Novelty

practically as he pleases, there seems little chance that the toe hold will be discarded. Anyone with championship aspirations must have this hold in his repertoire along with its guard."

It turned out that Roller was heavily foreshadowing the outcome of his bout with Vincent, as the West Indian grappler secured an inescapable toe hold on the former professor of physiology, and Roller was forced to submit after 32 minutes of wrestling.

Roller evened the fall tally five minutes later with a "half nelson and crotch hold," and then fully turned the tables on Vincent after another 21 minutes of grappling by submitting Vincent with a toe hold of his own, after so aggressively decrying its use just one day prior.

"The crowd, which was typically a Roller one, almost raised the roof with cheers after the final fall, and Vincent, although he cannot speak English, walked over to Roller and, extending his hand in good fellowship, jabbered a few words of congratulation, which were not understood, but appreciated nevertheless," concluded *The Springfield Union*. "This act by the Cuban, who had shown himself a clean wrestler throughout, got him in the good graces of the crowd, which gave him three hearty cheers."

Before ending the article, the writer for *The Union* apparently couldn't resist the opportunity to direct further commentary toward Vincent's appearance. After first complimenting Vincent by acknowledging how his "wonderful arm and shoulder development caused many to liken him to Jack Johnson," the writer added how Vincent "claims to be a strict Cuban" despite possessing "extremely dark skin and heavy profile" that led many of the people in attendance "to believe that he was a negro." Apparently, there were many who still hadn't realized that the two terms were not mutually exclusive, and that Cuban was a nationality rather than a racial designation.

Following the start of the First World War in Europe, Vincent's name was included on a list of several German wrestlers who would probably not be returning to Europe from the United States during the 1914 wrestling season. The war had disrupted international wrestling circuits and forced many European performers to choose sides or face suspicion in their adopted countries. However, Vincent inevitably *did* make the trip to Europe, which meant that updates as to his ultimate fate would have to be supplied by others.

When wrestler Ray Cazeau traveled to Springfield in 1920 to wrestle, he brought with him an update as to the postwar status of Vincent. The article commenced with a retelling of the dubious origin story of Vincent as a Cuban whose father was a "Hindu" and whose mother was a "Cuban Negro," and then added that Vincent's family moved to Pirmasens, Germany, along the French border. From there, the tale continued into rather peculiar territory.

"Perhaps the oddest turn of [Vincent's] strange career came when he married a white woman, the sister of Constans LeMarin, the big French grappler," added *The Springfield Union*. "He continued in the game as an active wrestler for a number of years and then conceived the idea of taking a troupe of women wrestlers to Russia. The receipt his venture received was astounding. No venture of the kind ever succeeded half as well as Vincent's, and the money began pouring in from the start. Vincent liked the country so well that he decided to remain there. He has given up his wrestling troupe, but remains as a man of parts, a man of wealth."

Given what is now known to have happened to men of wealth in Russia during the early 1920s, if any aspect of the latter portion of this story is true, one can only retroactively hope that Vincent managed to escape Russia with his life.

Fortunately, there is at least one report suggesting that Vincent managed to safely emigrate from Russia. When Tunisian wrestler and France resident Pete Ladjimi made his debut in Springfield a full decade later, he informed *The Springfield Republican* that he had been taught to wrestle by Illa Vincent after meeting the retired wrestler in Egypt.

The decade of the 1910s may have left the fate of Illa Vincent in doubt, but so was the state of Black American

A Decided Novelty

wrestling. Thankfully, help was on the way, as two Midwestern wrestlers would soon emerge to take up the mantle and carry it into the Roaring Twenties, with one of them becoming the first Black American wrestling star to make a name for himself from coast to coast.

5 – The Black Dutchman

In the aftermath of Illa Vincent's U.S. tours, there were a few more attempts made in the late 1910s to get Black wrestlers established in some pockets of the U.S. with little success. Very early in 1918, *The San Francisco Examiner* referred to a wrestler by the name of Elbert Williams as "the only colored wrestler in captivity" when he was slated to be the opponent for "The Russian Lion" William Berne at the Dreamland Rink in San Francisco. Williams doesn't appear to have lasted more than a couple of months in the business.

In March 1923, John J. Peri of *The Stockton Daily Evening Record* quipped that "Next to hen's teeth and left-handed third basemen, the scarcest things in the world are colored wrestlers."

With all due respect to baseball players and chickens, that statement by Peri was gradually becoming less true by the day, even as he wrote it. The 1920s would represent the first era when there was significant overlap amongst the careers of Black wrestlers who had some semblance of staying power, at least on a regional basis.

In fact, it was at the dawn of the Roaring Twenties when the development of the first recognizable generation of Black wrestlers began to take shape, and it would be kicked off by an event in Chicago that involved two Black wrestlers with very different backgrounds and trajectories.

Lee Roy Umbles was born in Kentucky in 1898 but was primarily raised in and around the area of Washington, Indiana. Umbles was undoubtedly a stellar athlete and was clearly an exceptional talent when it came to foot-based racing events.

In Washington, where the population was overwhelmingly White, having the high school athletic programs spearheaded by Black athletes was clearly out of the ordinary, and attracted special attention. When the track and field team of the local high school captured the Indiana state championship by half a point — relying heavily on the talents

A Decided Novelty

of two Black runners in particular — it was treated as a monumental occurrence.

"Washington is all agog since Saturday, and today two black Negro boys are the cynosure of the eyes of every feminine and masculine student in the high school, for to them goes the credit for winning the meet by a margin of one half a point over Crawfordsville," stated *The Vincennes Sun*. "Washington was a 'dark horse.'"

Umbles won Indiana's individual state championship in the one-mile run, and finished third in the half-mile race, while his teammate Hulley Ballau finished first in the half-mile, providing Washington with all the points it required to win the 1914 Indiana State Meet Championship.

The next year, Umbles was running on behalf of Ohio State University, but soon transferred to the University of Colorado at Boulder. It was there that he finished second in the Rocky Mountain News Marathon, and then won the News-Times Marathon in 1918.

Less than three years removed from seizing home state headlines for his exploits as a superb runner, Umbles was stepping through the ropes of wrestling rings in the Midwest, and actually found himself wrestling on the same card as a Black European wrestler who was apparently being brought into the Chicagoland area to fill the role left vacant by the departure of Illa Vincent.

The fleeting intrusion of Edward Geerd into the pro wrestling world often flies under the radar. Yet, Geerd's participation in wrestling is worth exploring for multiple reasons, including how he was advertised, what his presence was intended to accomplish, and how his efforts to wrestle eventually overlapped with those of the first identifiably Black wrestler whose name was carried from one American coast to the other.

Popular wrestler Johnny Myers of Illinois had been promoted as the world middleweight champion for several years, except that he had lost a match to legitimate Inter-Allied Games wrestling champion Ralph Parcaut in August and had been unable to secure a rematch. In order to restore some semblance of legitimacy to Myers' claim to being a world champion, Edward Geerd was imported from the Netherlands and advertised as the middleweight champion of Europe.

On January 8, 1921, Black American newspaper *The Chicago Whip* reported how Geerd was introduced by manager Virgil Williams of the Royal Gardens to a crowd at the Chicago Armory. Geerd was said to be 23 years old, and had "won matches in Holland, France, Spain, England," and "South and Central America."

The match between Geerd and Myers was scheduled to take place on January 31, 1921, and was advertised as a "world's championship wrestling match" with Geerd's unmistakably Black face used in the promotion of the show.

In the bout itself, Myers defeated Geerd twice in 45 minutes to "unify" his American championship and Geerd's European championship into a title of greater luster. The bout took place immediately following the show-opening match in which Lee Umbles — who had been training children to box, run, and wrestle at the Chicago YMCA on Michigan Ave. — defeated Hugh Gannon in the welterweight division.

The description of the bout between Myers and Geerd indicates that Geerd was comparatively uncomfortable with wrestling, and *The Whip* suggested that Geerd's confusion in the ring could be "explained by the colored man's unfamiliarity with the American style of wrestling."

"After the match, Myers, in a speech, said that Geerd was a sure comer, and with a few months of American training that there is not a man, to his knowledge, who would be able to flop the colored boy," added *The Whip*. "Myers frankly acknowledged that Geerd gave him a hard night's work."

This latter acknowledgement was of a rather dubious character, given how *The Whip* stated that Myers was "on top of his prey every minute of as long as it lasted."

Two days after Myers' title bout with Geerd, *The Urbana Daily Courier* upgraded Myers' American title defense against Paul Prehn to an international title bout "due to Myers' victory Monday night over Ed Geerd, the Holland colored grappler." From there, Myers continued to be advertised as the world middleweight title holder in Illinois once again without interruption.

This may represent the first case of a Black wrestler receiving a fabricated championship so that his loss of that title could further enhance a White wrestler's credentials.

Edward Geerd

Apparently, there was some difficulty booking Geerd in the aftermath of his performance against Myers. The next time his name was printed in the area's newspapers, it was in a June edition of *The Chicago Tribune*, when "an athletic and theatrical carnival" was being hosted at the Dreamland Gardens as a benefit for Geerd to help subsidize his return trip to the Netherlands.

While it's unclear if Geerd returned to the Netherlands, he definitely reached New Jersey. That's where *The Daily Press* announced that Geerd was advertised for an October match with Fred Meyer. For this occasion, Geerd was once again promoted as the outright middleweight champion of Europe, and also as "the colored middleweight champion of the world," but by the time of the bout, he had seemingly been demoted to being simply the "colored middleweight champion of Europe."

This time, Geerd would emerge victorious, and if his performance still lacked polish, it was masked by the shortness of the contest, which only lasted 13 minutes and concluded with a Geerd headlock.

"Meyer, who hails from New York, displayed exceptional fast work in the first few minutes of the affair, but later was checked by Geerd's effective toe holds, which were powerful," observed *The Daily Press*. "Geerd, claimant to the colored middleweight championship of Europe, secured the headlock hold on Meyer when the big fellow made an effort to throw his body atop the Holland champ while attempting to secure a scissor hold. Both contestants worked in rapid fashion and won the applause of the fans time and again."

At the same show in which Geerd battled Fred Meyer, established Black boxing star Bobby Dobbs also made an appearance as a grappler. A veteran of more than 200 fights, the 52-year-old Dobbs had gotten involved in the promotional and managerial aspects of boxing and wrestling, and offered an open challenge "that no Atlantic City colored boy" could defeat him in a wrestling match; the challenge was accepted by lightweight boxer Sammy Robinson.

Robinson was allotted 15 minutes to pin Dobbs, but was unable to do so, and Dobbs had a few other dalliances with wrestling that never amounted to anything serious. This once again underscores the association between wrestling and boxing during the early 20th century, and the overlap between the two sports would play a significant role in enabling some of the first true Black grappling stars to gravitate to the mat in the decade that followed.

After a one-month hiatus, Geerd was once again mentioned in *The Daily Press*, and was said to be fishing for a bout with Austrian wrestling star Henry Irslinger. Although the article was ostensibly floating Geerd for another wrestling match, its primary function seemed to be to present Geerd as a target for an experienced manager to promote his other talents, as he arrived at the publication with photos depicting himself in the application of his wondrous physical skills.

"One picture shows Geerd holding a two-hundred-pound dumbbell and five husky persons, a rather tough feat," disclosed *The Daily Press*. "He claims all sorts of tricks, such as bearing over eight hundred pounds on his chest and still displaying a smile. Geerd is after a manager in Atlantic City. He wishes answers, addressed to the Sporting Department of the Daily Press before six o'clock this evening."

During this period when Geerd had been contending with his career uncertainties, Umbles had been moving proactively to establish himself as a wrestler in other states around the Midwest, including his home state of Indiana.

In Richmond, Indiana in July 1921, Umbles posted an advertisement in *The Richmond Palladium and Sun-Telegram* under the name "L.R. Umbles, claimant of the colored light and welterweight wrestling championship of America." In the ad, he urged anyone in Richmond weighing between 140 and 150 pounds to reach out to him at his residence at 4 East Fourteenth Street in Washington, Indiana. He also engaged in mixed boxing-wrestling events.

Elsewhere in the Midwest during that summer, Ray Richmond emerged in Wisconsin, labeled as "the colored champion of Madison." *The Capital Times* of Madison reported how the city's "170-pound colored grappler" defeated George Connors of Beloit after attempting to apply a toe hold to his opponent for 23 minutes and then finally locking it in.

A Decided Novelty

"As a result of the injuries to his right foot, Connors was forced to forfeit the bout. Connors challenged Richmond to another bout," added *The Times*.

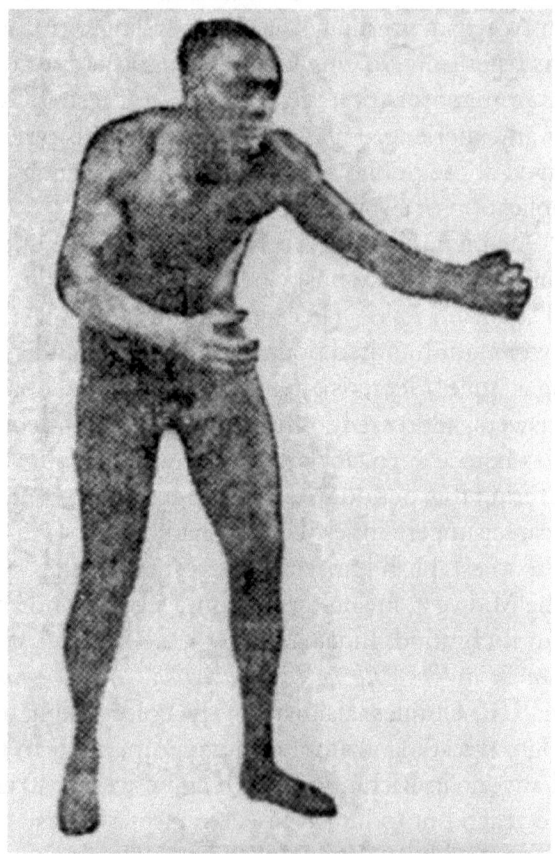

Ray Richmond

Later in the year, described as "a colored man of considerable wrestling skill," Richmond was included as one of two men taking on Jim Demetral in succession in a handicap match. With his skill and reputation, Demetral was perceived to pose an insurmountable challenge to his two competitors, even though both of them outweighed him by at least 10 pounds.

A Decided Novelty

"The champion has guaranteed to give each man two falls within two hours, each of the men to go one hour or less with him. If Demetral fails to drop each of the men within the hour he is with him, he will lose that match."

Predictably, Richmond was on the losing side of the December contest, although he gave a better accounting of himself than his White partner. *The Capital Times* opined that Richmond was "the toughest opponent of the two men," as it took far longer for Demetral to best him than it did his partner George Volkert.

"Demetral won the toss and chose Richmond as his first opponent," said *The Capital Times*. "The colored man stayed with him for 36 minutes and 40 seconds, when after a series of flops, Demetral held him on the mat for a period of three seconds with a body scissors and wristlock. After five minutes rest, Demetral took on Volkert, whom he forced to relinquish the first fall with a scissors hold. With another five minutes to get his breath, the champ appeared in the ring again with Richmond. A double wristlock was too much for the Negro, and after seven minutes, 10 seconds Demetral was his conqueror. He disposed of Volkert in four minutes, six seconds, with another wristlock."

If the objective had been to elevate Richmond by making him look slightly better than the White wrestler who was on his team, but still not nearly as skilled as the champion Demetral, it doesn't seem to have worked as intended. Richmond was advertised for two more shows — one in late December, and one in the middle of February 1922 — but reportedly refused to participate in the bouts. The first time, it was allegedly because he hadn't received main-event billing, and the second time it was seemingly due to his refusal to wrestle his chosen opponent.

Meanwhile, in early 1922 Umbles was being advertised as an undefeated competitor in the 142-pound weight division, and the reports from his matches generally presented him as a peerless ring technician. Such was the case of his victory over

A Decided Novelty

Jack Donahue in consecutive falls during yet another home-state appearance by Umbles.

"The first fall came after thirty-six minutes and forty-three seconds of wrestling with an arm scissors and a double wristlock," stated *The Indianapolis Star*. "Umbles won the second fall in twelve minutes and fifteen seconds with the same hold."

When Umbles won his next bout — a one-fall affair against Victor Brown — with the identical maneuver, there was a notable attendee in the audience to support Umbles, just as he had personally appeared to support Black wrestler Illa Vincent in the previous decade.

"Jack Johnson, ex-heavyweight champion of the world, was at the ringside and made a speech in which he said that he was within a stone's throw of condition and feared no boxer in the world," recounted *The Star*.

Eventually, defeat befell Umbles in the sort of way that leaves the audience unconvinced that his loss was the result of anything other than lousy luck. After pinning Kid Humphreys with a half nelson-headlock combination, Umbles reportedly fell prey to a very quick headlock and body scissors to suffer a pinfall loss of his own.

"The force of the fall broke Umbles' rib, and he was unable to appear for the third session," concluded *The Star*.

Overlapping with that activity from Umbles, another Black Midwestern grappler going by the name Harry "Tarzan" Wilson emerged from anonymity in the middle of March to try his hand at wrestling Demetral.

"Tarzan Wilson, dark-skinned wrestler of Detroit, will be Jimmy Demetral's opponent in a two out of three falls match at the Gayety theater Thursday night," reported *The Wisconsin State Journal*. "This is the first time a Negro has appeared in a mat encounter here in years, and the bout is expected to attract a capacity house. Wilson is said to be a clever performer and comes here with a fine record."

Each man scored a fall in the bout before it was ruled a draw when it failed to reach a conclusion before midnight. A

A Decided Novelty

rematch was scheduled at the Gayety theater, with Wilson now said to be the "negro wrestling champion" of Detroit. Wilson dropped two straight falls to Demetral in the rematch, but made quite an impression in the process.

"Tarzan Wilson broke hold after hold applied by Demetral, but after one hour and seven minutes the fast pace began to tell on him and he gave up when Demetral almost broke his leg with a twisting toe hold," printed *The Capital Times*. "The second fall came in twelve minutes with another toe hold and arm scissors. More than 2,000 witnessed the fray."

With that, Wilson disappeared from the limelight for an entire decade, but when he did emerge — assuming it was the same Tarzan Wilson — his performance would be both memorable and historically significant.

In the meantime, by summer 1922, it appeared that Ed Geerd had successfully landed the services of the manager he had sought, but his primary performance genre ceased to be mainstream wrestling. *The Evening Journal* of Wilmington, Delaware printed that Geerd, "the champion colored wrestler of the world and his all-African company," would be presenting three straight evenings of matches at Wilmington's National Theatre.

From there, Geerd apparently depended more heavily into entertaining audiences with his other talents. In October 1923, Geerd reportedly walked right into the Baltimore office of *The Afro-American* with a pile of photographs and demanded to speak to the publication's sports editor.

"In conversation with the caller, who spoke English with some trace of accent, we learned that his name was Edward Geerd, that he was a native of Amsterdam, Holland, where he was born and where his family still lives, and that his vocation, avocation, forte or profession, however he regards it, is that of a giant strong man and wrestler," relayed *The Afro-American*.

While Geerd presented the sports editor with the photos of himself juggling weights and holding pianos on his chest, the Hollander simultaneously complained about the lack

A Decided Novelty

of wrestling opportunities that he had been provided in the United States.

"Since coming to this country, he had not wrestled any because there were no colored wrestlers, and white men would not meet him," the article continued. "He has been in the country about two years and has been doing his strongman stunts in the South and West. He also took up boxing some time ago and says that he has had many workouts with George Godfrey, whom he praised highly. Geerd says he has engaged in nine bouts since taking up boxing and won eight of them."

One week later, *The Afro-American* included multiple illustrations of Geerd alongside Reginald Siki, who the paper referred to as "Wrestling Siki" to differentiate him from the Senegalese boxing star Battling Siki. The paper presented the 152-pound Geerd — "The Black Dutchman" — as tiny in comparison to the 6'2" and 217-pound Siki.

Following his invasion of *The Afro-American*'s office, it does not appear that Geerd returned to activity in a wrestling ring in a way that retained the attention of the press, but he seems to have been consistently booked as a strong man for shows in Pennsylvania for the remainder of December. From there, his only in-ring activity appears to consist of a handful of show-opening boxing events in the Midwest toward the latter end of the 1920s.

Even some of the most well-studied wrestling historians might be challenged to name any Black professional wrestlers prior to the debut of Reginald Siki. There are several reasons for this, including the distillation of the entirety of Black wrestling history down to a few pivotal figures for the sake of simplicity. Still, it appears that the overarching factor that propelled Siki beyond the Black wrestlers who preceded him to the point of historically effacing them has a lot to do with the company he kept.

Reginald Berry was born in Kansas City, Missouri on December 28, 1899. Eventually, he was drawn into the company of the traveling troupe of world-famous wrestlers led by the Zbyszko brothers, Stanislaus and Wladek. The Zbyszkos

A Decided Novelty

were among wrestling's biggest draws, as legitimate world champions who had helped transition the sport from purely competitive contests to entertainment spectacles that blended athletic skill with theatrical presentation. Over the course of time, several conflicting stories for how Berry came to find himself in the company of the Zbyszkos would be told, which will be introduced in the order that they were chronologically presented.

The portion of the American general public that followed wrestling first became aware of Reginald Siki in July 1923. Listed as a 21-year-old Senegalese wrestler, Siki was introduced by *The California Eagle* as being the latest sensation in wrestling who had recently made his debut in Chicago against Stanislaus Zbyszko.

"This muscular boy was sent to what old timers thought to be his death in a neat battle with the former world's heavyweight champion, Stanislaus Zbyszko, who has flopped the best grapplers in the game and knows every trick in the book!" printed *The Eagle*.

Berry's fictional Senegalese origin and 'Siki' ring name were carefully chosen, not random selections. In summer 1923, one of the most popular prizefighters in the world was Louis Mbarick Fall, a Senegalese light heavyweight who fought under the name "Battling Siki."

Beginning his boxing career with four losses and two draws before his first victory, and then improving to a mediocre record of eight wins, eight losses and two draws, Battling Siki went 41-1-1 in his next 43 bouts and earned a title shot against Georges Carpentier. During that contest, Siki stunned the world by knocking Carpentier out in the sixth round, and permanently ended the legendary fighter's campaign in the light heavyweight division.

Losing the light heavyweight title in his very next fight did nothing to stall the cultural momentum that Battling Siki had built, and he remained one of the hottest commodities in the world of legitimate fighting. The intent of the Zbyszkos

A Decided Novelty

was clearly to cast Reginald Siki as a branch that sprouted from the same Senegalese tree.

From his very first bouts, Siki was presented as "young champion of colored wrestlers," which was how *The Portland Evening Express & Advertiser* introduced him in the aftermath of his 30-minute draw at the Portland Exposition building against Frank Judson, who was once the wrestling coach at Harvard University.

The practice of introducing Siki as a champion of his race fit neatly into the pattern established by the Zbyszkos' crew. The traveling group of wrestlers were presented as a collection of all-stars from around the world, with each man being the champion of a nation or ethnicity. Presumably, this was intended to bolster the international appeal of the events, and also to inflame racial or ethnic passions in the populace in the hopes that they might pay to support the wrestlers who would serve as their avatars in the wrestling ring.

As a full-time wrestler traveling with world champions and other respected veterans, Siki's claim to racial championship status carried more credibility than similar claims by other Black grapplers.

For example, Bud Jones of *The Spokane Press* wrote in March 1923 that veteran pro boxer Sam "Tham" Langford had "recently left the ring after years of active participation, during which time he never succeeded in annexing any sort of title, and became possessed of a title almost immediately after he took up the mat game. The Boston Tar Baby's new title is what might properly be termed 'synthetic,' but it is, nevertheless, a title. 'Tham' is now colored heavyweight wrestling champion of the world, a title conferred upon him by Larney Lichtenstein, his manager. As far as we know, 'Tham' not only acquired a title by the shift, but he established a record as the first colored heavyweight wrestler the game has ever known."

Already a veteran of 282 fights at the time this announcement was made, Langford fought in a further 31 fights over the next two years without ever making a serious contribution to professional wrestling. Clearly, the ease with

A Decided Novelty

which a "colored heavyweight championship" could be conferred upon Langford simply by dint of his participation in wrestling betrays the dearth of Black grappling participants in general, especially within the upper weight divisions.

In Siki's case, it's unknown how much the Senegalese link was intended to attach him to the famous fighter bearing the same last name, or if the desire was primarily to present him as an exotic Black combatant. It's worth noting that every one of Battling Siki's 65 fights from the beginning of his career up until summer 1923 had been held on the European continent. As far as fight fans were concerned, watching Reginald Siki grapple was probably the closest they could ever hope to get to watching Battling Siki compete inside of a ring — or to personally watch someone of Senegalese descent do anything at all.

The *Collyer's Eye* news publication of Chicago hinted as much when it declared that Battling Siki had practically "faded out of the pugilistic picture," and a new Siki had emerged to take his place in a related sport.

"He is Reginald Siki and is referred to as the Abyssinian Panther," printed *Collyer's Eye*. "He stands 6 ft. 3 in., weighs 220 pounds, and is 23 years old. It is expected that Siki will make his debut in Chicago and will be pitted against some of the heavy trial horses to establish his worth."

This geographic confusion between Senegal and Abyssinia revealed either poor research or deliberate indifference to accuracy. While Senegal is known for its proud ownership of the westernmost port in mainland Africa, Abyssinia is a historical region within the Horn of Africa — unmistakably located in East Africa — and a term that is almost exclusively used to refer to Ethiopia. The distance between the two locations is well over 3,500 miles, which is roughly the distance separating Spain from Russia.

By fall 1923, Siki's presence in wrestling had already captured the attention of the Black news publications around the U.S., and *The New York Age* printed a detailed origin story of Siki for public consumption.

A Decided Novelty

"Reginald Siki, said to be a native of Abyssinia, but who has lived in Kansas City for the last two years, has come to New York and is now getting into shape for an extensive tour of the country this winter," wrote *The Age*. "Siki is said to have met the Zbyszkos, Gardini, Judson, Leavitt, Cyclop, and Manko in the West."

The Age didn't define what was meant by "the West," as nearly the entirety of the United States is situated west of New York, but the capitalization implies that the meeting took place somewhere along the West Coast. In the meantime, *The Age* also supplied the name of Siki's manager, Jack Stanley, and the location of his office, which was at 3 West 69th Street on New York City's Upper West Side.

In October, Siki lost a best-of-three-falls main-event bout to Wladek Zbyszko at the Gayety Theater in Baltimore. *The Baltimore Sun* reported how Siki had actually managed to score the first fall of the match on the American Heavyweight Champion from Poland in just over 31 minutes before Zbyszko recovered to win. It was the most public confirmation since the era of Illa Vincent that a Black heavyweight wrestler was capable of claiming a fall over a world-class White heavyweight.

That same month, *The Miami News* mentioned the opening of the wrestling season in New York City, and took special note of Siki's presence. After first clarifying that the 6'2", 208-pound "Abyssinian Panther" was no relation to Battling Siki the boxer, *The News* pointed out, "There are no colored wrestlers in America, and only two are known abroad."

At a minimum, Lee Umbles would have begged to differ with his omission from consideration as a Black American wrestler. Moreover, the statement from *The News* implies that Siki — who was clearly born and raised in Missouri and whose mother and father were born in Illinois and Tennessee respectively — was either Ethiopian or Senegalese, so as not to be factored into the tabulation of Black American wrestlers. It was a classification pattern that would

A Decided Novelty

persist later on, and which would ultimately prevent Siki from being fully appreciated as a homegrown American star.

An interesting follow-up to the announcement of Siki's involvement in wrestling came out of New York, suggesting that all of the top wrestlers on the tour, including Ed "Strangler" Lewis, Wladek Zbyszko, and Joe Stecher, had opted to "draw the color line" and refuse to wrestle Siki on account of his race.

Young Reginald Siki

It was certainly a unique tactic to imply that several of the most popular fan-favorite wrestlers of the era were openly racist, or at least prejudiced enough not to compete against

Black wrestlers. The report also offered a hedged position rooted in cowardice, stating that Siki — with his height inflated to 6'4" and his weight boosted to 237 pounds, while sporting a 52-inch chest — was "the most powerful-looking wrestler ever seen in New York," with the implication being that the other wrestlers wanted no part of him.

Ignoring the fact that Siki had apparently acquired two inches and nearly 30 pounds in the two days between these writings, the article flatly declared that Siki "is barred from a world championship bout on account of his color," comparing his situation to that of the famous heavyweight boxer "The Black Panther" Harry Wills.

Even if the report did Siki the favor of suggesting that all of the most acclaimed White grapplers were terrified of him, it also may have been intended to provide Siki with an excuse to hone his act away from the critical eyes of New York wrestling fans. As future reports would indicate, young Reginald Siki was a bundle of raw physical talent who required assistance when not being guided through his matches by some of the most experienced wrestlers in the world.

Back in Baltimore, an alternative origin story was supplied for Siki's participation in wrestling. Rather than discovering the faux Senegalese wrestler in the western United States, Ed Lewis had supposedly happened upon Siki while wrestling overseas.

"During a visit to Europe, Lewis saw Siki working out and persuaded him to come to this country," printed *The Evening Sun*. "He spent several months helping Lewis in preparation for his bouts and profited by his experience with 'The Strangler.'"

At the tail end of November, Siki was promoted for a bout in Chicago with Stanislaus Zbyszko, the elder of the Zbyszko brothers, and also a former world champion. Casually referred to as "the black panther" by *The Chicago Tribune* in what seems to have been an attempt to forge a link between the Black grappler and Harry Wills, Siki was once again presented as a major threat, as Zbyszko had supposedly been

A Decided Novelty

required to post a bond to guarantee that he wouldn't run from the fight, and even then supposedly held out in negotiations in an attempt to turn it into a one-fall bout.

The Tribune also went one step further and claimed that Siki was "the second colored man to make a try for fame in this country in the wrestling sport," declaring that Illa Vincent of "the Dutch Congo" had been the first.

"[Vincent] spent a number of years in America, but never got anywhere," stated *The Tribune*.

Apparently, the writer was also oblivious to the activities of Lee Umbles just one state eastward in Indiana over the prior two years, although it is understandably difficult to account for all wrestling events occurring in all states, especially when the outcomes of most matches never reached the mainstream.

Ahead of Siki's bout in Chicago with the elder Zbyszko, world champion Ed Lewis offered a comment about Siki that would contradict the story that he had been the one to discover and train the Black star. This contradiction was uttered in the midst of Lewis' assurance that he would demand every penny of the purse if he was to put his world title on the line in a bout with Siki, and that Siki should content himself with the honor of having a shot at a prestigious world wrestling championship.

"I don't take this stand because Siki is colored," Lewis told *The Chicago Tribune*. "But due to the fact that the challenger is a giant in size and weight, with what I understand tremendous strength, I don't propose to take a chance of losing the title without being well paid for it. Even if he cannot wrestle a lick — though my friends say he can go some — it is as much as a man's life and limb is worth to take holds with him, so if he thinks he can win the championship, I will give him the chance, but not a dime for his effort. This is final, and he can take it or leave it."

Undoubtedly, this was pure hyperbole for the sake of building interest in Siki, and selling the public on the inherent threat of competing against him. At a minimum, Lewis should be credited for his willingness to appear like a reluctant champion against a Black challenger, rather than insisting that the African import would present him with little in the way of resistance.

Additionally, this makes it clear how much the backstory of a wrestler could vary from one location to the next, at the discretion of the promoters, with little regard for the truth. In all likelihood, Lewis probably had a considerable hand in Siki's training, as did the other wrestlers on the tour. However, for the sake of selling the realism of the show, he was feigning social distance from the Black rookie.

Zbyszko went the extra mile to establish Siki as a credible threat when the two paired up for the young star's most high-profile outing to date. The opening fall extended to the one-hour-and-seven-minute mark before the Polish veteran finally won it with a combination jackknife and headscissor hold.

In its description, the bout resembled a hold-heavy contest intended to give the audience the impression that both grapplers possessed tremendous endurance, and that the young Black upstart was capable of dominating the former champion while displaying every tool required to be successful in the sport.

"During the first fall, Siki gave an interesting exhibition of defensive wrestling, his bridging particularly saving him from defeat on several occasions," reported *The Chicago Tribune*. "His great strength was also manifested, and time after time he picked up his opponent and slammed him to the mat with a resounding thud."

Flurries of action aside, Siki spent the bulk of the bout with the appearance of control, as he held Zbyszko in an arm lock on no fewer than seven different occasions while also trapping him in a combination body scissors and wrist lock for another long stretch. Once Zbyszko overcame Siki's dominance to wrap up the first fall, reports of the account suggest that Siki was physically worn out and mentally deflated,

A Decided Novelty

and soon surrendered the second fall after the comparatively short time of eight minutes had elapsed.

The result of the bout was sufficient to allow both sides of the racial divide to take solace. To the eyes of the burgeoning group of Black pro wrestling fans, Siki had proven that a Black heavyweight could compete with a former world champion and one of wrestling's biggest international stars for over an hour. Meanwhile, those hoping for White supremacy to be upheld within the upper echelon of heavyweight wrestling could be soothed by the fact that the most competent Black threat to date had failed to take even a single fall from Zbyszko.

In this regard, the reporting of the Associated Press was suspiciously selective, as most newspapers that received the AP's abbreviated account omitted all of the nuance, and simply stated that Zbyszko had "defeated Reginald Siki, a negro, in two straight falls."

Shortly thereafter, *The Free Press Evening Bulletin* of Winnipeg reported that Siki was advertised to face Canadian wrestling hero Jack Taylor on January 1, 1924. *The Evening Bulletin* stated that the Abyssinian Giant was known as "the gorilla man" in wrestling circles, and reiterated the claim that top grapplers like Joe Stecher and Ed Lewis had abruptly drawn the color line rather than risk their health and reputations against Siki in the ring.

"When Siki and Taylor meet, it will be the first wrestling match between a white and a colored man to be staged in this part of the country, and will no doubt create more than the usual interest among fans," added *The Evening Bulletin*. "Siki is a real giant, standing 6 feet 4, and weighing 237 lbs. He has a 49 inch chest, and according to New York papers, has won his matches by brute strength and aggressiveness."

Reginald Siki had captured the imagination of a significant portion of the American public as a Black heavyweight who could hold his own against the best White wrestlers on earth. Still, whether any wrestling promoter would

A Decided Novelty

allow Siki to benefit from consistent victories remained doubtful in the racially restrictive climate of the 1920s.

6 – Among the Darker Races

The Chicago bouts that followed Reginald Siki's headline-grabbing match with Stanislaus Zbyszko permitted Siki to make good on some of the promise he displayed before his consecutive-falls loss to the veteran star. He wrestled Renato Gardini to a one-hour draw in his very next bout, and then defeated Andre Anderson with a reverse body hold in a short 11-minute match.

However, Siki's momentum soon stalled, and he was quickly dispatched in front of a packed house at the Star and Garter by Japanese wrestler Taro Miyaki to close out his Windy City run of 1923.

"Siki never had a chance against the Oriental mat star, his only three grips, the stranglehold, the headlock, and the toe hold, being easily broken by the Jap," reported *The Chicago Tribune*. "The latter did not show much in the way of the horrible holds advertised, being content to pin the colored fellow with the old time scissors on the arm, with a little jiu jitsu twist for good measure. He won both falls with this grip, the first in 15:15, and the second in 8:30."

From there, Siki traveled to Winnipeg for his New Year's bout with Jack Taylor, and was greeted with a story in *The Evening Bulletin* that painted him as a very imposing figure, albeit with less than flattering imagery that made the wrestler sound far more like an attraction in a circus freak show than a professional athlete.

"The big black deserves the title of the 'Gorilla Man' for he resembles a huge gorilla more than he does a man, standing six feet five inches, with a pair of shoulders that can scarcely go through a door, a great barrel-like chest, and long arms that reach down to his knees, a bullet-like head, with eyes set close together, a flat nose, and an enormous mouth, give him anything but an edifying appearance," printed *The Bulletin*.

Through his manager Jack Stanley, Siki expressed confidence that he could defeat Canadian champion Jack Taylor, but *The Bulletin* reported that Taylor was "seldom in real danger" as he overcame Siki in two straight falls in front of 2,000 fans at the Board of Trade building. Apparently, the bout was wrestled in such a way that Siki — despite being the Abyssinian invader threatening to unseat the local champion — was thoroughly applauded by the Canadian fans.

"Though beaten, Siki uncovered a varied assortment of holds and displayed a good knowledge of the game," reported *The Bulletin*. "He is fast, and a willing worker who never lets up, and was in fine condition... Siki got out of numerous torturous holds, wiggling his legs and body like a fish taken out of water. It was his speed and ability to evade Taylor's holds that made an impression with fans, and they cheered him to the echo after it was evident that he was no set up."

Siki again wrestled for an hour, losing his falls in 35 and 25 minutes respectively. This established the pattern for his tour. As such, the model for Siki's debut tour seemed to have been established. He was to wrestle the top wrestlers in every location while demonstrating that Black wrestlers were capable of executing all of the same moves as White wrestlers. In the midst of this, he was to appear competent at a high level without ever posing a serious threat.

Back in Chicago, Siki lost a much shorter bout to Zbyszko than their initial Windy City encounter, turning a multi-fall match into a single fall match by being physically incapable of continuing past the 20-minute mark after being slammed onto the hard arena floor.

"The Abyssinian refused to go any further after the crash, and the veteran Pole, who will meet the giant Hans Steinke at Dexter Park pavilion on Tuesday night, was awarded the decision after 19:10 of wrestling," wrote *The Chicago Tribune*.

Ahead of a bout with Swedish wrestler John Freberg in Minneapolis, *The Minneapolis Sunday Tribune* printed yet another origin story for Siki, distancing him from the famous fighter that he had so brazenly lifted his faux surname from, along with the nation of Ethiopia that he was often said to represent.

"Siki is not related to the Senegalese fighter," stated *The Sunday Tribune*. "Reginald comes from South Africa and learned how to wrestle while serving in the World War with the French army. He displayed such natural ability that he decided to make wrestling his profession after being mustered out of service."

This story was implausible since South Africa, as a British Dominion during World War I, sent combatants to British rather than French military units.

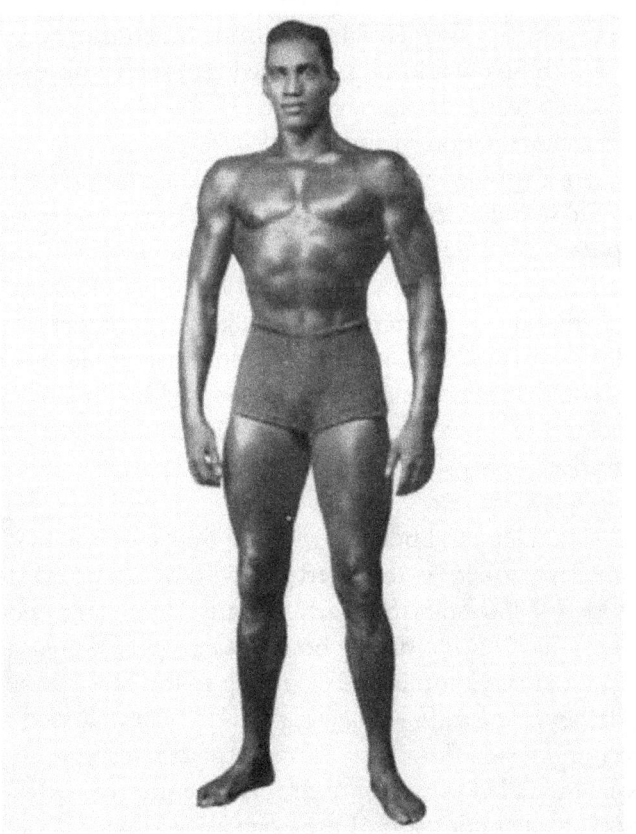

Reginald Siki

Incongruous stories aside, *The Star Tribune* also reported how "several hundred Negroes" were planning to attend the bout between Siki and Freberg at the Gayety Theater, with many having already reserved tickets well in advance of the match. Sadly, those hopeful Black fans who bought tickets hoping to view a Siki victory were disappointed; he lost the bout to Freberg in straight falls.

Siki's measurements continued to fluctuate wildly in promotional materials. The grappler who had been previously advertised as a nearly 240-pound, chiseled specimen at the beginning of January was advertised as a 190-pound wrestler just 20 days later ahead of his late January match against middleweight Jim Demetral in Madison, Wisconsin. Someone familiar with Siki would be astonished that such a physically impressive wrestler could have shed 50 pounds of lean muscle in such a short period of time.

As a stipulation for the match, Siki agreed to defeat the lighter Demetral twice in one hour or forfeit the entirety of his fight purse. *The Capital Times* predicted that Siki "should have little trouble" defeating Demetral, but the actual bout unfolded in a way that made Demetral appear like the far superior wrestler. Notwithstanding the stipulation that would practically necessitate that the outsider would score at least one pinfall on the undersized crowd favorite for the sake of building tension, Siki failed to gain a single decision over Demetral, and was nearly pinned himself.

The Demetral bout fit with the theme of Siki being sent into smaller markets as the hired gun with a high profile to lose to the local White stars. Similarly, in early March, Siki traveled to Columbus, Ohio to drop a bout to George Katsonaros at the Chamber of Commerce. According to the description provided by *The Lancaster Daily Eagle*, Katsonaros tossed Siki out to the ringside floor after 70 minutes of wrestling, and "the Abyssinian" failed to pull himself together and reenter the ring.

On the undercard of the exact same show, Siki's fellow Black wrestler Lee Umbles — whose wrestling career began two years prior to Siki's — defeated Ray Lancaster via referee's decision after 30 minutes.

It's difficult to tell if the criticisms leveled against Siki's outings during the month of March were critiques of his performance as if he was competing in a legitimate sport, or if

A Decided Novelty

commentators in the know were taking subtle shots at the wrestler's ability to uphold the appearance of legitimacy.

After Siki's bout with Renato Gardini in Michigan, *The Ironwood Daily Globe* wrote that Siki "was in a kindergarten stage when it came to showing any knowledge of wrestling." After another bout between the two in Wisconsin, *The Iron County Miner* stated how "the match proved to be pretty much a joke" because it was clear to everyone present that Gardini "could have forced Siki to the mat twice in five minutes had he desired to do so."

Siki spent the remainder of 1924 wrestling all over North America, with most of his bouts ending in draws or losses. Black newspapers, operating outside mainstream wrestling promotion networks, reported more accurately on wrestlers' actual physical dimensions and performances.

Evidence of this materialized in November, when *The Afro-American* of Philadelphia stripped several inches from Siki's advertised height, and dozens of pounds from his physique, declaring him to be 6'2" and just over 200 pounds.

"Although he has done some boxing, Siki has placed himself under the veteran trainer and fighter, Bobby Dodds, trainer of George Godfrey," reported *The Afro-American*, after Siki declared Philadelphia to be his future home. "Dodds hopes to have Siki ready for action in a month or so."

In light of future events, the connection between Siki and Godfrey would prove to be historically coincidental at a minimum, and certainly advantageous with respect to future booking opportunities.

Out in Indiana, Lee Umbles had been getting down to serious business, defeating Ollie Olson with his double wrist lock specialty in front of his hometown crowd in Washington. From there, Umbles began exchanging wins and losses with the top draws in his weight class around the Midwest. In March 1924 in Lancaster, Umbles defeated hometown boy Bob Eaton. The very next week in the same city, he lost a decision to his first opponent, Ray Carpenter, but then got right up and pinned his next foe, Young Patsey.

A Decided Novelty

Just two months later, Umbles was being advertised to face Carpenter once again, except this time Carpenter was the welterweight champion of the world. Oddly enough, Umbles was also being advertised to be a representative of Cuba, and the wrestling champion of the Caribbean nation no less, despite being born and raised in the Ohio River valley. In this fashion, he too fell into the tradition of Clarence Bouldin and Illa Vincent.

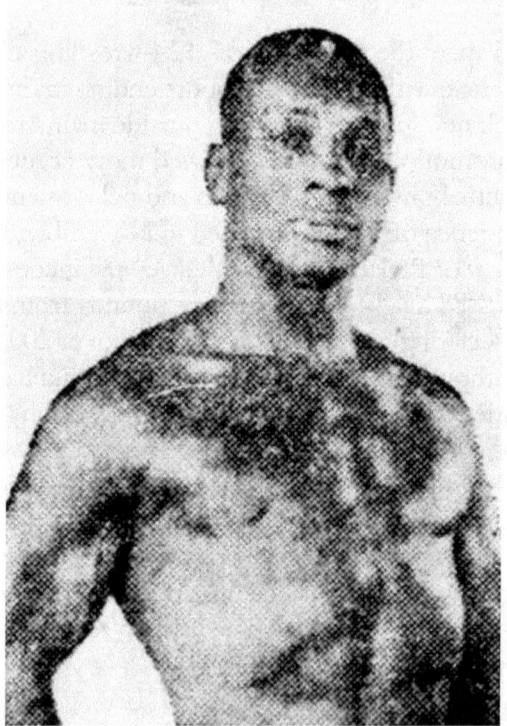

Lee Roy Umbles

This change to Umbles' place of origin was almost certainly a ploy to transform Carpenter into a wrestler who was competing to keep the hard-won championship of an American from falling into the hands of a foreign power. Holding up his end of the equation, Umbles made the local Ohio wrestler appear to be a champion capable of withstanding

A Decided Novelty

any onslaught, putting Carpenter through what *The Lancaster Daily Eagle* described as "78 minutes of agony."

"It was one of the speediest and hardest fought matches ever staged here, and both wrestlers were clean from start to finish," stated *The Daily Eagle*.

The report from *The Eagle* also noted that if "Cuban welterweight champion" Lee Umbles had "a little more finishing punch," he might be a world champion, but he lacked the ability to finish an opponent he had outwrestled. Nestled within this description is a compliment to Umbles, as he was clearly the wrestler dictating the majority of the action throughout the match.

In 1924, Umbles also tried his hand at legitimate boxing, only to be "severely trounced" by Jack Kirk, according to *The Dayton Herald*. Humorously, when acknowledging Umbles' background in less authentic combat, *The Telegraph-Forum* stated that Umbles was "a reformed Cuban wrestler."

After rebuilding his momentum with six straight victories, and while still being advertised as the champion of Cuba, Umbles rematched with Carpenter in Lancaster, and lost to a headlock in 25 minutes.

Now wrestling in the Northeast, and still labeled as "world's champion colored heavyweight wrestler," Reginald Siki continued to lose the majority of his matches. He was also quoted in *The Free Press Evening Bulletin* of Winnipeg as being "peeved" by his lack of activity in New York wrestling rings, which he believed was influenced by his race.

"Siki recently offered to wrestle Munn and Zbyszko, but the champion and ex champion both drew a rigid color line," reported *The Evening Bulletin*. "The big Abyssinian has been making rapid headway in the mat game the past year."

If there were regional prohibitions that restricted Siki's access to wrestling rings in the Northeast, he found the wrestling mats of the West Coast far easier to access. When the touring company of the Zbyszkos made its way out to San Francisco Bay in July 1925, Siki now had unfettered access to the ring, and to every member of the Zbyszkos' wrestling roster.

"Reginald Siki, a cousin of Battling Siki, will wrestle Wladek Zbyszko," printed *The Oakland Post-Enquirer*. "Six foot two in grappling pose, Siki weighs 220 pounds and is one of the most picturesque wrestlers ever to appear in the bay district. He speaks Spanish, Italian, French, Russian, and what have you, according to [Frank] Schuler. He holds a championship in India."

The Post-Enquirer added that Zbyszko could speak the same languages, and made a joke about how the two could "enliven the evening with a flow of language that could bowl of any linguist" without remarking about what a coincidence this was. Realistically, the international composition of the Zbyszkos' roster, combined with the frequent tours of Europe and other regions of the world, would have provided Siki with the perfect immersive environment to accelerate his education in several European languages.

While *The Post-Enquirer* didn't draw any special attention to Siki's dark complexion or his supposed African origin, *The San Francisco Bulletin* doubled down on both, stating that Siki had only been in the United States for about six months despite the fact that he had famously debuted almost exactly two years prior. The paper also repeated the erroneous claim that Siki was "the only colored wrestler taking part in contests in the United States."

A subsequent edition of *The Bulletin* amended this assertion, stating that Siki was the sole Black wrestler "in the *heavyweight* division in *this* country," which may have been intended to make allowances for the activities of Lee Umbles, Tarzan Wilson, and a few other regional Black wrestlers who competed in lower weight classes.

Siki made quite a splash during his Bay-area debut, wrestling Wladek Zbyszko to a draw, and repeatedly "had his muscular opponent in jeopardy." In the aftermath of the contest, Siki provided a lengthy statement to *The St. Louis*

Argus, one of the Black publications serving his home state of Missouri.

"It was a great surprise to the wrestling fans at Frisco when I climbed into the padded arena," Siki told *The Argus*. "These fans were skeptical of my ability; then too the notoriety that my cousin Battling Siki has created throughout the United States had a great deal to do with that attitude. When I was introduced to the referee the fans began to snicker and wisecrack about me not having a snowball's chance in hades, but after my hour of wrestling with the Pole they changed and were pulling for me to pin him. One hour was the time limit. At the end of the time, Wladek was completely exhausted. In five minutes more I would have pinned his shoulders to the mat. I am positive of this because he had to be carried to the corner."

Siki then won his next outing, downing Joe Kamareski in just under 36 minutes with a headscissors.

In his third outing, Siki managed to obtain a victory of sorts when captured a fall in a losing effort during his rematch with Zbyszko, capturing the second fall out of three with a flying half nelson after 45 minutes of total action had elapsed. The fact that Siki had evened the score appeared to light a fire under Zbyszko, who ended the bout less than six minutes later with a flying mare.

The way the bout played out made it crystal clear that Siki still would not have defeated Zbyszko if the bout had been a one-fall contest. Still, Siki had managed to pin a former world heavyweight champion's shoulders to the canvas, which boosted the perception that he was indeed a threat to the upper echelon of grapplers.

After Siki had a far easier time with Farmer McLeod — beating him with a full nelson in 31 minutes — *The St. Louis Argus* spoke about "the iron man of the wrestling game" in nothing less than glowing terms, and referred to his loss to Zbyszko in the best-of-three-falls match as "a fluke."

"Starting with his usual bang-up style of worrying his opponent, Siki had the former battling for his dear life," stated

A Decided Novelty

The Argus. "Seizing McLeod in a double wrist lock, he threw him to the floor, but McLeod refused to stay put and wriggled free time and again. Securing a flying mare which held the crowd spellbound, Siki caused the former to sail through the air and land on the mat with a sickening thud. After he had worried his opponent with a series of headlocks, he grasped him with a body scissors and pinned his shoulders to the mat."

The cultural importance of Siki being the sole Black heavyweight wrestling star of any renown was also acknowledged by mainstream publications. When Siki lost a bout to Hans Jaenke in San Francisco's Dreamland Rink — dropping consecutive falls in approximately 15 minutes and one minute respectively — *The San Francisco Bulletin* reported of the resulting devastation felt in the Black neighborhoods across the bridge in Oakland.

"A pall of gloom hangs today over West Oakland as Reginald Siki, the only colored wrestler in the world, is a shattered idol locally because of his defeat last night by Hans Jaenke in the main event of Frank Schuler's wrestling show at Dreamland Rink," reported *The Bulletin*.

As summer stretched into fall, Siki continued his practice of losing far more often than he won. This included a loss to Renato Gardini in Sacramento, after which *The Sacramento Union* attested that Siki's practice of wrestling shoeless made him especially susceptible to toeholds.

In the midst of all of these appearances throughout Northern California, Siki's name made it into the newspapers for an incident that had nothing at all to do with his wrestling prowess. In a scary episode, Siki was swimming at San Francisco's famed saltwater pond known as Fleishhacker Pool when he was caught in the undertow and nearly lost amongst the thousands of patrons in the water until he was rescued by lifeguard David Carter.

"Siki was about 100 feet out from shore when he was caught in the grips of the undertow that sweeps with irresistible force along the beach at that point," reported *The San Francisco Examiner*. "A powerful swimmer, he fought the current until he

A Decided Novelty

was exhausted. Then his cries attracted the attention of Carter. Siki was treated at the Fleishhacker first aid station, and later sent to his home at 1828 Webster Street."

While Siki was being physically tossed about by aquatic currents, his name was being tossed about more than 7,000 miles away in Australia. It was there that *The Referee* of Sydney was advertising Siki and at least one of the Zbyszkos to be among the wrestlers being flown in to entertain the locals.

Owning a less-than-stellar record did not prevent Siki from being advertised for appearances in Los Angeles by *The Evening Vanguard* as the colored heavyweight champion and "a giant black," who had been "throwing everyone sent against him."

A week ahead of his bout in Los Angeles against Abe Kaplan, in a bout included in one of Lou Daro's shows at the Olympic Auditorium, Siki was invited to participate in a festival held by Black residents of Los Angeles, where he was to be honored in front of 15,000 event participants.

"The colored sensation of the wrestling game will be introduced to the fans, and in turn will introduce the winner of the colored bathing beauty parade held recently," announced *The Los Angeles Evening Express*. "Siki will also start one of the eight auto races. Motorcycle races and airplane stunt flying will be included in the day's events."

Shortly thereafter, it was announced that Siki would be joined by heavyweight boxer George Godfrey, who had strung together 18 consecutive fights without being knocked out, and in his 14 victories during that time, he had knocked his opponents out in 12 of those fights. *The Los Angeles Times* clarified that Godfrey would serve as the official starter for the races while Siki would be on hand as the guest of honor.

Ahead of Siki's first major bout in Los Angeles, *The California Eagle* posed the question, "Is the colored race soon to have a world's heavyweight wrestling champion?"

"Standing 6 feet, three inches in height and weighing 220 pounds, Siki has lately proven what some are pleased to call a 'colored threat' to Joe Stecher's heavyweight wrestling crown, which has never heretofore rested upon the head of anyone but of the white race."

The article went on to mention that Siki had recently scored a "sensational victory" over Wladek Zbyszko in Philadelphia, and had captured everyone's attention when he pinned Zbyszko's shoulders to the mat "in jig time." Since no such Siki victories over Zbyszko had occurred, and certainly not in Philadelphia, the paper is presumably referring to the moment when Siki captured a single fall over Zbyszko in a best-of-three-falls match that he lost.

With all of the hype behind Siki for this appearance, and also in light of the fact that "The Abyssinian Panther" told *The California Eagle* he was "down to his best weight — 220 pounds of ebony-hued muscle," a casual fan might have assumed that Siki's victory was assured. Instead, the fans at the Olympic Auditorium watched Siki and Kaplan duel to a 30-minute draw.

After the bout, *The Eagle* remarked that Siki could take solace in the fact that he had "made friends" wherever he ventured in Los Angeles due to "his perfect manners." The publication also stated that Siki had been drafted into film work at the Hal Roach Studio during his time in Southern California, and was certain to return soon after fulfilling other wrestling commitments.

From there, the wrestling tour made a quick stop in Salt Lake City, Utah, where the "world's colored champion" was once again matched with Wladek Zbyszko in a multi-fall match. Owing perhaps to the losses Siki took in previous years that garnered national attention, *The Salt Lake Telegram* accounted for this, remarking "while [Siki] was beaten in some of his novice professional matches, he has been winning consistently for some time, and has worked his way to the first string of heavyweight tusslers."

Predictably, Siki lost his bout with Zbyszko, but while Steve Moloney of *The Salt Lake Telegram* reported that Zbyszko had "handily defeated Reginald Siki, colored heavyweight champion of the world," Siki broke new ground by scoring the first pinfall of the bout at the 17-minute mark with a leg split. From a visual standpoint, this demonstrated that Siki might be able to competently defeat one of the top White wrestlers in the world, provided it was a one-fall contest.

"Siki, the colored wrestler, was a revelation to mat fans," wrote Moloney. "The big boy, although decidedly inexperienced, showed that he had all the tussling tricks of a veteran, combined with the ambition of youth. He lacked, however, the polish and finish to his work to defeat such an experienced man as the great Pole."

Siki then returned to California and bookended a loss to Ranato Gardini with wins over Leo Pappiano and Jim Browning before being set to tackle Jim Londos in Los Angeles. Booked against a wrestler who was already being groomed to be the future face of pro wrestling, Siki was dismissed in two straight falls during their encounter at the Olympic Auditorium.

"Londos gained the first fall in 59 minutes and 20 seconds of torrid wrestling," reported *The California Eagle*. "A combination reverse headlock and body scissors turned the trick. After a five minute rest, Londos threw Siki in less than two minutes of wrestling. Siki was in distress from the first fall."

The middle-of-the-pack booking of Siki didn't escape the attention of the press, and as the year drew to a close, *The Los Angeles Record* assured its readers that Siki had been able to maintain his popularity with fans "even in losing battles" ahead of a bout against Martin Zikovitch, which also ended in a draw.

In the middle of December, the famous pugilist Battling Siki — the man who had inspired Reginald Siki's ring name — was gunned down on the streets of Hell's Kitchen in New York City. His body was discovered by a local patrolman, and a revolver with two spent shells was found in a nearby gutter.

"Twelve hours after discovery of his body with two bullet wounds in the back, the former barroom boy, decorated world war veteran, and participant in countless street and barroom brawls, lay in a morgue tonight while police combed haunts of the underworld for his slayer," reported the Associated Press.

The murder of Louis "Battling Siki" Fall was never solved. In its aftermath, as greater numbers of sports fans became aware that Siki was never Fall's true surname to begin with, Reginald Berry was forced to distance himself from Fall during interviews, while denying that he was any relation to the murdered fighter.

During the remainder of that same year, Lee Umbles continued to be depicted as a technically brilliant Cuban grappler who would push White Americans to their limits only to have them pull out the victories by the slimmest of margins. When Umbles lost by decision in Columbus, Ohio to Lee Fishbaugh, *The Lancaster Daily Eagle* declared "the Cuban" to be "one of the cleanest warriors to step into the local ring."

Just two months later in the same city, Umbles won a boxing match in impressive fashion, knocking out Oliver Allen in the second round of their fight.

Siki and Umbles weren't the only Black wrestlers making waves in the country during 1925. Down in Texas, wrestling fans were seeing the rise of a Black wrestling star who went by the name of White Noble.

Born July 12, 1892 to Sam Nobles and Rebecca Taylor, William Nobles eventually became one of the first Black wrestlers to regularly entertain audiences in the Lone Star State. Living in Taylor, Texas, Nobles spent at least a decade working as a local butcher, as he is listed as such in both the 1920 and 1930 U.S. Censuses. In his draft registration from the first World War, which did not give exact heights and weights, Nobles was described as tall and stout; later wrestling advertisements would fix his weight at 190 pounds.

When Nobles first emerged publicly on the Texas wrestling scene as "White Noble," it was established that he was the protege of another Taylor resident, the legendary Elmer "Pet" Brown. Brown was a renowned Texas professional wrestler who captured substantial media attention when he won perhaps the most respected version of the world middleweight wrestling championship from Mike Yokel in May 1914.

Subsequent reports would reverse the roles of Brown and Noble and allude to Noble as the trainer of Brown; this is unlikely, as Brown was four years Noble's senior, and was active in wrestling for more than a decade prior to Noble's first recorded bouts.

In an awful bit of prescience, Brown died under tragic circumstances in 1923 while still reigning as the world middleweight champion. At the site of his construction work camp, Brown was shot to death by constable L.J. Starkey, who was in the process of harassing a Black construction employee of Brown's (which the reporter unfortunately referred to as "his negroes") who were purported to have been involved in unlicensed gambling. Starkey was acquitted of murder, as the jurors discounted the eye-witness testimony of Brown's employees — *all* of whom were Black — and favored Starkey's self-defense claim, which rested on Starkey's belief that the famous wrestler could easily have broken his neck if he managed to get a firm grasp of him.

Brown's close relationships with local Black residents made him a natural mentor for aspiring Black wrestlers like Noble. By 1925, Noble was declaring himself to be the light heavyweight colored wrestling champion of Texas, but since there were so few Black wrestlers in Texas, Noble operated predominantly in his hometown area of Taylor, wrestling against White competitors like Speedy Johnson, Joe Montana, and Jack Bentley.

Although reports of Noble's match results are hard to come by, elements of his style can be gleaned simply by analyzing the few details that are available. In one of his main-event contests against Bentley, Noble emerged victorious from the 42-minute bout in two consecutive falls, and his two submission wins — by body scissors and armlock respectively — are indicative of a wrestler known for succeeding through technical prowess rather than brute force.

A Decided Novelty

Furthermore, as if 42 minutes wasn't a satisfactory amount of time to devote to a main-event wrestling presentation, details from some of Noble's other in-ring exhibitions reveal a wrestler who had few qualms, if any, about extending himself to the uppermost limit in order to send crowds home happy.

In 1925, Noble wrestled Joe Montana to a two-hour draw to prepare Montana to face Greek wrestler Gus Pappas. Then, in his own bout with Pappas, Noble engaged in an endurance session on the level of Illa Vincent when he sparred with the multi-time American middleweight champion for three hours and 45 minutes before the time limit expired and the referee rendered a decision in favor of Pappas.

Late in January 1926, Reginald Siki was credited with a victory over Jack Roller at the Olympic Auditorium "when his double wrist lock dislocated Roller's right arm and the latter was unable to continue," according to *The Illustrated Daily News*. While it's unknown whether it was a legitimate injury or not, the brevity of the rematch suggests that the outcome of the first match may have been unintended and possibly Siki's fault. Roller crushed Siki in just four minutes with "a combination arm and headlock."

The truth of Siki's past was supposedly exposed in January by famous syndicated sportswriter Frank G. Menke, who typed an editorial for his national column that sought to reveal the timeline of Siki's rise to prominence. Despite Menke's occasionally prejudiced language, his account offered the most plausible explanation yet for Siki's wrestling career origins.

"Not so long ago, Siki was a nice fat cook for the Zbyszko brothers," wrote Menke. "There came a day when the Curley combination needed some new rassler in a hurry. None was available. So appraising eyes were cast upon Siki. He had size, weight, and was the kind that would willingly follow orders. So they made a rassler out of him almost overnight by little more than the simple process of saying: 'Tag — you're a rassler.'"

A Decided Novelty

As there are zero indications that Siki was merely a chiseled, sculpture-worthy physical specimen during his first in-ring appearances, there is little chance that he went straight from being a "nice fat cook" to a pro wrestler without receiving any preparatory training, at least with respect to his conditioning. Moreover, it can be gleaned that Siki was already a wrestler prior to meeting the Zbyszkos if careful attention is paid to details that would soon be revealed about his origin.

Reginald Siki in peak physical condition

Menke continued, describing how Siki, who had been "nothing but a cook for the Zbyszko brothers up in Old Orchard, Maine," was placed in the ring with Wladek Zbyszko and allowed to win, before subsequently being booked against

Stanislaus Zbyszko for the world championship. Or to let Menke tell the tale, "They staged a match for the 'championship' between Stan and his former cook, and by clever press-agenting made it appear in advance that this negro, whom Stan could have tossed in about one minute, was a menace to Stan's reign as 'champion.'"

Although Menke went on to rather accurately describe the reality of a professional wrestling operation, inasmuch as the wrestlers received a weekly stipend with a share of the profits, and with headliners receiving a larger share, his details regarding Siki's development are off. Siki had not yet achieved an outright victory against either Zbyszko brother, save for a pair of single-fall wins in multi-fall matches. Moreover, he was nowhere near Stanislaus Zbyszko during his title reign, with his noteworthy straight-falls loss to Stanislaus in Chicago being a non-title match.

A couple of months later, an even less flattering anecdote about Siki circulated in *The Cincinnati Enquirer*, and it included an interaction between Siki and the man with whom he allegedly shared an agent, the world class Black boxer George Godfrey. To summarize the tale, the story begins with Godfrey inviting Siki to go horseback riding "in the hills near Los Angeles," resulting in the novice horseback rider Siki becoming so sore from the experience that he lost his next two matches as a result.

The story continues with the two athletes working out in a gym a few days later, with Siki applying antiphlogistine — a painkiller — to his hand afterwards. Godfrey inquired as to the purpose of "the mud" Siki was putting on his hands, and when he heard it relieved pain, Godfrey helped himself to a large dose of the ointment, which resulted in severe blistering of his hands, and a warning to the boxer from a physician that he should avoid fighting for a couple of weeks.

Elements of this story may very well have been true; Godfrey was forced to cancel a late-January fight against Manny Kaplan due to an injured hand. Then again, Godfrey was fouled so egregiously by Sully Montgomery throughout their January 6 bout that the latter was suspended indefinitely by the California Athletic Commission for his repeated use of blatant low blows, and injuries to Godfrey's nether regions may have been the true reason for the cancellation.

Speculative gym stories aside, *The Enquirer*'s retelling of the event quoted both Godfrey and Siki speaking in the very over-the-top, ungrammatically sound fashion of minstrel show entertainers ("Dat stuff'll just take the hide off'n your hand!").

While it's true that Godfrey was born in Alabama before moving to Leiperville, Pennsylvania, at this stage of his career, Siki was — by all accounts — a borderline polyglot raised in the Midwest, and whose mother was born and raised in the Upper Midwest. It was a stereotypical mischaracterization that spoiled the essence of what might otherwise have been a real downtime exchange between two notable Black sports legends of the era.

As Siki was having an unfortunate amount of artistic license taken with his speech patterns, Lee Umbles had been making major appearances in the Chicagoland area, notably losing to middleweight champion Johnny Meyers in consecutive falls that ate up a total of one hour and 15 minutes of ring time. The result of this match was syndicated and distributed by several news outlets, which spread the name of Lee Umbles around North America.

The Associated Negro Press, a Chicago-based news service, presented the report of Umbles' world title defeat with a very sympathetic slant, stating that Umbles had "lost a hard-fought struggle to the champion." They further humanized him through their reporting by adding that Umbles was a transplant from Indianapolis to Chicago, and was a physical education instructor at the YMCA on Wabash Avenue.

Following the Meyers match, Umbles' popularity increased enough that he was able to become an attraction in nearby Wisconsin. When promoting Umbles' Badger State debut against Jimmy Demetral on its front page, *The Wisconsin State Journal* noted that Umbles was "commanding the attention

A Decided Novelty

of promoters all over the country and is doped to win the title within the next few months."

When Umbles did receive a subsequent title rematch with Meyers in late May, this time at Turner Hall in Madison, he lost again, but gave another good account of himself by wrestling for 53 minutes against the world champion.

Lee Umbles ties up his opponent's arm

"Umbles made a great hit with Madison fans by his performance, and displayed more cleverness in his last bout than Meyers has shown in all the times he's appeared in Madison," declared *The State Journal*. "Johnny simply wore down his opponent; he didn't outsmart him."

In the aftermath of the Meyers contest, Wisconsin-based publications like *The Capital Times* began to refer to Umbles respectfully as "colored claimant to the middleweight wrestling title."

A Decided Novelty

Just like that, Umbles became an all-purpose combat draw in Illinois and Wisconsin, primarily wrestling, but also occasionally boxing. He also proved that he was able to adapt his repertoire of holds, defeating Rudy Stoll with a toehold at an Indiana Harbor event. In the aftermath, Stoll made an excuse through *The Lake County Times* that Umbles had taken advantage of a preexisting injury to his toe.

For the remainder of summer 1926, Reginald Siki suffered losses in all of his major bouts, including straight falls losses to Richard Schikat, George Kotsonaros, Jack Taylor, Renato Gardini, Wladek Zbyszko, and Stanley Pinta. At the tail end of that string of losses, *The Pacific Coast New Bureau* printed a very detailed biography of Siki.

While the bulk of the biography wanders aimlessly through make-believe territory, it shockingly contains the first authentic clues into how Siki's career and subsequent connection with the Zbyszkos unfolded.

After introducing Siki as "the only first class black heavyweight wrestler in America," the article insists that Siki's real name was Dejatch Tedelba, and that he was born in "Dir'e Douaha, Abyssinia." The city was almost certainly intended to have been Dire Dawa, Ethiopia, whereas "dejatch" is an Ethiopian word for "prince," and the surname Tedelba was completely invented.

"In 1915 he arrived in Montreal, Canada, where he resided 3 years, going from there to Kansas City, Mo. in 1918," continued the article. "He remained in Kansas City four years, one of which was spent at the Lincoln High School, the other three under the tutelage of Fred O'Day, former lightweight wrestling champion of the world."

From there, the article ventures into Siki's wrestling accomplishments, including a 1925 victory over Wladek Zbyszko in Baltimore, which never happened, and also a draw with Stanislaus Zbyszko on January 30, 1925, which also never happened. Siki was further credited with a victory in Los Angeles over "American Champion of the World" Jim Browning in November 1925. While Siki certainly boasted a win over Browning on his resume, "The Kansas Tornado" was neither an American champion nor a world champion on the night of their match.

On top of tacking a further two inches onto the peak of Siki's already exaggerated height and declaring him to be 6'6", the article also supplied a timeline to track Siki's progress as he worked his way toward a claim to the "catch-as-catch-can championship of the world among the Darker Races." In chronological order, Siki's supposed victims had been Negro champion William Briggs, Japanese champion Taro Miyaki, India champion Prince Goho Gobar, and Turkish champion Nulah.

The use of the name William Briggs is interesting, as there is no record of a Negro champion wrestler going by that name. However, there *was* a bout involving a Black wrestler with the surname Briggs and another Black wrestler that took place at the Kansas City Convention Hall on May 26, 1921, on a card headlined by Stanislaus Zbyszko and Joe Stecher.

The match in question was conducted between "The Snake" Leonard Rabinette and "Dusky" Briggs, further identified as "Lincoln High School student and Negro Champion of Greater Kansas City." *The Kansas City Times* reported that Rabinette defeated Briggs with a half-nelson body hold, and presumably won the championship.

This Kansas City wrestling scene likely provided Berry's introduction to professional wrestling before his transformation into Reginald Siki. This is further substantiated by the fact that Reginald "Siki" Berry *was* enrolled as a student at Lincoln High School — a Black-only institution for more than 100 years after its founding in 1865 — and evidence for the theory that Siki began his career as Leonard Rabinette rests in the fact that William Briggs is reported as the first victim of Siki during his "Darker Races" title conquest.

For half a decade, Siki had shouldered nearly the entire burden of favorably representing Blacks to the furthest extent permitted by wrestling promoters of the day. Despite the proliferation of losses on his record, his presence had been

A Decided Novelty

beneficial to the box office, and with only one Siki to go around, wrestling promoters would eventually get around to anointing new Black stars to elevate in his place.

7 – So Few Negro Wrestlers

When Reginald Siki disappeared from the ring for the latter part of 1926, his absence was attributed to some combination of rehabilitating an injury and the filming of at least one major motion picture. In December, the Associated Negro Press reported that Siki had been recruited into the filming of "Tarzan and the Golden Lion" while he was recovering from torn ligaments in his arm.

Siki resumed his wrestling activities — at least in the U.S. — in February 1927. During his major mat return to the Olympic Auditorium, he was one of three opponents defeated by former Harvard University wrestling coach Frank Judson, who pinned Siki in less than 10 minutes *after* Judson had already pinned two other wrestlers in under eight combined minutes.

Ahead of Siki's next match, the United Press writer appeared to have been mocking Siki's faux Ethiopian background, referring to him as the "Abyssinian wild man from Pullman, Illinois" prior to his bout with Chris Michaels. Siki lost yet again, this time because he failed to defeat Michaels within the agreed-upon 15-minute time limit.

In March, the Associated Negro Press announced that Siki continued to be in high demand in Hollywood due to his "great size and athletic prowess," and because he possessed a "heroic build." He was cast as an ancient Egyptian in "Sinews of Steel," a silent film starring Alberta Vaughn and Gaston Glass.

The arrival of summer saw Siki traveling to Vancouver for yet another rematch with Stanislaus Zbyszko, where *The Vancouver Sun* introduced him to readers under his alias of Dejatch Tedella, and at a height and weight of just over 6'2" and 218 pounds.

"Dejatch, etc., is a man of parts," offered *The Sun*. "He has boxed, wrestled, barbered, dived for pearls, chased the roaring lion through movie forests and done many things to turn the honest penny in his time. As a wrestler, he threw

Wladek Zbyszko twice, held Renato Gardini to a draw in two hours' brawling, and wrestled Romanoff in the south, only to have the thing end in a fist fight."

Reginald Siki in *Tarzan and the Golden Lion*

Not only had Siki *not* wrestled Tarzan Romanoff in the South, there is no evidence that the two had wrestled one another anywhere in North America at that point. Sadly, this editorial also quoted Siki in the stereotypical dialect attributed to most Black entertainers of the day. Siki had already expressed himself quite eloquently when interviewed in other publications, and his quotes in *The Sun* that include statements like "Ahm very peace-lovin', but iffen a man takes too much it ain't so good" do not jibe with his portrayals in other writings.

A Decided Novelty

While these mischaracterizations were unfortunate, their source was understandable. The Black population of Vancouver wouldn't surpass one-tenth of one percent for another 50 years. As such, it's entirely possible that the staff of *The Sun* had never had a single authentic personal interaction with a Black person between them, and believed that the minstrel show depictions of Blacks presented by traveling vaudeville stars who often performed in blackface were accurate representations of the race.

Far less forgivable were the headline and subheading from the day after the bout, which were "Dark Boy Slowly Crushed" and "Zbyszko Employs Craft to Puncture a Balloon From Africa."

Siki took the first fall of his bout with Zbyszko, with the overly colorful recounting of *The Sun* illustrating how Siki had "heaved the big Pole over his head, wrapped him in a leg scissors, taken a bar arm adjunct and pinned the stoutest shoulders in all of Poland to the blinking mat. Yassuh, Mistah Siki did just that."

Zbyszko evened the tally by clamping an armbar onto Siki and then inserting a thumb into a nerve in Siki's arm to force his adversary to submit. Zbyszko then pinned Siki three minutes later to end the match.

The Zbyszkos' wrestling tour reached New York in the fall, and Siki was hastily paired with Stanislaus Zbyszko once again. Presented as "the first colored man to be seen on the mat in the East in many years," Siki's recent accomplishments as the "Senegalese champion" were greatly embellished in order to depict him as a viable threat to one of the world's most successful grapplers.

"Siki comes direct from the Pacific Coast, where, during the summer, he won all of his matches, achieving victories over Ad Santel, Alex Lundeen, Paul Jones, Latrinda Gobar, and others," added *The Brooklyn Daily Times*. "He won a fall also over Renato Gardini, which is something few wrestlers can boast."

A Decided Novelty

Far from winning all of his matches, Siki had lost far more frequently than he had won during every year of his career up until this point, and summer 1927 was no exception.

With New York fans knowing nothing of Siki's less-than-stellar record in the West, Siki and Zbyszko wrestled to a one-hour draw in front of 2,500 fans at the New Ridgewood Grove. It was an encounter during which *The Daily Times* reported that Siki "grinned throughout and hurt Stanislaus plenty with grueling headlocks."

Siki followed this up by wrestling Cyclone Rees to a draw at the Ocean Park Casino in Long Branch, New Jersey, where Siki was similarly identified as "the first colored wrestler to appear before the local fans this season" by *The Long Branch Daily Record*.

Back across the Outerbridge Crossing, Siki beat Stanley Stickney in 19 minutes with a headlock, and then defeated Wladek Zbyszko on the technicality that the seasoned veteran was unable to down Siki within the agreed-upon timeframe of 30 minutes.

In the rematch held three weeks later toward the end of October, Zbyszko procured a headlock on Siki, who proceeded to lift the Polish wrestler completely off the ground and heave him over the top rope and into the laps of the reporters in press row. Zbyszko was saved from crashing directly onto the floor by the presence of several wooden chairs at ringside.

"Zbyszko clambered back into the ring, his knee bruised and bleeding, and implored Referee Earnest Roeber to allow the match to continue," reported *The Daily Times*. "Roeber refused, however, disqualifying Siki for unsportsmanlike conduct."

Following this "loss" to Zbyszko, *The Brooklyn Citizen* anointed Siki the "Black Menace of the Grappling Game."

"In many appearances at the Grove, Siki remains undefeated," printed *The Citizen*. "He was disqualified for tossing Zibby over the ropes, but if anything this has made him more feared than ever."

A Decided Novelty

The "Black Menace" title originated with Jack Johnson's threat to boxing's heavyweight division, then was later applied to any dominant Black fighter who represented a serious threat to the world championship in their weight class. Through the use of the term, *The Citizen* was underscoring Siki's viability as a world title contender in the sport of professional wrestling.

By the fall, Siki had moved on to New England, and following the pronouncement that George Godfrey had inherited the title of "The Black Panther of Boxing" from Harry Wills, Siki then began to be referred to more frequently as the Black Panther of wrestling, as Illa Vincent had been in the prior decade. Once again, Siki was introduced to a new set of fans by using a bout with Stanislaus Zbyszko to establish his credibility. The promoters also spun quite a yarn when unveiling Siki's backstory.

"Siki, whose real name is Dejatch Tedella, began wrestling in Africa when he was nine years old," reported *The Springfield Union*. "When he left Africa, he settled in Montreal in 1915. Although he wrestled in Canada for several years, he did not turn professional until 1923. Siki also lays claim to the colored championship of the world. Siki has never met Zbyszko in a mat tussle."

Local promoters apparently believed four years was enough time for fans to forget Siki and Zbyszko's famous 1923 Chicago bout. As usual, Stanislaus bested Siki, but Siki captured the first fall in 42 minutes with a headlock-bodyscissors combination. That's when Zbyszko gave the impression that he had begun to take the action far more seriously.

"The Pole got working, and after 46 minutes and 19 seconds, sent Siki down with a flying mare," reported *The Springfield Daily Republican*. "The Abyssinian was pretty groggy after this fall, and was an easy victim for Stan in the final fall, being pinned to the mat in 11 minutes with a flying mare."

In total, the two men wrestled for nearly one hour and 40 minutes, and Siki's popularity grew despite the loss. *The*

A Decided Novelty

Union reported that "Siki gained considerable prestige among local wrestling fans, his speed, cleverness, and strength winning for him rounds of applause at the close of the match."

Siki's popularity in the Northeast surged as he defeated Karl Vogel in New York, downed Fred Lieberman in Massachusetts, and then returned to New York to wrestle Wladek Zbyszko to a 30-minute draw. After Siki's bout with Zbyszko, *The Brooklyn Daily Times* remarked that so many holds and escapes were utilized that "at times it looked like an aesthetic dance."

After this particular bout with Zbyszko, *The Brooklyn Citizen* affirmed that Siki had developed quite a following among New York's wrestling fans, although no one could pinpoint precisely why he was so popular.

"Of course he has won all his bouts, but others have done as much," considered *The Citizen*. "He is so black they have christened him 'The Black Menace,' and his color may explain it. Albeit, his popularity transcends that of any other grappler, Hans Steinke excepted."

Siki closed out the year by taking both Jim Browning and Jack Taylor to draws in New York and Philadelphia respectively. *The Philadelphia Inquirer* touted Siki's bout with Taylor as Siki's Philadelphia debut. This officially put to rest any doubt that Siki's "sensational victory" over Wladek Zbyszko that allegedly occurred in Philadelphia early in Siki's career was anything other than a myth tendered by *The California Eagle* to raise Siki's stock.

"Siki, like his namesake who departed this world on the other end of a knife after having attained a world's boxing championship in the light heavyweight division, is a physical throwback to another age, being animal-like in strength and quickness," gushed *The Inquirer*.

Apparently, the writer of this article had forgotten the details of Battling Siki's murder; it was two bullets rather than a knife that led to the boxer's untimely demise.

In January 1928, the Zbyszkos' group slid back to New England, where they rekindled the angle of having it suggested

A Decided Novelty

by the local promoter — in this case, Jim Barnes — that Wladek Zbyszko and potentially other wrestlers in the organization would selectively draw the color line and refuse to face Siki out of fear for what the African star might do to them.

"Barnes believes that Zbyszko would gladly withdraw from his engagement with the Black Panther," stated *The Springfield Union*. "The boys have been telling Zbyszko just how good Siki is, and Brother Stanislaus has also been informing Wladek that Siki took a fall from him. That alone is reason for Wladek to take up the family cudgels."

Days later, *The Union* listed off all of the most noteworthy "Black Menaces" of boxing, including Peter Jackson, George Dixon, Joe Walcott, Jack Johnson, Harry Wills, and George Godfrey. This list of fighting luminaries was served up as a pretext to place Siki among them, as the first of such menaces in professional wrestling circles.

"The Negro race has turned loose plenty of good boxers, but until Reginald Siki broke into the wrestling game, there were few gentlemen of color inclined to submit to the punishment and grueling debates of the mat sport," proffered *The Union*. "Right now some of the leaders in the sport declare that Siki is truly a 'Black Menace,' and from the caliber of matches which have been made for him, they are intent on finding out just how good he really is."

Following that strong, glowing reintroduction to the New England market, Siki was immediately defeated by Wladek Zbyszko, albeit in what was, by all accounts, an epic encounter. After dropping the first fall to Zbyszko in 26 minutes, 40 seconds, Siki battled Zbyszko in a second fall that lasted one hour and four minutes, and wound up "pinning the broad shoulders of Wladek to the canvas with a body scissors and arm lock."

From there, the third fall added nearly 20 minutes to the total length of the match before Zbyszko won with a headlock. In total, the pair had struggled against one another for nearly two grueling hours.

A Decided Novelty

"It was a good battle all the way and witnessed by the largest crowd of the season," gushed *The Union*. "Siki gave Zbyszko a great deal of trouble and forced the giant Pole to show about everything in his wrestling kit before he was beaten."

Instead of following this magnificent showing against Zbyszko with a series of wins against lesser opponents, Siki wrestled to draws against Jack Ganson and Bud Myers, followed by controversial losses by decision and referee's stoppage to George Hill and Hans Steinke.

Even after all of this, *The Brooklyn Standard Union* still insisted that Siki had *never* been defeated "in the ring," taking great pains to explain that results ending with Siki being counted out of the ring — as he was against Hans Steinke — didn't count. Further, the results of matches taking place outside of New York City went undivulged in the area, and could therefore be overlooked if they might derail a promoter's intentions.

At the very end of February, Siki suffered his first irrefutable loss in New York City at the hands of Jim Londos. It took just over 50 minutes for Londos to pin Siki in front of a packed house at the 71st Regiment Armory, with the fall taking place after Londos had slammed Siki to the mat seven times in succession.

"Stunned after the seventh fall, Siki offered no resistance to Londos' efforts in applying his shoulders to the mat," recounted *The Yonkers Statesman*. "It took Siki three minutes to recover from the effects of the falls, and he was assisted to his corner."

Siki also lost to Dick Shikat in Philadelphia in March when "the undefeated champion of Germany" held Siki in what *The Philadelphia Inquirer* described as "a double overlocking toehold" where both of Siki's feet were "doubled up to the small of his back" for a full minute and 25 seconds until he surrendered.

Back in New York, Siki reportedly toyed with Tommy Lurich at Ridgewood Grove in New York before dismissing him in 17 minutes. Then he sat down for an interview with Alvin J. Moses of the Associated Negro Press.

Apparently Siki did not explain the tight control that was maintained over professional wrestling and who the fraternity within the sport granted admission, as Moses began his feature article on Siki by wondering aloud why so few Black American athletes "noted for their prodigious strength, do not go in for the wrestling game where prejudice is not as much in evidence as it is in fistic circles."

The interview allowed Siki to express that he was not concerned with weight differences between himself and heavier opponents, nor did he believe himself to be capable of defeating world champion Joe Stecher "at this stage of his development." This latter statement could be interpreted as Siki warning Moses that he should not get his hopes up that Siki would ever be placed in a position to win the world championship. Moses then revealed Siki's desire to instruct Black youth in wrestling, supporting this goal in hopes it would motivate young Black men to enter the sport.

After March, Siki departed for one of his European tours, during which he sent a postcard to the editor of *The California Eagle* dated March 27, 1928, and written in Oslo, Norway. It stated the following:

My Dear Friend:
    Just to let you know, I have had "bon voyage" so far. I am spending two days here with friends; shall sail tomorrow for Copenhagen. Will spend a day there and in Danzig, Germany, then on to my destination, Warsaw. I challenged the world in boxing and wrestling by radio aboard ship the 24th. The ground is covered with 4 inches of snow. Hope you received my photo. Give my regards to the boys and all Los Angeles friends.

REGINALD SIKI
(The Abyssinian Lion)

A Decided Novelty

While Siki was overseas, next to nothing was heard from him until the middle of October. That's when a telegram supposedly sent from Siki was brought to ringside and recited to the audience at the Olympic Auditorium in Los Angeles prior to a match between Ed "Strangler" Lewis and Marin Plestina.

"Siki wanted the winner, and judging from his past performances here for promoter Lou Daro, he is a dangerous opponent for either," opined *The California Eagle*. "Siki is about the only recognized wrestler of Negro blood in the game and always gets a big hand."

One and a half months later, with Siki still absent from American soil, Lou Daro's name was brought up yet again. This time the Associated Negro Press reported very early in December that Daro had directly asked representatives of the publication "if there was any logical reason why colored athletes do not seem to take to wrestling, but no definite answer could be given." The implication was that Daro would have happily booked such a wrestler if one could be found, but he had yet to locate any in Siki's absence.

A few days later, *The California Eagle* confirmed the story that Daro was anxious to welcome Siki back, adding that the promoter "deplores the fact that there are so few Negro wrestlers." In the meantime, *The Eagle* kept readers abreast of what Siki had been doing while he'd been absent from American wrestling rings.

"Siki has won several championships in Europe and Asia, and his picture is published surrounded by cups and medals," stated *The Eagle*. "He is now domiciled with Russowiki Foenden-heim, 5657 Stendamasto Koenigsberg, Deutschland (whatever that means)."

Apparently one wrestler did take Daro up on his invitation to Black wrestlers in Southern California. White Noble made his way from Taylor, Texas all the way to Los Angeles for a multi-month tour in 1929. While active there, the 190-pound Noble was hailed as the Negro Heavyweight Champion of America as he feuded with Al Baffert — a young actor-wrestler who had already appeared in two of what would eventually be more than a dozen Hollywood films.

Despite his out-of-state travels, Noble never dispensed with his day job. He maintained his employment as a butcher, and was still active in that role well into the 1930s.

For the entirety of 1929, Reginald Siki was absent from the United States in any capacity related to professional wrestling, nor does his name even appear to have been uttered publicly. In fact, the first time his name surfaced in 1930, it was the result of Lou Daro once again expressing his frustration with the absence of any great Black heavyweights to the staff of *The California Eagle*. *The Eagle*'s response was tantamount to a shrug, as they declared, "Regardless of the inducement, there is not a colored professional wrestler in the West."

The very next month, Siki returned to the United States, albeit on the polar opposite side of the country. In what was likely his Madison Square Garden debut, Siki upended John Gradowich in just over 11 minutes with a combination wrist lock and bodyscissors. Then, curiously going under the name of Reginald "Tiger" Siki, he wrestled Bill Bath to a 30-minute draw in Quebec City, Quebec.

Siki followed this up with a gallant loss to Al Baffert in Toronto, during which Siki seemed to have dislocated his knee at the 50-minute mark, only to have it audibly popped back into place by someone at ringside. Siki then proceeded to wrestle an additional 38 minutes before surrendering the conclusive fall to Baffert.

Leaving Canada, Siki ventured back out to Massachusetts, where he was reintroduced by *The Springfield Daily News* as the world's colored wrestling champion "who not only speaks fluently five different languages, but hails from an aristocratic Negro family which migrated to this country a score of years ago."

While Siki wasn't victorious in his return to Massachusetts, *The Springfield Union* reported that he so thoroughly manhandled Cyclone Rees during their match that

A Decided Novelty

"he was cheered to the echo for fully three minutes following the battle, while Rees was booed at length."

At the very end of October, Siki made his debut in Dayton, Ohio by earning a decision over Alan Eustace. Siki reportedly injured himself during the bout, and is said to have entered the following week's rematch nursing a fractured rib and torn muscles in his chest. Although he won the first fall with a giant swing in 28 minutes, Siki then lost the next two when Eustace strategically applied scissor holds to Siki's torso, ostensibly capitalizing on his injuries.

Siki quickly returned to Toronto, where he won a 30-minute decision over Tom Draak, then traveled to Dayton where he soundly defeated Dr. Strohosky in nine minutes with a bodyslam. Amid his Midwestern campaign, Siki also snuck in a bout against Abe Kaplan in New York City's Jamaica Arena. *The Standard Union* of Brooklyn reported that the Siki-Kaplan bout was prematurely halted at 11:00 p.m. due to a rule preventing wrestling from continuing beyond that time.

By 1929, Lee Umbles was back to wrestling primarily under his real name, and usually being touted as "colored welterweight champion of the world" despite seldom competing with any Black wrestlers. He had also added Michigan to the list of Midwestern states he appeared in.

The Wisconsin State Journal made note of the dearth of Black competitors Umbles was facing, and stated "Umbles is one of the few Negro wrestlers, and he has some trouble in betting matches because he is too rough for many of the white boys." A few days later, the publication underscored the point by adding "Umbles is one of few negro wrestlers in the country who has ever acquired much of a reputation."

It wouldn't be long after that statement was printed by *The State Journal* that Umbles would have a great deal more company on the wrestling scene from Black wrestlers than he likely ever envisioned.

When the wrestler who would eventually gain his greatest notoriety as "Tiger" Jack Nelson first appeared in Windsor, Ontario, Canada during summer 1930, the whiskers he symbolically wore were those of the dark-hued feline that was starting to become quite common where Black wrestlers were concerned.

As "The Black Panther of Memphis, Tennessee," Jack Nelson was introduced to Canadian wrestling fans as "the colored wrestling champion of the world" even though he supposedly hailed from a region where Black residents essentially did not wrestle due to legal restrictions.

"Because many of the big-time wrestlers have drawn the color line, Nelson has not been over-burdened with matches of late," insisted *The Windsor Star*, implying that White wrestlers had opted to duck a potentially dangerous opponent because of his skin color. They would soon be made aware that this particular Black Panther was going to be rendered effectively toothless by the booking decisions of local promoters.

While Nelson may have spent some time in Tennessee during his life, he was born in Austin, Texas on March 3, 1902 as Theodore Roosevelt Reed, son of Lee Reed and Hattie Pettit.

Nelson proved himself to be a capable ring opponent even while suffering his first defeat. Claude Kewley of *The Star* described him as "an ominous dark shadow" who pressured world light heavyweight champion Jimmy Logas during their match, and "threatened to swirl him from his throne, rend him limb from limb, and scatter minute particles of his anatomy to the four winds."

The Black Panther of Memphis unveiled a respectable arsenal of leg holds against Logas, but he was still defeated in straight falls. All the same, Kewley still furnished Nelson with a glowing review even though the bout would be entered into the record books as a definitive loss for Nelson, insisting that Nelson was "one of the greatest matmen who has appeared in a Border Cities ring."

Next up for Nelson would be a match with Jack Sampson, and *The Star* accused Nelson of taking his opponent far too lightly. As an outward display of this disrespect, Nelson "agreed to surrender his Tennessee state championship belt to Sampson" if the latter could defeat him. So it was that a championship belt that was said to represent the Volunteer State came to be defended in an Ontario wrestling ring.

"The Black Panther of Memphis" Jack Nelson

At the conclusion of his early August match with Logas, Nelson was forced to surrender his "handsome silver-plated belt" to his White opponent after suffering a loss. It was a transaction that would make less and less sense over time as the definition of what the belt was said to signify continued to change.

"I didn't figure Sampson was as good a wrestler as he turned out to be, and it was overconfidence more than anything else that cost me the decision," Nelson is recorded as telling *The Star*. "All I want is a chance to win back that belt."

That belt went through a sequence of identity changes over the next week. On August 11, what had originally been identified as a belt that symbolized the Tennessee state wrestling championship was now declared to be "emblematic of the colored wrestling championship of the United States."

Perhaps realizing how silly and possibly insulting it was to have a White grappler like Sampson in possession of a title belt solely intended for Black wearers, *The Star* once again altered the region that it symbolized, claiming it to be the belt worn by the champion of "the Southern United States."

Nelson was permitted to regain his cherished belt during the rematch with Sampson, but *The Star* opined that Nelson "probably did not get much satisfaction out of the victory." The reason stated for Nelson's disappointment was because the victory was acquired through an inconclusive count out win rather than a convincing triumph by pinfall or submission.

To his credit, Nelson did score the first fall of the bout in 46 minutes with a combination toe-hold and leg-stretch. Sampson evened the bout 22 minutes later, and the entire affair was concluded when Sampson struck his head on the hard floor and was counted out when he could not regain the ring.

By virtue of recovering the belt that he had lost to Sampson, Nelson was awarded a shot at the light heavyweight championship held by Logas. In front of a packed Windsor Arena house of 2,500 fans that included legendary wrestler Gus Sonnenberg and heavyweight boxer Primo Carnera, Logas once again defeated Nelson to affirm that the Black challenger was not a viable threat to his championship.

"Discarding his usual tactics, which consist chiefly of a varied assortment of leg holds, Nelson elected to stand up and wrestle with the champ, believing that margins in height and reach would give him the edge that might have resulted in victory," summarized *The Star*. "Logas once again proved, however, that he is one of the smoothest, most cunning and skillful wrestlers in the business. His tremendous strength also proved a great asset, and time and again it enabled him to wriggle from holds that would have downed a less formidable opponent."

Two weeks later, Nelson placed his championship belt on the line again — with his title altered once more to "colored wrestling champion of the Southern states" — as he faced yet another White wrestler in Benny Stefanski. By having Nelson put the title on the line against another non-Black opponent, the tactic seemed to have far less to do with crowning a representative champion, and far more to do with seeing who else could temporarily wrest the Black grappler's second-class bauble away from him.

The Star conveyed as much through its reporting, focusing far more on the tangible worth of "the handsome belt, which is valued at several hundred dollars" than what the trophy was supposedly constructed to represent. True to the pattern that had been established, Nelson once again found himself deprived of his belt after his match with Stefanski.

"The tireless boring in tactics of Stefanski and his opponent's tendency to be careless proved the downfall of Nelson," printed *The Star*. "Stefanski showed less aptitude in wiggling his way clear of the long, lean, spidery legs of the Tennessean and consequently took a great deal more punishment than in the previous bout. Nelson clamped on any number of toe-holds and leg spreads to telling advantage, but Stefanski threw them off and came bounding back in for more."

Now firmly established as fodder for the top wrestlers in Windsor, Nelson was characterized as "the big trial horse of matdom," in the next edition of *The Star*, and the quote was attributed to wrestling promoter Jack Milo, as he told inbound wrestler Pat Fraley, "If you can defeat Nelson, I'll give you some *real* bouts."

It was two months later that Nelson fully armed himself with the tactics of a heel, and *The Star* accused him of mauling his adversary Jack Felix while he "only showed occasional flashes of the form which made him a favorite with local wrestling followers not so long ago." Adopting rougher

A Decided Novelty

tactics didn't alter the end result; Nelson still lost the match to Felix in the end.

As Nelson was establishing himself in the exceedingly rare role of a Black heel in Ontario, the reputation that Lee Umbles designed for himself during the prior decade enabled him to be cast as a favorite opponent for the world champions in his weight class. In 1930, he lost two matches in Michigan to world welterweight champion Jack Reynolds — one in Jackson and one in Flint — with news publications seeming to express genuine surprise that Umbles could wrestle so well for so long in title match after title match without ever defeating the champions and capturing gold.

Apparently, none of these losses served to severely disrupt Umbles' momentum, as "The Colored Flash" continued to be hailed as "a sensation in wrestling circles" who had "met and defeated many of the leading welterweights in the country" before advancing to heavier weight classes.

Jack Nelson moved on to Hamilton and Toronto in early 1931, where he was introduced by *The Toronto Star* as a "colored grappler" who was "considered better than Reg Siki," although the publication neglected to say by whom Nelson was considered to be better, or by what measurement.

Comparing the heavyweight technician Siki with the leaner, rougher Nelson made sense only in terms of skin color. Further, while Siki's win-loss record was littered with blemishes, Nelson's was nearly bereft of any victories.

The Hamilton Spectator advised its readers that Nelson had "an inclination to rough matters" as he prepared to face California's cleverly named Railroad Route, but in their late April contest the two men spent the majority of their one-hour-and-23-minute match rolling on the mat. Nelson still lost the match after a flurry of activity from the bleeding Route to close the show.

"There were signs of real trouble when the pair came out for the third and deciding fall, and after both escaped the deadly splits time after time, Route became groggy and bled from the mouth after heavy punishment caused by headlocks, etc.," described *The Spectator*. "Despite this, however, Route cleared his head long enough, after nine minutes, to crash several times into Nelson, winding up by butting him at the end of a short, hard charge and pouncing heavily on the colored lad to slam him down for a fall."

Reginald Siki began 1931 in Dayton, Ohio, and he finally began to string together enough wins to have his most outwardly successful year in U.S. wrestling rings, at least with respect to the results of his matches.

Apparently, the members of the press had noticed Siki's relative lack of success in prior years, with *The Dayton Daily News* noting in the aftermath of Siki's defeat of Charlie Santon that Siki was "for the first time displaying what the fans have been expecting of him for months."

"Siki has shown signs in past bouts of being slightly muscle-bound above his shoulders, losing to men he should have butchered, but there were no complaints on his work Thursday night," added *The Daily News*.

The paper also noted that Siki used a pair of hip locks to capture each of his falls against Santon, and he would similarly use a hip lock to dispose of Hy Gandar in only six minutes the following week.

Siki dropped a pair of falls to John Pesek in about 48 minutes of wrestling, but seemed to collect himself and went on an admirable winning streak. He downed Jim Browning with a pair of giant swings, then defeated Alan Eustace with an airplane slam and a hip lock. Then he made his way to Camden, New Jersey for a memorable engagement with Andy Brown inside of the Camden Municipal Auditorium.

The Standard Union of New York reported that after Siki captured the first fall and donned his ring robe for the intermission, Brown sprang to his feet and attacked Siki, and found himself entangled in Siki's robe. When referee Frank Potts attempted to sort out the issue, he was struck hard in the face by Brown, and fired back at him.

"For a few seconds, they swung toe to toe, and then the referee proved his superiority by knocking Brown down for a long count," reported *The Standard Union*. "Scores of spectators started to converge on the ring. City policemen stationed in the house forced their way through and got inside the ropes."

What had likely started as a way of enlivening the wrestling show yielded unfortunate results when Brown sprang up and attempted to reignite the brawl in the presence of policemen who hadn't been clued in on the act.

"Brown was showing signs of reentering the fray, whereupon one of the policemen quieted him with a blackjack," continued the article. "This had a deterring effect upon the rest of the crowd, and presently the police succeeded in restoring order. When the time came for the second session between Siki and Brown, the announcer informed the gathering that the club physician had refused to sanction the further appearance of Brown in the ring because of the condition of his head, and Siki was awarded the bout by default."

News of the story extended well beyond the Northeast, as the Associated Press carried the details of how Andy Brown had been unceremoniously "beaten into submission" by the combination of Siki, Potts, and a Camden police officer.

In the fallout from Siki's victory over Brown, the Associated Negro Press published a feature on the Abyssinian Panther that crafted yet another origin story for him. Rather than immigrating to Canada as a youth and then finding his way to Kansas City as a teen, Siki was instead a jungle tribesman of an unnamed African nation who was persuaded to leave his home by an Italian sculptor in 1921.

While modeling in Italy, Siki supposedly grew flabby from lack of exercise. His sculptors suggested wrestling to develop his physique. They specifically requested that he wrestle out of the concern that he would become physically "asymmetrical" if he worked as a laborer.

As with the other feature articles on Siki, a great deal of ink was dedicated to detailing his mastery of French, Spanish, Italian, and German in addition to English. The ANP's article went the further step of disclosing that Siki's favorite authors were Shakespeare, Byron and Shelley, and that the Odyssey of Homer was among his favorite literary works.

After the encounter with Brown, Siki defeated Baffert in Dayton, bested Glen Wade in front of 6,000 fans at the Philadelphia Convention Hall, and wrestled to a draw against Charlie Santon on ladies' night at the Cadle Tabernacle in Indianapolis. Then he defeated Joe Komar and Gus Hanson in Milwaukee, and returned to Dayton to earn another convincing win over Santon.

It was around this time that an association between Siki and Ohio State University was published, and he was introduced as an Ohio State University student in multiple advertisements. This sort of allusion was also made when he began making appearances in Iowa, and *The Daily Times* of Davenport divulged that Siki had supposedly been educated in the United States "before returning to Abyssinia to take care of his father's imported rug business."

What proceeded from there was one of the most inaccurate representations of Siki's resume ever submitted, starting with the suggestion that Siki first developed an interest in wrestling by participating in the gym class at a YMCA in Los Angeles.

"He broke into professional wrestling in Newark in 1927, but decided to return to Abyssinia in 1928 to go into business," printed *The Daily Times*. "Early in 1930, he forsook the merchandise business and went to Europe to resume grappling. He has participated in many matches in Estonia, Latvia, Poland, Germany, France and Spain, and is the proud possessor of a championship belt which he is now displaying at the Puff Cigar store gym here. Siki is a student of languages and speaks his native tongue, Amharic, English, French, Spanish, Polish and German."

Siki's international wrestling exploits notwithstanding, this alternate timeline omits four years of very public activity from Siki's career, including the majority of the campaign that had helped to establish him as the most famous Black professional wrestler in the world up to that point.

However, it correctly states that Siki captured a regional championship during his European exploits, and he frequently carried the symbolic title belt to the ring with him. Also, Siki's relationship with Ohio State University was atypically authentic for a pro wrestling biography of the era.

The Ohio State registrar's office confirmed that Reginald Berry was enrolled in the College of Arts and Sciences from April 11, 1931 to June 8, 1931, although no major was listed, and no degree was ever awarded to him.

As for the actual match in Davenport, *The Daily Times* illustrated how Siki had "tossed the Caveman" George Mack out of the ring with such force that Mack decided to call it quits at the 35-minute mark and simply turned and walked the rest of the way to the dressing room.

The Moline Daily Dispatch offered additional insight into the bout, revealing that Siki had a new weapon in his arsenal that he mercilessly administered to Mack.

"Siki used his head throughout the match, butting it against Mack's forehead with apparent telling effect," described *The Daily Dispatch*. "He employed about ten other unique tricks to trouble the caveman, having George at his mercy almost the whole route."

This use of headbutting by Siki was so infrequent in its use that it was seldom mentioned again. Still, future outings by other Black wrestlers would suggest that someone might have been paying attention to Siki's rare flashes of headbutts during his time in Illinois.

As 1931 drew to a close, Siki traveled to Calgary for a match with Canadian champion Jack Taylor. *The Calgary Daily Herald* labeled Siki as "the Jack Johnson of the wrestling game," which is noteworthy for the simple fact Johnson had lost the heavyweight boxing championship more than 16 years prior. The dated nature of the reference drew attention to the fact that it had been more than a decade since a Black fighter had

A Decided Novelty

even had so much as an opportunity to box for the world heavyweight championship.

The Daily Herald also stated that Siki "has not met any of the several world champions that are now on parade," which couldn't have been more false. Siki had lost a match to John Pesek — the still-reigning world champion of the Midwest Wrestling Association — in September of that very year.

Most interesting of all was *The Daily Herald*'s revelation that Siki had married "the daughter of famous English jockey and trainer Thomas Sydenham." The publication stated that Siki and his wife intended to settle in a new home that they had already purchased in Paris, France sometime within the next two years.

The implication that Siki had wed a White woman was a move that was itself reminiscent of Jack Johnson, who had famously forsworn relationships with Black women at the height of his boxing career and had wed White women on three separate occasions. Siki's actual marital status at the time remains unclear; no famous English jockey named Thomas Sydenham existed. In fact, that particular name belonged to a famous 17th century physician, regarded by most as the father of English medicine, and its use suggests that either Siki or his publicist was having some fun at *The Daily Herald*'s expense.

This was also the case with a subsequent biographical piece about Siki published by *The Daily Herald*, which alleged that "Papa Berei" — Siki's father — moved the African tribal family to Los Angeles when Siki was only eight years old. As Siki's father established a local business as an exporter of fine goods, Siki excelled as a *seven*-sport high school athlete, who was a standout in track and field, football, baseball, basketball, swimming, boxing and wrestling.

While Jack Nelson had emerged alongside Siki and Umbles as yet another Black wrestling standout, victories were still few and far between for at least two of the three men. However, several young Black grapplers were set to emerge on the scene to help them carry the load, including a Black star from another sport who would transform the idea of a

A Decided Novelty

victorious Black wrestler in the main event of a wrestling match from an anomaly into an expectation.

A Decided Novelty

8 — Boss of the Colored Middleweights

While Reginald Siki achieved unprecedented multiregional stardom, his success alone didn't increase the number of Black wrestlers on major wrestling cards. The true turning point occurred in 1931, which marked the emergence of a new generation of young Black wrestlers, sparked by an unlikely catalyst.

Reginald Berry had already drawn inspiration from the popular boxer Battling Siki when creating his Reginald Siki persona. It's doubtful that anyone could have imagined the outcome when one of the most dominant and popular Black heavyweight fighters of the era — and someone who Siki occasionally shared managers with — decided to take up professional wrestling as a means of continuing to earn an income.

In a fitting turn of events, Feab Smith Williams would draw inspiration from mid-19th-century Black Canadian fighter George "Old Chocolate" Godfrey and borrow that name for the duration of his own professional boxing career. Although he rapidly stockpiled victories throughout the 1920s, Godfrey was dogged by accusations that he accepted bribes to extend the lengths of fights, or would throw obvious low blows in order to get himself disqualified during fights that he had doubtlessly been winning.

Such was the case when Godfrey fought Primo Carnera, and George threw a left hook to the groin in the fifth round against the future world heavyweight champion after Godfrey had dominated the early action. An independent review of the fight decreed that the fight had been fixed, and that Godfrey's low blow had been intentional. As a result, George was suspended from boxing in the majority of the major states where fights were held.

In the aftermath of his suspension, Godfrey was forced to fight outside of the lucrative fighting states of New York, New Jersey, Pennsylvania, Massachusetts, and Illinois. It was at this stage that George was presented with another option for making money inside of the squared circle.

According to Jim Rooney of *The Springfield Union* who interviewed Godfrey, the fighter was "hanging around a gymnasium one day, doing nothing as there was nothing to do," when a wrestling promoter approached George and asked him if he had ever wrestled before. Godfrey replied that he had wrestled while serving in the Navy, presuming that traditional folkstyle grappling was the sort of wrestling the promoter had been talking about.

"The Black Panther of Leiperville" George Godfrey

The announcement of Godfrey's wrestling debut was made on January 16, 1931 from Mexico City. He was said to be competing the very next night against American wrestler Jack Russell.

"I'm through with boxing," Godfrey was quoted by the United Press. "The best white fighters in the United States

A Decided Novelty

absolutely refuse to meet me, and I'm fed up on just shadow boxing."

Godfrey was not actually through with boxing by any means. Two weeks earlier, he had knocked out Salvatore Ruggirello just over two minutes into round one of their 10-round fight, and he already had his next fight booked in February for the vacant Mexican heavyweight boxing championship. Still, the idea that the highest ranked Black heavyweight fighter in the world would completely forsake boxing for professional wrestling certainly added weight to the announcement.

George won his debut wrestling match, and when the word of his pro wrestling debut was carried all across North America, promoter Carlos Henriquez immediately announced his plans to bring Godfrey to the United States because his drawing power would be best utilized there.

By the time Godfrey finally made his American wrestling debut, he would already be beaten to the punch in at least one respect. Ten days after "The Black Panther of Leiperville" had announced his intention to wrestle and subsequently made his in-ring debut in Mexico, a very different Black Panther — who also just so happened to be a Black wrestler — was suspiciously rushed to the ring in Centralia, Washington to compete against Mervin Barackman.

It's important to make a note about the significance of the Black Panther title when applied to Black American fighters. In August 1927, a major Associated Press editorial from Bill Ritt appeared in newspapers all across the United States to explain in detail how in every decade of the early 20th century a "Black Panther" had emerged to stalk and hunt the reigning world heavyweight champion. Jack Johnson had carried the title unofficially, Harry Wills had formally carried the title, and George Godfrey had now positioned himself as being worthy of the name.

"George Godfrey is the new Black Panther's name," wrote Ritt. "George is a great hulking chocolate-hued boy who hails from Leiperville, Pa., a 224-pound fighting man with maybe not so much science, but possessing great punching power and the build to take it. Though he's new to the top of the business, Godfrey is a veteran of many years of fighting."

Two months after this editorial ran, Reginald Siki began referring to himself as "The Black Panther of Wrestling" for a three month stretch in Massachusetts before abandoning the Panther title. Nearly two decades earlier, the name had also been used by Illa Vincent during his brief U.S. campaign.

These are important details to note, because what had once been a title that had been inspired by boxing, only to be briefly used and discarded in pro wrestling circles, was about to become ubiquitous within a pro wrestling context.

When Godfrey arrived in New Jersey for his U.S. grappling debut, he did so while carrying his newly won Mexican heavyweight boxing championship belt, earned through a 53-second knockout of Ricardo Rosel.

"The Philadelphia negro scored fourteen victories in a Mexican wrestling tour and hopes to win a place among the performers in one of the eastern mat trusts," reported *The Atlanta Journal*.

Once the opponent for Godfrey's U.S. debut in Newark, New Jersey was declared to be John Grandovich, "the heavyweight champion of Yugoslavia," Dixon Stewart of the United Press wrote a syndicated piece that received wide-scale circulation. In the article, while referring to Godfrey by one of his most prominent nicknames, Stewart made a prophetic statement about how the boxer was likely to be presented during his wrestling venture.

"Promoters are undecided as to Godfrey's billing, but the unwritten rules of wrestling require that all performers be titleholders, and the 'Black Panther' probably will become Negro heavyweight champion," prophesied Stewart.

Stewart's prediction about billing Black wrestlers as champions would prove prophetic. In the meantime, Godfrey was getting down to the serious business of preparing for his American wrestling debut.

A Decided Novelty

The Pittsburgh Courier reported that Godfrey's ring entrance paid tribute to his triumphant Mexican tenure, as he walked to the ring with "a beautiful Mexican shawl" draped over his broad shoulders, and "a 30-gallon sombrero decorated with crimson tassels" on top of his head.

George had promised to unveil a mystery hold, but that pledge went out the window when Grandovich slapped him in the face and kicked him in the shins. Godfrey then unleashed his fists, knocked out Grandovich, and covered him for a pinfall win in just over 19 minutes.

That match was followed by a bout in Jersey City, for which UP correspondent Dixon Stewart was present.

Clearly amused by the fact that Godfrey had "metamorphosed into wrestling's first 'black hope,'" Stewart added that Godfrey's wrestling career would benefit from his "long years of holding up ring opponents" and carrying them into the latter rounds of fights, presumably for the benefit of the bookies.

"Big George cannot wrestle, but that is not a serious handicap," joked Stewart. "After a Mexican tour in which he scored 14 consecutive victories in as many cities over his chauffeur, who appeared under 14 different names, Godfrey made his United States debut in Newark, N.J. Monday. He won his bout with a 'mystery' hold, which consisted chiefly of a right hook to the jaw."

Stewart then explained what happened at the Jersey City event, including a sequence that began when Godfrey slugged Tommy Draak and sent him sailing out to the floor and into the audience. Draak refused to continue, and was replaced by Jack Arnold. When Godfrey ended the match with Arnold in only three minutes without resorting to fisticuffs, Stewart mockingly suggested that this "gave rise to the suspicion that Arnold may be the multinamed chauffeur" from Godfrey's Mexican tour.

Then Stewart mentioned what he conceded was the most crucial feature of the Jersey City show — the packed stadium.

A Decided Novelty

"Whereas such stars as Londos, McMillan, Sonnenberg, and Don George never have been able to draw more than 1,100 fans at Jersey City, Godfrey's appearance resulted in a sellout of the 6,000 capacity arena, and more than 5,000 fans were turned away," Stewart wrote.

A similar story emerged from Godfrey's debut in Camden, where 5,500 fans packed the Camden Convention Hall to watch Godfrey dispose of Andy Zaharoff in straight falls. Despite the incessant tease that Godfrey had a mystery hold to unveil, no such unveiling occurred, as Godfrey won both falls with bodyslams according to *The Every Evening* of Wilmington.

It was apparent that Godfrey may have had difficulty recalling the name of whatever hold he might have used, let alone how to execute it in the heat of battle. In *The Knoxville News-Sentinel*, sports editor Joe Williams stated how after one of his first U.S. wrestling matches, "the snarling, snapping, vicious black panther" admitted that it was "impossible for him to recall any of the technical phases" of his matches, nor did he know what holds he had used.

"I just grabbed hold of the man and threw him," said Godfrey.

According to *The Philadelphia Inquirer*, that's exactly how Godfrey disposed of Nicholas Samarof in front of a record crowd of 2,500 fans in Bridgeton, New Jersey.

"The Black Panther required just seven minutes and eight seconds to dispose of Nicholas Samarof, who weighs 215 pounds and mixes slugging freely with his tussling," explained *The Inquirer*. "Nick started tossing high-hand leads and Godfrey retaliated in kind. Then George grabbed the socking Samarof with a body slam, crashed him upon the mat, and it was all over."

Ever the showman, Godfrey even mixed wrestling into his legitimate boxing activities. In July, Godfrey participated on a mixed boxing-wrestling card, and did both on the same night. Essentially using wrestling as a pre-match warmup, Godfrey lost a 12-minute bout to the original Stanley Stasiak via

A Decided Novelty

bodyslam. When it came to Godfrey's wrestling ability, the Canadian Press reporter noted that Godfrey "seemed to know little about the sport except headlocks, which he used frequently."

Godfrey brushed off his pinfall loss, and knocked out George Gemas in the second round of their six-round main-event encounter after opening a cut above Gemas' right eye in the first round.

The Black Panther of boxing's first real encounter with his legacy occurred in November when he wrestled on the same Salt Lake City card as "The Black Panther" Alexis Kaffir. By that time, Godfrey had recovered his claim to the world colored heavyweight boxing championship by knocking out Seal Harris in August. While Godfrey lost a 10-round decision to Jack Gross earlier in November, his boxing record since the commencement of a full-time wrestling schedule was 3-1, which was rather outstanding all things considered.

Alexis Kaffir was more frequently referred to as Alex Kaffner, and he got his start in the wrestling business as the Black Panther who wrestled in Centralia, Washington in January of 1931. This particular Panther was not mentioned by name at first, but his place of origin was offered as Birmingham, Alabama, and it wouldn't be until two decades later that Tacoma wrestling promoter Nick Zvolis confirmed that this Northwestern iteration of the Black Panther was indeed Alex Kaffner.

"As not one man in a thousand has ever seen a colored man on the mat, it is probable that many Twin City enthusiasts will be on hand to watch the man 'strut his stuff,'" wrote the reporter from *The Chehalis Bee-Nugget*.

The Panther's first match against Mervin Barackman ended in a draw, but the newspapers reported that the 6'1", 180-pound Panther had clearly outwrestled Barackman in their multi-round affair. In his next major effort, the Panther defeated Oscar Butler in consecutive falls.

By March, the Panther was cemented as a main-event competitor. Prior to his bout against Marvin Westerberg, it was noted that the "195-pound colored boy" had created a sensation in the southern portion of Washington, and that his presence added significant interest to the card.

The scarcity of Black residents in many 1930s regions had the side effect of automatically transforming the few Black wrestlers who appeared there into novelty attractions. The very next month, coincidental with the disappearance of the Black Panther from Washington came the first appearances of "The Black Panther" Alex Kaffir in Utah.

"Kaffir, colored sensation, tips the beam at 215 pounds and is said to be the toughest man in the game to take off his feet," printed *The Salt Lake Tribune*. "He claims to have the strength of a couple of bulls, and no man can take him to the mat unless he cares to have them do so."

It didn't take long at all before the news publications of Utah had tacked a syllable onto Kaffir's forename, now rendering it as "Alexis." They also asserted that his technical approach to grappling would be a welcome change from the methods employed by the influx of bruisers to the sport.

"Kaffir is said to have made quite a remarkable record in the ring," said *The Salt Lake Telegram*. "Wherever he has performed, he has drawn large houses simply because he is something new. Football players have been a boon to the mat game in the past six months. Kaffir should be a change from the bunting type of wrestler."

In making his Salt Lake City debut, Kaffir was introduced as hailing "from Egypt" and quickly disposed of Charley Frisbie. *The Tribune* noted that all Frisbie received for his efforts "was a thrust to the mat at 11 minutes by the powerful black panther of the ring."

Perhaps recognizing that Kaffir's dark skin was incongruous with the skin color of 20th century Egyptians, the promoters made a hasty modification to Kaffir's stated place of origin. He was quickly given the alternate origin of being a "Senegalese grappler from Egypt."

In that respect, Kaffir now appeared to be borrowing heavily from both Reginald Siki and George Godfrey, since the former had been touted as a hyper-technical Senegalese grappler, while the latter had rapidly popularized the use of the Black Panther title by Black wrestlers.

Following the victory over Frisbie, Kaffir was quickly served up to local favorite Ira Dern, who bested Kaffir with an airplane spin in a 16-minute match. Alexis then returned to the ring later in May to wrestle Billy the Bear, an *actual* wrestling bear.

"The Black Panther" Alexis Kaffir

In the early summer months, Kaffir continued to compete unsuccessfully in main-event matches against Dern. All the while, the local papers played up Kaffir's darkness as a means of enticing fans to watch him wrestle. Perhaps no illustration was more inventive than the one supplied by *The*

Box Elder New Journal, which described the Black Panther as being "blacker than two black crows."

By August, the Black Panther had returned to Washington and once again shed the name of Alexis Kaffir. The Washington newspapers began referring to the Panther as either a "Seattle Negro" or a "Tacoma Negro," which is likely to be the truest reflection of his point of origin. They also mockingly referred to him as a "cullud boy" during the promotion of some of his matches.

Returning to Utah in the fall, the Panther reclaimed the name Alexis Kaffir and feuded with local roughhouser Leo Papiano, along with Mike Collins and Dean Detton. Following the pattern of Reginald Siki, the majority of Kaffir's outcomes were either losses or draws, as he was now finding clear-cut victories quite difficult to come by.

This time around, the Utah press acknowledged that Kaffir emanated from the Pacific Northwest while still insisting that he was ethnically Senegalese. As such, he was the sole representation of Black wrestlers in a state with just over 1,000 Black residents amongst a total population of more than 500,000, and the first Black wrestler of note to appear in Utah since Siki's brief swing through the state in the prior decade.

Still operating in the Midwest and Ontario, Jack Nelson was about to run headlong into another Black newcomer to the pro wrestling profession. Nelson had added the prefix of "Tiger" to his stage name by the time he made his debut in Niagara Falls in August. *The Niagara Falls Review* cast Nelson in a different light than he had been presented during the earlier stages of the year, describing "the colored bon-bon" as "one of the cleanest men in the game."

The "coffee-skinned demon" who was purportedly "feared by all the white boys in his class" managed to defeat Pete Kopfer in 18 minutes with a reverse arm lock. The next week, Nelson went straight back to losing his matches, as he was downed in straight falls by Stan Rogers with "little difficulty."

A Decided Novelty

Nelson also began making a fair number of appearances in Michigan and Ohio during summer and fall 1931. In Sandusky, he was identified as "the Black Panther from Butte, Montana." In Battle Creek, he was advertised as "the Black Panther of Memphis, Tennessee," and "the first colored matman to appear on a Battle Creek canvas."

The Battle Creek Enquirer included the true statement that "there are few colored matmen in the sport today," then added that "Nelson is reckoned among the toughest canvas artists of them all." Given the dearth of Black wrestlers with any sort of name recognition who were making appearances in major venues, this was a reasonable deduction even if Nelson had been less successful than Siki in terms of his win-loss record.

Nelson's losses continued to mount in Michigan, where he showed that he was adept on the canvas, but not in the same class as his opponents. When frustrated, Nelson would also resort to biting portions of his adversaries' anatomies, like when he "seemed to delight" in biting the toes of Duge Marcel in the course of losing two straight falls to the Canadian in Battle Creek. In this way, he continued to confirm himself as the first Black wrestler with a sustained career to openly wrestle in a heel-like manner in front of White, Northern audiences.

As Nelson's activity in Michigan and Canada extended into the fall, he was set on a collision course with new Black wrestling star Gorilla Parker. It amounted to one of the first significant clashes of headline-grabbing Black wrestlers ever to take place, and one of the first clear instances of what had previously been pondered and then dismissed three decades earlier as "a decided novelty" actually playing itself out inside of a wrestling ring.

While Black wrestlers had competed against each other before, this marked perhaps the first legitimate match between two well-trained Black wrestlers who had been groomed to be stars rather than a novelty sideshow between untrained brawlers.

A Decided Novelty

Whether or not it is a fair representation of what he was truly like in his youth, Henry "Gorilla Parker" Daniels of Frederick, Oklahoma was memorialized as a hot-tempered youngster in his hometown newspaper. In late November 1923, the basketball player for the Consolidated No. 2 High School team was required to appear before Frederick Mayor E.U. Gamblin, and he paid a $7.50 fine as a penalty for a fight he had instigated during a Saturday night basketball game.

"Daniels, a member of the No. 2 basketball team, which played the Demolay team here Saturday night, was several times penalized for fouling and put out of the game, it is said, and then manifested a disposition to cause trouble by visiting the dressing room and baiting the Frederick players," reported *The Frederick Leader*.

Apparently, Daniels was also irritated by the fact that his jacket had gone missing during the scuffle, and *The Leader* printed a follow-up report four days later stating that Daniels' jacket had "mysteriously reappeared in the gymnasium, Tuesday, according to the janitor of the building."

It seems remarkable that Daniels would return to his town of 4,000 residents as a conquering hero a little more than a decade later, but he would manage to do so by maximizing his muscularity, entering the world of professional wrestling, and borrowing elements of his presentation from one of the most celebrated Black boxers of the era.

By October 1931, William "Gorilla" Jones had amassed 81 professional boxing wins and was considered to be one of the best middleweight fighters in the world. That's when Gorilla Parker debuted in Detroit's wrestling rings, claimed to be a Motor City product, and quickly drew the attention of all who beheld him.

As Gorilla Parker, Henry Daniels was described as "a Detroit Negro, who can look more sinister than Public Enemy No. 1 when he wants to." When Parker made his debut in Ontario, the press was a bit more complimentary, saying that he "resembled a ball of muscle" when he overwhelmed his

A Decided Novelty

opponent Ray Meyers and tossed him all over the Grand Opera House of Hamilton.

"When the two first met in the ring, Parker immediately circled his muscular arms about Meyers and pinned him to the mat with a bear hug to win the fall in just thirty seconds," reported *The Hamilton Spectator*.

Even though the bout had been advertised as a one-fall match, the fans were apparently so outraged by the bout's brevity that referee Hughie Hayes requested a restart to the contest simply on the grounds that the fans were upset. Parker obliged, and pinned Meyers a second time in under six minutes to win two falls of a bout that had never been expected to extend beyond one.

"Parker displayed abnormal strength during his short exhibition, picking Meyers up and tossing him around like a bag full of air," continued *The Spectator*. "Against such Atlas-like strength, the Kentucky grappler was powerless."

When Parker made his subsequent return to Hamilton to wrestle Bobby Samson, *The Spectator* lamented how easily he "tore through his opponent" the prior week, but described him as a "one-man tank," and declared him to be "one of the most powerful and attractive men ever to work here."

"Parker, boss of the colored middleweights, is a combination of a dusky Samson and Adonis," stated *The Spectator*. "He is one of the finest built men in the wrestling ring, and power just oozes from him."

The Spectator continued to pile on the praise in subsequent printings, while also providing Parker with the first name of William, cementing the connection with his namesake William "Gorilla" Jones, the popular fighter who had just secured his 82nd victory inside of a boxing ring.

"Parker's advance notices didn't half do him justice," glowed *The Spectator*. "He came here touted as the 'boss of all colored middleweights,' but that notice should have been augmented considerably. If Parker's not the boss of the majority of all middleweights, colored and otherwise, we could eat last year's straw hat, if any."

During the match with Samson, Parker reportedly broke out of all of Samson's early holds "with ridiculous ease" as a showcase of his great strength, until Samson applied a leg scissors around Parker's body to gain the advantage, and then dropped him to the mat with shoulder tackles.

"Parker took this rough treatment for just a short time, after which he went after Samson with venom in his eyes, tossing and butting him around until it seemed almost impossible for the Californian to stand such punishment," recounted *The Spectator*. "After 15 minutes, Parker hurled Samson viciously to the mat, smothering his shoulders down to score his second successful local victory."

In the aftermath of this battle, *The Spectator* suggested a bout between Gorilla Parker and Jack Nelson to determine the true colored middleweight champion. Just days later, that bout was confirmed, although it's noteworthy that between the two wrestlers, Parker was the one identified as the reigning colored middleweight champion "of North America."

After all, Parker can only be confirmed to have been wrestling for one month at this point, with no established victories over Black wrestlers on his resume, while Nelson had been claiming to have been the champion of his race for at least a year, and carried around a physical belt to back his claim.

Just as quickly as the bout between Parker and Nelson was advertised, it was scrapped.

"Matchmaker [Sammy] Sobel originally intended to have 'Gorilla' Parker, colored sensation, battle Jack Nelson, the Memphis grappler, in the semi-final, but the latter increased his demands at the last minute, and he was cut from the card," stated *The Spectator*.

A short time later, the Parker-Nelson title bout was resurrected, with *The St. Catharines Standard* describing the bout as "a natural, bringing together two middleweight mat stars for the jeweled belt that goes to the champion."

The language employed by *The Spectator* suggested it would be a massive upset if Jack Nelson could defeat the newest Black wrestling star. The best it could muster was to suggest that "the elongated Nelson" *might* be just clever enough to defeat a wrestler with Parker's superior physical gifts.

The chiseled physique of Gorilla Parker

"Few wrestlers who have appeared here since wrestling became popular have had as much appeal to the fans as Parker," gushed *The Standard*. "Willing to mix at any and all times, the colored flash combines speed with science and vast strength, and his favorite method of wearing down opponents is to toss them helter-skelter about the ring and wave them over his head."

On the night of the actual bout between the two Black wrestlers who were both positioned as being of championship caliber, Parker scored a dominating straight-falls victory at the Grand Opera of Hamilton to win "the colored light heavyweight championship."

"It took the Gorilla only 23 minutes to pack in two falls and win the light heavyweight championship," reported *The Spectator*. "While Parker was forced to do a little more wrestling than in previous matches, he was a popular victor, for the moth-eaten darkie from Memphis failed to show anything bordering on championship form."

According to the report, Nelson's demeanor during the match appeared to be one of desperation, as he "did everything from biting Parker's toes to heaving a stagehand at him" before Parker won consecutive pinfalls with flying mares.

The fact that something tantamount to a legitimate championship may be construed to have changed hands from Nelson to Parker is significant for historical purposes when considering this event in isolation. However, at the moment, the intention of the promoters appears to have been to legitimize Parker's claim to a championship so that he could serve as a more attractive challenger to world middleweight champion Gus Kallio, who was also active in Ontario at the time.

In order to present Parker and Kallio as wrestlers competing on a level playing field, the name of Parker's championship was changed just five days later from light heavyweight to middleweight, and the intrigue of the match was whether or not the Black champion would be a worthy contender to a race-neutral title in his weight division.

The answer to that question turned out to be a resounding no. While Parker had been presented as an overwhelming powerhouse during his first few bouts in

A Decided Novelty

Hamilton, Kallio slowed him down and defeated him in straight falls with a pair of leg-based submission holds — "the Frank Gotch toe hold" and the "figure four toe hold" — in only 35 total minutes.

Kallio had been dominant, but the Hamilton crowd had seemingly grown quite fond of Parker, as *The Spectator* reported that "the game effort of the young challenger in the second go grew the crowd's approval," leading to Parker being "roundly encouraged and cheered by the packed house" even though he was clearly outmatched.

Back in Michigan, Parker was simply "the Negro with the bulging muscles" and fulfilled the role of being the incumbent Black wrestler filling out the cards. He drew frequent praise for his physique, his aggression, and his athleticism, with multiple reports describing how he would leap completely out of the wrestling ring to topple opponents who were standing out on the arena floors.

As entertaining as these sights may have been to witness, Parker rarely ascended beyond the preliminary matches of shows he wrestled in. This was regardless of the fact that Parker may have had the most commanding introduction to pro wrestling audiences of any Black wrestler of the catch-as-catch-can era besides George Godfrey.

Then there is the matter of Jim Mitchell. While the timeline for Mitchell's formal entry into a professional wrestling ring is somewhat murky, he was certainly active by summer 1930. That's when he was one of the "two Negroes" who were set to open the July 3 show at the Savoy Theater, as identified in *The Courier-Journal* of Louisville.

Competing against fellow Black wrestler Wildcat Carter, Mitchell wrestled within his adopted home state as the Black Panther, and would continue to perform show-opening duties late in the year when he tussled with another Black wrestler who went by the name of Buck Weaver.

It was late in the summer of 1931 when Mitchell's sustained participation in professional wrestling would become evident, as would the difficulty in differentiating between promotional tactics and true-life events in connection with his development and discovery.

Much of the confusion stems from the veracity of statements made by Indianapolis wrestling promoter Jim McLemore, who had reportedly been in the midst of a four-month European wrestling tour with a company of wrestlers in July of that year. Upon his return to Indiana in October, McLemore consented to an interview with *The Anderson Daily Bulletin*, in which he spent a great deal of time defending himself against unfounded allegations that he had been deported, and had only recently been allowed back into the country.

"On his trip, McLemore took six wrestlers, one of whom, Buck Weaver, former Indiana University football star, is well known here," elaborated *The Daily Bulletin*. "He reports that he staged wrestling matches in ten different countries and on three ocean vessels."

The Daily Bulletin's report noted that McLemore's most recent wrestling show to that point had been staged in July. In the meantime, both Buck Weaver — who was different from the Buck Weaver who wrestled in Louisville — and Jim Mitchell had participated in matches in Indianapolis during the late summer months while McLemore was supposedly overseas.

The reason these details are consequential is because of the way McLemore formally introduced Mitchell to Indiana's wrestling fans during the earliest months of 1932. *The Anderson Herald* reported that McLemore identified Mitchell as one of the wrestlers he took with him to Europe during summer 1931.

"James Mitchell, wrestling instructor of the Louisville Colored YMCA, known as 'The Black Panther,' downed Scotty Scott of Jackson, Mich., in the preliminary," submitted *The Herald*. "Mitchell accompanied Promoter Jimmie McLemore and a group of Indiana wrestlers on a tour of Europe, Asia, and Africa last summer. Mitchell won all of his matches during the tour."

A Decided Novelty

Notwithstanding the fact that a wrestling company could technically tour parts of all three of these continents without ever leaving the Mediterranean Sea, the underlying goal of grouping Mitchell with the participants of the tour seemed to be to present him as a worldly and well-traveled Black wrestler on the level of Reginald Siki.

"The Black Panther was introduced not only as a wrestler, but a baseball and basketball player, a physical director of the colored Louisville YMCA, and a linguist who 'knows enough of a dozen languages to at least order ham and eggs,'" declared *The Kokomo Tribune*.

Mitchell's supposed linguistic abilities were never mentioned again after Indianapolis, suggesting promotional exaggeration. This stands in stark contrast to the marketing of Siki, whose mastery of languages was a frequent talking point amongst the press, and who was probably routinely put to the test by the reporters who interviewed him.

More important is the fact that Mitchell showed "a clever knowledge of scientific wrestling holds," displayed incredible speed, and recorded a fall after multiple shoulder butts despite losing his multi-fall match to Speedy O'Neal at the Kokomo Armory.

For his return engagement with O'Neal, Mitchell was said to have requested a no-holds-barred matchup. During the bout, both O'Neal and Mitchell displayed "terrific slams, ripping leg splits, blood-stopping arm locks, butts, and numerous other damaging holds." At the conclusion of the final fall, O'Neal was felled by a headbutt from the Panther, rose from the campus, and was knocked back to the mat with a second headbutt for the final pinfall.

"Hats flew in the air and the wildest demonstration of the year was staged," remarked Deke Noble of *The Tribune*. "Mitchell hopped out of the ring amid great cheering, and O'Neal clambered to his feet and staggered out to the accompaniment of jeers and hoots."

Aside from this rare flourish of headbutts in a limitless contest, Mitchell soon fell into the habit of ending his matches

A Decided Novelty

with variations of shoulder tackles, with his flying version often lauded as a move befitting a panther. Almost overnight, the 5'9", 150-pound grappler developed a reputation for being possibly the fastest competitor in the state of Indiana.

Simultaneously, Mitchell garnered praise as one of the most competent technical wrestlers in the state, whose cleanliness often worked to his detriment. To wit, when Johnny Carlin found himself being "clearly outclassed at straight wrestling" in the opening fall of his bout with Mitchell, falling prey to the Panther's "flying holds," Carlin then proceeded to "brutalize" the Panther for the remainder of the bout, with Mitchell losing due to his unwillingness to return the favor.

These introductory bouts for Mitchell in Indiana overlapped with the temporary cessation of his appearances in Kentucky. In the middle of February in Louisville, Mitchell wrestled against "Lightning" John Byrd in a bout hosted by the AAA Club, and which was said to be held with the Negro middleweight championship of the world on the line. This match ultimately served as Mitchell's swansong in Louisville for several years.

Continuing in Indianapolis, the Panther earned the unfortunate reputation of being injury prone. In mid-April, Mitchell was supposedly diagnosed with a broken breastbone, which was administered by the errant knee placement of Blacksmith Pedigo during a bout at the Indianapolis Armory. *The Indianapolis News* detailed how the misplaced knee abruptly ended the third fall of the main-event match.

Dr. C.E. Hadden of the Indiana State Boxing Commission stated that the broken breastbone was diagnosed through an X-Ray, and promoter McLemore seized the opportunity to propose that the injury — which some patients healed from in as little as four weeks — might somehow spell the end of Mitchell's wrestling career. McLemore added that if such an injustice were to occur, it would leave Mitchell with a career record of 63 wins and two losses, even though the Panther had just lost at least three matches in the month of March alone.

A Decided Novelty

In an apparent medical miracle, Mitchell was back in action the very next week, although the notion that he may have still been suffering through the ill effects of the injury was blamed for Mitchell's subsequent defeat at the hands of Johnny Carlin during his return bout.

"The Black Panther of Louisville" Jim Mitchell

A genuine injury to Mitchell may have postponed a cross-generational dream bout between the Black Panther and Indiana's homegrown Black wrestling legend Lee Umbles. The two were scheduled to wrestle each other at the Indianapolis Armory on Friday, May 20, but Mitchell was pulled from the bout due to a reported injury. This spoiled what could potentially have been the only opportunity Umbles would ever have had to share the ring with a Black wrestler of similar size and acclaim.

After several weeks out of commission, Mitchell returned to action in mid-July, and *The Anderson Daily Bulletin* credited a shoulder injury suffered during a wrestling show in Terre Haute with keeping Mitchell hospitalized and out of the ring for well over a month.

The month after his July ring return, Mitchell traveled north to Western Michigan and began wrestling in Battle Creek.

Umbles, who had been enjoying one of the best runs of his career when he was scheduled to share the ring with Mitchell, had made his debut in Racine, Wisconsin earlier in 1932, and it was treated as a huge deal. *The Racine Journal-News* ran an extensive bio on the "colored champion" as he made his arrival.

"Known as the 'wizard of the mat,' Umbles is rated as the most scientific wrestler, and is rated as the foremost contender to the world's title at 158 pounds," stated *The Journal-News*. "He is a physical director, trainer and masseur, a teacher of boxing, wrestling, and jiu jitsu. He has been wrestling for four years, meeting all comers, conceding 15 to 25 pounds, and winning."

In Racine, Umbles played his role to perfection, dropping a best-of-three-falls affair to local hero Duke Rupenthal while dictating the pace of the main-event match, and headlining a program that *Journal-News* reporter Wash Cain called "the most attractive and sensational wrestling program ever held in this city."

"Umbles won the first fall after 39 minutes and 40 seconds of the most spectacular wrestling with a vertical leg split, and the crowd roared its approval," noted Cain.

Lee then lost the second fall by count out when the action spilled out of the ring, and then was ruled unable to continue due to the discovery of two broken ribs following the

A Decided Novelty

fall. In essence, Umbles had displayed his usual wrestling skill, yet technically lost the bout without being seen to have suffered any direct damage from his opponent.

One of the most vital takeaways from Umbles' wrestling matches is that he was almost always described as the most technically proficient wrestler in every match, even in defeat. This is typified by the review of his bout against Jack Jefferies of Detroit.

"The bout was fast, clean, and aggressive for the first 10 minutes, but then Jefferies started a few rough tactics, then Lee retaliated and Jack stopped his rough stuff," reported Wash Cain of *The Journal-Times*. "Umbles won the first fall after 19 minutes and 20 seconds of fast action with a double wrist lock and headscissors. Jack started his kicking and slapping tactics early in the second fall, but Lee weathered each session and finally clamped on a cradle hold to win the second and deciding fall in eight minutes."

Cain also added that Jefferies was "roundly booed" for refusing a post-match handshake with Umbles. On top of being a superior grappler, Lee was apparently also quite a good sport.

In two short years, Lee Umbles and Reginald Siki had watched as the emergence of a clowder of panthers and a single gorilla had breathed new life into the Black American wrestling scene. The best was arguably yet to come; Siki's home state was about to toss yet another wrestling prodigy into the mix, while in Massachusetts, a chiseled middleweight was preparing to break boundaries in his very first year as an active wrestler.

9 – The Kansas City Negro

Several states south of where Lee Umbles, Jack Nelson, Jim Mitchell, and Gorilla Parker were busy entertaining audiences, wrestling fans were also getting their first taste of Elmer "Jack" Claybourne, the native of Mexico, Missouri who first landed on the radars of most wrestling fans in January 1932.

The quotation marks around the name Jack are appropriate, as it was a nickname rather than a middle name. Even though Claybourne's full name was often written as Elmer Jack Claybourne in later years, he had no legal middle name.

When Claybourne made his wrestling debut at the age of nearly 22-years-old, *The Minneapolis Tribune* and *The Minneapolis Journal* described how local middleweight wrestler Harry Kamatchas of Mankato — billed as the world champion of the 156-pound weight division — had defeated the "Kansas City Negro" Jack Claybourne in consecutive falls to conclude an exhausting match. The first fall went over 37 minutes, and the second fall lasted an additional 42 minutes.

That same month, Claybourne began wrestling in a few locations inside of his home state of Missouri, within a reasonable drive of his hometown of Mexico. In the town of Moberly, he debuted under his actual name of Elmer Claybourne, and *The Monitor-Index and Democrat* of Moberly proclaimed Claybourne to be "best of his race at the mat game in this section of the middle west."

Competing against Billy Wolfe, Claybourne lost a multi-fall match that lasted well over an hour, dropping the first fall in 29 minutes and the second in 39 minutes. *The Monitor-Index and Democrat* observed that the 21-year-old Claybourne "possesses great strength, but lacked the skill and knowledge of the grappling game to successfully combat the punishing holds that Wolfe continuously fashioned on him."

Jack also wrestled that month at the City Hall of Chillicothe, and after he "vanquished Charles Knoche with a

A Decided Novelty

toe hold," Claybourne was described by *The Chillicothe Constitution-Tribune* to have "evinced more speed than local fans have seen in some time and proved himself a favorite with the crowd."

This speed was also displayed during a bout emanating from Council Bluffs, Iowa, in late March 1932. Pulling curtain-raising duties, Claybourne impressed the audience of 2,000 fans while sparring with Curley Smith, and *The Council Bluffs Nonpareil* cited Claybourne's performance as a highlight of the show.

"A crackerjack opening bout between Curley Smith and Jack Claybourne, Kansas City Negro, went to a draw and drew a big hand from the crowd," reported *The Nonpareil*. "The colored boy was the favorite and kept Smith well in hand by tossing him from the ring occasionally. According to Promoter Grace, the Negro will be seen again in the local ring."

However, wrestling wasn't the only ring-based endeavor that Claybourne was involved in at the time. In a pattern that would play out repeatedly during the early years of his career, Jack would find himself donning the leather gloves and participating in boxing matches that were often inserted into wrestling cards, and which featured combatants who were ostensibly competent at both disciplines.

While boxing matches on wrestling cards were commonly staged — *especially* when at least one of the fighters was a professional wrestler — Claybourne's earliest recorded bout appears legitimate based on its description. Unfortunately for Claybourne, it also suggests that he wasn't a particularly gifted boxer.

At the Athletic Hall in Moberly, Claybourne boxed under his real name of Elmer Claybourne, and lost decisively to Cyclone Williams in their 10-round match. The writer for *The Monitor-Index and Democrat* made it clear that Elmer "could not trade punches successfully" and that Williams "was taking it easy" throughout the contest.

"Williams proved a remarkably clever boxer, with a lot of power to his punches," added the fight report. "He jolted

Claybourne severely in the third round, putting him down and all but knocking him out. Claybourne rallied some in the latter rounds, but Williams was master of the situation at all times."

Young Elmer "Happy Jack" Claybourne

    Back in Wells, Minnesota in April, and competing against Harry Kamatchas yet again, Claybourne was defeated in straight falls even after putting forth a valiant effort and displaying a commendable level of conditioning.

    "Harry Kamatchas, called the 'Greek Demon,' defeated 'Happy' Jack Claybourne in straight falls, the first fall taking 24

A Decided Novelty

minutes and the second coming after 32 minutes of the fastest wrestling ever seen in Wells," stated *The Wells Mirror*. "Kamatchas, the champion, was, as usual, the master of the situation most of the time, but Claybourne displayed some wonderful showmanship as well as some fast, clean wrestling."

As Claybourne became a regular participant in shows at the Memorial Building in Kansas City, the promoters followed what was a common practice of billing Claybourne from one of the areas in which he had most recently wrestled. This is why throughout his first year of wrestling regularly in Kansas City, the Missouri native was introduced as being a resident of Minneapolis, Minnesota, a Northern city with a Black population of less than one percent in 1930.

Elsewhere in the Midwestern states, Gorilla Parker had left Michigan and traveled south to Ohio, where he was introduced as an Alabama native who had claimed the middleweight title of the South, similar to the way Jack Nelson had been briefly billed in Canada. This claiming of a race-neutral Southern championship remained provocative, as mixed-race pro wrestling bouts were still banned — either by law or informal agreement — in the majority of Southern states.

In what was retroactively a huge historical letdown, a Louisville showdown between "Black Panther" Jim Mitchell and Gorilla Parker was advertised in what resembled an authentic unification of Black wrestling titles into an intercontinental championship.

"[Allen] has signed Black Panther, recognized in eight countries as the Negro welterweight wrestling champion of Europe, to meet Gorilla Parker, New York, who boasts recognition in New York State as the Negro welterweight wrestling champion of America, in a finish match, the best two out of three falls, at a class weight," stated *The Courier-Journal of Louisville*.

The very detailed recognition of Mitchell as a Black champion recognized in eight distinct European countries is humorous in retrospect, because Jim Wango — a popular and very active Black wrestler in Europe at the time — never claimed a status as being any sort of Black European champion, but was instead alternatingly advertised as being either the champion of South Africa, or of the entire African continent.

The particulars of who held which fictitious championships turned out to be entirely irrelevant, as what would have been a dream match between two of the best active Black wrestlers of the era in their youthful primes never took place. In a massive letdown, Parker never made it to the show, and Mitchell defeated replacement wrestler Rough House Williams in a match of substantially less historical value.

The very next month, Parker surprisingly lost a rematch with Jack Nelson on the undercard of a Detroit show headlined by Frank Wolff and Fred Lyons. While the bout between the two in Hamilton was treated as a near-main-event match, this particular Nelson-Parker bout was a non-title affair that practically went unadvertised, and Nelson's victory over Parker was reported without any details. To add insult to injury, Nelson was misnamed in *The Detroit Free Press* as "Jack Burns" in the report from that evening.

After parting company with Parker, Nelson continued to wrestle in both the eastern and western portions of Michigan throughout 1932, while still losing most of his matches. Nelson still retained his penchant for roughhousing behavior, and *The Battle Creek Enquirer* highlighted Nelson's fondness for nibbling on the thighs of his adversaries. Before losing to big Texan Stanley Roberts, Nelson was flagged for "continually biting that part of the cowboy's anatomy."

One opponent Nelson was not accused of biting was the bear owned by Charlie Polzin, who Nelson sparred with in exhibitions in both Michigan and Ohio. Then in Canada late in 1932, Nelson was accused by *The Windsor Star* of failing "to display anything like the form that made him one of the most feared wrestlers in these parts two years ago," leaving knowledgeable readers to scratch their heads as to how amassing fewer than five victories over roughly a five-month

A Decided Novelty

period could ever have been sufficient to make Nelson a feared wrestler during the early stages of his Canadian tenure.

Meanwhile, George Godfrey spent the first months of the year still actively involved in wrestling, but he also solicited other money-making offers, including an opportunity on the West Coast that kept him front and center in the professional boxing world.

"In his newest robes as a wrestler, George Godfrey, the black panther of the prize ring, will appear before Sacramento mat fans tonight in what may be his last grappling exhibition until after Jack Dempsey concludes his latest comeback attempt," reported *The Sacramento Union*. "Dempsey, in training here for a week, declared Saturday he held a contract with Godfrey and said he probably would exercise same by drafting the giant negro from the wrestling ranks to train him for the next few weeks."

Dempsey had retired from serious fighting several years earlier, but the boxing legend still participated in a seemingly endless string of post-retirement exhibition fights. According to the International News Service, Dempsey had lined up 20 exhibition fights during the first two months of 1932 alone, and was soliciting Godfrey's assistance to train for them.

Fully understanding the uniqueness of what he offered to fans, Godfrey continued to make a habit out of double-dipping in early 1932, as he would both wrestle and box at several shows. His fights at these events were often authentic enough to be listed on his official win-loss record, even if the majority of his opponents during this stretch could best be classified as "tomato cans" who were either making their debuts, or entering their fights with Godfrey as the holders of losing records.

In virtually all instances, Godfrey's wrestling matches ended in one of two fashions. Either George would hoist his opponent into the air with a crotch lift and slam him to the mat for a pin, or he would throw a dramatic right hand to his rival's chin, and then cover their unconscious body on the mat. Regardless, Godfrey's clearest contribution to wrestling was his drawing ability, aided by the fact that his wrestling tenure overlapped with a period in which he was still seen by many boxing fans as a viable world heavyweight title contender.

Speaking of titles, in March 1932, an article appearing in *The New York Age* suggested that Godfrey's entry into the world of professional wrestling immediately piqued the interest of promoters who wanted to turn the idea of a world colored heavyweight championship into a real thing.

George Godfrey with gloves on

"Joe Fox, former boxer and well-known masseur and trainer, plans to promote a wrestling contest between George Godfrey and Reginald Siki for the colored heavyweight championship of the world," the article began. "The locale of the proposed contest has not been finally decided upon, and Mr. Fox is desirous that all readers of *The Age* who would like to see the contest staged in New York write him in care of this paper."

A Decided Novelty

The article added that Fox had already reached tentative agreements with the respective managers of Godfrey and Siki to stage the event, and had also secured the services of Harry Wills — a former Black Panther of the boxing world in his own right — to serve as the special referee for the bout. Presumably, arranging such a match should have been a cinch because both athletes often found themselves in one another's company, and for a time had even shared the same manager.

In fact, that same year, *The California Eagle* reported on the opening of a health farm by Billy McClain. Among the accomplishments listed for McClain in the article is that he was "trainer of Jack Johnson, manager of Sam McVey, discoverer of Reginald Siki, and for a number of years trainer of Wladek Zbyszko."

That statement alone was enough to explain how Siki, who was presumably wrestling on a Zbyszko-headlined card in Kansas City during his rookie year, came to be recruited into the Zbyszko's camp. However, the same article also went on to state how McClain had taken over the management of George Godfrey and Seal Harris, with Harris also being a famous Black heavyweight boxer who Godfrey had knocked out when they faced one another in August of the previous year.

At least in the United States, no match between Godfrey and Siki would ever materialize. Yet, even without a "colored wrestling championship" to claim, Godfrey could leverage his legitimate fighting accomplishments to lend enhanced credibility to any wrestling titles he chose to claim.

The idea of a rivalry between the most famous Black wrestler and boxer-wrestler would continue to build. In one instance, *The Springfield Daily News* would erroneously claim that Siki had made himself available to settle the dispute with Godfrey, but that George "politely sidestepped with the excuse that other engagements would not permit him to meet the Abyssinian."

The dream match would eventually come to pass, but it would be held in a setting far removed from any of those that were originally offered.

A Decided Novelty

In the meantime, Siki was still quite active in the ring. The Associated Negro Press reported of Siki's disappointment with a new rule that had gone into effect in the wrestling world, and its immediate effect on the outcome of an early May bout held in Buffalo between Siki and Ed Don George. After 35 minutes of action dominated by Siki, George caught his opponent by surprise with a flying tackle that knocked Siki completely out of the ring and onto the cement floor.

"As Siki fell, his back struck the edge of the table on which the newspaper correspondents were writing," stated the ANP's report. "George followed him but was unhurt by his fall and clambered quickly back into the ring, but Siki lay quiet as Referee Coffee, a novice referee, began his count."

The referee counted to 20 and ruled that Siki had lost the bout, and the disappointed fans complained that the brand-new rule requiring that wrestlers beat the referee's 20-count and return to the ring was unfair and didn't provide the competitors with nearly enough time to collect themselves.

"The count was over before I realized the referee had begun," Siki told the ANP reporter, while George added that he was unsatisfied to have won the bout in that fashion.

Also added to the story was the detail that Siki had immediately driven home to New York City with his German wife, which suggests that if Siki was indeed married to a woman from England at the end of December — as had been previously reported — then he had divorced and remarried within a five-month period.

While Siki had been wrestling in several locations throughout 1932, he was spending the majority of his time in New York City, bodyslamming his way through what was usually lower-tier competition, like Al Beverage and Paul Finsky.

In a full-circle moment, wrestling fans in Wisconsin were treated to a short-lived round of appearances from a brand-new Siki — Donald Siki — in September 1932. Introduced as an "Abyssinian Negro," Donald Siki was

A Decided Novelty

declared by *The Racine Journal-Times* to have been "following in the footsteps of his noted cousin Reginald Siki."

This was a fitting bit of turnabout being fair play, as Siki had himself debuted as a cousin of Senegalese fighter Battling Siki when he began his wrestling career. However, Siki had been in the habit of distancing himself from Battling Siki since 1925 when the fighter was murdered, and it was made clear that the fighter's real name was Louis Fall.

Since Reginald Siki had long since made use of several alternative aliases, including Dejatch Tedella, Dejatch Tedelba, and Reginald Berri, attempting to link Donald to Reginald by use of Siki as a surname was a misguided effort that clearly didn't work. However, the attempt does reinforce the notion that wrestling promoters were scrambling to create their own versions of Reginald Siki, especially as he appeared primed to accept an increasing number of engagements in Europe.

Siki's final bouts of the year were punctuated by bizarre occurrences. During the first such event in Boston, *The Boston Globe* reported how Siki ended his bout with Lloyd Stewart during the sixth minute of action when he casually hoisted Stewart off the ground and tossed him over the ropes. Lloyd went crashing down on top of a chair and was unable to return to the ring, allowing Siki to achieve a count out victory of his own.

Two weeks later, in his final bout of 1932, Siki was awarded a victory that received publicity around the country. In front of an estimated 10,000 fans in Boston Arena, both Siki and referee Al Pierotti were punched in the face by Bull Martin, resulting in vengeance-seeking fans swarming the ring, and the police being summoned to restore order.

By this point, it was clear that professional wrestling had taken a vastly different approach to booking Black wrestlers than the business Siki had first entered. So many regional and territorial wrestling promotions had sprouted up that the business as a whole was far less reliant on just a few traveling troupes of performers.

A Decided Novelty

Moreover, as Siki — and arguably George Godfrey to an even greater extent — had proven the viability of Black wrestlers as box office attractions when showcased properly, 1932 would be the year that their metaphorical offspring truly began to come into their own as dependable draws.

It may also be for this reason that 1932 became Siki's final year of serious in-ring activity in North American rings for more than a decade. As an increasing number of Black wrestlers entered the sport of pro wrestling in featured positions, the intrigue of seeing a Black man inside of a wrestling ring in something other than a pre-show scramble dwindled in several major cities.

As far as the skillful execution of matches is concerned, it's unlikely that any other Black performers could have competed with Siki's mastery of the craft at that time, and his size, musculature, and reputation still enabled him to stand out. However, for fans who simply wished to gaze upon the form of a Black man as he competently executed wrestling holds and throws, that particular longing could now be satisfied by watching a handful of wrestlers other than Siki during the 1930s.

For example, while the annals of history are silent on "Tarzan" Harry Wilson's activities for a full decade, either he or someone bearing his name managed to reemerge for a show in Madison, Wisconsin in 1932. At this point, Wilson was inexplicably advertised as "a nationally known wrestler" despite the fact that there are no clear records of any Black grapplers wrestling under that name anywhere other than Wisconsin, and nowhere at all for 10 full years.

"Wilson, a 205-pounder in the heavyweight class, has met some of the best wrestlers in the country and is one of Chicago's outstanding candidates for national honors" said *The Capital Times*. "Only his color, his backers are sure, prevents him from being recognized as a grappler who rates with Lewis, Sonnenberg, DeGlane and Savoldi."

This version of Wilson would make appearances with only slightly more regularity. As he prepared to engage in combat with George Mack, *The Wisconsin State Journal* characterized Wilson as "one of those ebony-hued grapplers who likes it rough, and makes a specialty of butting head with anyone who will take a chance of ramming their cranium against that kinky-thatched, reinforced concrete dome of his."

It's worth noting that this is one of the earliest allusions to a "son of Africa" — as *The Journal* described Wilson — having a supernaturally hard head, and relying on a headbutt-heavy attack. The move had been popularly introduced to wrestling a few years earlier by Michigan wrestling legend Gus Sonnenberg, but was not yet widely utilized. When it was, it was generally regarded as a heel tactic, and usually used quite sparingly. Meanwhile, *The Capital Times* added that the Wilson-Mack match would be "the first 'mixed' bout to be staged in Wisconsin in some years."

Ahead of his bout with Mack, Wilson provided reporters with a public workout, which the reporter from *The State Journal* described as "impressive."

"Wilson, a husky colored mat star who is rapidly gaining a prominent place in Chicago wrestling circles, worked out here Wednesday afternoon and was impressive," printed *The State Journal*. "His drill lasted more than half an hour, but he kept going at top speed throughout."

Mack downed Wilson in consecutive falls, but not before Wilson reinforced the notion that it could be a foolhardy strategy to initiate a headbutting exchange with a Black wrestler.

"Early in the match Mack tried butting heads with his colored opponent and fell into a trap, for if there's anything that Wilson liked, it was butting heads," reported *The State Journal*. "Once Mack was knocked groggy when 'Tarzan' pushed him back and then pulled him in, striking both of their heads."

Wilson was then advertised for a match with Jimmy Demetral, which was a rematch of their encounter from 10 years prior. *The State Journal* referenced a drinking song, stating that when Greek meets Greek, it always ends in a tug o' war,

A Decided Novelty

but "the same song does not tell you what happens when Greek meets Negro," hence the intrigue of the bout.

The event was postponed, and it was later reported by *The Capital Times* that Wilson had been forced to call off the match because he had been diagnosed with a cold. The event was hastily rescheduled, which allotted *The Times* another opportunity to promote the bout by referencing Wilson's peculiar fondness for head-on-head contact.

"Wilson is probably one of the only wrestlers in the game who cracks his own head against that of his opponent, at least intentionally," stated *The Times*. "Other wrestlers may do it, and regret it, occasionally, but Wilson, when he appeared here about three weeks ago, used the unusual method of subduing his opponent time and again. He seemed to take pleasure in cracking his own skull against that of George Mack, whom he wrestled on that previous occasion."

Back in the Rockies, in January 1932, a writer from *The Sun Advocate* referred to Alexis Kaffir as "the big black mass of muscle" and a "Senegalese giant negro." It was during that month that the Panther of the Northwest wrestled his final match in Utah, dropping two straight falls to Ira Dern.

It was in February 1932 that Kaffir would materialize in Colorado for a match against Mike Collins and debut his most familiar pseudonym of "Alex Kaffner." For his first appearance in Colorado, Kaffner was advertised to have had "a long list of impressive victories to his credit" despite actually having rather few. The pattern that established itself in Utah repeated itself in Colorado, as Kaffner was defeated by Collins in two straight falls.

In Cheyenne, Wyoming, Alex earned a win against Randell Hicks in a June match that was notable more so for where much of the action took place. The writer from the Associated Press noted that Kaffner and Hicks departed from the ring and brawled through the front row on three different occasions before Kaffner finally tallied his win.

The AP carried the story of the Panther's bout all over the country, spreading his name to a degree that was

A Decided Novelty

unprecedented up to that point. The next week, Kaffner was referred to as "heavyweight colored champ" for the first time prior to a match against Jack Anderson in Greeley, Colorado. Similar to other cases, it was a title that carried little weight inasmuch as there was no record of Kaffner engaging in any matches with Black wrestlers prior to being awarded his so-called championship.

The field of Black wrestlers became even more crowded in 1933. February of that year marked the debut of Joseph Alvin Godfrey of Malden, Massachusetts as Ed Flowers, "a dusky middleweight from Cuba." Known varyingly as Ed Flowers and Nick Flowers, and often with "The Black Panther" added to his name, Flowers was thrust straight into the mix with Ted Germaine, Joe Costello, and the rest of the top wrestlers of New England.

Details from Flowers' matches throughout the spring and early summer months are difficult to come by, but a report from *The Boston Globe* in early May indicates that he had "stripped Al Vantres of his middleweight crown" during a match in Fall River.

Since the middleweight championship of the region that was offered by promoter Charley Gordon was listed as a world championship, Flowers became perhaps the first openly Black wrestler of his generation to be granted a run as an advertised world champion, and during his rookie campaign no less.

Flowers' first reign as a world champion appeared as if it would not last more than two weeks; Vantres defeated Flowers in Boston's Mechanic's Building in early May to reclaim the championship. Apparently, promoter Gordon changed his mind, and informed *The Boston Globe* days later that Vantres was "over the middleweight limit" at the time of the match, and that Flowers was still the world titleholder.

In these early stages of his career, Flowers was touted as a masterful wrestler. *The Greenfield Daily Recorder-Gazette* described his opponent Marshall Muse as being of no match for "the Cuban from Salem," as Flowers dismissed his challenge in straight falls with an armlock-bodyslam and a "back fall."

After two months of dueling with Ted Germaine, the top star in the region regained the world middleweight championship from Flowers on July 7 in Salem by winning the first and third falls.

Joe Godfrey as Ed "Tiger" Flowers

Flowers continued to war with Germaine — a notoriously rough wrestler — and the rest of the grapplers on Charley Gordon's roster, as they engaged in a promotional war with the roster of competing promoter Paul Bowser.

One of the best displays of Flowers' early competency as a wrestler was showcased at the very end of November.

A Decided Novelty

That's when Flowers wrestled Paul Adams for one hour and nine minutes in Greenfield's Washington Hall before emerging victorious.

"Wrist locks, double arm holds, spread eagles and numerous other holds never seen here before were applied," reported *The Recorder-Gazette*. "Flowers finally won the bout after Adams had tried a couple of holds that Flowers broke out of. As quick as a flash, Flowers applied a reverse arm hold on Adams, the South Hadley mat artist tried to break away, but instead Flowers brought his arms between his legs and like a shot of lightning flopped Adams over backwards and landed on him for the fall, the time being 69 minutes."

Right in the middle of Flowers' rookie year in New England, a Black wrestler by the name of Joe "Chocolate" Gans was briefly introduced as the light-heavyweight colored champion. It was a seemingly superfluous title considering that Flowers had already held the top race-neutral championship of the region without any qualifications based on skin color.

While new Black wrestling stars were making their debuts, the standard bearer for Black pro wrestling was in the process of phasing himself out of the domestic scene. The most interesting stateside news about Reginald Siki early in 1933 involved a new addition to his family. The Associated Negro Press reported the birth of "a fine baby girl weighing eight and one-half pounds" who was given the name "Margellen Regina Berri."

Siki didn't resume his in-ring activities in the United States until April, when he dueled to a draw with Leo Pinetzsi in New York.

Although he was now a ring veteran of 10 years, there were still plenty of markets that Siki had not yet appeared in. He made his debut in Portland, Maine during the month of May, and *The Portland Evening Express* presented him as "one of the top-notchers of the game, regardless of race."

"Siki, who is 33 years old and a native of Abyssinia, has been wrestling professionally for 10 years, the greater part of the time in Europe, although he is a citizen of California," added *The Express*.

At the end of October, Siki had one final match with Yvon Robert in Holyoke, Massachusetts, which he lost in consecutive falls. After that, he retreated to Europe, where he would wrestle almost exclusively for the next decade.

There were far greater misfortunes occurring in 1933 than Siki's departure. The spring was punctuated by a tragic incident in Taylor, Texas. At 9:15 p.m. on Saturday, March 18, White Noble was admitted to the Doak & Stromberg Clinic-Hospital in critical condition. He had a bullet lodged in the left side of his abdomen that had traveled a significant distance through his body before decelerating to a stop.

"He was shot in the right arm just above the elbow, the bullet penetrating his right side and passing through his body, lodging in his left side above the waist," read the report in the following day's edition of the *Taylor Daily Press*.

The shooting incident had reportedly been sparked by an argument between Noble and an unauthorized tenant at his rental property, 30-year-old Mary Felix, who had moved into a house owned by Noble on Bland Street without his permission. Noble was conscious when he arrived at the hospital and described to authorities what had happened from his perspective.

"Who gave you authority to move into this house?" is what Noble explained that he said to Felix when the two were standing on the front porch of the house. The 4'11" Felix subsequently produced a .32-20 pistol and fired three shots, with only one of the bullets striking Noble.

With her culpability undeniable, Felix was quickly taken into custody and sat confined to a jail cell while Noble fought for his life. Nearly 12 hours after he was pierced by Felix's bullet, Noble succumbed to his injuries. Ten years after the shooting death of world champion Pet Brown, the same fate had befallen Brown's most promising pupil.

Felix was immediately charged with murder and held on a $1,500 bond. Funeral services for Noble were held just

A Decided Novelty

three days later at Mount Calvary Baptist Church, and his body was interred at City Cemetery. On May 25, slightly more than two months after Noble's death and burial, Mary Felix was sentenced to just five years in jail for his murder, with no further explanation provided for the relative leniency of the sentence. The light sentence Felix ultimately received was consistent with the era's *de jure* devaluing of Black lives, even when the victim was a successful local businessman and athlete.

Once the murder, burial and sentencing had come and gone, so did the legacy and potential historical placement of a man who certainly played a pioneering role in the legitimization of Black wrestlers in Texas and elsewhere.

After Noble's death, Texas wrestling segregation intensified. Black wrestlers were relegated to separate matches, then separate promotions, while facing increased public ridicule. One Texas district attorney suggested that participants in "negro wrestling matches" ought to be "promised a watermelon each to stimulate the action."

The Texas Boxing Bill, passed that summer, included specific language that prohibited "boxing, sparring, or wrestling between a person of the white race and one of the negro race." Profit-oriented wrestling promoters would then spend the next two decades trying to circumvent this law's highly specific language.

During this period in Texas, All-Negro wrestling shows would sprout up across the state, featuring wrestlers like Reckless Red, Yellow Jones, Ben Coates, Dynamite Dan, and the Corsicana Kid. Coverage of these events was sparse, but the one name mentioned during this era of Black wrestling in Texas that would turn out to have any staying power into the coming decades would be that of Johnny "Cyclone" Cobb.

In the meantime, the tragic and untimely murder of White Noble would eliminate him from any future discussions of Black wrestling pioneers, both in his era, and any that followed it.

A Decided Novelty

That same year, Gorilla Parker visited Indiana for the very first time in a professional capacity, and was surprisingly billed as a heavyweight. One of his first Indiana appearances, which took place at the Armory in Anderson, coincided with a showing from "The Black Panther" George Godfrey.

Right before Parker wrestled Bill Honeycutt to a 30-minute draw, Godfrey stood in the ring holding "a ruby-studded belt, valued at $2,500, emblematic of the heavyweight championship of Mexico," and matchmaker Jay Gardner announced that Godfrey would be present in two weeks to defend that belt against a yet-to-be-named opponent.

This appearance by Godfrey was accompanied by a fantastical claim that the boxer-wrestler "won both the heavyweight wrestling and boxing titles of Mexico recently in one evening." As reported by *The Anderson Herald*, Godfrey had defeated his boxing opponent, then immediately challenged the nation's boxing titleholder and conquered him as well.

The to-be-named opponent turned out to be Jack Baxter, and he and Godfrey split the first two falls of their title fight before Godfrey ended Baxter's evening with what was depicted as one of the most vicious body slams in history.

"For the final fall, Godfrey picked Baxter up and slammed him on the mat, breaking several boards in the floor of the ring," reported *The Herald*. "Baxter was unconscious for a short time."

Earlier on the same card, Parker defeated his opponent Ken Gibbs in five-and-a-half minutes with a "Japanese leg strangle."

Two nights later in Indianapolis, a nearly identical pattern would play out. Godfrey put away Bill Moss with a bodyslam to cap their best-of-three-falls match, while Parker submitted Bill Honeycutt in 14 minutes with "an Indian footlock."

In the fall, Parker and Jack Nelson wrestled each other once again, this time in Windsor. The two Black wrestlers were described as "bitter rivals" in *The Windsor Star*, and they

A Decided Novelty

wrestled to a 20-minute draw as a lead-in to the headlining match between Gus Kallio and Les Fishbaugh.

Aside from drawing with Parker, Jack Nelson more or less continued his losing ways in Ontario, Michigan, and a few other parts of the Midwest that year. Greater insight into Nelson's background was provided in September, when he sat for a thorough interview with *The Detroit Tribune*. The feature article opened by stating that Nelson hailed from Beale Street in "good old Memphis town," and that he learned the fundamentals of professional wrestling right there "on the banks of the Mighty Mississippi."

"This was back in the late 1920s," continued the article. "In the succeeding years, when the big fellow who answers to the 'Black Panther,' 'Black Bear,' 'Dark Flash,' 'Bearcat,' and other euphonious appellations had become proficient in his craft, the wanderlust struck him and he began to roam about the country, seeking matches with other artisans of the craft."

According to the article, Nelson arrived in Toledo and entered a tournament "to decide a colored heavyweight champion of the universe," and when it was over, referee Raymond Laraux of Montreal "was tapping him on the shoulder" to present him with "the gold belt, emblematic of the World's colored heavyweight championship. This was in 1930."

The tournament was allegedly hosted by "the Terminal Athletic Club of Toledo" and was sanctioned by the National Wrestling Athletic Club of Toledo, within which Nelson was purportedly "one of the seven Negroes holding membership."

In case it wasn't obvious, no such tournament ever took place, and there was never such an organization as the National Wrestling Athletic Club operating in Toledo. Moreover, there was no referee operating anywhere in the wrestling world at the time who went by the name Raymond Laraux or any of the name's alterations.

Even so, the origin of Jack Nelson's claim to Black world championship status is important to establish because of how other prominent Black wrestlers would subsequently attach their own title claims to Nelson's, while appealing to far more authentic sanctioning bodies than the spurious Toledo-based organizations first cited by Nelson.

Late in 1933 is when Gorilla Parker first ventured out to the East Coast and made his inaugural appearances in the New England area. After one of Parker's earliest bouts in Lewiston, Maine — a draw against Jack Perry — *The Lewiston Evening Journal* affirmed that the grappler had clear potential if he cut back on his theatrics as a "wild acting negro."

"And right here we want to go on record as feeling that the colored boy, who packs much more color than that in his skin, is a far better wrestler than the result of the match showed last night," espoused *The Evening Journal*. "Now and then he cut out his fancy falls and dramatics long enough to do a little work and proved that against someone where he didn't have so much time to be an actor, he might prove a fine mat man."

In Lynn, Massachusetts, Parker was billed as world light heavyweight champion without racial qualifiers. While this is an intriguing fact for multiple reasons, one of those reasons is the way in which other Black wrestlers were showcased on the very same cards.

"The battle royal will be between five colored boys — Kid Lipson, Cyclone Whip, Alabama Snowball, Stanley Dixon, and Buzz-Saw Stanley — and a humorous contest is in the offing as the quintet knows nothing about the wrestling pastime," explained *The Daily Evening Item* ahead of a mid-December event at the Lynn Arena.

Even on a show where Gorilla Parker was presented as a Black wrestler of world-championship caliber, the promoters still presented "colored battle royals" between unskilled wrestlers for the sake of offering entertainment intended to be brutish, buffoonish, or both.

The reported results of the show confirm that the same event in which Gorilla Parker expertly disposed of his White opponent Charlie Perry with a flying mare also included a

A Decided Novelty

multi-wrestler comedy act composed entirely of Black performers.

"Cyclone Whip and Kid Lipson shared honors in the battle royal, both being counted out after tiring from their exertions," reported *The Evening Item*. "Stanley Dixon, Buzz-Saw Stanley and Alabama Sam were other entries and the latter, a colored boy, gave the fans a laugh as he defended himself against the onslaughts of the other quartet."

Without explanation, Parker was either upgraded or downgraded — depending on your perspective — from the world light heavyweight champion to the world colored heavyweight champion within the pages of *The Press Herald* of Portland, Maine.

Displays like the "colored battle royal" would soon become less commonplace as the number of Black wrestlers in Parker's class grew. Just one year earlier, matches between Parker and Jack Nelson had helped to normalize the idea of proficient Black wrestlers dueling with one another in a select few Northern cities. A surprising move by a West Coast wrestling star would soon result in the Central States region being treated to the same rare sight.

10 – Eightball Can't Take It

Even though he won 50 percent of his matches at best in 1932, Jack Claybourne still emerged as a situational world champion by the end of the year. Labeled as the "colored world's champ" from Montgomery, Alabama, Claybourne wrestled in a select number of small towns around his actual home region of Missouri and Kansas, displaying incredible athleticism and resourcefulness, and becoming the first Black wrestler to appear in several of these towns.

This included the city of Emporia, where Claybourne was reportedly the first Black wrestler to perform. In his second bout in the city, Claybourne competed against the man who was presumably the *second* Black wrestler to appear in Emporia when he met "the Black Panther of Ft. Worth" in the main event of the evening.

This inbound Black Panther was *not* from Fort Worth, Texas by any means, but was actually Alex Kaffner, who had relocated to the Midwest from the Rocky Mountain area. Kaffner's billing as a Kansas City resident was accurate since he had established a residence at 1831 Troost Ave. In the Kansas City address book, Kaffner was listed as "Alex Caffener" along with Helen, presumably his wife. His occupation was provided as "wrestler."

With both Claybourne and Kaffner present, the newspapers had a field day advertising the presence of two different claimants to colored championships from two separate weight classes, with Kaffner listed as the negro heavyweight titlist, and Claybourne as the negro light-heavyweight champion.

The two rotated through other opponents, but they were pitted against one another several times, with their shared skin color allowing them to treat many fans to a sight they had never seen before: Skilled Black grapplers competing against each other in fast-paced wrestling action.

Few descriptions of the encounters between the pair of pioneers in their youth successfully made it into print, but the surviving accounts suggest that the bouts were stellar. During a main-event affair between the two at the Royal Theater in Emporia, *The Daily Gazette* described how Alex and Jack traded the first two falls with separate alligator clutches before Claybourne closed the show with a back-body slam.

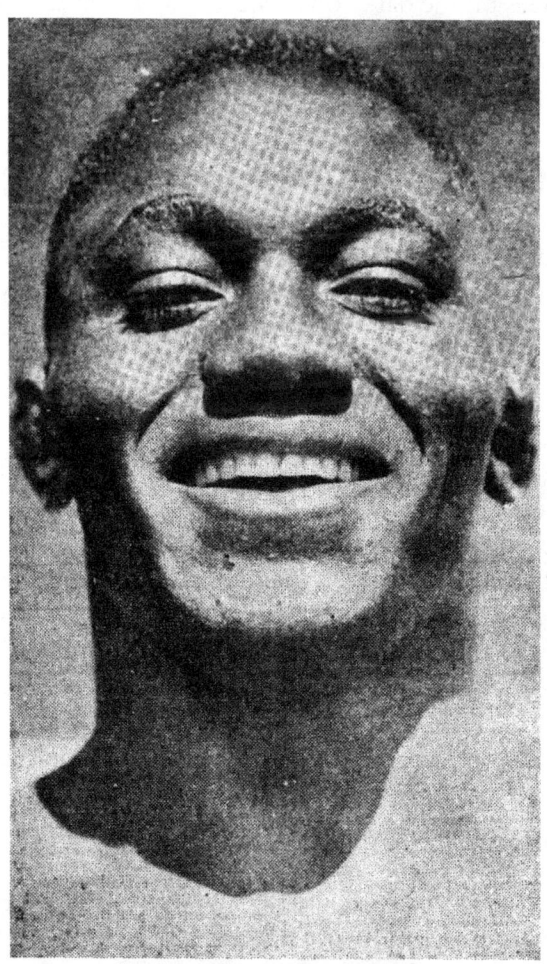

Smiling Jack Claybourne

A very colorful description of a different bout between the two was printed in *The Council Grove Republican* in the aftermath of a show in Council Grove, Kansas, albeit one punctuated by analogies of an era that relied heavily into the use of derogatory racial imagery.

"Customers at the wrestling matches last evening came to the conclusion that Happy Jack Claybourne and the 'Black Panther,' the two colored headliners, were raised on the milk of rubber trees on the dark continent. It was a logical conclusion," began the report from *The Republican*.

The article proceeded to describe a multi-fall contest in which the two Black combatants bounced one another off of the mat with little regard for one another's personal safety. After Claybourne secured the first fall with a "double Japanese toehold," Kaffner rallied to win the second fall with an airplane spin. That's when the action truly became frenetic.

"In their try for the deciding fall, the colored wrestlers literally wrestled all over the armory," continued *The Republican*. "Spectators, with aid of (referee) 'Tiny' Elza, heaved the pair back in the ring without bothering to untangle them. After Claybourne had dented the platform several times with the Panther's head, the latter's shoulders stayed on the mat for the official count of three."

Chaos seemed to be the norm whenever Claybourne and Kaffner squared off. Kaffner struck fast during their April rematch and took the first fall with a Boston crab, which required Claybourne to score a pinfall to even the tally. With the score tied, the action predictably spilled outside of the ring once again.

"The two wrestlers and the referee, Les Holzapfel, were staging a track meet around the ring with Holzapfel in the lead," reported *The Republican*. "The latter took a corner too fast, skidded and went down. Alex stumbled over him and fell flat on the mat. Taking advantage of his opportunity, Happy did a dive onto the Panther, knocked out his wind, and pinned him for the required count of three."

At the conclusion of his feud with Claybourne, Kaffner would head north to the state he would become synonymous with — Wisconsin. Early in his stay there, Kaffner was mistakenly referred to as "The Black Panther of Louisville,

A Decided Novelty

Kentucky," which observant wrestling fans would have regarded as an unmistakable reference to Jim Mitchell.

The Journal Times of Racine, Wisconsin published information about Kaffner's background. Unsurprisingly, the majority of it was not factually accurate. It stated that the "colored heavyweight champion" was 27 years old and had been wrestling for nine years. If accurate, that would make 1906 the year of Kaffner's birth, but the reality was that Kaffner was likely born in 1901, therefore placing him in his early 30s.

The writer added that Kaffner was known in "the east" as the Black Panther. In truth, it's likely that Kaffner had never competed in a match east of the Mississippi River prior to arriving in Wisconsin, let alone in any states along the Atlantic shore.

Kaffner's entry to Wisconsin's wrestling scene was accompanied by a published endorsement of his presence from Lee Umbles, representing a tacit passing of the torch from one Black star to another as Kaffner took up the mantle as the most active Black mat combatant in the state.

Elsewhere in the Midwest, Jim Mitchell began the year wrestling in Michigan before extending the range of his appearances into Northern Ohio, and primarily the town of Marion, with its population of just over 30,000 residents.

The wrestling fans of Marion quickly took to the Black Panther of Louisville, who was described by Karl McElroy of *The Marion Star* as "rough and fast" while possessing "the grace that is characteristic of that jungle beast."

It was also at the Marion Steam Shovel Arena that Mitchell received an opportunity to wrestle against recognized world middleweight champion Gus Kallio in June. Before that bout, he was declared to have been a product of Algeria. As an extension of the French Republic based in North Africa, the country had been a source of uprisings and unrest among the native population early in 1933.

With a new African nation in the news, wrestling promoters followed their established custom of affiliating their

Black wrestlers with that country. In this instance, they improperly linked a descendant of Sub-Saharan Africans like Mitchell with an Algerian populace that looked quite dissimilar from him.

In his battle with Kallio, the "Algerian" Panther used his famed shoulder butts to even the match at one fall apiece, and he appeared to have the champion on the brink of defeat after connecting with a series of flying shoulder tackles in the match's third fall. However, Kallio weathered the storm and managed to emerge victorious from the encounter by applying a wristlock to Mitchell.

"The Panther struggled and almost broke the hold several times, but was finally forced to admit that Kallio was the better man. The fall lasted 13 ½ minutes," reported *The Star*.

The following month, plans were made for Mitchell to debut in Sandusky, a locale that would eventually become the site of one of Mitchell's crowning career achievements. Local promoter Dan Morris introduced residents of a town famous for the Cedar Point amusement park to the latest Black wrestler to tour the state.

"Mitchell is known from coast to coast, Morris says, and is a big gate attraction," stated *The Sandusky Register*. "His lightning speed and unusually clever ability wins the approval of the fans. Several years ago, he made a successful tour of Europe, centering most of his work in Greece under the managership of Jimmie McLemore of Indianapolis, Morris said."

If Mitchell had actually participated in McLemore's tour of Europe, he was only two years removed from it as opposed to "several years." Moreover, it would have been a stretch to say that the Black Panther was known from coast to coast at the time even if the only coastline in question had been that of the Great Lakes.

However, Morris' plans to have the Panther debut in Sandusky were apparently derailed by yet another injury to Mitchell, who was said to be convalescing at the Fostoria City

Hospital after dueling Martonio Angelo of Buffalo for an hour and a half.

"According to word received here, the Panther remained on the mat, unable to get up after Angelo had pinned him for the deciding fall," explained *The Register*. "He asked that he be left alone so that he could rest a few minutes. A short time later, the Panther rolled over unconscious. He was carried to a dressing room and given medical attention. His physicians said that his condition was caused by a concussion of the brain."

Mitchell eventually debuted in Sandusky two weeks later to wrestle Leo Donahue to a one-hour draw, and then defeated MarAlla the following week, ending the affair in 27 minutes by dropping him in the conclusive fall with "a series of body butts."

As the year progressed, Mitchell continued to tour both Ohio and Michigan, establishing his series of consecutive shoulder butts as one of the most reliable match-ending sequences in the region. At the same time, while the Black Panther was dominant in victory, he retained his tendency to appear conspicuously brittle in defeat.

In the middle of an October bout in Grand Rapids, Mitchell was ahead in the fall count when he submitted to Les Fishbaugh's "twisting crab hold." *The Grand Rapids Press* revealed that the Panther was examined in the locker room by Dr. Harold Mitchell, who "found a dislocation of a vertebra at the hip joint and ordered the wrestler to St. Mary's Hospital for an examination." The Panther was deemed the loser of the bout by default.

One month later at the same venue, Mitchell was also winning his match against Martino Angelo when he attempted a flying shoulder tackle, missed his target, and "landed head down on the floor four feet below the mat." *The Press* called readers' attention to the fact that this was "the second time the Panther has defaulted because of injury in recent weeks."

Just a few weeks later, during a December bout in Sandusky against Jack Kennedy, Mitchell found himself in a similar scenario. As the first fall of the match neared its conclusion, Kennedy climbed atop Mitchell's back, wrapped a figure-four body scissors around the Panther's waist, and squeezed. Mitchell was seen to pass out, fell backwards onto Kennedy, and the referee counted to three.

"The Panther won the fall, but that was only the work of lady luck as he happened to be on top of the heap after the fall, which rendered both semiconscious, and finally found Kennedy the stronger of the two and the least hurt," observed *The Sandusky Register*. "The bout had been so evenly matched that only some break as this could possibly terminate the battle, which seemed as though it would go on forever without a decision. The fall came at the end of one hour and five minutes. When the Panther found he could not answer the bell, he conceded victory."

Far more significant was the fact that the Panther finally tracked down Lee Umbles in Flint, Michigan in December so that the two could have their dream match. In front of 1,200 spectators at the Industrial Mutual Association Auditorium, Mitchell took two falls from Umbles in under 40 minutes with "full body holds," and acquired a symbolic victory for his generation of Black wrestlers by defeating one of the major Black standard-bearers of the 1920s.

The year 1934 opened with the wrestling promotions of California still searching for a worthy replacement for Reginald Siki. The absent Senegalese-Abyssinian's name was invoked in an article in *The New Pittsburgh Courier* as a means of introducing a wrestler named Isiah, or "Blondy," as Siki's heir apparent.

Isiah was identified as a student "under the direct supervision of Jim Browning," who had wrestled his way to three victories in a row and was now off in San Francisco getting more matches under his belt. The article concluded with the invitation that there was "plenty of room on the Coast for colored wrestlers."

Tiger Jack Nelson would be among the first to take up that invitation, but he would first garner some of the most impressive attention of his career when he was listed by *Brooklyn Eagle* writer Eddie Forbes as one of three wrestlers — including Ghafoor Khan and Ayub Kahn — with whom Jim Browning was training for his world title unification match against Jim Londos at Madison Square Garden in New York City. Nelson's name was appended to identify him to the masses as "the acknowledged Negro champion of America."

Further east in New England, another Black wrestler who would one day make significant waves on both coasts was making his debut. George Hardison made his first pro wrestling appearance as "Big George Hoddison" in spring 1934. From the very beginning, he was labeled as a resident of Greenfield, Massachusetts by no less of an authority than *The Greenfield Daily Recorder-Gazette*.

Even in those early stages of his career, "the colored strong man of Greenfield" established himself as a leglock specialist, as he opened an early April show by making Jack Miller of Philadelphia submit to "a punishing reverse leg hold" in 13 minutes.

Several different labels were applied to Hoddison based on his size and complexion, but the name that resonated enough to stick was "The Black Demon." It was under that name that he would be known throughout most of Western Massachusetts, and other areas of New England where he eventually worked.

Unsurprisingly, the Black Demon name had been another of boxer-wrestler George Godfrey's most common sobriquets, underscoring the extent to which the participation of Godfrey in professional wrestling had been influential in legitimizing Black wrestlers as attractions, even as those wrestlers continued to borrow from generous portions of his promotional repertoire.

Hoddison soon made appearances in the areas around Holyoke and Springfield, and it was at that point when he first began carrying the synthetic title of "Massachusetts Negro Heavyweight Champion."

A Decided Novelty

The championship was artificial on two counts; the Black Demon doesn't seem to have encountered much in the way of Black opposition, and he also seemed to be one of the few wrestlers truly carrying around more than 200 pounds of body weight during the heart of the Great Depression, Black or otherwise. This unfortunate feature of the times — specifically a lack of abundant food resources on American dinner tables — limited the possibility that Hoddison would ever have encountered another Black wrestler large enough to challenge him for that particular heavyweight title.

On the basis of his size and strength, if not his still-developing wrestling ability, Hoddison quickly became a standout amongst the wrestlers performing in the region. *The Springfield Daily Republican* declared Hoddison to be "the most popular wrestler to appear in Chicopee" in the middle of October 1934, right before one of the many main-event appearances that Hoddison made at the Union-Canadian Hall.

By this stage, Hoddison had also begun experimenting with other moves that would become trademarks of his. A powerful body slam had been added to his arsenal, presumably as a means of demonstrating his prodigious strength. To showcase his agility, he also added a "rope bound," a maneuver requiring him to stand on the outside of the ring apron with his hands on the top strand of the rope, and vault over it to tackle his opponent and cover him for a winning fall.

In the Midwest, Gorilla Parker's return to Michigan was accompanied by at least one anecdote that betrayed how even Black babyface wrestlers were subjected to racist taunts.

Against heel wrestler Alex Kasaboski in Port Huron, a combination of kicks, knees, bites and holds secured the first fall for Parker, at which point Kasaboski sprang to life and clamped on a hold referred to as a "car twist." *The Port Huron Times Herald* described how several fans in attendance shouted "Eightball can't take it" as Parker writhed in agony, with "eightball" being an early 19th century derogatory term for a Black person. Kasaboski then defeated Parker to win the second and third falls with a flying mare and a leg twist, respectively.

Later in the year, Parker made his earliest appearances in several Ohio cities, and the methods used to promote him varied from night to night and location to location. In Dayton, he was billed as "the Cuban wonder." In Akron, he was described as a "sepia wrestler from Detroit" just one day before the paper added that he was the holder of the colored light heavyweight championship of the world. No matter what backstory was imagined for Parker, he impressed all onlookers with his actions inside of the ring.

"Lending some color to the show, a sepia star, Gorilla Parker, of Havana, used a back body drop to toss Tiger Walker, of Georgia, in the second preliminary," printed *The Akron Beacon Journal*. "It was by far the most interesting bout on the card, and the Gorilla guy lacks nothing in showmanship."

Ahead of his Cleveland debut match in mid-September, Parker had apparently made such an impression on at least one of the promotional writers that *The Plain Dealer* swore that he was "the greatest colored grappler in the history of this universe."

Charley Pauly of *The Dayton Herald* certainly thought himself clever when he described the ending to one of Parker's mid-October matches in Dayton, and illustrated how Ray Carpenter "flying-tackled a white ring post instead of his negro opponent," and suffered an injury as a result.

"Whether Ray was a bit colorblind, near-sighted, or both, it has not been determined, but his plunge, which was calculated to catch Parker squarely, missed Parker entirely, damaged the finish of the painted post, and gave the rugged Carpenter a cut ear and a mean bump on the head," wrote Pauly. "Parker took advantage of his opportunity and clamped on a top body hold to win the single-fall feature event in exactly eight minutes."

While it's true that blading was already a common practice for self-inducing the flow of blood in wrestling

A Decided Novelty

matches at the time, it is unlikely that Carpenter sliced his own ear in order to produce a bleeding effect. Therefore, it is entirely possible that he misjudged his leap and legitimately injured himself. Still, since Parker was on a winning streak, it is not only probable that his victory is what the booker had intended, but that the conclusion to the bout went precisely as planned, save for Carpenter's bloody ear.

After Parker was booked for a bout with "Blacksmith" Welch in Chillicothe, Ohio in mid-October, *The Scioto Gazette* treated it as if the region had lucked out tremendously by acquiring "one of the most sensational stars in the ranks of the world's light heavyweights" on short notice.

"When asked if he would spot Welch 20 pounds and wrestle him, Parker said, 'Bring him on. I'm just as strong as he is, and I can take care of myself,'" reported *The Gazette*.

The Plain Dealer of Cleveland may have been overdoing it by playing up the fact that Parker was still undefeated in the Cleveland area, but *The Gazette* took even greater liberties prior to the Welch match, claiming that Parker had only lost one match in his *entire* career — as the result of an inadvertent foul by world light heavyweight champion "Midget" Fleischman.

"Parker is literally a mass of muscle, with tremendous, bulging arm and shoulder development, which he uses to good advantage on the wrestling pad," gushed *The Gazette*. "He couples his strength with an aggressive, driving offensive, and a thorough knowledge of the science of the game to form a combination which has proved almost unbeatable in the past year and a half."

Although *The Gazette* heaped considerable praise upon Parker prior to his appearance, the reporting of his two-falls-to-one victory over Welch contained some descriptions of Parker that weren't particularly flattering.

"Several times the colored boy — who incidentally, really looked like a gorilla when his ire was aroused — broke holds with his sheer strength," recounted *The Gazette*. "The second fall went 16 ½ minutes with Parker winning with a pin after holding a powerful headlock on the Blacksmith for several minutes. Welch was quite groggy. The last fall started out with a bang, both boys dashing out for the kill... after a series of hard slams, Welch picked the black boy up and slammed pretty hard, and as he dropped on him for the pin, Parker simply rolled over and held the blacksmith's shoulders down for the count."

One of the rare occasions in Parker's career when his race factored directly into the angle being presented to fans occurred in Mansfield, Ohio, after Parker lost a bout to Stanley West of Nebraska. Following the bout, Parker openly criticized referee Gene Gordon, and hinted that racial prejudice may have contributed to Gordon's failure to officiate with impartiality.

"I've been the victim in Mansfield of loose, if not prejudiced officiating by Gordon," Parker told *The Galion Inquirer*. "Get me a square deal in the officiating and I'll take West out every time, and my dough says so."

The "dough" Parker spoke of was in reference to a $200 side bet he had apparently placed on a rematch if such a bout with West was to ever take place. Well, when the bout *did* take place, it was made to appear as if Parker's complaints about officiating tinged with a racial bias were all hot air, as he was decidedly thrashed by West, who repeatedly shoulder-butted Parker to the ground before pinning him.

Like Parker, Jim Mitchell also continued to tour what were becoming his familiar Midwestern haunts during 1934, and the descriptions of his matches reveal a wrestler who was going out of his way to portray the most squeaky-clean image that he possibly could. In a January bout against Billy Londos at Battle Creek's Masonic Auditorium, Mitchell reportedly "took his abuse like a good panther" and actually "waved aside the referee when he offered to disqualify Londos for fouling."

"The Panther took the first and only fall in 21 minutes with a series of his favorite aerial shoulder butts and a full body hold. The remaining time passed with no decision," stated *The Battle Creek Moon-Journal*. "Londos worked unmercifully on the negro's arm during the second fall, leaving the Panther in such a state of chaos that it was necessary for the referee to straighten out his arm and put it back in front of him so he could find it — and in the next few moments the Panther was smacking Mr. Londos most emphatically with the arm that had just been converted into a dish rag."

One week later in the same venue, Mitchell had a match against Wildcat Pete of Oregon, in front of an audience that *Moon-Journal* sports reporter G.B. Dolliver Jr. described as being evenly split along color lines, and with both groups of fans ultimately being "satisfied that their boy won." The ending to the contest commenced when Pete and Mitchell both collided with referee John Staffen, resulting in all three men lying in semi-conscious states on the canvas.

"While John is trying to regain his lost equilibrium, the Wildcat (George Pertulla by name) flops on the Panther (name unknown) with a full body hold, and what seems like the count of three expires — with nobody there to count him out but the by-now half crazy fans," illustrated Dolliver. "Staffen comes back to the party about now, but by this time the Panther has rolled over on top of Pete, and John pats the canvas three times quick-like and the show is over, with the Panther the winner. So Pete wins first, and the Panther wins last — but last is for keeps."

Western Michigan was seemingly the location where the Panther mastered the art of appearing utterly defeated in victory. At the end of a February bout in Battle Creek, Mitchell received a devastating uppercut from Les Fishbaugh "that knocked the Kentuckian into oblivion and off the mat as well." *The Enquirer*, which still characterized the triumph as genuine, drew attention to the way in which Michell required the referee's help to "help him climb a bit shakily back onto the canvas-covered planks in order to have his hand raised in a token of victory."

The following month in Kalamazoo, Jerry Hagan of *The Kalamazoo Gazette* detailed how Mitchell was similarly rendered unconscious by Fishbaugh after being "bunted on the jaw and knocked over the ropes" before slamming his head on the cement floor outside of the ring. The Panther was initially counted out of the ring, but when he was deemed unable to continue in the final fall, the referee reversed his decision and awarded both the fall and the match to Mitchell.

On the other side of the Detroit River in Windsor, Ontario, Canada, Mitchell was portrayed as far less susceptible to damage. In October, he took consecutive falls from Danny McDonald to earn a world championship match against Gus Kallio. The Panther battled back from a one-fall deficit, felling McDonald with "a reverse overhead slam" to claim the second stanza, and then opening the final fall by "following up a series of flying tackles with a series of shoulder jolts and head butts," before putting McDonald away by "hitting him with a number of hard tackles."

In the world title match one week later, *The Windsor Star* described Mitchell as "a better wrestler than the champion" who offered "his usual clean and speedy performance," but was outsmarted by a champion who was "not averse to using illegal tactics." This included antagonizing the challenger with "the way in which he slapped Mitchell's face and pushed his hand into the challenger's dark-skinned visage."

Mitchell took the first fall "by means of his shoulder hoists and a body pin," but submitted to Kallio's toehold twice over the proceeding 34 minutes to lose the match.

Mitchell and Parker weren't the only Black wrestlers active in the Midwest during 1934. Harry "Tarzan" Wilson had made only one 1933 appearance of note, wrestling against Dan Brown in Madison, Wisconsin. He entered the news cycle once again in 1934, with a minor — yet common — modification made to his moniker, as *The LaCrosse Tribune and Leader Press* labeled him "Harry 'Tarzan' Wilson, 'The Black Panther.'"

"The Memphis boy has proved to be to wrestling what George Godfrey once was in boxing," opined *The Tribune*, adding Wilson to the growing list of Black wrestlers compared to Godfrey. "He rates with the best but cannot get bouts with the top-notchers because of his color."

A Decided Novelty

The Tribune added that Wilson was "known throughout the midwest as the Black Panther" because he was "lightning fast with sinewy strength" and "as agile and clever as the animal after which he is named." This was a wild exaggeration, as Wilson seldom made appearances of any sort, and was a very late adopter of the Black Panther title.

Speaking of which, Jack Claybourne assumed the Black Panther title himself during his first outings in Montana. In one of his earliest matches in Great Falls, Claybourne exchanged falls with "Totem Pole" Anderson through submission holds in the early rounds, with wrestling's latest Panther taking the first fall with a surfboard hold, and Anderson forcing Jack to yield to a short-arm scissors. Then Anderson resorted to dirty tactics and started choking the Panther in the ropes with "a noose hold."

"When the referee objected, Anderson concentrated on him. The result was that [referee] Higgins, a heavyweight mat man in his own right, took a couple of swats at Anderson and sent him spinning," stated *The Great Falls Tribune*. "The black boy took advantage of Anderson's momentary dizziness and put on a Boston crab and rolled the Totem over for the finish."

In his very next outing in Great Falls, Panther Jack continued along his winning trajectory by taking two falls from Lou Kotonen with a bodyslam and a toehold. Then the action shifted to Montana's capital city of Helena in October, where *The Daily Independent* described Claybourne's feet as being "longer than a mule's ears," while also clearly identifying "the 168 pounds of brawn and ivory" as the babyface in his bout with Totem Pole Anderson. *The Independent* insisted "there will be plenty out there hoping the colored boy smears Totem all over the Arctic Circle."

By all accounts, Jack's actions that evening in Helena satisfied the bloodlust of the audience. Claybourne lost the first fall to Anderson with a "rolling keylock," but then the Panther "used a flying Dutchman and a body press" to even the fight. Then, in the fifth round of the battle, the Panther hoisted Anderson onto his shoulders, spun him around with an airplane spin, and turned him over to "send Anderson crashing to the canvas on the back of his neck, knocking him out."

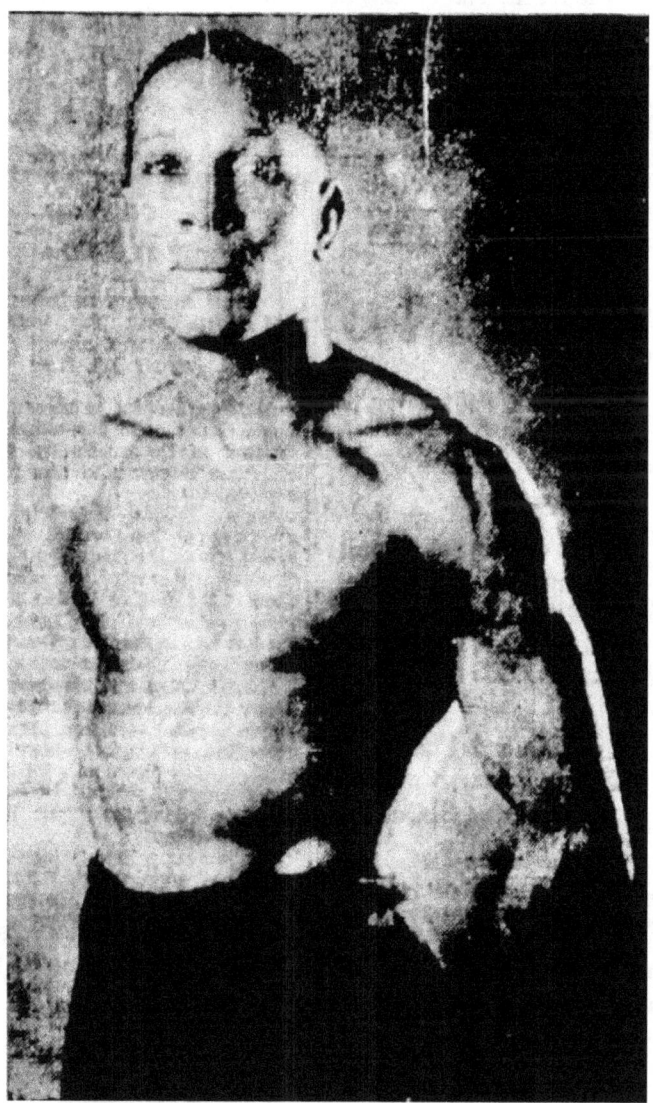

Jack Claybourne as "The Black Panther"

Back in Great Falls, Claybourne was given the appearance of being the most dominant wrestler in all of

A Decided Novelty

Montana when he won a six-man "wrestle royal" to begin the evening, and then destroyed Tiger Backley during their bout later in the night. *The Tribune* described the Panther as spinning Backley around in the airplane spin "in the most approved roller-skating fashion," after which, "Backley went down hard and failed to come out for the start of the next round."

Once the Panther had successfully pulled off this herculean effort in front of a Great Falls audience, a follow-up edition of *The Daily Leader* described him as "apparently invincible."

Meanwhile, Ed Flowers had been phased out of action in New England, as was his name. Surprisingly, Flowers then wrestled at least twice under his real name of Joe Godfrey, in what appear to be events promoted outside of the Charley Gordon banner. It's possible that Godfrey wanted to avoid any unnecessary feather-ruffling by wrestling under his established name in opposition to the promoter who helped him gain traction in the industry.

The two matches were held in Saugus, Massachusetts at the Cliftondale Community House, very close to Godfrey's hometown of Malden. One of the bouts concluded in a brawl with Bill Anderson that needed to be broken up by representatives from the Saugus Police Department.

These two appearances by Godfrey under his real name were interspersed between the initial matches wrestled by Godfrey under the name Tiger Flowers in New York.

In February 1934, Tiger Flowers recorded a victory over Otto Van Burg at the Jamaica Arena in the borough of Queens in New York City. This initial reference to Flowers the wrestler only referred to his stated nationality of Cuban rather than his race. Almost immediately, Flowers had his status nominally upgraded to that of the Cuban light heavyweight champion in keeping with the international all-star nature of pro wrestling from that era, and especially in New York City.

Perhaps out of the necessity of distancing the pro wrestler Tiger Flowers from the countless boxers making use of the same name — which was a tribute to the beloved Black boxer Theodore "Tiger" Flowers who had died tragically on the operating table — the first addition was made to Godfrey's pseudonym prior to a New York bout in March, with the addendum of "Johnstone" tacked onto the end. This would only be the first of several concurrent names employed by the same wrestler in different locations around various East Coast locales.

Flowers then wrestled to a draw with a grappler that he would have several encounters with, Maurice LaChapelle. Although he was often stated to have been of French extraction, LaChapelle was actually Zoltán Kájel of Hungary. This is representative of the fact that the use of false national origins within the wrestling world was broad, and applicable to wrestlers of any race.

During a follow-up appearance by Flowers in Camden, *The Courier-Post* made it clear to readers that the "clever colored foe" of Johnny "Popeye" Carlin was also Black in addition to being of faux Cuban extraction.

"In jousting with Flowers, Carlin is facing another worthy rival," glowed *The Courier-Post*. "The colored youngster is one of the cleverest light heavies ever to appear in this city, having won his first bout and drawing in his second with Maurice LaChappelle of France last Monday night. The latter bout was a whirlwind match from start to finish, and the draw decision met with popular approval."

The article elaborated that it should be no surprise to fans if Flowers won his bout with Carlin, given that he was "built like a young Hercules" and "displayed great ability as an orthodox wrestler." A later *Courier-Post* piece would refer to Flowers as "a perfect specimen of humanity" due to his chiseled physique.

Aside from displaying tremendous technical prowess within a powerful figure, another trait Flowers soon presented to the fans was his remarkable toughness. In a 30-minute Convention Hall draw with Pat Faletti, he made his ownership of that attribute crystal clear by exchanging stiff shots with

Faletti in front of 3,500 fans, leaving both men the worse for wear.

"It was a fast, rough match, and Faletti finished with a deep gash over his left eye, while Flowers was bleeding from the mouth," described *The Courier-Post*. "Faletti, who was making his debut, started slugging early in the bout, and dropped the colored youngster on numerous occasions with terrific rights to the head and body. Flowers finally met the Italian at his own game and gave him as good as he received."

Later, *The Courier-Post* would say that Faletti was so aggressive during the show-stealing bout that "Flowers finally reached the stage where he either had to punch back or be knocked out, with the result that the bout became a brawl."

Flowers' Camden Convention Hall loss to Harry 'Speedy' Schaffer revealed other characteristics of the young wrestler. Tom Ryan of *The Courier-Post* emphasized Flowers' insistence on maintaining a squeaky-clean wrestling style no matter how dirty his opponents' tactics became, which was very similar to how Jim Mitchell was cast.

Ryan wrote that "2,800 fans witnessed Schaffer subject the clean-cut colored youngster to a savage, off-color beating before winning each fall," noting how Shaffer "could have been disqualified at least 50 times for biting, punching, kneeing, and using strangle holds."

While Flowers had shown his great reluctance to get down and dirty with his opponent during that match in South Jersey, he also displayed a physical trait that caught Tom Ryan's attention when the writer noticed what the specific target of many of Schaffer's illegal punches had been.

"A punch early in the match opened Flowers' left ear, which is one of the finest 'cauliflowers' in the mat industry, yet, despite the painful injury, the colored youth stuck to his guns and went down fighting gamely each time he was pinned," noted Ryan.

On top of his musculature, the strikingly cauliflowered left ear of the original Tiger Flowers would become one of the principal means of identifying him. For what it's worth, the legitimate fear held by wrestling promoters that the heelish actions of a wrestler might spark real conflict with the audience is justified by the outcome of this very bout.

Philadelphia Inquirer reporter Ronald Friedenberg observed that a "burly fellow" who "was particularly abusive" challenged Schaffer to a fight after the wrestler had finished abusing Flowers. This led to Schaffer stripping off one of his two pairs of tights and inviting the fan to fight him in the ring. Fortunately, the fan declined the invitation.

In April, Flowers began wrestling in New York with greater regularity, and extended his appearances to different venues around the city. This included what would retroactively be an ironic ending to a match that took place inside of a small venue in Manhattan.

"A head-on collision between Tiger Flowers Johnstone and Herman Donchin resulted in both of them being counted out and a draw being rendered at the St. Nicholas Arena last night after 28 minutes 20 seconds," reported *The Brooklyn Daily Eagle*.

As a new Black entrant to the entertainment scene of New York City, Flowers was simply keeping pace with the zeitgeist of the city. Just one month before Flowers made his debut, the 125th Street Apollo Theater reopened as a performance venue catering to Black audiences with Black entertainers and an all-Black staff. It would soon become a cherished symbol of Black art, entertainment and culture.

May would be the month that the first in a slew of fake baptismal names would be bestowed upon Flowers, with one New York promoter labeling him Charley "Tiger Flowers" Johnstone. While this was the most common spelling of Flowers' surname, Johnston and Johnson also became common alternatives. For example, the Johnston spelling was used when describing Flowers' act of brutalizing Axel Madsen after the latter had bridged his way out of half a dozen pinning attempts.

"Shortly after the 25-minute mark had been reached, Madsen scored with flying mares," observed *The Brooklyn Time*

Union. "However, Johnston whipped back from a mare to score with a flying tackle, and that was the beginning of the end. Battered by tackles, Madsen fell easy prey for the series of slams which followed, and was easily pinned by the body slam."

Tiger Flowers flexes for a photo

Changes to the names that bookended Tiger Flowers weren't the only alterations that were made to the wrestler's title. Also in May, Flowers was squarely inducted into the pantheon of Black wrestlers who would be forced to wear the name of "Black Panther" when *The Bergen Evening Record* described him as "Tiger Flowers Johnstone, The Black Panther," making Flowers a bearer of the name in two different states.

Using both 'Tiger' and 'Black Panther' awkwardly combined two separate big cat species in one persona. It was far from the only time that the labels would be paired so clumsily.

Flowers would also be lumped into the company of the other Black stars of his era in another way. In the promotion for a Hasbrouck Heights show in New Jersey, in which half the wrestlers on the roster were touted as the representative champions of their respective nations, Flowers at least temporarily shed his false Cuban identity and was advertised as the "colored champion."

Of course, there were inevitably descriptions of Flowers that combined all of those identities, like when *The Bergen Evening Record* labeled Flowers as a grappler "who lays claim to the light heavyweight championship of Cuba and Harlem, is one of the most subtle, scientific grapplers of the present age. He is as spry as a panther and just as foxy. Moreover, he's a great showman, and that is a great addition to a grappler."

Regardless of how he was advertised prior to the opening bell, Flowers developed a favorable reputation for being one of the standout wrestlers on the card once his matches were underway. Reporting favorably about Flowers' match with LaChappelle in Teterboro, *The Bergen Evening Record* noted that "the bout lacked the tragedy, clowning, burping, and grunting associated with the other bouts, but was waged scientifically. There wasn't a rough moment in it, but the masters put on an excellent show that was called a draw. Both were given a wild ovation."

So noticeable was Flowers' reliance on his technical wrestling prowess at this early juncture that promotion for him began to lean all the more heavily into spotlighting those abilities. *The Evening Record* anointed him as "an expert wrestler with all the science and ring lore of a Londos or a Lewis — and just as tough when opponents try to spread him."

It was quite premature to compare Flowers to full-fledged legends like "The Golden Greek" Jim Londos or Ed "Strangler" Lewis, both of whom were beloved White champions whose names were recognized across the continent and around the world. Moreover, making such comparisons carried other potential risks, like offending White wrestling fans who wouldn't take kindly to having a Black wrestler juxtaposed so favorably with their heroes.

A Decided Novelty

Given the palpability of the underlying racial tension that lingered in many of the urban metropolises of the United States in the 1930s, it was seemingly inevitable that someone would make an overt threat to the proprietors of any form of combat theater in which a Black wrestler was even occasionally seen to be getting the better of his White opponents.

In June, prominent wrestling promoter Jack Pfefer of Teterboro submitted one of those threats for public consumption through *The Bergen Evening Record*.

"Guess you haven't been reading the Bergen County newspapers lately, else we don't think you would have the nerve to bring Tiger Flowers Johnstone over to wrestle at Teterboro Saturday night," began the letter. "We still have a few more crosses to burn and we never run out of matches. This is just a friendly tip so take it while the taking is good and call the match off. (Signed) K.K.K."

The letter was published by *The Bergen Evening Record* along with the response from Jack Pfefer, who declared that he would not be intimidated by "night prowlers" with "pillowcases and bed sheets over their heads," and that Flowers would indeed be appearing as advertised.

In addition to addressing the threat made by presumed members of the Ku Klux Klan, the article by *The Evening Record* also delved into the fact that Flowers had been picking up "a lot of easy money posing for some of the most noted sculptors in the country."

As tempting as it might be to attribute bravery to both Pfefer and Flowers for insisting that the show must go on beneath a cloud of intimidation, the aforementioned threat must be taken with a huge grain of salt considering its alleged target.

Over the course of the next decade, Jack Pfefer would gain a reputation for being something of a swindler and charlatan in promotional circles. While credited as one of wrestling's original innovators with respect to the use of pageantry to attract fans, Pfefer would likewise be cast as someone who would stoop to any level to garner attention for his wrestling product.

The threat's authenticity remains questionable, particularly since Pfefer himself publicized it while responding with theatrical defiance.

When Flowers appeared in the Pennsauken Township Arena and wrestled under the auspices of promoter Charley Grip, he would have his name modified again. This time, the surname of Johnstone was dropped altogether, and he was provided the first name of Ted — a common abbreviation for Theodore — to make him a closer match to the original Theodore "Tiger" Flowers, the boxer who inspired his name.

By the conclusion of 1934, Reginald Siki had effectively abandoned the United States, but the talent pool of Black talent was beginning to swell in his absence. This meant that Black stars were going to be bursting through racial barriers at an accelerated rate as a byproduct of their mere presence. In some instances, well-meaning wrestling promoters would stretch the boundaries of good taste in order to expedite that change, or often merely as a byproduct of it.

11 – The Black Demon

In January 1935, Reginald Siki and George Godfrey finally squared off in Brussels, Belgium in a match to conclusively determine who the world colored heavyweight champion was. Godfrey emerged victorious.

Now theoretically possessing a solid claim on the title of best Black heavyweight wrestler in the world, Godfrey was asked whether boxing or wrestling was a more strenuous sport. George answered as if wrestling was a joke that everyone was in on, and his response was included in the nationally syndicated column of John J. Romano.

"Why man, wrestling is like a parlor game," Godfrey was reported as answering. "I just plays with the boys. When they gets tough, I just clips them on the chin and then rolls 'em over."

In fairness, the essence of Godfrey's boxing career hadn't been much different. He had spent the prior year fighting primarily in Brazil, Belgium, and Romania against boxers with abysmal records. His lone fight against a quality opponent — Motzi Spakow of Bucharest — resulted in Godfrey being disqualified for throwing low.

The quality of Godfrey's recent competition pool may have been lacking, but he was still selected to fight Belgian boxer Pierre Charles for the world heavyweight championship of the International Boxing Union after the IBU stripped Max Baer of the title for refusing to fight Charles in Europe.

Many sports reporters treated the fight between Charles and Godfrey as a joke, and some issued statements about George that greatly mischaracterized his career in the process. In one instance, an unnamed reporter for the Associated Press wrote that Godfrey "has been knocked out by every heavyweight of any importance," which was patently false.

Godfrey's most recent knockout loss at that point had occurred in 1923. Since that time, Godfrey had competed in

106 fights over the course of 12 years without suffering another defeat by knockout.

Reginald Siki and George Godfrey in Belgium

On October 2, 1935, Godfrey outpointed Pierre Charles in Schaerbeek, Belgium — in the latter's home country no less — to win the IBU World Heavyweight Championship. Returning home with a semi-legitimate claim to world-title status in boxing, Godfrey quickly announced his desire to wrap up his wrestling obligations and return to boxing exclusively.

"I don't intend to be like other heavyweight champions," Godfrey told Universal Service sportswriter Murray Goodman. "I won't wait a year before defending my laurels. Of course, I didn't get much mazuna for licking Charles, nor do I intend to hold up any promoters here. I believe a match between me and Louis would draw well. Should Joe decline the bout, I would be glad to give Braddock a chance to win undisputed right to the heavyweight title."

The "Louis" introduced by Godfrey was Joe Louis Barrow, a young Black fighter who had exploded onto the scene and surged to world title contention. Between the middle of 1934 and the end of 1935, Louis would reel off a staggering streak of 23 victories with zero defeats, knocking out former world champions Primo Carnera and Max Baer in the process. Staying true to form, the Associated Press christened Louis as "the new Black Panther of the ring."

Perhaps feeling as if there was no longer any point in protecting his status as a championship-caliber wrestler as he sought a fight with Louis, Godfrey went on an atypical losing streak when he resumed his grappling appearances. He lost quick falls to Danny O'Connor and Casey Berger on back-to-back nights in New Jersey, and seemed laser focused on making a defense of his IBU world title against Leroy Haynes in Los Angeles on Christmas Eve. However, Godfrey withdrew from the event two days before the fight, claiming a hand injury.

As Godfrey had managed to resurrect his name within discussion about the upper echelon of heavyweight boxing, Henry Daniels finally returned to his hometown of Frederick, Oklahoma, and was treated as a conquering hero in the prelude to his bout with Elton Eubanks, who hailed from the town of Duncan within the same state. Daniels then made the first advertised appearance under his authentic name while also making it clear what stage name he had been using when wrestling in other regions.

"Daniels played on the basketball team of Consolidated No. 2 school in 1923 and 1924," disclosed *The Frederick Leader*. "Daniels has been wrestling professionally for the past six years under the name of 'Gorilla' Parker, and from the clippings in his scrapbook, he has met the best welter and middleweights in the country. He is a colorful showman of the type who can either rough it or wrestle."

While Daniels had been a main-event performer in several locations where he wrestled, promoters apparently believed his exploits as Gorilla Parker would carry greater significance if he was presented as a West Coast attraction. Consequently, the local man who was "formerly a resident of Tillman County" was falsely stated to have moved to San

A Decided Novelty

Diego, California, while also having his years of wrestling activity inflated by a couple of years, unless he had previously wrestled under a different name.

"Daniels is the roughest wrestler to appear in the local ring yet, and is also the most colorful showman," declared *The Leader*. "He is strictly of the rock 'em, sock 'em type, and has been taking the West Coast wrestling centers by storm."

Such praise in the hometown newspaper — even if gently exaggerated — represented a drastic improvement for a man whose previous headlines in *The Leader* had been limited to his instigation of fights during high school basketball games.

Given the success he had acquired in more established and respected wrestling territories, Daniels was quite generous with his Oklahoma opponents. This included losing a match in front of his hometown crowd to Elton Eubanks on a card that offered a mixture of boxing and wrestling bouts.

On most occasions, Daniels was only generous enough to surrender single falls in best-of-three-falls matches in front of his townspeople. "Bull Dog" Adkisson was a frequent opponent of Daniels, and the Frederick native usually emerged victorious with bodyslams and full nelsons.

Ahead of a late March victory over Bob Spangler, Daniels was introduced by a new name as Henry "Bad Boy" Daniels, perhaps as an allusion to his real-life reputation as a high school troublemaker from Consolidated No. 2 High School.

The month of March required some rather heroic traveling efforts on the part of Daniels, as he traveled back and forth from Oklahoma to Wisconsin repeatedly, and without the luxury of a modern freeway system. It's remarkable that he went to such trouble to appear in a town of 5,000 residents — his hometown — in between bookings in Wisconsin cities with 70,000 people, where he was convincingly touted as "colored light heavyweight champion of the world" with a reputation that backed up his title.

For example, he wrestled on Monday, May 11, in Frederick as "Bad Boy" Daniels, then drove to Racine,

A Decided Novelty

Wisconsin, to wrestle Jim Demetral as Gorilla Parker on May 14. No matter how tired he may have been from 1,000 miles of travel, he didn't shortchange the fans on his effort level, as his actions that night in Racine nearly started a riot after Demetral began chasing him around the ring during the deciding fall of their 35-minute bout.

"Parker stopped long enough to lock one of Jimmy's legs in the ropes to take his second fall with a body press in 17 minutes," recounted *The Journal Times*. "About five minutes elapsed before the fans would permit the Bostonian to leave the ring."

Parker was rewarded for this victory with a shot at "Midget" Fischer's world light heavyweight championship. Parker succeeded in winning the first fall, only to have his legs mangled so badly by Fischer's leglocks that he surrendered the following two falls by submission and had to be carried bodily back to the dressing room.

In late May, Parker made his debut in the New York City borough of Queens at the Ridgewood Grove Arena wrestling as "Zimba Parker of Africa" against Whitey Wahlberg. He then wrestled as "Zimba Gorilla Parker" when he captured a decision victory over Bobby Risko at Jamaica Arena. From that point onward, Parker shed his "Gorilla" sobriquet, and exclusively competed under some version of Zimba Parker when appearing in the Empire State, and in the surrounding states.

As usual, promoters focused on Parker's prodigious muscles. In New Jersey, *The Courier-Post* described him as "built along the lines of a small Hercules" and the owner of "two of the most powerful arms in the bone-bending business."

Parker's strong physique implied explosive potential that he frequently exhibited even in losing efforts. Because of this, Parker received the reputation for being a fast starter, like when he torched fan-favorite Leo Wallick in just 25 seconds to take an early one-fall lead.

"At the bell, Parker rushed across the ring to flatten Wallick with a flying tackle to stun his rival," reported *The*

A Decided Novelty

Courier-Post. "Five more tackles and a body press enabled the colored grappler to score the first fall."

Unfortunately for Parker and whatever fans he may have had in attendance, Wallick quickly evened the score with a series of dropkicks, and then extended the match past the 31-minute mark to wear Parker down and finish him with a body slam.

Henry "Gorilla Parker" Daniels

In July, Parker was labeled "The Black Panther" before a match in Montclair against Max Martin, adding another star to the long line of Black wrestlers who were temporarily given that title. In Zimba's case, it was indeed a rare association, but it would appear in the most unlikely of places.

A Decided Novelty

For example, in fall 1935, *The Honolulu Advertiser* began to make promises that "Zimba Parker, Black Panther" would soon arrive in the South Sea Islands. It's possible that plans changed, or that Parker was simply mistaken for one of the other popular Black Panthers involved in wrestling. Either way, neither Parker nor any of the other panthers would materialize in Hawaii during the remainder of 1935 or in all of 1936.

In other locations where members of the Black Panther fraternity had established themselves, Parker was being compared favorably to them as a means of building interest for his appearances. These comparisons often led to some unintentionally amusing connections.

"The new colored sensation, Zimba Parker, of Kentucky, appears in the semi-final against that contrasting shade of epidermis, Drop-Kick Murphy, the fair-haired Alabama college boy, who went south from Medford, Mass. for his schooling," printed *The Portland Press Herald*. "Parker is said to be even more sensational than the Black Panther, heretofore considered tops in the Joe Louis section of the mat game."

To wit, on one of the rarest of occasions when Zimba Parker — an occasional Black Panther — was declared to have been a product of Kentucky, he was being compared to "Black Panther" Jim Mitchell, who was *actually* from Kentucky. In another instance, Zimba was described as "a colored villain" who was "a serious threat to the Black Panther for honors in the ebony action of wrestling."

At some point along the way — likely after the first time he was named as "Zimba Parker, The African Lion" — Parker was reported to have worn a Lion's pelt as his pre-match garb, with *The Springfield Daily News* connecting the choice of entrance attire to Parker's African identity. After the bell rang to commence his matches, Parker's wrestling style surpassed the colorful nature of his attire. An example of this was when he wrestled New York police officer Sammy Fitzpatrick Cohen in Greenfield, Massachusetts.

A Decided Novelty

"Officer Cohen began the proceedings by pulling his ebony rival's nose, but the act only inspired the black warrior to get a stranglehold on the New Yorker's own schnozzle," stated *The Greenfield Daily Recorder-Gazette*. "Enraged, Sammy Fitzpatrick next tried pounding Parker's wooly skull, but his only reward was a bruised hand and a solid thump on his own cranium."

The Recorder-Gazette then explained that Parker "resembled Joe Louis" as he assaulted Cohen with punches to the head and body. Helpless, Cohen trapped Zimba against the ropes and choked him until the referee called for a disqualification.

Parker was eventually elevated to contention for the unofficial title of the top "bad man" in Northeastern wrestling, as he began to rack up victories as an "Ethiopian mat warrior" or an "Ethiopian savage."

This time, aligning Zimba with Ethiopia had less to do with any specific actions of Haile Selassie and more to do with fascist Italian dictator Benito Mussolini's imperialistic ambitions. Mussolini launched an invasion of Ethiopia in fall 1935 after relocating hundreds of thousands of troops to the Horn of Africa during the preceding months.

As the Ethiopian situation grabbed international headlines, wrestling promoters found it fashionable to keep presumed Ethiopians on their rosters, and Zimba became one of many Black wrestlers touted as Ethiopian imports.

Described as "the Ethiopian black panther who has yet to meet defeat in this section," Parker tackled "former navy middleweight champion" Steve Karras multiple times in Greenfield and made short work of him.

The label of Ethiopian was even slapped on the least likely of targets. By 1935, it was perceived in at least some circles that Lee Umbles' wrestling career was over. That at least appears to have been the impression of the Associated Negro Press, which published a report of a grammar school wrestling tournament to be held in Chicago that February. The organizer of the tournament, which was being handled by the Chicago

A Decided Novelty

Board of Education, was Lee Umbles. The ANP identified Umbles as a "former wrestler."

In fact, Umbles was still wrestling — and often winning — primarily in Wisconsin and Indiana. Surprisingly, in the state where he first made a name for himself, Umbles was identified as "the 180-pound Ethiopian champion, Lee Umbles." Clearly, even Umbles wasn't immune to the booking fallout caused by the Italo-Ethiopian War, as it was stated that promoters were looking to book Umbles against an Italian wrestler, which "may result in an embargo on banana oil."

With even more credibility to back his title claim stemming from his brief flirtation with New York media exposure, Gorilla Parker's former nemesis Tiger Nelson headed west in 1935 after another round of Midwestern losses, and he brought his belt with him. However, Nelson garnered the bulk of the attention from his first year of activity in California's wrestling rings from his proximity to a killing, coupled with the accusation that he may have incited it.

The undisputed details are that during an early July wrestling show at the Olympic Auditorium in Los Angeles, 35-year-old World War I veteran William V. Focher hurled a whiskey bottle into the wrestling ring. This led to Focher's extraction from the audience, and a face-to-face meeting between Focher and promoter Lou Daro, who allowed Focher to remove himself from the premises.

When he submitted a statement about the night's events during a commissioner's inquest, Daro stated that "he asked Jack Nelson, a Negro grappler, to remain with him as he feared Focher would attempt to kill him." It's unclear whether or not Daro requested that Nelson stick by his side before or after Focher had later approached Daro with a friend, cursed at Daro, and threatened "I'll fix you for this."

Shortly thereafter, Focher was gunned down by a volley of bullets fired by policemen J.E. Chase and T.R. Welch, who had overheard the word "holdup" being shouted from Daro's direction, and fired upon Focher as he was fleeing from the scene. According to The United Press, the policemen blamed

Nelson for calling out to them that "it was a stickup," thereby prompting their swift and deadly response.

When he actually climbed into the wrestling rings in and around the Los Angeles region, Nelson was hailed as "a colored wrestler who is touted as one of the most colorful and action performers in the mat game" by *The San Bernardino County Sun*.

Within his first month wrestling along the California coast, Nelson's act drew rave reviews despite his consistent defeats. Upon learning that Nelson would be facing Hugh Claphan in an upcoming bout, Carl Johnson of *The Bloomington News* praised Nelson's overall presentation, if not his technical prowess.

"The match I shan't miss is the opener between 'Tiger' Nelson and Hugh Claphan," wrote Johnson in the June 14 edition of his sports column. "I have never seen Claphan, but I have seen the 'Tiger.' As a hair-pulling, riot-causing nut, he is tops. As a wrestler, he isn't much, but he is fun to watch."

True to form, Nelson lost his bout with Claphan in short order, but he accomplished just enough in that short time to be remembered. As the writer from *The San Bernardino County Sun* recounted, "Jack 'Tiger' Nelson proved a strong attraction despite his defeat by Hugo Claphan, the strong Canadian. Nelson proved to be a flashy and speedy grappler, and at times had Claphan in a bad way, but lost the scheduled 30-minute joust in less than six minutes as the result of a body press."

Aside from the fatal shooting incident involving Nelson, one of the chief newsmaking events concerning a Black wrestler during 1935 focused on a wrestler who may never have set foot on North American soil during his lifetime.

It appears that Jim Wango crossed the threshold into the European public's awareness for the first time in 1923. This occurred when famous Black fighter Battling Siki was in Paris, France preparing for a fight against Marcel Nilles, and had enlisted the aid of "two blacks" as sparring partners — Paul Haws and Jim Wango.

A Decided Novelty

Understanding the frequency with which professional wrestlers were recruited from boxing ranks, and provided that Wango — when he didn't identify as a South African wrestler — was frequently labeled as French, it is certainly reasonable to assume that this Jim Wango who helped to train Battling Siki was the same Jim Wango who ultimately wrestled as "The Black Devil" in several European venues.

Wango had apparently already established himself as a wrestler possessing some degree of talent by late 1931. When Wango was defeated by Atholl Oakeley at the London Sport Club in 1931, *The Daily Mirror* declared it to have been "Wango's first defeat by a white wrestler."

The Sunday Sun described what Wango looked like in victory when he downed Harry Brooks in Newcastle in mid-December of that year, after emphasizing that the 6'4", 15-stone (210-pound) wrestler was regarded to be colossal in size.

"Despite his weight, the coloured man was wonderfully agile and escaped with ease from all the attempts by Brooks to pin him down, and in the second round, Wango pinned his man down with a leg and arm lock to win in 13 minutes and a half," described *The Sun*.

Even though he was introduced under a most menacing nickname, "The Black Devil" was also shown to be gracious in victory, as demonstrated when he defeated Jack Ansell in Liverpool that same month.

"Jim Wango, the coloured South African champion, was so elated after defeating Jack Ansell, a sixteen stones Londoner, that he repeatedly kissed Ansell when the latter offered his congratulations," noted *The Liverpool Post and Mercury*.

With Wango frequently labeled as a product of South Africa, British publications like *The Sunday Dispatch* described how the "Negro Colossus" Wango would pound his chest at the beginning of his matches, eliciting direct comparisons between that pre-match ritual and the actions of African gorillas before they engage in combat.

A Decided Novelty

In reality, Wango's place of residence was Marseilles, France, which was a fact that came to light when a formal complaint was made in the House of Commons about Wango's participation in a mixed-race wrestling event at the Victoria Palace Theatre in London in March 1932.

"Mr. Roland Jennings, Conservative M.P. for Sedgefield, Durham, is to ask a supplementary question that Wango should be barred from entering the country or appearing on the stage," printed *The Daily Herald*.

A representative from the Victoria Palace immediately denounced Jennings' attempt to bar Wango from appearing, citing the precedent set by other combat sports, and invoking reasoning similar to that used in the laws restricting the commingling of Blacks and Whites in the wrestling rings of the Southern United States.

"There have been boxing matches between coloured and white people, and these have received official sanction," the official remarked to *The Herald*. "Why not wrestling matches?"

Wango's colorful nickname attracted much attention, especially when paired with his size. Even English skeptics of the credibility of the modern "all-in" wrestling style of the 1930s were impressed by Wango's intimidating physical dimensions.

"Now, I have seen a good deal of all-in wrestling, so let me state here and now that by far the most brutal thing about it are the names affected by the various champions," began the writer from *The Sunday Dispatch*. "Even these cannot bear too close an inspection. Jim Wango, 'The Black Devil,' is six foot four and weighs 17 stone; he would probably keep that nickname even if he were selling flowers."

When Wango arrived in London from Paris for a series of matches, he was met at the airport by the press, and a contingent that included British wrestling champion James Wolfe, who hoisted Wango into the air to the delight of the nearby photographers.

A Decided Novelty

Wango's foremost reason for venturing into London on this trip was to wrestle against British all-in heavyweight wrestling champion Atholl Oakeley. Given the size disparity between the two wrestlers, many pundits did not care for Oakeley's chances.

"There is something sinister about Wango's sobriquet of 'The Black Devil,' but the folk who have seen him tell me the man himself is even more sinister, and if the ex-Public Schoolboy can obtain the verdict, he will worthily uphold his title, never mind the claims of [Bert] Assirati and a few other fancied challengers," printed *The Football Post* of Nottinghamshire."

The Nottingham Evening Post similarly afforded Oakeley little chance of winning against his overpowering competitor, who was labeled the "champion of all Africa."

"Wango, who is the first coloured all-in fighter to appear in Nottingham, has already made a big reputation in British rings with spectacular victories over a number of leading British and Continental heavyweights, stated *The Evening Post*. "The negro has a complete mastery of the holds under the new rules, and this skill, allied to great strength and aggressiveness, will make him a most formidable opponent for Oakeley."

As a prelude to his showdown with Oakeley, Wango first defeated King Curtis, and in an ironic twist, Wango's ethnic origin was offered as Senegalese, which in his case was probably accurate.

"A fine specimen of Negro physique, Wango against Curtis not only showed himself to be possessed of exceptional strength, ability, and stamina, but revealed style and skill of a high order," opined *The Evening Post*. "Oakeley has not yet been beaten in Nottingham — where he has made four previous appearances — but there is a conviction amongst many of those who saw Wango outclass Curtis that, if there is a wrestler at least to take the British title holder's measure, it is the 'Black Devil.'"

A Decided Novelty

In front of more than 4,000 spectators who filled New Victoria Hall to watch a match scheduled for 10 rounds of 10 minutes apiece, Oakeley pulled off a stunning come-from-behind victory over the wrestling champion of Africa.

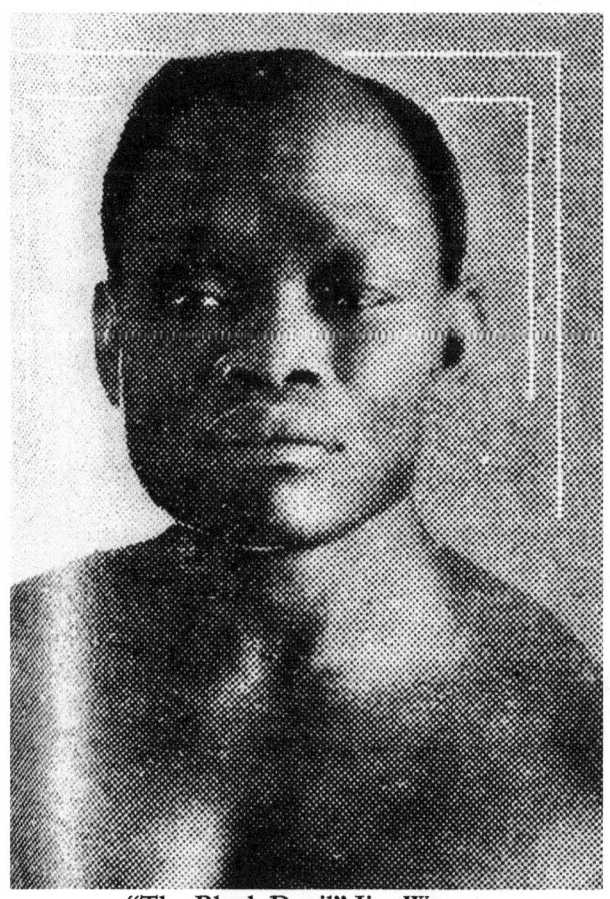

"The Black Devil" Jim Wango

"Wango's face at all times added dressing to the crowd's salad, for he bared his teeth and shouted when in difficulties, and was wreathed in broad smiles what times the tide flowed his way," described *The Evening Post*. "One of these periods arrived in the third round, which saw the white man driven out of the ring and the balance of difference squared, but in the next the battle terminated abruptly, Oakeley securing a pinfall to win, with a full nelson and body press. The bout had then been in progress 34 min. 10 sec."

In 1935, Wango participated in a wrestling tour of Europe through Switzerland and Germany that moved him from total obscurity on the other side of the Atlantic Ocean to a major political talking point.

After Wango won or drew all his tournament matches in Nuremberg, Germany, police prevented him from continuing to wrestle there, claiming his appearance caused "public unrest."

"This occurred after Julius Streicher, the anti-Semitic propagandist, had visited the hall and delivered a speech to which he declared that it was only 'an advertising stunt,' and 'an appeal to the inferior when a nigger was allowed to compete with whites,'" reported *The Newcastle Evening Chronicle*. "Respect was due to every race, said Streicher, but it would have been better if the negro had been left at home."

Greater elaboration of Streicher's statement was provided when the full report from Nazi newspaper *The Fränkische Tageszeitung* was made available to the Associated Negro Press.

"Those who organize wrestling matches between Negroes and white men are damaging the white race," Streicher was translated as having said. "It is contrary to the spirit of Nuremberg to see white men defeated in wrestling by black men. People who applaud when a black man has floored a man of our race are not of Nuremberg. Moreover, a woman who applauds no longer can have anything to do with Nuremberg."

The Nazi publication added that the key factor contributing to Wango's in-ring success had been the fact that Wango's skin "being oily and smooth, permitted him to slip literally from the clutches of his adversaries."

As the international plight of Black wrestlers was becoming tied to mounting tensions across the globe, Jim Mitchell had one of the most important years in Black wrestling history in 1935, although contemporary commentators might be tempted to dismiss the significance of his achievement on the basis of its parochial nature.

That February, Mitchell was granted the rare privilege of reigning as the top titleholder of a region or territory as a Black wrestler. Then again, referring to Sandusky, Ohio as either a region or a territory is rather generous — at least in wrestling parlance — and the same could be said about acknowledging the Sandusky junior light heavyweight championship as a consequential wrestling title.

Wrestling championships bearing major city names were relatively rare, let alone one exclusive to the light heavyweight division of a municipality with fewer than 25,000 residents. In essence, the Panther won a championship that had been in existence for less than one year, and that symbolized an area that fell well short of the 50,000-resident mark often used to distinguish cities from towns.

Even so, being recognized as the champion of a locale with so few Black residents to speak of was no small feat in a business where the process of crowning champions was entirely beholden to the whims of the booker or promoter in charge. As such, promoter Dan Morris was under zero obligations to place a championship belt around the waist of Mitchell, and should be commended for doing so, regardless of the circumstances.

Mitchell collected the Sandusky title by seizing it from Martonio Angelo. The first fall was a dominant display by the Panther, as he responded to Angelo's rabbit punches "with his favorite shoulder bucks, applying them very hard and following with the usual body pin." Angelo won the second fall, then began the third with flagrant cheating.

"Angelo showered Mitchell with a handful of sawdust he gathered out of a hole in the canvas," illustrated *The Sandusky Register*. "He came back with his favorite hold, the hammer lock, and while having this hold he kept throwing sawdust in Mitchell's face. It looked as if Angelo had the fall,

A Decided Novelty

but suddenly Mitchell got a French Savote and a body pin to take the fall in 13 minutes, and win the 'championship.'"

Mitchell's first title defense was against Danny McDonald, and the Panther secured the only true fall of the encounter 55 minutes into the match with what *The Register* identified as a "European crab lock." Prior to this, there was a role reversal from the established script, as Mitchell sidestepped a McDonald flying tackle, and the challenger sailed through the ropes and into the second row of reserved seats.

Mitchell also escaped from McDonald's version of an Indian deathlock before applying the European crab lock, leaving McDonald unable to answer the bell for a second fall due to a leg injury.

Mitchell continued to wear the red, white, and blue belt symbolic of the Sandusky junior light heavyweight championship for months despite losing matches in Sandusky rings, presumably because the matches were simply non-title bouts, or because his opponents exceeded the weight requirement. By the time he got around to defending his championship again, the Panther had been handed an additional pseudonym, and *The Register* was labeling him as Jimmie "Dark Folks" Mitchell.

What was probably Mitchell's only match under the atypical ring name was made memorable by the antics of referee Johnny LaCount and wrestler Sly McLain, and especially by the moment when McLain ripped off LaCount's trousers.

"The referee, blushing furiously, scampered for the dressing room, and Dan Morris jumped into the ring to take charge of things," illustrated *The Register*. "In the confusion, the Panther pounced on McLain, gave him a series of high shoulder bucks, and then pinned him for the third and deciding fall. McLain was raging mad and swarmed into the dressing room where, according to reports, he laid LaCount among the sweet peas with a right to the chin."

The following Tuesday, Mitchell returned to Fisher's Hall still in possession of his title belt — but absent his short-

A Decided Novelty

lived nickname of Dark Folks — to duel with Danny MacDonald yet again. The Panther fell behind early after succumbing to the Scottish Canadian's Indian deathlock in 21 minutes. A further 26 minutes elapsed before Mitchell evened the score with a series of body slams to set the stage for a thrilling climax.

After being on the receiving end of a series of shoulder blocks from MacDonald, the Panther was seemingly out on his feet. However, when MacDonald went for one final shoulder tackle, Mitchell caught him with yet another body slam before collapsing to the mat.

"Referee Dan Morris began counting both men out," added *The Register*. "At nine, Mitchell rolled over and slid on top of MacDonald to take the fall. Then he rolled off and went back to dreamland. Fans ganged around the ring and watched Morris and his aides bring the gladiators back to consciousness after several minutes."

Two weeks later, in early June, Mitchell lost a match to Joe Wood, but managed to keep the championship belt of Sandusky around his waist despite the defeat. Wood was conveniently said to have weighed in at 178 pounds, which was seven pounds heavier than Mitchell and the 171-pound cutoff for junior light heavyweight title candidacy.

Mitchell was theoretically at a considerable weight disadvantage, but he managed to display his mat prowess by reversing Wood's crab hold into an Indian deathlock for a submission in the bout's second fall. Seemingly learning from this maneuver, Wood reversed the Panther's crab hold into a crab of his own 11 minutes into the third fall and forced Mitchell to submit.

The Panther's reign as the top dog in Sandusky came to an abrupt end after four months when he lost his championship to Danny MacDonald, a wrestler he had defeated previously inside of the Fisher's Hall ring.

It was a match that was described as "a beautiful exhibition of science, strength and skill," and Mitchell opened the scoring with a series of body slams to conclude the first fall in 19 minutes. From there, the bout was all MacDonald, who won the second fall with a backdrop in four minutes, and then finished the match with a simple kick to the stomach.

MacDonald wouldn't defend the junior light heavyweight championship of Sandusky again until January 1936, at which point it had its name shortened to the Sandusky light heavyweight championship. The Scottish Canadian would continue to defend the local title until June, when it would be completely phased out and abandoned. With that, the wrestling championship of Sandusky, Ohio would cease to exist after a brief two years, as did one of the first race-neutral championship belts to adorn the waist of a Black American wrestler.

Following the loss of his title, the Black Panther left the Midwest and made his first appearances in New England, including in Maine. *The Portland Press Herald* referred to him disparagingly as "the homeless colored boy," and he was occasionally billed as an Ethiopian. He was also placed on the same cards with Zimba Parker on a few occasions, with Parker positioned as the Black villain who was searching for an opportunity to supplant Mitchell as the top performer in what *The Press Herald* referred to as "the Joe Louis section of the mat game."

Elsewhere in New England, a fictitious backstory was added to the tale of the Black Demon's origin, and it would serve as a harbinger of a substantial reshaping of George Hoddison's image that would transpire a couple of years later. An October edition of *The Springfield Daily News* identified Hoddison as "The Black Demon of Ethiopia," which no doubt startled wrestling fans in the area who had grown accustomed to Hoddison's identity as a Black American resident of Greenfield.

Out west, Jack Claybourne made his debut in Oregon as "Jack 'Snowball' Clayton," while simultaneously being labeled as the Black Panther. Fortunately, the use of this objectionable nickname and an altered surname only persisted for a short time, as "snowball" was a derogatory term for American Blacks that extended back to the 18th century.

Sadly, the ethnic slurs didn't end there. In Salem, Claybourne was stamped as "Mose" by *The Oregon Statesman*. One of the sources for the term "Mose" came through the comic strip "Musical Mose," which was written and illustrated by mixed-race Louisiana Creole cartoonist George Herriman — a man for whom questions of racial identity always occupied a prominent place in his work.

In the syndicated strip, the Black American protagonist Mose was a musician who repeatedly attempted to impersonate other ethnicities — usually Whites — only to suffer regular, harsh beatings as a consequence of having his Black identity found out.

Fortunately for Claybourne, his wrestling talent appears to have been respected from the moment he arrived, and he swiftly piled up victories. In Corvallis, the "jet-black colored chap who is built like an Olympic athlete" was immediately given a win over a former football player from Oregon State University.

"[Claybourne] met Bill Kenna, former State College football guard, but the ex-collegian was no match for the smooth working Claybourne, and after dropping the first fall, the colored grappler returned to the ring to annex the next two falls and the match," recorded *The Daily-Gazette Times*.

When Claybourne was booked for return engagements in Corvallis, *The Gazette Times* was tasked with offering readers a deeper dive into Jack's backstory, and also the appearance of "the dynamiting negro middleweight."

"Claybourne is around the six foot mark and weighs a little over 170 pounds," described *The Gazette Times*. "He is the blackest, liveliest negro grappler that has ever shown his wares in Corvallis, said local promoters here today. Everywhere Claybourne has wrestled, the fans have packed the arenas upon the occasion of his return engagements. He resorts to a very clean type of wrestling, breaking cleanly and conducting a tough but clean campaign throughout his entire match."

A Decided Novelty

In April 1935, *The Sunday Oregonian* of Portland included a large photo of Claybourne with his eyes directed off to the reader's left and his palms pressed together at chest level. The caption-writer for *The Sunday Oregonian* saw fit to interpret this as a prayerful posture, and captioned the photo "Fevven Sakes, Lawd, Help Me."

Jack Claybourne presses his hands together prayerfully

The clear intent was to suggest that Claybourne was offering up to God "a fervent plea for divine protection" from the other participants in the battle royal he was set to engage in at Portland's Labor Temple.

A Decided Novelty

However, by rendering the sentence "For heaven sakes, Lord, help me" as "Fevven sakes," the caption writer was imposing the catchphrase of Mushmouth — a character from the *Moon Mullins* comic strip — onto Claybourne. In the comic strip, Mushmouth is the morbidly obese, lazy, oafish, Black sidekick of the White titular character.

Along with the radio sitcom *Amos 'n' Andy*, in which White voice actors Freeman Gosden and Charles Correll offered up their best minstrel show exaggerations of Black speech patterns, comic strips were often the sole sources of exposure that many Whites living in isolated regions of the United States and Canada had to representations of Black people.

Because of this, harmful stereotypes of Blacks established during the era could reach households that actual Black people would never have been invited into, resulting in wrestlers like Claybourne being forced to contend with these prejudices — and often to cater to them — in the hopes of ingratiating themselves with paying audiences composed exclusively of White patrons.

As for the article itself, it can be extrapolated from the writing that promoter Herb Owen was using the late addition of the man who was now occasionally being called "the Black Panther from Michigan" into the battle royal to test the waters of including a Black wrestler in the main events held in Oregon's largest city. In the process, he explained away the absence of Claybourne from prior main events as being the byproduct of racist attitudes harbored by some of the wrestlers on his roster.

"Bulldog Jackson, Rod Fenton and other 'meanies' wanted nothing to do with the Michigan blackbird, giving the color line as a flimsy excuse," stated *The Sunday Oregonian*. "But Promoter Owen outsmarted the dodgers by signing them for the free-for-all and then unexpectedly substituting Claybourne when it was too late for the 'villains' to back out."

Claybourne gave a decent showing in that April battle royal, outlasting four other men and making it to the final pairing before he was pinned by Del Kunkel after "a series of body slams and piledriver holds."

Citing Claybourne's bravery as justification for including him in more main events in Portland, Owen immediately thrust Claybourne into a main-event bout with villainous Rod Fenton, "holder of the mythical meanie championship."

"The Black Panther showed in the battle royal that he fears no one," said *The Sunday Oregonian*. "He slugged toe-to-toe with the villains and dealt out more punishment than he received. This factor makes the 'experts' give him an even chance to topple the detested Fenton."

The elevation of Claybourne in Oregon provided an example of how a wrestling promoter could equate racism with cowardice in order to improve the perceptions of a Black wrestler. Just a few months later, a wrestling promoter located 1,600 miles away would attempt to book Claybourne while sidestepping racism that had been enshrined in the law, and the results would be far less favorable.

12 – Color for a Show

Toward the end of Jack Claybourne's tenure in Oregon, *The Daily Journal* had very abruptly begun to describe the dark-skinned Claybourne as being "very Ethiopian-like in color," and when he soon departed from Oregon and traveled to the Texas-Mexico border, that was a facet of his characterization that survived the journey.

In Juarez, Mexico, in October 1935, the ersatz Ethiopian Claybourne was enthusiastically embraced by the Mexican fans when he made his debut there.

"Juarez wrestling fans shouted 'Viva Ethiopia' and lifted 'The Black Panther,' Negro wrestler, to their shoulders last night at the Pan American Stadium when he won a match from a wrestler billed as Renato Garibaldi, Italian," reported *The El Paso Herald-Post*. "'Down with Mussolini' shouted the fans, when the Negro pinned his opponent's shoulders to the mat."

The punchline to the article arrived in its closing sentence, when it was revealed that the "so-called Italian wrestler" was "Jack Purdin, blond American."

In stark contrast to the way he was received in Juarez, Claybourne was outright banned from appearing on the other side of the Rio Grande in El Paso, Texas, per the state's prohibition against mixed-race combat. Even though Claybourne had been previously advertised to appear, promoter Jack McIntosh pulled him from a late-October show once he "discovered" that the wrestler was Black.

In his vain attempt to reacquire his position on the card, Claybourne reportedly made a statement to *The El Paso Times* that he "isn't a negro" in the classic sense of the term because he was of "Cuban lineage." Apparently, this was born out of the belief that culture trumped skin color with respect to racial designations in the Texas law, and possibly because Afro-Cuban fighters like "Kid Chocolate" Montalvo had been observed to achieve greater public acceptance than Black American fighters.

A Decided Novelty

This was further discussed in the November 8 edition of *The Times*. Promoter McIntosh expressed his own confusion over the situation — likely for show — stating that he hired the Panther thinking that he was bringing in a Cuban, only to discover once Claybourne reached Texas that "he was as black as the traditional ace of spades, and had all of the earmarks of an American negro, barred from wrestling and boxing rings in Texas."

The far more likely scenario is that McIntosh himself attempted to pass Claybourne off as a foreign wrestler to sidestep the ban on the U.S. side of the river, but was unsuccessful. McIntosh was probably quite familiar with the fact that the population of Cuba was approximately 10 percent Black in the mid-1930s, and therefore knew that a Cuban with a dark complexion was nothing out of the ordinary, least of all in Cuba.

Around the same time as his appearances in Texas, Claybourne wrestled in New Mexico for promoter Johnny Flaska as "the Black Panther of Portland," or "La Pantera Negra" in Spanish. *The Albuquerque Tribune* introduced him as "the Joe Louis of the wrestling world," who was seeking an opportunity to capture the light heavyweight championship.

Writing about the Panther in late October, a sports columnist operating under the pseudonym Mahatma Gandhi dedicated his column to recent events in local wrestling, and referred to Claybourne's iteration of the Black Panther as "The Black Panther, colored boy, from points in Ole Kaintuck."

Whether Gandhi was encouraged to list Kentucky as Claybourne's origin by someone else or was making it up entirely, this represents a classic example of the red herrings that have caused tremendous confusion among wrestling historians hoping to keep the activities of different Black Panthers neatly arranged.

With Jack Claybourne, Alex Kaffner, Jack Nelson, and Jim Mitchell — who was *actually* from Louisville, Kentucky — all making the rounds, it can be quite easy to mistakenly credit certain Black Panthers with matches that took place several time zones away from where they were active.

When he actually offered accounts of Claybourne's matches in Carlsbad, Gandhi continued to play into racial imagery. When Claybourne would defeat a White opponent, Gandhi would issue a remark like "a black panther had a nice white meat supper last night."

Gandhi also reinforced the classification of the Black Panther as an "Ethiopian warrior," and referred to a show-opening battle royal consisting exclusively of untrained Black "wrestlers" as "proteges of the Black Panther."

As previously noted, it was common practice in some areas — *especially* Southern states — to open wrestling shows with untrained Black youths seeking cash prizes who resorted to fisticuffs to violently batter one another until only one remained standing.

The advertisement for this particular show referred to this collection of Black young men in far less flattering terms than Gandhi initially selected, and instead identified them as "five burly black boys banging away."

In a later promotional piece, Gandhi mockingly referred to his favorite fighter amongst the five Black young men featured in the forthcoming battle royal by the name "Dempsey Tunney Firpo Louis" — a mishmash of the names of four famous fighters. To be clear, Gandhi never actually identified which of the fighters he believed would win, but in the aftermath of the show, he simply wrote, "My boy won the battle royal."

Reaching Michigan for the first time in 1935, Tiger Flowers dropped the 'T' and 'E' from his surname and simplified his ring name to Tiger Flowers Johnson. He would also seemingly dabble in some new wrestling tactics, as he "butted his way to victory" over Fred Kimble during his debut at the Arena Gardens roller rink on Detroit's Woodward Avenue.

When Flowers moved on to the Western Michigan, he followed in the tradition of the Black wrestlers who had preceded him in those rings, like "The Black Panther of Tennessee" Jack Nelson, Gorilla Parker, and "The Black Panther of Louisville" Jim Mitchell, by also assuming the title of colored heavyweight champion.

Additionally, Flowers benefitted from the common promotional tactic of being favorably compared to his Black peers in a way that ran the risk of simultaneously diminishing them in the eyes of the same fans. To accomplish this, *The Herald Press* of St. Joseph informed fans that Flowers had defeated both the Black Panther and Gorilla Parker prior to his arrival, when there is no evidence Flowers had even been within shouting distance of either man.

During the same tour, multiple Western Michigan news publications like *The Battle Creek Enquirer* and *The Herald-Press* called out the overuse of the Tiger Flowers name in combat sports, and referred to the wrestler Flowers as "another of the scores of professional athletes named Tiger Flowers," while clarifying that this Flowers, like the others, had "copied his name after the brilliant Negro boxer, now dead."

Wrestling in Oakland County north of Detroit, Flowers was involved in an incident the Associated Press carried to several states. Throughout his match with Frank Malciewicz, the clean-cut Flowers endured repeated fouls, with the Pontiac crowd growing increasingly more infuriated by Malciewicz's cheating. When referee Charles Southerland finally threw the match out and awarded the decision to Flowers after one final foul, the crowd decided to exact revenge on Flowers' behalf.

"The fans, irked by the methods Malciewicz used against his opponent, Tiger Flowers Johnson of Cuba, charged the ring," reported the AP. "Malciewicz was badly bruised before police could quell the rioting patrons."

In many ways, the most significant and enduring event that would occur for Tiger Flowers in 1935 would be in September, with the reveal of an artistic production that lent credence to the claim made during the previous year that Flowers' modeling services were in high demand.

A Decided Novelty

At the 27th annual Stockbridge Art Exhibition, one of the "notable pieces" reported on by *The Berkshire Eagle* of Pittsfield, Massachusetts was a bust of the head of "Tiger Flowers Johnstone, a colored wrestler" by Emily Winthrop Miles. The bust of Flowers would include a peculiar feature that would truly distinguish it from similar busts — the severely cauliflowered left ear of Joseph Godfrey, which would be one of his signature traits throughout his career.

Miles's works were later displayed in several art museums across the northeastern United States, including the bust of Flowers, which eventually found a home in Harvard University's Fogg Museum.

The reveal of the bust of Flowers' head would rekindle the flattering discussions of his features, with *The Herald-News* of Passaic stating that "[Flowers'] physical makeup is one that would create envy, so much so in fact that recently he was voted the most perfectly developed athlete his weight in America at a meeting of sculptors for whom the 'Tiger' has been a model for some years."

Miles also completed drawings of both Tiger Flowers and his young wife, but the drawings were incorrectly identified as the boxer Theodore "Tiger" Flowers and his wife Willie Mae. Since Joseph Godfrey was serving as the model for both the bust and drawing under the name Tiger Flowers, the model identified as the wife of Tiger Flowers is very likely to have been Godfrey's wife Ursaline.

The same month the bust of Tiger Flowers was unveiled to art aficionados, *The Moncton Daily Times* informed readers that local favorite Vic Butland had become a huge hit in Montreal and was set to wrestle Tiger Flowers, revealing that Flowers had taken his act to Canada.

Few match results are available from Flowers's Quebec tour, but one important match description survived. An October edition of *The Montreal Gazette* reported how Tiger Flowers had been disqualified from his bout against Fred Slavik at the Mount Royal Arena. In an outcome that strongly foreshadowed events that were to come, Flowers was disqualified "for butting the referee with his head."

As 1936 opened, the man who had amplified Black participation in wrestling was again slated to defend his version of the world heavyweight boxing championship against Leroy Haynes, but George Godfrey postponed the fight, claiming that his hand had been reinjured during training.

When Godfrey finally did return to the ring in a boxing capacity, both his opponent and their eventual fight were underwhelming. Weighing 253 pounds — nearly 30 pounds heavier than he weighed in his prime — Godfrey dwarfed his 196-pound tune-up opponent Billy Wells.

According to *The Afro-American*, approximately 2,000 spectators at Washington's Griffith Stadium booed the action between Godfrey and Wells. The rookie fighter clipped Godfrey on the chin in the opening round, but did nothing substantive to follow up on it. The fight then ended under dubious circumstances in the second round.

"The second round was a brief, rough-and-tumble affair with the two fighters clinching about six times," described *The Afro-American*. "In the sixth mix-up, Godfrey uncorked one of his mysterious inside rights that carried Wells down for the count. Few observers around ringside actually saw the blow, but Wells apparently felt it for he took the full count."

Prior to the fight, boxing promoter Jeff Dickson offered Godfrey a $25,000 guarantee for three fights in Europe. However, after Godfrey's embarrassing outing against Wells, the International Boxing Union opted to strip Godfrey of his world title, citing his failure "to pay within three months the fine imposed on him for appearing late in the ring."

The timing was suspicious. Before his IBU title fight against Pierre Charles, Godfrey held up the IBU for delivery of his fight purse and refused to walk to the ring until he was paid. While the IBU publicly reported that it had fined Godfrey for the incident, the organization's decision to wait a full year after the fight to strip him suggests his poor showing and

A Decided Novelty

shoddy conditioning against Billy Wells may have influenced the decision

Deprived of both his world boxing title and any opportunity at a three-fight deal in Europe, the nearly 40-year-old Godfrey went back to work as a professional wrestler. In Allentown, Pennsylvania, George made short work of Joe Gotch, ending the match in under 5½ minutes on a card that also featured Tiger Flowers.

"Gotch might have fared a bit better had he not made the mistake of trying to get rough with Godfrey," reported *The Morning Call*. "He stuck his fingers in the colored man's eyes once or twice before Godfrey really got peeved, and then 'Big Gawge' smacked him down with a right hand swing. When he got up, a left smash to the neck put him down again, and Godfrey just sat on him to end the match."

Down in Frederick, Oklahoma, Gorilla Parker had returned to his hometown yet again, where he resumed activity under his real name of Henry Daniels while adding a clear allusion to the gimmick he had popularized in far more prominent wrestling territories. As Henry "Gorilla" Daniels, he spent the better part of a month facing local competitors.

At the end of January, Daniels appeared in Massachusetts for a match as Zimba Parker, and then came right back to Oklahoma for one more appearance as Gorilla Daniels. Afterward, Parker returned to his familiar stomping grounds in the Midwest and reacquired his primate sobriquet on a full-time basis.

During summer 1936, Parker learned to apply a new technique in order to win his matches. In Dayton, Ohio, it was described as a "bulldozing headlock" that Parker used to dispatch Johnny Carlin. In Lima, Ohio, the name of the move was amended to a "bulldog headlock" when he used it to defeat Jack Conley in the first fall of their encounter.

He also employed what sounds like a unique variation of the bulldog headlock when he "started to apply a flying mare grip on his opponent, but shortened the pressure, dragging Conley face downward on the mat" to win the final fall, according to *The Lima News*. It was a hold that sounds quite similar to what wrestling fans of later generations would describe as a crusher, cutter, or stunner.

Parker dealt with Conley similarly in a subsequent match. After leveling his bout with Conley at one fall apiece, Parker applied what had seemingly become his new favorite hold to devastating effect.

"In jig time Parker came back to win the match with his second fall after Conley had sent his fists swinging wildly," said *The Coshocton Tribune*. "The Gorilla got to Conley and slammed him around the ring. Then he sent Conley to slumberland with a series of bulldog headlocks. Exhausted and groggy from the jolt he received when his head hit the floor in the bulldog headlocks, Conley was unable to leave the ring for several minutes after the bout. The crowd that filled every corner of the bowl cheered wildly as Gorilla left the arena victoriously."

When summer 1936 came to a close, Parker shifted his focus eastward, and returned to using "The African Lion" Zimba Parker as his ring name. This time around, even more attention was garnered by his choice of ring attire.

"Zimba often wears a leopard skin in place of trunks when he wrestles, but some states have banned this, and Parker is often requested to refrain from using the skin," wrote *The Reading Times*.

The Times also fixed Parker with the familiar compliments, saying that "his physique would amaze Reading fans" because "Zimba's muscles bulge out, and he resembles Joe Louis, the celebrated 'Brown Bomber,' in many ways."

Clearly intended to give Parker significance and dignity, this dime-a-dozen compliment was already showing its limitations and may have been hierarchically applied. Specifically, when Parker appeared on a November card with Tiger Flowers — this time referred to as Ed "Tiger" Flowers — it was Flowers who was declared to be "wrestling's latest Brown Bomber" while Parker was almost derisively referred to as "the so-called 'African Lion.'"

A Decided Novelty

In the West, Parker's former nemesis Jack Nelson had ventured outside of California and into Utah. It was there that *The Salt Lake Tribune* added some further wrinkles to Nelson's career backstory when he made his debut there in March 1936.

"Tiger" Jack Nelson

It was explained that Nelson had acquired the "colored championship" of the National Wrestling Association — the wrestling counterpart to the National Boxing Association — during a 1929 contest in New York City. Like Nelson's original story about acquiring his colored championship, this story was also false. However, the story about being awarded his title by the National Wrestling Association sounded far more credible

A Decided Novelty

and impressive than Nelson's original tale about winning a multi-man wrestling tournament in Toledo, Ohio.

The Tribune also reaffirmed Nelson's role in training Jim Browning for his 1934 match with Londos, and listed Nelson's place of origin as Seminole, Oklahoma, which was far closer to his actual birthplace in Austin, Texas than any cities or towns that publications had previously offered.

Further, *The Tribune* also provided Nelson with a signature hold: The Flying Wristlock. The inclusion of this detail is curious inasmuch as Nelson had not yet been granted a victory in any of his West Coast matches. He wouldn't be victorious on this occasion, either. Although he locked Del Kunkel in his patented wristlock to secure the first fall, Nelson immediately lost the following two falls via bodyslam and piledriver.

While Nelson was the loser of the bout, *The Tribune's* reporter did credit him with looking and moving very differently than most heavyweight wrestlers.

"Unlike most heavyweights, Nelson is neither bulky, nor ponderous," stated the writer, identified by his initials as J.C.D. "Contrariwise, he is lanky and exceptionally agile."

As the year progressed, Nelson earned fewer draws, and was allowed to tally losses in a more dignified manner, often by way of disqualification. He also resumed the use of his old Black Panther nickname, but pairing it with "Tiger Jack" made the name glaringly redundant. *The Daily Herald* made note of it, declaring, "It is not clearly known which of these two animals, the panther or the tiger, that Nelson resembles most, but if it is a cross between them, then (his opponent) Papiano is a marked man."

Through May 1936, Nelson was still a "colored world champion" who was winless against White opponents, and the press took note of it while pointing out the quality in Nelson's performances. As *The Deseret News* pointed out, "Nelson has been scuffling around here most all season to the horrification of the ringsiders. He usually loses, but he makes a great show of it."

A Decided Novelty

Nelson finally rose above the level of lovable loser for the first time in early June in Casper, Wyoming when he pinned Lou Mueller in a best-of-three-falls affair. Stating that Nelson had "lived up to his reputation as The Black Panther," *The Casper Star-Tribune* described how Nelson had finally secured a legitimate double-pinfall victory over a White wrestler for the first time in his career.

Two months later, Nelson secured a second multi-fall victory in Casper, downing Jimmy Smith with a Boston Crab and a flurry of punches and kicks. He then achieved his first pinfall victories in front of California crowds one week later in early September when he pinned Bernie Spiel in Pasadena, and Roughhouse Burney in Bakersfield.

Over in New England, Jim Mitchell was being shortchanged by the same scenario that worked to his advantage while he was holding gold in Sandusky. Against New England middleweight champion George Myerson, the Panther waged what *The Daily Item* of Lynn referred to as "a strict defensive type of battle," and won the bout in one hour and 18 minutes. Prior to the bout, the fans were already made aware of the fact that Mitchell had weighed in above the weight limit, and therefore his nearly 80-minute effort did not result in a championship victory.

Later, *The Daily Item* described the Panther's style as lacking spectacular elements, but being fundamentally grounded. Specifically, they stated he "has no lethal flying tackle or dropkick," but added he "boasts a most deadly headlock" that he uses to wear down his opponents over the course of long matches.

In Maine, the Panther had dropped the Ethiopian label, and Austin Goodwin of *The Portland Evening Express* ran a biographical special on Mitchell's wrestling career filled with dubious content. Goodwin opened his piece by asserting that Mitchell had once engaged in "bootblacking" — or shoe shining — and indulging "in any other occupation by which he could earn an honest penny."

A Decided Novelty

From there, Goodwin described a scenario in which Mitchell was taken under the wing of a few veteran wrestlers who taught him the fundamentals, qualifying him to become their training partner on the basis of his "fine physique." It was further stated that Mitchell was asked to fill in one night by an Indiana promoter when he was short on participants for the preliminary card, thereby giving Mitchell his first official match beneath the lights.

"The chocolate colored Kentuckian didn't know anything about the strategy of the game, such as letting an opponent stay in there for awhile to give the public a run for their money, or holding himself under wraps to make the other chap look good," wrote Goodwin, perhaps inadvertently describing the process of "working" a wrestling match. "He figured he was expected to win if he could, and quicker than you can pronounce the familiar name of Jack Robinson, he clamped a head-hold on his rival, clasped the unfortunate victim into a state of dizziness, and pinned him for a fall in less than 10 minutes. This victory made a great hit with the crowd, and started Mitchell on a career that paid him far better than bootblacking or running errands for the wrestling moguls."

Goodwin concluded by detailing how Mitchell had never known where his next meal was coming from, and rode a secondhand pawn-shop bicycle from town to town, but now drove from city to city in an expensive eight-cylinder car while living off "the fat of the land."

This tale's concluding sentiment rings true if Mitchell's weight increases are any indication. Described as a wrestler who barely qualified for the middleweight minimum of 154 pounds just five years earlier, Mitchell was now being advertised as a 195-pound grappler who was flirting with the boundary of the heavyweight division.

Before one of his bouts at the Bar Harbor Casino of Bangor, Maine — a victory in which Mitchell secured his falls over Fred Kupfer via flying mares and a double-wristlock and headscissors combination — Mitchell was asked to predict the outcome of the forthcoming Joe Louis fight against Jack Sharkey.

The prognosticating Panther expressed his belief that Louis would "flatten" Sharkey inside of five rounds. Making Mitchell look like a clairvoyant, Louis knocked Sharkey down twice in the second round of their August 18 fight before knocking him out just over one minute into the third round.

Looking at the results of matches from 1936, it's clear that New England stalwart George Hoddison had become comfortable enough in the ring to work his way through a match of significant length. In front of 900 fans at the Brightwood Wrestling Club Arena, Hoddison and Steve Brady dueled to a 90-minute draw, with the Demon recording his only fall 52 minutes into the session with his rope bound and tackle.

At this stage of his career, Hoddison had received a superficial status upgrade to New England Colored Champion, but it was still not obvious that he had ever even encountered another Black wrestler in the dressing room, let alone inside of a wrestling ring.

That all changed during summer 1936 when Hoddison made his first appearance in Canada. During this tour of Ontario and Quebec, Hoddison first dropped the approximation of his true surname in favor of a new identity as "the Ethiopian champion, Zelis Amhara." It was also here that George Hoddison was first advertised on shows alongside Joseph Godfrey, who was still wrestling in his Tiger Flowers persona.

In several ways, Flowers had preceded Hoddison as a Black wrestling star in Massachusetts, having been the standout Black attraction in Boston, as well as capturing the world middleweight championship belt that had adorned the waists of many of the top draws in the state. By this time, Flowers had long since moved on to New York, New Jersey, and Pennsylvania, leaving Buck Jones as the top Black wrestler in and around Massachusetts Bay.

A Decided Novelty

Not a great deal is known about Buck Jones, aside from the fact that he wrestled from 1934 to 1938, isolated himself to New England for the entirety of his career, and seemingly served as the replacement for Tiger Flowers in Boston as the Black challenger to Ted Germane and other White wrestlers.

Usually described as a tall, 195-pound heavyweight, Jones was a wrestler who became a standout for his proclivity to use his head as an offensive weapon, just as Tarzan Wilson had been described during his few Chicago appearances.

While this method of combat would have stood out to a greater degree in almost any other part of the country, in the region where headbutting innovator Gus Sonnenberg had once been such a massive gate attraction, Jones was just one more in a long line of headbutters.

It can be argued that the most important event within Black pro wrestling circles that occurred during 1936 stemmed from the debut of one of the wrestling genre's most underrated performers.

LeRoy Howard Clayton was born June 23, 1911, in Cincinnati, Ohio. He is perhaps the perfect embodiment of the relationship between boxing and wrestling during the era in which professional wrestling was developing into its modern form.

The earliest traces of Clayton's athletic success are found in the results of amateur boxing results in Illinois in 1931, where he appeared to have been in the nascent stages of developing his potential as a combat athlete. From there, he is found once again boxing his way through the Southern states, and most frequently in Tennessee and Virginia.

The Register of Danville refers to Clayton by his nickname of "The Black Bearcat," which was possibly a reference to his Cincinnati roots, as the Bearcat is the mascot of the University of Cincinnati.

In acknowledging Clayton, *The Register* stated that he "once held the heavyweight title of Ohio, and has 103 fights to his credit, having won 89, lost 8, and fought to a draw in 6. He weighs 180 pounds." Published accounts indicate that Clayton

A Decided Novelty

slugged his way through the South, more or less brutalizing all opposition he faced.

Clayton had at least two early brushes with professional wrestling during his boxing career, or at least the essence of pro wrestling. During an April 1934 boxing card Clayton headlined in Bristol — a twin city that straddles the border of Virginia and Tennessee — the detestable practice of the Negro battle royal was presented to a Bristol crowd that had gathered together from a pair of adjacent towns that were both well over 90 percent White in the early 1930s.

"Preceding the regular boxing events, ten husky local negroes will be tossed in the ring to engage in what promises to be the most exciting 'battle royal' ever staged here," stated *The Bristol News Bulletin*.

Clayton's other clear exposure to wrestling took a far less controversial form when he fought in the opening match of a police day pro wrestling card in Kingsport, Tennessee the very next month. *The Kingsport Times* informed its readers that Clayton had still never lost a bout during the professional leg of his boxing career.

Before long, *The Bristol Herald Courier* had dubbed Clayton "The Black Ring Panther," and when Clayton made his way to Elizabethton, Tennessee for a fight with Eddie Steppon, *The Elizabethton Star* reported that Clayton had "fought and defeated some of the best Negro fighters in the south, and Clayton has wreaked havoc in the white ranks on more than one occasion."

When Clayton quickly dismissed Steppon via first-round knockout, *The Watauga Spinnerette* reported that Clayton "showed the fans that the fight in which he tied (Joe) Louis, present contender for the heavyweight title, is no accident."

For the record, there is no evidence that Clayton ever directly crossed paths with Joe Louis, who had just defeated Primo Carnera by technical knockout five days prior to this victory by Clayton. Regardless, *The Roanoke World-News* had declared Clayton to be "the colored heavyweight champion of the South."

A Decided Novelty

Unfortunately, Clayton's rampage through the South's boxing rings would be cut short by an ankle sprain received in training during October 1935. Clayton ultimately made his way to Los Angeles, where *The Los Angeles Times* labeled him as the latest find of local promoter Sid Marks. The promoter described Clayton as "a 198-pound Negro slugger who has 'it.'"

"Roy (King Kong) Clayton, five feet seven inches of windmilling colored energy, breaks in under Sid Marks' banner against Danny Alberts, Escondido heavy, in the second spot," reported *The Times* when Clayton made his debut in Southern California.

Clayton dropped Alberts three times on the way to a decision victory, and appeared to be well on his way to continuing his winning ways. It was then that any dreams Clayton might have had that boxing would be as easy for him on the Pacific Coast as it had been in the South were violently dissolved. Just two weeks after his impressive debut, Clayton was knocked out in the second round of his fight with Moose Irwin.

It's unknown precisely what transpired behind the scenes in the wake of Clayton's devastating defeat at the hands of Irwin that led to his career being rerouted toward wrestling, but educated guesses can be made considering the fact that Sid Marks was a promoter of both boxing and wrestling events. What is certain is that Clayton made his pro wrestling debut just a few months later, and started notching victories immediately.

"Leroy Clayton, first negro wrestler to appear in Stockton in years, mauled Ted Sarris to the canvas in five minutes for an impressive start here," reported *The Stockton Independent*.

Over the next few weeks, Clayton tried different stage names, some of which had become hackneyed to the point of being stereotypical.

"Leroy Clayton, the Black Panther of the wrestling profession, disposed of Bronco Valdez with a kick in the groin to win the affair at 4:30," said *The Stockton Independent*, confirming that Clayton was at least temporarily saddled with the same nickname held by half a dozen men before him.

LeRoy "King Kong" Clayton

"The Dark Destroyer" and "Black King Kong" were also names used by Clayton until he finally settled on "King Kong" Clayton as his official ring name. That was the name he used when he debuted in Salt Lake City in December, defeating Jack Romero of Minneapolis to make a solid first impression in the Mountain West.

Upon his arrival in Utah, Clayton was assigned a familiar point of international origin, and labeled as a "giant

A Decided Novelty

Ethiopian" by *The Provo Evening Herald*. This was as Clayton's inexperience was skillfully obscured by a clever bending of the English language as he was advertised for bouts against wrestlers like Vic Hill.

"King Kong Clayton, probably less skilled in wrestling science than Hill, is strong as an ox, and is liberal in his use of rough tactics," explained *The Herald*.

The story that Clayton was a direct transplant from the African continent was not applied with much consistency. *The Ogden Standard-Examiner* stated that Clayton was from Chicago, along with the fact that he was "the premier of all colored heavyweights" despite his having logged less than half a year inside a wrestling ring.

Jack Claybourne returned to Oregon early in 1936, and was placed in the bizarre position of representing "the Ethiopian side of a mat battle" against Italian wrestler Ernie Piluso, in a match that Herb Owen claimed to have arranged "as the result of many requests" from fans. In a very clumsy bit of ad hoc politicizing, Owen rushed the pair together to play out the ongoing military hostilities between Ethiopia and Italy inside of a wrestling ring.

When Piluso won the match due to some clever maneuvering that landed him on top of Claybourne as the latter was applying a full-nelson, *The Oregonian* stated that Piluso had "won a major battle for his countrymen in the Italo-Ethiopian controversy," and without any of the "atrocities of war" being evident in the wrestling match.

Apparently seething due to the outcome of the bout with Piluso — presumably because he was mortified at the thought of having let down his adopted countrymen — Claybourne demolished Al Aho in only 32 seconds during his next appearance in Portland. The Panther tapped into his background as a boxer and flattened Aho with a series of uppercuts, recording "one of the shortest falls on record at the Labor Temple" in the process.

Claybourne returned to Albuquerque, and then found himself in Northern California wrestling as "the Black Panther

A Decided Novelty

of Alabama," with *The Morning Union* of Grass Valley acknowledging him as "one of the first Negro wrestlers to appear in the local ring," as well as describing him as a wrestler with "a national reputation for cunning and viciousness."

After a very successful tour of the San Francisco Bay area's outskirts, Claybourne returned to Oregon, where *The Statesman* greeted him as "the grinning snowball from Missouri."

In December, wrestling fans of Eugene were presented with the most direct display of presumably staged prejudice yet, when middleweight champion Jack Lipscomb "attempted to draw the color line" so that he wouldn't be forced to defend his championship against Claybourne.

According to *The Register-Guard,* Lipscomb said his intent was "making the wrestling business safe for the white race," and that it was an injustice that a champion "should be forced into a match with a contender of another race." The article concluded that Claybourne would enter the affair with a seven-pound weight advantage and "plenty of righteous wrath on his side."

Once again, with the stage perfectly set for a symbolic accomplishment through a Black wrestler's conquest, the booker went in the opposite direction. Even though Claybourne drew even with Lipscomb in the second fall with "a blasting series of dropkicks," Lipscomb caught the Panther by the legs in midair when he attempted the same sequence in the third fall, and forced him to submit to a Boston crab."

Returning to the East Coast from the Midwest, Tiger Flowers resumed his practice of losing the overwhelming majority of his matches. Ironically, even in the midst of his extended losing streak, he drew the same repeated comparisons to Joe Louis as his more successful Black contemporaries.

The irony of the situation stems from the fact that Louis had lost only one of his first 27 fights up until that point, whereas Flowers only occasionally emerged from his bouts as the winner. Despite the clear disparity in the success rates of the two competitors, Flowers was quoted in *The Lancaster New*

A Decided Novelty

Era suggesting that comparisons to the most highly ranked Black heavyweight fighter since Jack Johnson were beneath him.

"They tell me that I'm following in the footsteps of Joe Louis, but I'm a few steps ahead of Joe," Flowers allegedly remarked. "It will be perhaps a year or so before Louis ever gets a crack at the [Max] Schmeling-[Jim] Braddock winner, but I plan to win the heavyweight title within the next six months or whenever the promoters can get [Dave] Levin to meet me."

Considering that Flowers had never wrestled in the heavyweight division, let alone strung together many victories as a light heavyweight, the notion that he would suddenly move up a weight division and then win that division's world championship — all within six months — probably sounded preposterous to fans who followed his career closely.

Unmistakably, 1937 would be the year that would make it clear that several of the most prominent Black wrestlers in the world were in the process of making their exit from the wrestling business. In some cases, it would appear to be voluntary. In others, the moves were seemingly prompted by political decisions, or physical limitations.

In February, a special benefit show in Chicago featuring professional wrestling was presented, and part of its clear intention was to feature Black wrestlers. Of the five matches included on the show, at least four involved Black participants. This included headliner Lee Umbles, who was once again billed as "colored welterweight champion."

Also wrestling were Black wrestlers Jim Monette, "Wild" Bill Hooper, and Oran Lovett, but none of them would make a significant splash in the business. This would turn out to be one of the final domestic showings of Umbles, as appearances by him became increasingly rare after he had dedicated a sizable portion of the prior 15 years of his life to pro wrestling.

Lamenting the fact that Umbles had never received the respect that he was due, and acknowledging that he was clearly on the downside of his career, Dan Burley of *The Chicago*

Defender wrote a scathing rebuke of "an unrelenting determination on the part of the promoters to keep our boys from getting anywhere as a wrestler."

"Little as it may be known, the [Black] race has hundreds of prospects who may be termed 'diamonds in the rough,'" said Burley. "They never get a break because there seems to be a system organized to keep them in the place of being just 'color' for a show."

Likewise, in the summer, the downfall of George Godfrey commenced in earnest. It all began when Godfrey applied for and received a license to fight in the state of California. *The Los Angeles Times* reported that Godfrey had received a clean bill of health during his physical from Dr. Harry Martin of the California State Athletic Commission, but *The Times* also noted that George offered his age as 35. Godfrey was clearly attempting to sneak beneath the age limit of 38 years set by the Athletic Commission; he had celebrated his 40th birthday earlier that year.

The fight with Hank Hankinson went disastrously for Godfrey, with the Associated Press reporter stating that Hankinson pounded Godfrey "back into oblivion" when the erosion of the once proud Black Panther's skills truly began to show. The bout was temporarily halted for 10 minutes when a glass bottle thrown from the balcony shattered in a corner of the ring, and actually inflicted a cut on the arm of the wife of Chico Marx of the famous Marx Brothers comedy troupe.

Even that lengthy delay — which occurred in the middle of the seventh round — was unable to prevent the inevitable from transpiring in the eighth round.

"Tiring badly, Godfrey walked into a steady rain of head blows," reported the AP. "A left and right caught him at the opening of the eighth, sending him down for a nine count. His seconds threw in the towel after he got up."

If the loss hadn't been embarrassing enough, to add insult to injury, Godfrey received a lifetime suspension from the California State Athletic Commission just two days later for showing "no ability" during his bout with Hankinson. Thus

A Decided Novelty

ended George Godfrey's boxing career after 126 official fights. In the pages of *The Los Angeles Times*, George was described as "a pitiful picture of futility."

"If nothing else, Godfrey's sorrowful exhibition should serve as a grim warning to other old-timers that have outlived their usefulness in the prize ring, but feel that they can still come back," said Commission inspector Bill Smith.

Although Godfrey was reinstated one month later due to the pleas of his manager Frank Garbutt and a promise that Godfrey "would appear before boxing inspectors prior to his next fight to prove he was in condition," no comeback fight ever took place.

Similarly, Gorilla Parker also seemed to be headed toward the conclusion of his wrestling career in 1937, but for a very different reason. In May, it was printed in *The Piqua Daily Call* that Cleat Kauffman had been required to serve as a substitute for Parker, since the latter had been recently injured in an automobile accident.

Parker had previously been in New York for a very short time wrestling as Zimba Parker, with his only notable result from that period being a loss to Jesse James. Whether the automobile accident was a true story, or it was being used to cover for an injury that occurred during a match, Parker sat out the entire second half of 1937.

Unfortunately, two of the top Black wrestling attractions of the early 1930s found themselves sidelined due to vastly different circumstances. Luckily, one of the remaining stars, whose career had seemingly been trending downward, was about to reinvent himself into one of the most enduring wrestling attractions of the era, regardless of race. Elsewhere, two others were about to find their dark-hued waists brightened by the rare sight of gold.

A Decided Novelty

13 – An Unethical Wrestler

While Gorilla Parker was spending 1937 recovering from an injury, his old rival Jack Nelson was making an awkward debut in Hawaii. The wrestling veteran apparently divulged the true identity behind his gimmick to the press the instant he arrived on the island, thereby preemptively eliminating whatever mystique might have accompanied the Ethiopian gimmick he had brought to the island with him.

On April 22, 1937, *The Honolulu Advertiser* explained how the latest wrestling import from Ethiopia, a wrestler by the name of Amnerus Selassie, was "known as Black Panther on the Mainland and comes here with a fine reputation." With this in mind, it's difficult to imagine that what occurred when "Selassie's" plane landed was approved by Hawaii promoter Al Karasick.

Referring to himself as "Juan Selassie Amnerus" to the reporter from *The Honolulu Star-Bulletin*, which was already a reshuffling of the name that had been assigned to him just two days earlier, Amnerus revealed that he was actually Jack Nelson, and had gotten his start as a boxer before shifting his focus to grappling.

"In 1929 they showed him that money flowed in pro wrestling and he turned grappler," reported *The Star-Bulletin*. "Amnerus made such a showing that year that he took the world's colored heavyweight championship. He has been kept busy since, performing from coast to coast and meeting the headliners, including Man Mountain Dean, Chief Little Wolf, Ernie Dusek, Casey Berglund, Pat Fraley, and Nick Lutze. Amnerus specializes in the blind wristlock, regarded a most effective hold."

Nelson had been effectively outed as being a Black American playing the role of an Ethiopian, but the ruse was maintained in subsequent reports. Two days later, *The Star-Bulletin* added that "Juan Selassie Amnerus, known as the Black Panther… claims to have come to the U.S. from Ethiopia at the age of 12," implying that Jack Nelson had been a pseudonym temporarily adopted by the Ethiopian national.

For all of the creative hoopla surrounding the debut of Amnerus, he was not particularly successful. His debut against Bob Kruse was said to be "too scientific for most people" even though the bout "had more honest to goodness wrestling" than the rest of the matches on the card combined.

After making his debut, Amnerus recorded one victory by disqualification, and then tallied a series of losses to close out his time in Hawaii by the end of June. Throughout the roughly two-month string of activity, Karasick and his team never bothered to report Nelson's Ethiopian name with consistency, as it vacillated between Juan "Selassie" Amnerus and Amnerus Selassie, with Selassie used as either a nickname or a surname with seemingly no rhyme or reason behind it.

Following an early portion of 1937 spent in Oregon, California and New Mexico, Jack Claybourne returned to the Midwest for the first time in several years during the summer, still going by the name of the Black Panther, and sowing greater confusion as to which Panther was which. In Illinois, Claybourne wrestled as the Black Panther in a state where Illa Vincent had popularized the name in a wrestling context way back in 1911.

In parts of Wisconsin, Claybourne grappled as the Black Panther in a state where Alex Kaffner had consistently gone by the name "The Black Panther of Milwaukee" for four straight years, and was continuing to wrestle under that name in cities like Milwaukee and Racine. While most of those cities referred to Claybourne as a product of Portland, Oregon, he was known as "the Australian Black Panther" in Green Bay.

Meanwhile, when "Black Panther" Jim Mitchell entered Oregon in 1937 in the aftermath of Claybourne's tenure there, local promoters had to go out of their way to assure fans that Mitchell was "the original" and "the real McCoy," not to mention a superior Panther to Claybourne in general. For full context, this attempt at clarifying that Mitchell was the truest of the Black Panthers was transpiring just a few hours south of

A Decided Novelty

Washington, where Alex Kaffner had debuted under the Black Panther name in 1931.

Fortunately, Claybourne was soon granted several new nicknames, including one that stuck: "Jumping Jack." His stretch of activity through the Rust Belt states saw Claybourne introduce a new set of Midwestern fans to his high-risk, high-reward style. However, his presence also contributed to controversy.

When Claybourne and Kaffner reconnected for a bout in Gary, Indiana in December, they were initially banned from sharing the ring with one another. According to reporting from the Associated Negro Press, Indiana state athletic commissioner Sam Wurbarger stepped in and prohibited the match from taking place.

"It is the policy of the state athletic commission to refuse permission to colored athletes to wrestle in the state of Indiana in mixed matches," cited Wurbarger.

Apparently, Wurbarger could not fathom that the two headliners of the charity affair were *both* Black, and that no mixed-race matches in violation of Indiana law were being staged. The enforcement of a restraining order was necessary for the bout to continue as planned.

Just a few months earlier, Kaffner had made the news for something that had nothing whatsoever to do with wrestling. *The Capital Times* of Madison reported that the wrestler and his wife were fishing on a trestle on Lake Monona around 9:30 a.m. on September 14, when Laura Sorenson — a 68-year-old woman who was also fishing from the trestle — was struck by a passing North Western railroad freight train and killed instantly.

"Her body, hurled into the lake, was recovered by Alex Kaffner, 744 W. Washington Ave," stated the article. "Mr. Kaffner saw the train, a freight train enroute from Madison to Lancaster, approaching the trestle. The Kaffners saved themselves by stepping onto beams supporting the tracks."

Having taken over for Jack Claybourne in the Pacific Northwest, Mitchell did his best to live up to his billing as the

Panther who "is not Jack Claybourne of Missouri, who was seen in these parts last year, but is a new, one and only panther, black as tar, shapely and smooth."

Similarly, *The Oregon Statesman* identified Mitchell as "The Original Black Panther, otherwise known as the Dark Mystery or the Smiling Senegambian." *The Eugene Guard* described Mitchell as a grappler "built like a dusky version of Hercules."

Fans who watched Mitchell operate in the ring could easily distinguish him from Claybourne for several reasons. Aside from the fact that Claybourne was four inches taller than Mitchell, with darker skin and a more chiseled physique at the time, their wrestling styles were also vastly different. While Claybourne favored a flashier aerial attack, Mitchell's approach was usually far more technical, as exemplified by his preferred means of dispatching his opponents, with body scissors, wristlocks, and Indian deathlocks.

After spending the early part of his summer in Oregon, Mitchell traveled to Southern California. He was immediately praised as the colored world champion; *The Merced Sun-Star* went so far as to describe him as the "holder of three world's titles for wrestlers of his race."

Mitchell was present when *Santa Cruz News* reporter Carroll Williams was granted firsthand access to backstage events taking place at the Watsonville Arena. Upon entering the dressing room, Williams noted that the Panther was smoking a cigar. When Williams subsequently asked Mitchell how the Panther had first gotten involved in wrestling, he stated that Mitchell's face split into "one of those big grins such as you associate with a Negro boy who spots a ripe watermelon."

Mitchell answered Williams by explaining that he had once been bullied in school and then took up wrestling, and the school's football coach saw him in action and advised him to become a wrestler. No doubt, if this story is true, the football coach was probably suggesting that Mitchell join the high school's wrestling team, not that he should seek to join the ranks of wrestling's professionals.

"And the funny part of it — so help me — is that my opponent in my first professional match I ever had was the same kid who used to beat me up in school," added Mitchell, later including that he "got even" with the young man who had previously bullied him.

Mitchell supposedly stated that his professional debut took place 13 years earlier, which would place his first match in 1924. At this point, the Panther was 16 years old at most, making it more than likely that Mitchell was inflating his experience level.

From there, Mitchell continued his story, stating that the worst injury of his wrestling career was suffered in Athens, Greece. The Panther insisted that it was in this country bordering the Mediterranean Sea that he was knocked out during a match when he was tossed to the ground, adding that his head struck the ground so hard that "I was blind when I recovered consciousness."

"I went to a doctor in Paris, and after about four weeks, I recovered my sight. But he told me that if ever again I happened to hit my head on that particular spot, I'd probably be blind the rest of my life," added Mitchell. "If you notice, the boys don't ever give me one of those airplane spins and dump me down on the floor hard."

Apparently, there were no competent doctors in Greece, as Mitchell had been required to seek a diagnosis from a doctor 1,500 miles away from where he suffered his alleged injury, at least according to his story.

Regardless, Williams conceded that he had never seen Mitchell on the receiving end of an airplane spin, and concluded that this was either because the Panther was too clever to be caught in the hold, or that it was the result of an honor-among-thieves agreement by which Mitchell's opponents did not believe a victory was worth achieving at the potential expense of Mitchell's eyesight.

A Decided Novelty

In comparison to Jack Nelson's mismanagement in Hawaii, it would be difficult to imagine a career rebranding being handled more expertly than Joe Godfrey's transition from Tiger Flowers to Rufus Jones in summer 1937.

Although there was an influential theologian named Rufus Jones whose lifetime and career overlapped with Godfrey's and the creation of the Rufus Jones wrestling identity, the inspiration for that stage name was certainly the 21-minute film *Rufus Jones for President*, which starred Ethel Waters and marked Sammy Davis Jr.'s debut.

Late in summer 1937, Godfrey re-debuted in Michigan as "Rough" Rufus Jones of New York City. However, his characterization as Detroit's newest Negro star from the Northeast didn't last long. Within weeks, Jones was being billed as "an unethical wrestler" from "Red Run, Georgia."

Jones made quite an impression during his first month in Michigan with his far dirtier grappling style. Within two weeks, *The Detroit Free Press* was already reporting that Jones had fouled young Babe Kasaboski so much during their match at Detroit's Arena Gardens that the venue's fans got fed up and stormed the ring to intervene.

Throughout summer and fall, Metro Detroit newspapers fleshed out Jones' fictional backstory as an ex-minister-turned-wrestler who hailed "from the cotton fields of Georgia." He had been wrestling on the carnival circuit since the tender age of eight, and had engaged in more than 1,000 matches by the time he'd reached Detroit. His repertoire consisted almost exclusively of roughhousing tactics, and he had a special weapon at his disposal — a "flying headbutt maneuver."

After two months of disturbingly dirty wrestling, Jones received a massive endorsement from a key figure in Detroit's Black community when Harold "Poppa Dee" Johnson was introduced as his manager. Johnson was well known in Detroit's boxing circles as a manager to Black fighters, while also serving as a ring announcer for many local fights. Being linked to Poppa Dee had the net effect of causing Jones to be

A Decided Novelty

embraced as the unofficial in-ring representative of Detroit's Black inhabitants, despite his disreputable behavior.

From a character perspective, the loveable Poppa Dee was there to curb Jones' tendency to turn every contest into an unstructured free-for-all, which would play out in front of local audiences in an intentionally comedic fashion.

On the night of the announcement that Jones' career was under new management, Dee arrived at the Garden Arena accompanied by Roscoe Toles, a local heavyweight boxer who had amassed a stellar record since being taken in by Dee. Once he arrived, Dee spoke to Jones within earshot of the media and explained how he could be of assistance to him.

"You can give those wrestling fans plenty of action without making yourself out [to be] such a mean devil," the avuncular Dee explained to Rufus in front of reporters from *The Detroit Free Press*. "What you need is a manager like Poppa Dee."

Prior to Jones' bout that night with the Great Mephisto, Dee reportedly climbed into the ring and explained to referee Philbin that his new protege was going to become "Gentleman Jones," and would conduct himself in a manner befitting that new title.

"A moment later, the match was on, and Rufus Jones forgot every instruction that Poppa Dee had whispered," continued *The Free Press*. "Roscoe Toles at the ringside shook his head in chagrin as Rufe violated every known rule of wrestling. He had the crowd jammed against the ring shouting curses and threats. Nobody was in his seat after the match was underway for 10 minutes. Mr. Jones didn't have a friend in the house except Roscoe, Poppy, and a twelve-year-old sister, Henrietta Jones."

A more in-depth explanation of the relationship was offered by the city's Black newspaper, *The Detroit Tribune*. It was through this publication that Metro Detroit's Black fans were informed that Jones had "left the old plow 'a-tumbling down in de fiel'" in pursuit of the riches that were presumably earned by those who participated in wrestling contests in the big cities.

A Decided Novelty

Poppa Dee told *The Tribune* that Jones had heard the tale of Illa Vincent, "the only colored wrestler who ever attained national honors among the heavies," and that Rufus was attempting to emulate Vincent's mat exploits.

For this story to be true, Jones would have needed to make the acquaintance of someone with an exceptional memory. As headline-grabbing as Vincent's wrestling activities in the United States were, his entire Stateside career was confined to a two-year period that concluded two months before the now 25-year-old Jones was even born.

In addition, both Reginald Siki and George Godfrey — to the extent that the latter could be classified as a wrestler — were certainly more recent and prominent examples of Black wrestling heavyweights who had attracted mainstream attention, and at levels that superseded those of Vincent.

Continuing, *The Tribune* elaborated as to how the fact that Jones was now a main-eventer in the area's wrestling rings was "testimony of his ability to grapple with the best in the country," while citing how "the large throngs which pack out the Arena to pray for his defeat" only translate into greater popularity for Jones.

"In the rasslin' game, the more unpopular the rassler is with the fans, the larger the crowds will be when he grunts and groans," insisted *The Tribune*.

In the meantime, Jones was allegedly training in seclusion alongside Dee, who was teaching him to master a hold called "The Lemon Squeezer," which Dee had supposedly taught to Vincent years earlier.

If there was any presumed link between "The Lemon Squeezer" and any tactics that Jones would soon add to his repertoire and unleash upon his opponents, it apparently came in the form of a specific type of headbutt. This move, which would eventually become commonplace, was still not yet widely practiced as an intentional offensive maneuver, and certainly not in abundance during matches.

By mid-November, *The Lansing State Journal* had elaborated on Jones's use of a "flying head-butt," during which he left his feet to gain momentum before bringing his skull crashing down atop his opponent's scalp.

Jones' creative use of the headbutt was noteworthy, but it was not yet a maneuver that singularly defined him. As he blazed a trail of carnage through the state of Michigan, Rufus would still conclude most of his matches with accepted wrestling techniques, like when he downed Mike London in December, planting him in the center of Lansing's Prudden Auditorium with an airplane spin followed by a body slam.

Joseph Godfrey wouldn't be the only Black wrestler to undergo a major renaming during this time. By 1937, George Hoddison was headlining his share of matches in and around Springfield, and was evenly splitting the wins with Steve Brady, whom he had been wrestling consistently for years at this point.

Then, late in November, Hoddison made a career-redefining move of his own when he traveled from Springfield to Boston to wrestle for Charley Gordon, and changed his name to a variant of his Canadian alias Zelis Amhara. Adopting a far more alliterative pseudonym, Hoddison would thereafter be known as Seelie Samara.

At this time, Samara joined a talent roster that still included Ted Germaine, but which was now running as a distant second to that of promoter Paul Bowser. Within two weeks of his arrival in Boston, Samara — who Gordon advertised in *The Boston Globe* as "nothing less than the strongest Negro in the world" — received a major status upgrade.

Through a somewhat convoluted series of statements attesting that Samara was "recognized by Massachusetts Wrestling Association, Inc." and carried the "wrestling title and belt of the United States Wrestling Association," Samara emerged "as claimant of the world's heavyweight championship" just before 1937 ended. Remarkably, it does not appear that he acquired this lofty distinction through any traceable in-ring activity.

A Decided Novelty

While Jones and Samara enjoyed incredible debuts in their new wrestling homes, considering what he would come to mean for Montana, it's difficult to fathom a more mismanaged debut in a region than King Kong Clayton's, at least in some parts of the state.

When *The Great Falls Tribune* trumpeted the arrival of the inbound Clayton, "a colored boy from Salt Lake City," it's unlikely that either Clayton or any of the Montanans who watched him realized he would eventually come to symbolize an entire era of wrestling in that region.

Clayton was victorious in his Montana premiere, but it was hardly an impressive victory. He won two falls of a best-of-three-falls match when his opponent Ike Cazzell was disqualified for punching him excessively. Cazzell then took a fall from Clayton with an airplane spin, and was disqualified again in the final act.

The trip to Montana also offered Clayton his first taste of the wrestling scene in Alberta, where he was described in *The Edmonton Journal* as "a beautiful wrestler" whose work in the ring was "as clean as a whistle." A few liberties were taken when describing Clayton's ring experience; barely half a year into his wrestling career, it was said he had "burnt the trails along the length and breadth of the Pacific Coast and is still in great demand."

"King Kong Clayton, oftimes tagged as the Black Panther, is a clever colored grappler who hails from Alabama," declared *The Journal*. "He comes to grips with the old rascal Indian Ike Cazzell of Mexico in the semi-windup."

Upon returning to Montana, Clayton was given a more impressive means of victory, taking two falls from Klem Kusek by way of a Boston Crab and a "back body press."

When one of Clayton's matches in Edmonton saw him backflip from the ring and crash onto the ringside table, writer Ken McConnell of *The Journal* partook in some very uncomfortable imagery to describe what Clayton must have been feeling as he "crashed to the floor as the table was smashed to bits."

A Decided Novelty

"To record that King Kong was enveloped in a very thick fog is putting it mildly indeed," began McConnell. "He probably heard the deafening roars of old Nums in darkest Africa, and the sweet music of the banjo-strumming cotton pickers in Alabama."

This sort of imagery is precisely in line with what would have been expected from a sportswriter in the mid-1930s who was serving the readership of a Canadian province with a Black population that was roughly one-tenth of one percent, or fewer than 1,000 total persons.

The most awkward and bizarre aspect of Clayton's arrival in the region took place in areas of Montana like Helena, where Clayton was quite literally introduced as Tiger Jack Nelson. The promoters seemed to believe that no one would notice if they introduced a completely different Black wrestler to the region under Nelson's name, even though Nelson had toured the Mountain West region just one year earlier.

Not only was Clayton about a decade younger than Nelson, but he was also at least five inches shorter with a far thicker frame. Frankly, the only thing the two wrestlers shared was a similar complexion; for anyone who had ever seen both men in person, there was no confusing the two.

The Helena Daily Independent was forced to retract its identification of King Kong Clayton as Tiger Jack Nelson in a rather embarrassing and misleading statement.

"It is well known that the colored man wrestles under two names," argued *The Daily Independent*. "Some promoters bill him as Tiger Jack Nelson while others prefer the more spectacular name of King Kong Clayton, a moniker dubbed onto him during the heyday of the King Kong movies. Regardless of what name he wrestles under, Tiger Jack is a wrestler of the first division, and many of the boys have found out to their sorrow that he beats them either at straight wrestling or in the more spectacular antics of the matmen."

After setting the stage for the misuse of Tiger Nelson's name to be phased out in favor of Clayton's common alias, the writer then made a curious comment about Clayton's in-ring style and how it applied to Black wrestlers in general.

"The reason [Clayton] does not win oftener is his racial habit of allowing the other boy to get in plenty of rough stuff and illegal holds and tactics before he cuts loose with even so much as a good solid forearm blow, something absolutely legal in the wrestling game today," *The Daily Independent* continued. "Some of these boys can hit as hard with their forearms as many men can with a full knuckle punch."

The writer appeared to be arguing that Black wrestlers had a habit of being more reluctant to break rules than the in-ring representatives of other races and ethnicities. If anything, it was being implied that the conduct of Black wrestlers was either too gentlemanly, or too passive. Either way, the argument seemed to be that the appearance of being too polite once matches began resulted in an otherwise avoidable accumulation of losses by Black wrestlers.

There is also the matter of how writers insisted on quoting Clayton as if he bordered on illiteracy, as when *The Helena Daily Independent* published an alleged statement from Clayton expressing his reluctance to wrestle against Ike Cazzell.

"I sho don't want no part of that bad man," began the quote attributed to Clayton. "I fights whatever boy else Mr. Alley done says I gotta, but no Indian Ike — no man — I sho don't want ma eyes dug out by de sockets. Dat Indian Ike fella sho is poison to me. Take him away!"

Considering that Clayton was a high school graduate born and raised in a major Midwestern city, it's unfathomable that he would have spoken like this, especially since subsequent interviews would contradict the notion that he conversed like a man who lacked formal education. Yet, as bad as the first volley was, the follow up was even worse.

"Mista Alley, sir," Clayton allegedly said, "I always been a clean rassler and I don't like this Indian Ike business. No boy can wrestle him clean and get a break. If'n I rassles him an I got to slug it out wif him an' I'm afraid de white folks mob me if'n I does. I jes nachally am gonna lose ma shirt no matter what happens."

Ironically, this statement appeared to have been planted in the service of assuring the residents of Helena that they could be impartial enough to accept a non-Black wrestler as a fan-favorite.

"Most fans are fair-minded and believe that when two boxers or two wrestlers enter the ring on common ground, they are to be accepted on an equal basis," stated the writer. "In fact, the negro athletes are usually given more than a fair break by the fans in these times of colored champions in nearly every sport."

This was a very aspirational statement for a city of around 15,000 total residents, fewer than 150 of whom were Black. This is especially true when juxtaposed with a fictional interview that would have catered to lingering assumptions that those Black residents were complete imbeciles.

Notwithstanding the attempts to establish Clayton as something of an uncultured brute within the context of his fictional backstory, inside of the ring, he was apparently nothing short of spectacular in blending raw athleticism with technical wrestling. *The Great Falls Daily Leader* described him as a "scientist" inside of the ring.

In one best-of-two-falls match against Klem Kusek, Clayton won his falls with an Indian deathlock and a skin-the-cat reversal from the ring ropes. He also scored a fall against the Red Shadow with an "upside-down pretzel hold." In writing about Clayton for *The Northwest Enterprise* of Seattle, L.A. Howard reported of Clayton, "He has acquired a host of friends and well wishers among both whites and negroes for his clean sportsmanship in the ring."

Outside of the ring, things were apparently different. In April, *The Standard-Examiner* of Ogden reported that Clayton had been arrested on a petty larceny charge during a trip through Utah. The Associated Press carried additional details of the charge, in which a man named Monroe Berger alleged that Clayton had taken his suitcase, returned the contents of

A Decided Novelty

the suitcase to him, but retained possession of the physical suitcase.

Upon his release from custody, Clayton seemingly retreated back to Montana and wrestled exclusively in the Big Sky State and Alberta for the remainder of the year. That's when some alternative origin stories for Clayton arose, with one of the most creative coming from *The Butte Daily Post*.

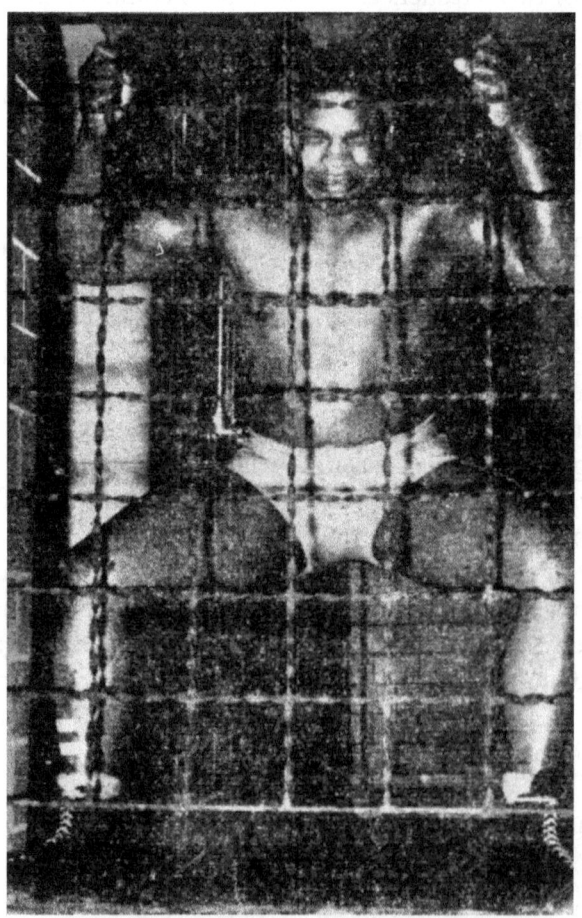

"King Kong" Clayton hangs from a cage

"King Kong Clayton, Negro grappler... was once a chauffeur for Stanislaus Zbyszko, world heavyweight champion in 1921 and 1925," claimed *The Daily Post*. "It was during this employment with Zbyszko that the Negro mat star received his early training as a 'grunt and groan' artist."

This was obvious nonsense, and a clear rehash of the story used to link Reginald Siki with the Zbyszkos, only with Clayton's name inserted in Siki's place.

In a pairing that was definitely a product of its era, Clayton spent a chunk of his time during fall 1937 feuding with a middleweight said to be of German extraction who went by the name "Young Hitler." With World War II still two years away from its official initiation, but with the anti-Black policies of Nazi Germany being publicly divulged, in-ring combat between a Black American wrestler like Clayton and a surrogate for the German dictator was clearly a low-stakes representation for a far more serious social conflict.

In most of their bouts, Clayton "took the measure of Young Hitler of Germany" despite frequently falling behind by losing the first fall as a consequence of Hitler's cheating. Once he trailed in the matches, Clayton would mount a furious comeback using a flurry of maneuvers — not so coincidentally identical to those used by Jack Claybourne in Montana years earlier — to overpower the smaller Hitler, just like he did in Great Falls.

"In the fourth round, Clayton started firing dropkicks at his foe," reported *The Great Falls Tribune*. "Hitler survived two attacks, but when the Negro cracked him with three in a row and followed with a body press, the German was in no condition to argue. Clayton followed up in the next round with more kicks and quickly slammed Hitler into submission."

By defeating Hitler in convincing fashion, Clayton was rewarded with a shot at the Montana light heavyweight title of Billy Spendlove. Even as the papers played up Clayton's role as a hero, they seemingly couldn't do so without resorting to disparaging language. In instances where writers were obviously attempting to compliment Clayton, he would still be labeled as "that handsome, black-as-coal hero, King Kong Clayton," as he was in *The Edmonton Bulletin*.

A Decided Novelty

Then there was the language used by the writer for *The Calgary Daily Herald*, who referred to Clayton as "Mrs. Clayton's rassling pickaninny" well after the term had been plainly understood to be derogatory.

The fact that Clayton defeated Spendlove in the ring for his title in Butte — fair and square — is yet another standout moment in an era where Black wrestlers were usually limited to honorary titles specific to racial identity. Clayton then won his rematch against Spendlove in Butte the following week. This time, Clayton won two falls against Spendlove by way of a bodyslam and a "leg strangle and body press."

"The wily Clayton drew lengthy applause with his smashing tactics, and staged one of the fastest fights in the local arena," printed *The Montana Standard*. "Both Clayton's and Spendlove's lips were bleeding in the final round."

To close out the year, Clayton participated in the first-ever mud-slinging match in Montana's history. Held in Butte, the concept was borrowed from a match held between Joe Parelli and Pat O'Dowdy in California, which required competitors to wrestle in a ring caked with thick mud. Clayton and the Mountain Hermit waged war in the Montanan version of the match, which Clayton won.

"The novel attraction provided mat followers with plenty of excitement," reported *The Butte Daily Post*. "The ring contained more than six inches of cold, slimy mud, which splattered over spectators at the ringside. Many of the spectators wore raincoats."

Having been absent from wrestling for nearly the entirety of 1937, Gorilla Parker resumed his wrestling career in New England in January 1938, with the papers urging Parker and Jim Mitchell to come together and finally settle who the one true Negro wrestling champion was.

The fact that Parker was promoted in weight class to the status of "world colored heavyweight champion" may have been a byproduct of post-injury weight gain. From this point onward, the once frequent references to Parker having a herculean or chiseled physique more or less came to an end.

A Decided Novelty

Midway through the year, Parker disappeared from the ring once again, and would not return for several years, as the Gorilla Parker who wrestled in Alabama during 1940 was undoubtedly an imposter.

Speaking of imposters, Reginald Siki ostensibly made a single appearance in a U.S. wrestling ring in late January 1938 as one of many participants in a three-hour boxing-and-wrestling show presented at the Sports Arena in Washington, D.C. Siki reportedly teamed with Little King to defeat Battling Barry and Joe King in a team battle royal.

The primary reason to suspect this was an imposter is that an appearance by Siki — whose name was fairly well known to wrestling fans across the nation at the time — was never alluded to in the buildup to the show. Moreover, it was apparently the *only* newsworthy appearance made by Siki in North America during the entire year, and the small-scale character of the event makes it unlikely that Siki would engage in intercontinental travel solely for this event.

That same month, it was reported that George Godfrey had suffered a stroke, and had supposedly been recovering in Long Beach Hospital in New York for several weeks before anyone realized who he was. It had apparently taken the keen eyes of Long Beach police chief Edward J. Agnew — himself a former middleweight fighter from Leiperville — to recognize the most famous athlete his hometown had produced.

"On hospital records, the man is listed as George Giudrey, 56, with a Freeport, Long Island address, but Dr. J. Alexander said that when asked, the man admitted he is Godfrey," reported the AP.

The physician who updated the press about Godfrey's condition added that Godfrey was recovering, but other publications exaggerated several of the details of Godfrey's hospitalization. Some went so far as to refer to Godfrey as a "destitute patient" who was in "critical condition" and "rapidly losing his eyesight." Others added that his plight has been the result of a "cerebral hemorrhage."

A Decided Novelty

However, it appears that none of this was true. The real George Godfrey emerged in Los Angeles two days after this report to dispel the rumors that anything was wrong with him at all — although he had apparently packed on an additional 40 pounds since his final appearance inside of a boxing ring, and now tipped the scales at north of 300 pounds.

"That Godfrey back East must be two other gentlemen, not me," laughed George. "They've had me dead, blind, and all washed up, but ain't none of it true. I never felt better in my life. I feel like I can go 15 rounds right now with that Joe Louis fellow. No, I haven't got any fights lined up right now, but I'm in training, just the same."

In April, Godfrey resumed making appearances at wrestling events when he served as a special guest referee for a show at the Mission Club in Santa Barbara, California, and followed that up by refereeing another bout in Las Vegas.

September actually saw Godfrey climbing into the ring to wrestle once again, with stops in Utah, Washington, Oregon, and British Columbia. Frequent attention was called to Godfrey's immense size, as he still maintained his 300-pound physique, and was often described as immobile.

In Wisconsin, "Black Panther" Alex Kaffner had been participating in a memorable series of matches against the masked wrestler known as the Shadow. The first of these bouts took place at Breese Stevens Field in Madison during July. The referee was forced to rule the match a draw — with the fall total tied at one apiece — because it had begun raining too hard over the outdoor venue for the match to continue. The reporter covering the event wrote that Kaffner had been beating the Shadow "from puddle to puddle" right before the action was brought to a halt.

Kaffner supposedly received an injury during a different match against the Shadow that same month. The Black Panther was the recipient of a "reverse body slam," which caused him to land on his neck and damage his vertebrae. Whether or not the injury had any legitimacy is

A Decided Novelty

unknown, but Kaffner was out of action for a month, and then returned for a series of revenge bouts against his masked rival.

These matches were so unruly that at least one required police intervention, as the repeated rule-breaking from the Shadow incensed the Madison crowd to such an extent that they were ready to storm the ring in Kaffner's defense.

"Kaffner lost the third fall in 12 minutes when 'The Shadow' strangled him with the ropes and then kept the referee too busy to allow Kaffner to be freed until he was an easy prey for a body slam," reported *The Capital Times*. "Again, there was confusion in the ring, and police stopped angry fans from taking part in the melee."

To the extent that Kaffner was engaged in an extended feud with anyone during his time in Wisconsin, it was definitely Greek wrestler Jimmy Demetral. The two faced each other on several occasions throughout Kaffner's Wisconsin tenure, as Demetral had an apparent fondness for defeating Black challengers. Prior to Kaffner's arrival, Demetral had attracted large crowds to his victories over both Lee Umbles and Tarzan Wilson.

Taking everything into consideration, Demetral's comparative success perfectly underscores the difference in treatment between White and Black wrestlers of similar ability during the era. Retrospectives on Demetral note that he reigned as the officially recognized world middleweight champion and world light heavyweight champion in Wisconsin for large stretches of the 1920s and 1930s. In Kaffner's case, all of his supposed championships during that era, during which he was highly active in the Badger State, were essentially imaginary.

Speaking of championships that may or may not have been official, during the early stages of 1938, some concessions were being made in the wrestling war between Charley Gordon and Paul Bowser, and not of the sort that favored Seelie Samara's tenuous standing as a world titleholder.

As *The Boston Globe* reported that Bowser "had finally recognized the penetrating wails" for a match between

A Decided Novelty

Gordon's "Negro champion" and a suitable opponent from Bowser's camp, it also announced that "Louis Thesz" was being imported from the Midwest in acknowledgement of the "consolidation of champions policy" that had begun to take shape in wrestling.

George "Seelie Samara" Hardison

    In short, young headliner Lou Thesz was being brought in to help whittle down the number of champions in the wrestling industry by consolidating the world titles of different cities into individual, regionally recognized world championships. Samara's title claim would be the first to go.

    Predictably, Samara did surrender his championship, albeit mostly through an absence of allusion. After a Boston

A Decided Novelty

Arena match against Hans Steinke in late February, Samara's claim to world title status was simply never mentioned again.

In March, the Associated Negro Press offered its account that Bowser was permitting Gordon to bring Samara to the Boston Garden — the superior venue — for a match with Bowser's recognized world champion Steve "Crusher" Casey. It was a bout that was being advertised as "the first official world's heavyweight championship match featuring a Negro challenger."

Adding context, ANP reporter Mabe Kountze recounted how Bowser had "in effect told Promoter Gordon to cease his title claims from the rival sports palace, the Boston Arena," and while the bout between Casey and Samara would have the appearance of an interpromotional battle, it would more closely resemble a conciliatory act by Gordon to satisfy Bowser.

In short, Samara was identified only as the challenger for Casey's title in the prelude to their Boston Garden contest rather than as a former titleholder, and he surrendered two straight falls to the Crusher in under 40 minutes to informally abjure any claim he might have had to being a world champion.

Due to the semi-national attention the bout between Casey and Samara attained, the staff of *The Greenfield Recorder-Gazette* apparently thought some clarification was in order. Samara had been publicly labeled as an Algerian before his title bout, but *The Recorder-Gazette* cut straight through all of the promotional deception.

"The 'Seelie Samara,' billed as the 'Algerian strong man,' who was flattened by Steve Casey at the Boston Garden last night in straight falls, is George Hardison of 12 Washington Street, Greenfield," they reported.

Following his drubbing at the hands of Casey, Samara was severely downgraded in the way he was presented to the public. Before his next match, which would be against "Dazzler" George Clark, *The Globe* described Samara in generally unfavorable terms, betraying the new reality of how Samara would be booked in his home state.

A Decided Novelty

"The lethargic title holder of the St. Botolph St. guild, after much beating of the promotional tom-toms, was tossed in against Steve Casey a while back, but on that occasion he came out a rather distant second to the good 'Crusher,'" observed *The Globe*.

At this point, Samara appeared to become a fully ingrained participant in the wrestling affairs of the Boston Metro area. When he made his mid-April debut in Lynn, the "Algerian" Samara was described as "a giant of the wrestling ring" in *The Daily Evening Item*, owing to the thick muscles that adorned his six-foot frame, amounting to an advertised weight of 225 pounds. This was sufficient size to render Samara amongst the largest wrestlers of the Depression era, no matter where he appeared.

The Evening Item also included the bizarre insistence that Samara was "called the uncrowned heavyweight wrestling champion of the world" even though this claim was immediately followed by a reference to "[Samara's] recent defeats by the title holder Steve Casey and George Clark on the Boston mat," which should have been adequate to nullify any such claims.

Then, in a move that was jarring but not without precedent, Seelie Samara disappeared from wrestling cards in the Boston area, followed by the instant reemergence of the Black Demon George Hoddison in wrestling rings around Springfield.

It was very similar to the manner in which Joe Godfrey temporarily abandoned the name Tiger Flowers in Massachusetts while wrestling for a competing promoter in Lynn, and just before he began making his first showings in New York. The difference in this case was that the Black Demon's appearances in Boston as Seelie Samara had been disclosed by the Springfield-area press. Yet, *The Springfield Union* neglected to print his African-inspired name, instead simply stating that the Demon "was a popular figure in the West Street ring a few years ago" and "has been active in the eastern part of the state."

A Decided Novelty

Although the two cities are less than two hours apart by automobile, Boston and Springfield were apparently worlds apart with respect to the audiences that attended wrestling matches in each area of Massachusetts.

Soon, Hoddison would be on the move again, resuming the use of the name under which he had held a highly disputed claim to a world heavyweight championship. In the process, he would not only claim additional gold, but also complete the assembly of an iconic collection of Black wrestling talent, the likes of which would have been unfathomable just a few years prior.

A Decided Novelty

14 – Gentleman Jack

Out in Montana, King Kong Clayton abruptly lost his light heavyweight championship to Speedy Warren at Miner's Hall in Butte on January 3, 1938. The falls were knotted at one apiece when Clayton was tossed from the ring, became injured, and couldn't resume the competition. When Clayton tumbled out of the ring, he landed in the lap of a spectator, which set off a sequence of extracurricular events.

"As the wrestlers were leaving the arena, Warren was attacked by several overzealous fans," reported *The Montana Standard*. "Within a brief period of time, there were several free for alls in progress in the hall."

It's endearing to think that a Black wrestler could inflame the passions of an overwhelmingly White wrestling fanbase in the mid-1930s to such an extent that his loss of a championship would spark a violent spectator eruption.

By now, Clayton was so popular that the once unflattering exaggerations of his background tended to drift in the opposite direction, away from accentuating the least flattering stereotypes of 20th century Blacks, and more toward presenting him as a cultured gentleman who excelled in all aspects of life.

"Hailing direct from ol' Alabama, Clayton is a college graduate, and with several seasons as a professional football player, is rated among the nation's leading all-around athletes," stated *The Lewistown Democrat-News*.

Several claims related to Clayton's athletic prowess were made both before and after his death, yet there is no evidence that he ever played professional football, and he self-reported to be a high school graduate in the 1940 U.S. Census, and not a graduate of any college of university.

By April, Clayton had moved up to the heavyweight division, at least for the sake of his objective in Helena, which was all about snatching the Helena heavyweight title away from Nick Bozinis. *The Helena Daily Independent* reported that 2,000 fans — well over 10 percent of the city's population at the time

A Decided Novelty

— "rocked with applause for the colored by who really opened up for the first time in Helena."

"The final fall went to King Kong with a shoulder pin after he and Nick exchanged heavy blows, a headbutt or two, and a flying dropkick that failed to land full force, but which did knock Bozinis out of the ring and down among the first pew holders," reported *The Independent*.

It was announced on April 26 that matchmaker Tom Alley was attempting to secure wrestler George Craig to face Clayton for his newly won city championship the following week. However, the very next day, Alley reneged on the announcement, citing the racial prejudice of Craig as the reason a title match between he and Clayton would not be taking place.

"Craig claims that prejudice against mixing with colored grapplers made it extremely obnoxious for him to meet King Kong," reported *The Daily Independent*. "He said, 'Highest regard for Clayton as wrestler and sportsman, but I am very much opposed to meeting him in Helena or anywhere else.'"

Instead of wrestling Craig, Clayton would defend the championship of Helena in a rematch against Bozinis. This time, 3,500 spectators packed the Algeria Shrine Auditorium in Helena — an assemblage of more than 30 percent of the city's populace. Once again, the townspeople went home happy when Clayton successfully defended his title.

"The agile negro slipped his legs free and secured a head scissors on the Greek just when he looked doomed, and managed to win the match two falls out of three," reported *The Daily Independent*.

Because Clayton's proven boxing background had been referenced consistently in his promotion throughout 1938, he was eventually lured into the York Hotel gym in Edmonton to spar with Eddie Wenstob, a light heavyweight fighter from Viking, Alberta. Wenstob was the reigning light heavyweight champion of Western Canada, with a record of 8-1 in his prior nine fights, and 16-2-1 in his previous 19.

"Eddie went two slam-bang rounds against Leroy "King Kong" Clayton, 193-pound negro boxer and wrestler," reported *The Edmonton Journal*. "He cut Clayton's lip for two stitches; peppered Clayton's body with right-hand smashes, and at least once King Kong seemed to be on the way to the canvas."

"King Kong" Clayton spars with Eddie Wenstob

It is unlikely that Clayton had dedicated himself to any serious boxing training for the better part of three years; he was certainly no match for a seasoned fighter who was only six months away from winning the outright light heavyweight boxing championship of Canada.

A Decided Novelty

"One time I thought I would be a pretty good boxer," Clayton told *Journal* reporter Ken McConnell. "I fought a good boy in Jersey. He beat me; near beat me to death. He broke my nose; a couple of ribs, and cut my face to pieces. But I learned how to fight that fella, and we met next time at the Coliseum in Chicago. I gave it to him good that time, and that's the way you learn."

One week later, Clayton returned to the ring and fought on the undercard of a boxing event headlined by Wenstob against Emilio Martinez, who was ranked as the fourth-best light heavyweight in the world by the National Boxing Association at the time. Weighing in at 189 pounds, Clayton knocked out 205-pound Eddie Shelton of Spokane, Washington after dropping him twice.

When commenting on the fight, *Edmonton Journal* sports editor George MacKintosh stated, "The semi-windup featuring King Kong Clayton and Eddie Shelton was a proper bust. I wouldn't know whether Clayton can fight, never having seen him inside a boxing ring until last night, but I'll take my oath that Shelton can't. He hasn't any business in there as a principal in a semifinal joust."

Whether Clayton was considering a full-time return to the boxing ring or was just feeling confident because of the battering he gave Shelton, there is no way of knowing. What is known is that Clayton genuinely returned to fight once more — this time in Kalispell, Montana — and was promptly knocked out by intermountain champion Tommy Lynch.

"King Kong Clayton proved to be a less effective boxer than he was a wrestler in a fistic match with Tommy Lynch of Deer Lodge," printed *The Missoulian*. "Clayton went down for the count of eight only to arise and be smacked down permanently."

Undaunted, Clayton signed up for a rematch against Tommy Lynch in early 1939, and this time the fight was held in Edmonton under the oversight of promoter Fred Osborne.

"Osborne looked long and carefully into the Lynch record, and he promises that King Kong, who used to spar

A Decided Novelty

with Mickey Walker, will really know whether he is a wrestler or a fighter when the bout is over," reported George MacKintosh in *The Edmonton Journal*.

No reference to their previous encounter was made during the leadup to the rematch between Clayton and Lynch, ostensibly for the sake of not revealing Clayton's earlier loss. When interviewed prior to the contest, Lynch claimed a remarkable professional record of 58-6, with 34 wins coming by way of knockout. Presumably, Clayton had been added to that list of knockout victims during their December skirmish.

In the only taste Edmontonians had received of Clayton acting in the capacity of an authentic fighter, he had looked like a world-beater. As the day of the fight approached, Clayton continued to wrestle a full-time schedule. Then the public pre-fight workouts began, and knowledgeable onlookers conceded that Clayton appeared to know what he was doing with a pair of boxing gloves on his fists.

"In workouts in preparation for his joust with Lynch, Clayton has looked better than a lot of others who have worked out in the same gym," admitted MacKintosh. "He is better known as a wrestler than a boxer, but he may have more fistic ability than he has been credited with."

Then the rematch between Clayton and Lynch occurred, and the unthinkable happened — Clayton won by decision. Granted, Clayton outweighed Lynch by a solid 20 pounds, but Lynch had been the overwhelming betting favorite going into the bout.

"Tommy Lynch, a pretty fair junior lightheavyweight, slugged with all his might Tuesday night at the Memorial Hall, but try as he did, he could not make any impression on King Kong Clayton, and the latter won a well-merited decision in the 10-round main event of a high class professional boxing card," reported *The Edmonton Journal*.

According to reports, Lynch had needed to come on furiously in the final three rounds of the fight simply to close the distance on the scorecards, as Clayton consistently stepped

A Decided Novelty

forward throughout the fight and methodically piled up points in the early rounds.

"But Clayton, the plodder, a man with a magnificent physique, just was too tough," added *The Journal*. "He had a cut-up face in the end and probably showed more damage than Lynch."

Far east of where Clayton had been flirting with a full-time return to fighting, Jack Claybourne had been in Ohio, where he picked up his iconic name of "Gentleman Jack" right before a bout with supposed former UCLA football player Alonzo Wood.

"One of the cleanest wrestlers in the business, Claybourne has been called the finest piece of mat machinery the colored race has ever produced," glowed *The News Journal* of Mansfield, Ohio. "'Gentleman Jack' is a spiffy dresser, colorful both in and out of the ring, and wears a perpetual smile as big as his face."

The newly minted Gentleman Jack had little trouble with his opponent Wood, as *The Journal* reported that Claybourne moved around the ring "with the speed and grace of a lightweight," and that Wood "ran directly into the feet" of Claybourne in the final stages of both falls, becoming yet another victim of Claybourne's dropkick barrage.

This period of activity in the Midwest saw Claybourne listed as weighing anywhere from 175 pounds to 195 pounds. Capitalizing on these phony and drastic weight fluctuations, Jack might wrestle as a heavyweight in Illinois one night and then compete as a light heavyweight in Ohio the next. *The Dayton Daily News* actually went to the trouble of pointing this out.

"Claybourne... has been appearing mostly against heavyweight opponents," observed the publication. "Bordering on the heavy and light heavyweight line, he can swing into either division with ease and without sacrificing any change in wrestling technique."

This valuable ability to convincingly straddle two weight divisions was owed to Claybourne's brand of acrobatics, which was atypical even among wrestlers far lighter and shorter than he was, as the majority of wrestlers conformed to a straightforward grappling style. At the same time, Claybourne's 6'1" frame placed him within the 95th percentile of the tallest wrestlers of his generation, regardless of race.

The foremost gentleman amongst the era's Black wrestlers was about to have his first meeting with the most violent Black heel in the business. While Claybourne had been wowing audiences with his technical brilliance and high-flying athleticism, Rufus Jones had been carving a path of destruction through Midwestern wrestling rings.

After memorably feuding with fellow rulebreaker Bull Curry for the title of Detroit's chief "bad man," Jones made his way to new venues in Southwest Michigan, appearing in Battle Creek, the home of the famous cereal-makers at the Kellogg Company.

In the aftermath of Jones' bout with English wrestler Walter Percy, *The Battle Creek Enquirer* remarked that Jones "as expected did just about everything except wrestle" during a match in which Jones captured the only fall with a body slam. Still, *The Enquirer* caught on to the fact that in-ring acumen was only one aspect of the value Jones brought to his performances.

"Percy landed several drop-kicks, but most of the entertainment was furnished by Jones' grimaces in feigned anguish when in one of Percy's figure four scissors or crotch holds," noted *The Enquirer*.

Future reports of Jones' activity would lend credence to the idea that he was gradually grasping the concepts that would make him one of wrestling's premier showmen. In the meantime, C. Lavern Robbins of *The Battle Creek Moon-Journal* would focus on the post-match antics of Jones, who he said "lived up to his advance publicity of being a mean mat villain."

"As the bell sounded the end of the time limit, Percy cracked Jones with a left uppercut," recounted Robbins. "Jones tried to hit back, and then Percy knocked Referee Vern Clark

A Decided Novelty

of Detroit down for trying to interfere. Jones and Percy squared off again, and then Jones knocked Clark down."

Seeing his referee being pinballed around the ring by the two wrestlers, promoter Farmer Nick entered the ring only to be knocked down by Percy, and then inspector Earl Brutche entered the ring, grabbed Jones, and with the help of Nick, pulled him out of the ring.

"The affair ended without any injuries, but the fans had entertainment galore for a few seconds," concluded Robbins.

When the wrestling season opened across the Ambassador Bridge in Windsor, Ontario in February 1938, Jones took part in a remarkable main-event bout against the Great Balbo to kick things off. When Balbo captured the initial fall with flying tackles, Jones "heaved a chair at him to show he didn't like being pinned," in the words of *The Windsor Star*.

After falling behind on the fall tally, Jones evened the bout with punches, kicks, and flying tackles, while growing increasingly dirtier with his choice of tactics as the match progressed. As was his custom, he turned every object at his disposal to his advantage.

"Jones had come out for the bout with his right wrist taped, but apparently he wore the tape as a weapon rather than for protection of any injury or sore," continued *The Star*. "He rubbed it across Balbo's eyes at every opportunity, till finally, in the third set-to, Balbo grabbed his arm and yanked the tape off."

With the tape in his hands, Balbo retaliated against Jones with tactics identical to those that had first been employed against him. Unfortunately for Balbo, he was not as gifted at shielding his illicit activities from the view of referee Johnny Banks, who disqualified him and awarded the final decision to Jones.

"Balbo 'burned up' over the decision and was loath to let up in his wicked offensive," continued *The Star*. "He kept after Jones for several minutes after the bout ended, despite attempts by Referee Banks and a ringsider to calm him down. When last seen, Jones was in full flight headed to the dressing

A Decided Novelty

room, with Balbo tearing after him and a highly excited crowd of fans licking their chops after the somewhat bloodthirsty finish."

The following month, Jones and Balbo had a rematch in Windsor and were tasked with presenting an exciting main event to the Windsor Chryslers — champions of the Michigan-Ontario Hockey League — as well as the players' wives and girlfriends. To accomplish their appointed task, the two wrestled for a full 90 minutes without either man scoring a fall.

According to *The Star*, the pair "stuck to orthodox wrestling" for the first 60 minutes before the contest devolved into something that more closely resembled a typical Rufus Jones match. The dramatic change in the tone of the bout occurred when Balbo grabbed Jones, hurled him out of the ring, and followed him out to the Windsor Arena floor with his fists flying. From there, both wrestlers cheated with impunity, and took turns declining offers from referee Ted Greise to disqualify their opponent for the use of exceedingly rough tactics.

"Jones had Balbo almost out on his feet in the last minute or so by butting Balbo's head with his forehead, and Greise wouldn't go for that, stepping in to rescue the Italian," continued *The Star*. "Since this rescue act was perhaps instrumental in saving Balbo from defeat, Jones was quite angry, and showed it. The outcome was that for a few minutes after the final gong, both Balbo and Greise belabored the Negro, Greise even going so far as to take off his shirt."

On his very next trip to Saginaw, Jones was described as "the black villain" by *The Saginaw News*, in comparison to Patrick Finnegan, who was characterized as "lily-white," and "heroic." Jones lived up to his villainous billing during the bout, losing the final fall by way of a disqualification ruling handed down by referee McGregor. That's when the real action started.

"Rough Rufus objected so strongly that he felled the referee with a lusty jab, and the fiasco was on" described *The News*. "During the melee, Jones tore a leg from McGregor's pants and used it to wrap around his adversary's head in a well-acted attempt to throttle him. If McGregor's efforts lacked the sincerity and showmanship of the finished mat artists in his match with Rufus, he nevertheless provided a packed audience with a novel ending to an otherwise mediocre card."

In Port Huron, *The Herald Palladium* had to remind its local wrestling fans of exactly what had transpired that had caused Jones to be absent from their local rings for an extended period of time.

"Jones is the grappler who gained headlines all over the country six months ago when he introduced a new dodge in the wrestling art," said *The Herald Palladium*. "The colored man pulled a police nightstick from his trunks and tapped an opponent upon the head during the heat of the match. Rough Rufus was set down by the state boxing commission for three months for the little trick, and was threatened with a life ban if he ever tried it again."

At this point, the feud between Jones and Claybourne kicked into high gear. The claim that the two were natural adversaries was buttressed by the insistence that there was an authentic colored world light heavyweight championship that both wrestlers were attempting to acquire.

In the absence of such a title, it would be presupposed that Black wrestlers could not coexist without at least satisfying their curiosity as to who among them was the best combatant of that shade.

The Hamilton Spectator declared "Jones was looked upon as a speedster, but when Claybourne appeared on the scene, he began to steal Jones' thunder." To those who perceived this statement to be true, Claybourne usurped an even larger share of that thunder when he forced Jones to submit to a Boston crab to win the semi–official colored title.

Before the pair clashed just across the Detroit River in Windsor, Ontario, *The Windsor Star* elaborated on the heated rivalry that had been brewing between the two, beginning its article by opining that "rivalry between colored athletes often reaches an amazingly high point." *The Star* also added that it was "very seldom that colored men meet in wrestling or boxing," with the point regarding boxing being easily disproven.

"Rough" Rufus Jones

"Claybourne, from South Africa, is an amiable, easy-going grappler not easily angered; Jones, from Georgia, is an excitable and troublesome rascal," added *The Star*. "Claybourne is proud of his position in the mat world; Jones is envious of it. Claybourne is a hero, whereas Jones is a villain. Where Jack gets cheers, Rufus gets jeers — and criticism in physical forms less pleasant."

The two fittingly dueled to a draw during their first meeting in Detroit, with the match ending on a "head-on collision" between the two that resulted in a double knockout. Regardless of the official result, all of the talk after the match was about the sensational "hurdle hold" employed by Gentleman Jack to nearly score a fall against Rough Rufus just prior to the bout's conclusion.

"Rough Rufus was hiding behind the six-foot-two frame of Referee Verne Clark. Time and again, Gentleman Jack tried to circle Referee Clark, but try as Mr. Clark would, he could not get out of the way. Rough Rufus dodged with Clark," described *The Free Press*. "Disgusted, Gentleman Jack, unable to get around Clark, suddenly gave a leap, vaulted nimbly over the referee's head, and came down with a body scissors on the surprised Rufus. Jones eventually broke it, and a moment later the collision occurred."

Claybourne won the Detroit rematch between the two Black grapplers, along with their first bout in Canada. Their next bout, hosted by the Hamilton Sporting Club, was billed as a multi-fall match for the colored light heavyweight title, and Claybourne landed the only fall of a fight that was described as "so intense that neither grappler paid the slightest attention to the final bell and had to be pried apart when the limit was up."

Jack defeated Rufus by taking him down with a series of flying headlocks and then locking him in a crab hold. Seemingly infuriated by losing a fall to the Gentleman, Rufus escalated the violence of the match to suit his style.

"On his return to the ring, Rufus continued his rough tactics, using eye gouges and rabbit punches on the South African, and resorted to the ropes frequently," stated *The Spectator*. "Jones applied a punishing self strangle, but Claybourne returned the favour with a series of elbow smashes. Running the ropes, Jones jumped out of the ring followed by Claybourne, continuing the bout for an interval on the ground. On their return to the ring, neither man was able to secure the

A Decided Novelty

advantage, and Claybourne was banging Jones' head against the posts at the gong. The bell had no effect as they continued to trade elbow smashes a short time after the gong."

Jack had temporarily emerged as the victor, but the momentum would swing when the scene shifted to Kentucky. When Jones arrived in Louisville intent on battling Claybourne, *The Courier-Journal* lauded his "unblemished record" of "300 victories in four years of competition."

Rufus's phony undefeated streak was kept intact when he bested Claybourne, whom *The Courier-Journal* described as "the fastest thing since Jesse Owens" who "kept the crowd in an uproar, with his rubber-legged antics and kangaroo kicks."

Jones smashed Claybourne to the canvas to take the first fall, and Claybourne retaliated with his dropkicks to take the second. In the third, Claybourne missed a dropkick and landed on his head, allowing Jones to retain the Negro heavyweight championship that he had allegedly arrived with.

Later in the year, Jones lost a main-event, best-of-three-falls match in Battle Creek to Abe Greenberg, which would rank as just one of many main-event bouts by Jones in the state of Michigan if not for the description of the bout's second fall. Down one fall to zero, Jones used his head in an unorthodox fashion to even the score.

"Jones won the second fall in five minutes with a body slam and press after butting Greenberg in the head several times," recorded *The Battle Creek Moon-Journal*.

It's true that Jones had drawn attention to the leaping delivery of his headbutts before, but this report from *The Moon-Journal* describes one of the first instances of Jones stringing together several headbutts in succession to overwhelm his adversaries.

While Jones continued to cause mayhem in Michigan during fall 1938, the New England area was graced by the presence of Tiger Flowers, or at least someone wrestling under the name Tiger Flowers.

This version of Flowers appeared at the show of Sam Price at the Boston Arena on October 19 and remained in the

A Decided Novelty

region until winter ended in early 1939. This would be the first of multiple imposter Flowers who would appear over the years, as "Tiger Flowers" — like "The Black Panther" — had figuratively fallen into the public domain of names that any Black wrestler could apparently use.

As 1939 opened, George Godfrey's relative inactivity had some wrestling promoters attempting to tear him down to build others. In trying to elevate Seelie Samara before one of his appearances in Harrisburg, Pennsylvania — in Godfrey's home state, no less — *The Evening News* repeated the claim that Samara was the most successful Black wrestler since Reginald Siki, while adding that Godfrey had tried his hand at wrestling, "but was pinned too often by fourth- and fifth-raters and soon gave up the idea of becoming a grappler."

This retelling of Godfrey's career intentionally overlooked the fact that George had actively competed as a pro wrestler multiple times every year since 1931 and had usually been booked as an unstoppable force. Moreover, Godfrey was announced for a multi-month series of wrestling appearances in California the very next day after this insulting summary of his wrestling career was set in ink. However, the statement about Godfrey having been pinned by fourth- and fifth-raters would prove to be uncomfortably prophetic.

It soon became apparent that the 300-plus-pound Godfrey was now utterly lacking in ring stamina, mobility, and interest, and seemed to care about the quality of his wrestling even less than he had when he was younger and lighter.

In San Francisco in late January, the International News Service reported that Godfrey defeated Al Billings in three minutes with a right-hand punch to the stomach. Three days later in Oakland, he bested Art Shires in two-and-a-half minutes with a bear hug. In Modesto, he downed Shires two falls to none in a best-of-three-falls encounter in under three minutes with bear hugs. In Sacramento, he similarly submitted Charles Rainere with a bear hug in 2 minutes, 19 seconds.

Whether the promoters and bookers changed their minds about Godfrey, or whether George made the decision to pull the plug on his wrestling career and be generous on his way out is unknown. What is clear is that the enormous ex-boxer soon started to lose nearly every match he was involved in, and in times as alarmingly short as those he used to win with. This is best exemplified by a bout he lost to Hardboiled Haggerty in San Francisco in late March, which culminated in Godfrey being pinned in just 56 seconds.

During this period, what might have been a bright spot for Godfrey's legacy went unreported. A bout between George Godfrey and Tiger Jack Nelson was booked in Los Angeles in July and was billed as being for Nelson's "colored title belt." The reports from the aftermath of the event do not reveal the result of the Godfrey-Nelson bout, if it even happened. There were other advertised bouts from the show for which no results were provided; the match also appears to have been the last of Jack Nelson's career.

For what it's worth, Godfrey showed up in Arizona a few months later claiming to be the colored champion, but there is no further information provided that would suggest he acquired the right to claim that title at Nelson's expense. Regardless, reviews of the once proud fighter's matches from this period of time onward frequently included the word "disappointing" in their descriptions. This was true of one of Godfrey's bouts at the Phoenix Madison Square Garden against the Turk, which *The Arizona Republic* referred to as "the biggest disappointment," and a showing that was "in the flop class."

It was at the conclusion of this short run of appearances in Arizona that Godfrey's in-ring career was essentially over, save for some exhibition bouts at Army benefit shows during World War II, which also occasionally included some wrestling.

When assessed in terms of its overall significance to Black wrestling history, 1939 was all about Seelie Samara. In March, *Le Devoir* of Montreal reported that promoter Ray Lamontagne had contacted wrestling star Heinie Olson and was attempting to bring him in for a bout with "the famous

A Decided Novelty

Negro athlete Zelis Amhara." This served notice to wrestling fans in the Montreal region that Amhara was being brought back for what was becoming a semi-regular series of spring and summer appearances.

Le Devoir described Amhara as significantly tougher than he had been presented in other territories, offering that "before being a wrestler, the Ethiopian was a boxer of great value" who "is able to take the hardest blows."

Amhara arrived alongside fellow returning wrestling star Harry Madison, and the two were quickly placed on a collision course with one another, with *Le Devoir* referring to Amhara as "the scientist, and fast colored wrestler."

After defeating Madison on April 12, Amhara was rewarded with a world junior heavyweight championship match against Clement Durocher the following week on Monday, April 17. It was on that date that Samara defeated Durocher to record his first attainment of a nominal "world" championship that occurred inside a ring.

Moreover, following a title defense one week later, *Le Devoir* reported "Amhara demonstrated last night at the Saint-Jacques Market Hall that he truly has the right to be the junior heavyweight champion by triumphing over Graham Stockton in the main event prepared by promoter Ray Lamontagne, because after losing the first fall to the Verdun athlete, the Ethiopian was able to take the other two falls without being put in danger."

Now being booked as a dominant wrestler, Amhara still expressed his public displeasure with promoter Lamontagne, whose booking of a Black wrestler like Amhara had been downright progressive by North American standards. After signing a contract to face Jack Remillard, Amhara was quoted as making unkind statements about Lamontagne.

"Lamontagne promised me a match with [Victor] Delamarre, but he seems to have forgotten everything," complained Amhara to *Le Devoir*. "Is he afraid of seeing me defeat your strongman, or is it Victor who is afraid? I beat Madison, Durocher, Stockton, and Monday night it will be

Remillard's turn, with all due respect to the latter, and then I sincerely hope that Lamontagne will match me against the strongman from Lac Bouchette."

Amhara strengthened his title claim with a mid-May victory over former champion Durocher at the Marche Saint-Jacques Hall, as *Le Devoir* chalked it up as just another win for "the junior heavyweight champion," who was being booked unprecedentedly well for an unmistakably Black wrestler in a North American wrestling territory, with the lone exception of George Godfrey.

"After losing the first fall to his opponent in 17 minutes, the Black champion came back to the charge to take the other two decisively in 12 and 10 minutes respectively," stated *Le Devoir*.

Amhara's championship reign was stopped after just over a month when he was defeated by Harry Madison on May 29, but it was far from a definitive victory. *Le Devoir* recorded how Madison won the first fall in 18 minutes, only for Amhara to injure his leg three minutes after the action resumed. The referee then awarded the fall, the match, and the championship to Madison.

The unsatisfying finish only served to fuel demand for a rematch, and the return engagement was held on June 26. In a lengthy encounter, Amhara scored what *Le Devoir* described as "an amazing revenge" by recapturing the world junior heavyweight championship.

"It was only after 51.14 minutes that the famous Ethiopian managed to secure the first fall of the fight, but 34.06 minutes later, the brutal wrestler from Verdun equalized the exchanges, with the Boston Crab hold," described *Le Devoir*. "In trying to apply this hold again, Madison was trapped by the Negro, who was on his guard, and Amhara took advantage of it to secure the decisive fall in 3 minutes."

An underrated feature to Amhara's tenure as a world champion in Montreal is how seamlessly it was squeezed into the rest of his touring schedule. During the same time period, Amhara was making appearances in Ontario and Michigan as

Seelie Samara, and regularly competing in the ring against Rufus Jones. The two had been waging a particularly brutal war with each other in Battle Creek, where both men were said to be "representatives of the Southern race."

In fact, on the very night Amhara recaptured the world title from Madison, Jones was booked for a rare reappearance in Montreal under his restored identity as Tiger Flowers. Both wrestlers resumed their familiar Ontario and Michigan stage names of Samara and Jones the following day.

Now a two-time holder of Montreal's version of the world junior heavyweight championship, Amhara's appearances in Montreal became more sporadic as the summer wound down. The Ethiopian, who would have been far more accurately described as a Georgian transplant from Western Massachusetts, spent the bulk of his summer making appearances in Michigan and Ontario with nary a mention of his world title status in the French-Canadian province being uttered in other territories.

One of the cruel ironies of this world title reign is that Samara was receiving far more bookings around the Midwest than he was in Canada, but the manner in which he was depicted elsewhere wasn't nearly as favorable as it was in Quebec. While he may have been the chief headliner in Montreal as Zelis Amhara, Seelie Samara was simply another unsuccessful challenger for the light heavyweight title defended by the Great Mephisto in Ontario.

The migration of Samara out of New England and into Ontario and the American Midwest marked the beginning of what could either be called the "Murderer's Row" era of Black American wrestling, or less ominously, the "Four Kings" era.

Both are terms borrowed from specific eras of boxing history. The former is a reference to a set of phenomenal Black boxers spearheaded by Charley Burley, Eddie Booker and Lloyd Marshall.

All were Black fighters who were considered among the best of their era, yet these feared fighters were never given opportunities to compete for the sanctioned world titles, and instead were relegated to continually fighting one another for what amounted to the championship of their personal peer group.

The Four Kings designation is a term applied to Ray Leonard, Marvin Haggler, Thomas Hearns, and Roberto Duran — the four boxers who waged war with each other in the 1970s and 1980s, and dominated the boxing scene in the weight classes below the heavyweight division.

In professional wrestling, a variation of both themes can be applied to the grouping of Jack Claybourne, Rufus Jones, Jim Mitchell, and Seelie Samara.

The four members of this group would spend the better part of the next 12 years in constant engagement with one another — as both allies and adversaries — as they traded mythical championships that were spontaneously created for them. Each was a Black wrestler who was routinely excluded from winning championships for the bulk of their careers, which was owed to the widespread reluctance on the part of promoters and bookers to crown Black grapplers as the supreme stars of their territories.

On the occasion of Samara's first U.S. appearance under that name outside New England, *The Courier-Post* referred to him as "the only Negro heavyweight in the U.S." Although this was only true in a technical sense, predicated on the choice of Reginald Siki to wrestle in Europe, and the nebulous status of George Godfrey as a serious wrestler, Samara was clearly the truest heavyweight out of all the serious wrestlers in his peer group.

The Patriot of Harrisburg, Pennsylvania added further seasoning to the discussion after shaving a full decade from the 34-year-old Samara's age by referring to him as a "24-year-old lad from Boston."

"Only one other Negro, Reginald Siki, has been as successful as Samara in the rough and tumble sport," added *The Patriot*. "Big George Godfrey, a former pugilist, tried his hand at wrestling but was pinned too often and gave up the idea of becoming a grappler."

For all intents and purposes, *The Patriot* had its story backwards; Siki's win-loss record was not particularly favorable during his time in the U.S., and he had essentially abandoned the U.S. for Europe. Meanwhile, George Godfrey, despite his lack of mastery of the finer points of professional wrestling, had tasted defeat with far less frequency, and for a brief moment had been one of the most impressive and consistent drawing cards in U.S. wrestling history.

Continuing its description of Samara's background, *The Patriot* described him as a protege of John Pesek, who had allegedly discovered Samara while the Black grappler was working as the strongman of a traveling circus, and "marveled at the Negro lad's feats of strength."

The Pesek story was an appeal to the great popularity of Pesek in the Tri-state area. With the activity of "The Nebraska Tiger Man" confined primarily to Ohio, New York, New Jersey, and Pennsylvania during the years of Samara's discovery and development, there is no way to make a connection between Pesek and a Black wrestler who spent his earliest years wrestling in relative obscurity in Springfield, Massachusetts.

Given his general inactivity in Montreal, it was almost a foregone conclusion that Amhara's mid-September match against Larry Raymond would signal his surrender of the world junior heavyweight championship. After a two-and-a-half-month world title reign that involved very few appearances in Quebec as champion or otherwise, Amhara lost his world championship in Montreal to Larry Raymond.

Upon making his exit from the circuit of Michigan, Ontario, and Quebec that had become the norm for him, Samara ventured to Illinois, where *The Freeport Journal-Standard* introduced him as "The Ethiopian Menace," "a real strong man," and "the best in the business at anticipating the movements of his foes and outguessing them."

News reports would suggest that this final description was apparently untrue, as Samara's fellow wrestler Charles "Gorilla" Grubmeyer would allegedly learn. In mid-November, it was reported that during an October 2 match between the two men, Samara and Grubmeyer were involved in one of the most shocking episodes of biting ever depicted inside of a wrestling ring.

According to reports from the International News Service, Samara and Grubmeyer were engaged in a "minor brawl" at the White City venue in Chicago, during which Grubmeyer allowed his fingers to linger in Samara's mouth for too long. The end result was that Samara's teeth clamped down on Grubmeyer's right middle finger, nearly removing it in a single bite. Six weeks later, Grubmeyer's infected finger was formally amputated by the medical staff of Chicago's John B. Murphy Hospital.

The problem with this tale is that *Le Devoir* reported Samara was still busy wrestling as Zelis Amhara that very same night in Montreal against Harry Madison — a match that Amhara lost by disqualification. In essence, unless there was serious confusion with respect to the dates involved, the story was fabricated to turn the unrelated misfortune of Grubmeyer's lost finger into a future wrestling angle intended to attract fans.

Predictably, the story of Grubmeyer's lost finger and Samara's alleged role in its loss carried the news at least as far as Southern California, roughly 2,000 miles from the westernmost extent of Samara's wrestling activities up until that time.

With the core quartet of Black wrestling talent from the era squarely established, Black wrestlers were now racking up wins at an unprecedented pace, and even occasional championships. Still, on a continent with as many wrestling territories as North America, there was plenty of room for even more influential talent to make its mark, and the unveiling of perhaps the most aggressive social boundary pusher of the era was on the horizon.

A Decided Novelty

15 – The Dark Angel

For Jim Mitchell, 1939 was punctuated by victories over two of his key contemporaries. This included his first interaction with Rufus Jones, which would ultimately lead to a long-term on-again, off-again, partner-adversary relationship that would last for more than a decade.

The first bout between the two took place in Dayton, Ohio, in what was advertised as "marking the first time two colored wrestlers have been brought together into the same ring locally" by *The Dayton Daily News*. Meanwhile, *The Dayton Daily Herald* upgraded the significance of the bout by declaring it to be a contest with the colored light heavyweight championship on the line.

Curiously, which of the two men was supposed to have been the reigning titleholder on the evening of the bout was never mentioned, but by the end of the night it didn't matter. *The Herald* reported that the "extremely cagey Negro" known as the Black Panther had taken Rufus to task with "a series of rope flips" to win their bout in 13½ minutes.

Mitchell also made his triumphant return to Louisville in April to battle "Gentleman" Jack Claybourne. A feature article in *The Courier-Journal* offered what was probably a reasonable timeline for the start of the Panther's wrestling career by stating that the "ebony-hued lad" had begun wrestling nine years earlier by occasionally filling in on local wrestling programs.

Known for his snow-white trunks and apparent absence of a catchy nickname, the Panther was said to have been referred to by fans as 'The Black and White.'

"He was plenty green, too, back in those days, but certainly not 'yellow'; very smart, also, for a wrestler, but not the smart-alecky type like most beginners, and World Welterweight Champion Jack Reynolds, Joe Parelli, and many of the other topnotchers of the era took a liking to him, and taught him the trade tricks," continued the article.

A Decided Novelty

This article served as one of the first clear resources linking Mitchell's training and development to Reynolds and Parelli, which would be a story that was repeated in several other publications in the years to come.

Mitchell's hometown return was successful, as he took two out of three falls from Jack Claybourne at the Columbia Gymnasium. Ironically, the lone fall that Claybourne captured from the Panther came by way of an airplane spin, the one move that Mitchell insisted in Los Angeles that there was a gentleman's agreement to never wield against him.

Right before his September bout against Claybourne, *The Courier-Journal* described Mitchell as a "former valet service employee" who had overcome humble beginnings to forge a successful wrestling career.

In August and September, Mitchell could be found working on the same shows as Claybourne in both Dayton and Cincinnati, albeit with the Cincinnati shows containing the odd wrinkle of Claybourne performing under the name Pablo Hernandez and being labeled as a "Cuban Negro."

Claybourne would later claim that this name change was necessitated by a Cincinnati law prohibiting American Blacks from entering local wrestling rings; that restriction had apparently been lifted by April 1939, when Mitchell appeared in Cincinnati listed as an "American-born Negro" while Claybourne retained his fake identity as a Cuban national.

Following George Godfrey's 1931 announcement that he would soon begin wrestling as a means of maintaining his in-ring activity despite being suspended by major boxing commissions, some municipalities passed laws banning the participation of Blacks in wrestling primarily as a means of targeting Godfrey. The temporary Cincinnati restriction on Black wrestlers appears to have been the result of one of these anti-Godfrey rulings.

Mitchell and Claybourne would reconnect in Akron during the month of June, wrestling to a 30-minute draw in a setting with considerably less fanfare attached in comparison to their Louisville meeting. The pair also worked collaboratively in

A Decided Novelty

a match against Stacey Hall and the Great Mephisto, with their team failing to operate cohesively as a unit.

"The Black Panther" Jim Mitchell

"The Negro team was moving along on even terms when a misguided punch started the fireworks and set the stage for its defeat," declared *The Dayton Daily News*. "Claybourne drew a bead on Hall's jaw and let fly, but the blow went awry, landing instead on the Panther, who figured the wallop intentional and a double-cross. It was an easy matter then for Hall and Mephisto to nail the disorganized pair."

A Decided Novelty

After having his falling out with Mitchell, Claybourne would also find himself engaged in combat with Samara, except that these matches would take place in Louisville, and the first in-ring meeting between Samara and Claybourne in August 1939 ended in a Claybourne victory. *The Courier-Journal* illustrated how Jack rebounded from surrendering the first fall to Samara by capturing the two successive falls with a "kangaroo kick" and his own version of a "monkey shake."

Coincidentally, since Samara was the reigning world junior heavyweight champion of Montreal at the time of the match, Gentleman Jack would have been able to claim a clean victory over a reigning world champion if Samara's status as a titleholder had been advertised at the time. For quite a while, Claybourne found victories over former and current champions to be altogether elusive.

Jack would then have another match at the Allen Athletic Club of Louisville against Mitchell, with advertisements stating that both men were hoping to win the bout and move on to "a return engagement with the recognized world's Negro heavyweight champion, Rufus Jones." The multi-fall bout was contested with a 55-minute time limit in place, and the lone fall registered was awarded to Mitchell shortly after the 40-minute mark, as he caught Claybourne with a flying mare for the pin.

In October, Michigan welcomed another young wrestler who is rarely connected with the core group of Black talent that started wrestling in the early 1930s, Don Blackman, who was wrestling as "Dynamite" Blackman.

Don Blackman was born on May 12, 1912 in Alabama, and the feature article on Blackman that appeared in *The Michigan Chronicle* referred to Blackman as a five-year mat veteran who was 26 years old.

In actuality, this would have been a far more accurate description of Jones, who was 26 years old with just over five years of ring experience at the time the article was written. Meanwhile, Blackman was actually 27 years old. There was no evidence that he had wrestled anywhere prior to his appearance

A Decided Novelty

in Detroit in fall 1939, at least not under any variation of his real name.

At the same time, Blackman's general size and appearance, coupled with his reported presence on the East Coast of the United States, makes him an excellent candidate to have been the wrestler who appeared briefly as Tiger Flowers in the Northeast during that latter part of 1938 and very early in 1939.

In an interview years later, Blackman would claim to have caught the bus from his hometown of Birmingham, Alabama to New York City when he was only 17 years old, at which point he began training to be a professional wrestler "just to get in shape." If true, this means that Blackman would have been a fully trained wrestler by 1930, and physically capable of performing in the Tiger Flowers role.

Over the course of his feature article from *The Chronicle*, Blackman made a few statements that would support this theory. He cited New York, New England and Cuba as three locations that were critical to his development. New York was the most frequent wrestling area of the original Tiger Flowers, New England was the region where the Tiger Flowers who emerged in 1938 and 1939 had all of his matches, and Cuba was the original nation offered as a birthplace for the Tiger Flowers character.

The same article saw Blackman denouncing Rufus Jones — who had played the most iconic version of Tiger Flowers — as "one of the dirtiest wrestlers he has ever seen," after Blackman had concluded a public training session at the YMCA of Saginaw.

Despite what seemed like an aggressive callout of Jones, Blackman didn't last in Michigan for more than a week before heading out to the West Coast to wrestle under the name of "The Dark Angel" — another one of Joe Louis' recurring nicknames.

Instead of battling Blackman, Jones engaged in further battles with Gentleman Jack, with the most vivid descriptions of their matches being supplied by Canadian publications.

A Decided Novelty

The Daily Record described one of the matches between Jones and Claybourne as "the wildest show of the night, with Gentleman Jack leading Jones on a merry parade." With Claybourne leading the bout one fall to zero, Rufus grabbed Jack by the hair and tossed him out to the arena floor. When the incensed Claybourne climbed back into the ring and returned the favor to Rufus, fill-in referee Meniaci disqualified him and awarded the fall to Jones.

"Claybourne was furious," added *The Daily Record*. "He sent Jones reeling with a hard smash and then turned on the referee. Jones recovered and gained his feet only to go smashing back to the mat with Meniaci following suit. Finally, Jones made a dash for the dressing room and Jack followed, jumping over the ropes. At this point the brawl was halted by police officers who separated the two."

Jack and Rufus were also on opposing sides of an elimination tag team match in Windsor, with the writer of the promotional piece for *The Windsor Star* having the rare wherewithal to recognize that ethnic differences applied to Blacks just as plainly as they did to other groups.

"[The match] pits two Negro-White teams against each other, and to add to its colorful qualities, it brings into contention four different nationalities," the article explained. "Hart is a Hollander, Kasaboski is a Polish-Canadian, Jones is an American Negro, and Claybourne an African Negro. With all those spices, it should prove a tempting dish before the expiration of the hour time limit that has been allowed for its consumption."

The bout itself was a further display of Jones' versatility as an entertainer. Early in the match, Jones played the role of the cowardly instigator, and urged his partner Kasaboski to attack Claybourne while Rufus kept a safe distance. On two of those occasions, Jones actually shoved his partner forward, and both times Kasaboski's chin was met by the raised feet of Gentleman Jack. Kasaboski understandably grew weary of this tactical approach.

A Decided Novelty

"If words couldn't convince Rufus that Kasaboski didn't like the Jones strategy, action could. He turned on his partner in crime, gave him a mighty elbow sock, and crashed him to the mat," illustrated *The Star*. "It was Claybourne's big chance. He took it. He piled on top of both his opponents, and before they knew it Jones had been pinned."

Claybourne was ultimately awarded the victory when Kasaboski got fed up, attacked the referee, and drew the disqualification.

Jones may have suffered the loss, but *The Star* would credit him with being "unquestionably the most entertaining team wrestler yet to be seen in these parts — and there have been more than a few of them."

In Hamilton, Jones had continued to tweak elements of his wrestling style to accentuate one move in particular. It was a style that would eventually come to define him, and *The Journal Times* noted that his style had "no buts about it, but plenty of butts." Dizzy Davis became one of the primary victims of Jones' evolving offense, which depended heavily on the use of his head.

"Dizzy had been up to his usual tactics of hair pulling and use of the ropes, and it finally got on the wrong side of the dusky lad's skin," the paper explained. "At the first opportunity, Jones grabbed Davis by the ears and soundly rapped him on the head, using his own noggin as a battering ram. Davis took about five good solid knocks like that and then went down on his knees. He got up once more, and again Jones battered him down by socking his head against Davis'. This time, Dizzy stayed down for the count."

Davis mounted a comeback in the second fall, choking Jones, and inspiring *The Journal Times* to employ the racialized humor of likening the image of Jones' tongue sticking out of his Black visage as being as conspicuous as "the white spot on the eight ball." Once he managed to free himself from Davis' grip, Jones returned to his headbutting attack.

"Again and again, he pounded his solid head like a sledgehammer against Dizzy's head, battering him to the floor," the article continued. "Then he picked him up and pounded some more, until the referee raised the colored boy's hand in victory."

This bout introduced a standard Jones trope, involving a marked overreliance on headbutts to pummel opponents into submission, along with a method of winning matches dishonorably, by forcing a referee's stoppage due to either concussion concerns, or blood loss.

Following that sudden outpouring of headbutts, *The Journal Times* took to referring to Jones as "Knothead," suggesting that the wrestler's butting explosion would become an ordinary occurrence.

"Rufus, whose name might be spelled 'rough house,' uses his head when he wrestles, but not in the manner others do," stated the article. "Rufus uses his head as a battering ram to beat his opponent to the floor by bumping his head."

The end of 1939 treated fans to a sight so rare that it had never been seen before, and would never see again, when Jack Claybourne, Rufus Jones, Jim Mitchell and Seelie Samara all competed against one another at the Detroit Arena Gardens in a blindfold battle royal.

While it may have been intended as a callback to the racist practice of having a group of unskilled Black combatants brutalize one another at the outset of a pro wrestling event, this moment in 1939 is best viewed through the lens of progress. After all, a considerable amount of change had to occur within the wrestling industry in order for four full-fledged Black wrestling stars to simultaneously compete within the same wrestling ring. Just one decade earlier, promoters had considered it a luxury to find even one.

Way out west, it was announced by *The Seattle Star* that King Kong Clayton, "the top negro matman in the United States," was among the performers that wrestling fans in the Evergreen State should expect to see soon.

Despite this announcement, Clayton was looking far more like a wrestler who was on his way out of the business. Motivated by the box office success of Clayton's clash with

A Decided Novelty

Tommy Lynch, Calgary fight promoter Darby Melnyck quickly lined up another fight for the region's most active boxer-wrestler. This time it was a heavyweight fight against "Young" Tunney Lust.

In the words of *The Edmonton Bulletin*, Clayton relied on a "two-fisted attack" to score a third-round technical knockout over Lust. In the wake of Clayton's third victory inside of a Canadian boxing ring in the space of five months, *The Albertan* declared Clayton to be "the man who rules heavyweight boxers in Southern Alberta" even when promoting his wrestling appearances.

Following his victory over Lust, Clayton was recruited as an official sparring partner for Eddie Wenstob as he prepared for this Canadian title fight with Tiger Warrington. Before joining Wenstob's training camp, Clayton took part in a notoriously brutal match in Edmonton against Bob Cummings.

"Half a dozen chairs were broken — one of them by Cummings over the negro's head — as they took time out of the ring to give the nearer customers a close-up of the grunting game," stated *The Edmonton Journal*.

In the middle of Wenstob's training camp, Clayton appeared for his fourth sanctioned boxing match on Canadian soil, this time against Joe Lindgren. Analyzing Clayton's pre-fight workouts, the writers from Canadian news publications were now taking Clayton deathly seriously as a fighter, having now watched him defeat three fighters, two of whom had respectable resumes.

"Clayton, in three rounds of shadow boxing, showed all the trickiness that has carried him to victory after victory in a long career in the ring," opined *The Calgary Albertan*. "In three rounds with the heavy bag, he thrilled onlookers with the power of his one-two, fake-and-hit K.O. blows that make most of his record a list of knockouts over clever opponents."

Between the time Clayton migrated from the South to the West and made his debut inside of a Canadian boxing ring, he had added at least two knockout losses to his record, which

A Decided Novelty

went unmentioned by the Canadian press. If the promoters had intentionally hidden those losses from public consumption, there would be no way to hide the third such defeat, as Lindgren knocked Clayton out in the sixth round of their bout.

"Joe Lindgren stopped the colored puncher, King Kong Clayton, ex-sparring mate of Joe Louis, later wrestler, now heavyweight boxer, with a knockout in the sixth round at Calgary the other night, the day the king and queen were in that Canadian town," reported *The Missoulian*. "King Kong had stopped Eddie Shelton and Tunney Lust at Calgary and was such a big card that the promoters are now provoked at Joe for knocking King Kong into a loop."

In the end, Clayton may have been a victim of his own refusal to devote himself wholeheartedly to improving his boxing conditioning. Remaining true to form, Clayton started fast and knocked Lindgren to the canvas in the first round of their bout, only for Lindgren to recover, drop Clayton for a nine-count in the fifth round, and then end the fight with a two-punch combination in the sixth round.

With the loss to Lindgren presumably ending his brief run as a featured boxer in Alberta, Clayton returned to wrestling in Montana briefly before departing from the region where he had spent the bulk of his wrestling career to make his debut in Oregon. His arrival touched off one of the most direct acknowledgements of racial discord ever displayed during a professional wrestling angle.

When Clayton made his appearance at the Armory in Eugene, Oregon as the mystery opponent recruited by promoter Herb Owen to face Babe Small, the villainous Small announced to the crowd of 2,150 spectators that he would "be damned if I wrestle a nigger," and stormed out.

Instead of facing Small, Clayton defeated Georgie Kitzmiller in two falls, using "a combination arm and leg stopper" to win both. Small then purportedly received an edict from National Wrestling Association president Harry Landry, declaring that Small's wrestling career would be forfeited if he refused to face Clayton one-on-one.

Small accepted the offer, but doubled down on his racism, telling fans to remain in their seats while he "annihilates the nigger."

"If I have to wrestle a nigger, I'm going to do it my way," Small told *The Register-Guard* of Eugene. "I'm going to beat him so bad that yellow streak will show up like a state highway center line. That's why I'm bringing my friend Joe Gosky with me to keep the fans from stopping the murder."

To the credit of Herb Owen, the over-the-top racist in the feud was plainly cast in the role of villain, and on the night of the big match, 3,000 fans packed the Armory in Eugene to watch Small receive his comeuppance. The match certainly began with disappointment, as Small assaulted Clayton from the outset and quickly captured the first fall.

"There wasn't anything Small left untried as he pummeled the negro about the ring and finally downed him in 8 minutes with a figure-four toe hold," reported *The Register-Guard*.

At the tail end of the second fall, Clayton was knocked out of the ring and into the ringside seats, but re-entered and peppered Small with punches before evening the fall tally with a "leg corkscrew." The ending to the match may have required improvisation from the match participants, as fan involvement possibly threw off the execution of the third fall.

"During the final fall, Small's second was attacked by spectators after he tried to pass a 'gimmick' to his partner for a second time during the match," continued *The Register-Guard*. "Elton Owen and Ernie Piluso led him through the crowd unharmed."

The ending of the match, while technically a victory for Clayton, surely left many of the people in the crowd disappointed, as Small was ultimately disqualified for kneeing Clayton in the groin, and then attempting to blind him by grinding peanut shells into his eyes.

A Decided Novelty

Days later, a tag team contest that would immediately rematch the pair was announced, as Small requested just one more shot "at that nigger, and any other guy that's as black as him."

For the rematch, Clayton was given Ernie Piluso as a partner, while Bob Cummings sided with Small, and Clayton and Piluso got their hands raised when Cummings and Small were disqualified.

As the hullabaloo surrounding his arrival died down, Clayton settled into what was primarily a middle-of-the-card role in Oregon, although his presence was still played up for historical purposes. *The Medford Mail Tribune* reported in October how a popular vote was required to authorize Clayton's appearance. When Clayton showed in Klamath Falls during that same month to wrestle Pete Belcastro, he was declared to be "the first colored wrestler ever to appear in Southern Oregon."

In Medford, Clayton resumed his practice of beating up Adolph Hitler analogues when he defeated Hans Hitler Schultz, with *The Mail Tribune* specifically referring to Schultz as a Nazi after Nazi Germany had already invaded the western half of Poland and split the now occupied nation with the Soviet Union.

As he prepared to face Schultz in Klamath Falls, *The Evening Herald* noted that the foremost obstacle working against Clayton upon his entry to Oregon was "a feeling that he is considered an inferior grappler because of race prejudice."

Before his Klamath Falls bout with Schultz, Clayton was also said to have been a master of the headbutt, which is the first time the signature maneuver of Rufus Jones was ever directly named as a favorite of Clayton's. More to the point, the writer seemed to be preemptively inserting the promoter's suggestions for how Clayton had been advised to wrestle into the pre-match coverage, because King Kong went on to defeat Schultz with a flurry of Claybourne-style dropkicks, and with no Jones-style headbutting mentioned in the match report.

A Decided Novelty

Once again adopted as "the Joe Louis of wrestling," except this time by Oregonians, Clayton was set to face off with former world champion Bob Kenneston. In the meantime, he began wrestling in Northern California as well. When Clayton made his debut in that region, he was described in far less flattering terms, like "The Congo Giant."

"King Kong Clayton" grapples with Bob Kenneston

"Clayton, who has been dubbed the Gorilla because of his likeness to the animal, and because of his gorilla-like backbreaker, will meet all he can handle in [Herb] Parks," remarked *The Chico Record*.

In Klamath, Clayton's "thick skull" finally came into play, albeit as much for its resilience as it was for its offensive effectiveness. As Clayton chased Kenneston out of the ring and "down into the laps of the ringside customers," Kenneston hoisted a chair aloft and "konked the negro over the head with the steel rungs." Clayton struggled to climb back into the ring, and when he did, he was easy prey for Kenneston's uppercuts, and the subsequent three-count pinfall.

A Decided Novelty

In Marysville, California, Clayton got his revenge. *The Appeal-Democrat* reported that after Kenneston won the first fall with a backbreaker, Clayton responded by "slamming Kenneston with a 'chin hold' and finished him off with four backflips. Kenneston was subsequently disqualified for fouling Clayton.

Finally, in their Klamath Falls rematch, "the ivory-skulled Alabaman" finished Kenneston off quickly in a bout *The Evening Herald* called "the wildest main event Klamath Falls has seen in many a day." The entire best-of-three-falls match reportedly lasted a total of four minutes.

"Kicking and jumping like an enraged colt, the chocolate-colored southerner was too cagey for the southern Oregon swivel hold artist," stated *The Herald*. "Clayton picked him up like a sack of spuds and tossed him over the ropes, but Kenneston dragged himself back into the ring. Then Clayton clamped on a headscissors to win the initial tumble in just 3:30 after the bout began."

Enraged at surrendering the quick pinfall, Kenneston charged Clayton in the corner and uppercutted him during the intermission, but Clayton retaliated in kind. When the bell finally sounded to signal the start of the second fall, Clayton quickly whipped Kenneston to the canvas headfirst with a snapmare. Then Clayton sent Kenneston high into the air with a move that sounds like a high backdrop, and then covered him for the second pinfall.

That December, Clayton teamed up with another Black wrestler in Eugene, who was known simply as "The Angel," to compete against the villainous tandem of Bob Kenneston and Prince Ilaki.

"'The Angel,' a Harlem importation, proved to be all Clayton promised and kept the meanies in hot water during the first minutes of the match," declared Jack Wells Jr. of *The Register-Guard*.

The match was all even at one fall apiece when "The Angel" fell prey to a series of hard dropkicks and was dismissed with a body press while Clayton struggled in vain to save his partner." As inauspicious as it may have been, the Eugene crowd had just witnessed one of the first matches in the career of Don Blackman, who had just made his way westward after his match in Michigan against Rufus Jones never materialized.

When Jim Mitchell traveled back to Southern California in 1940, he also ran into Blackman, who had amended his nickname to "Dark Angel." He and Mitchell were declared in *The Los Angeles Time*s to be the first Black wrestlers to wrestle at the Hollywood Legion Stadium.

Because Mitchell had begun to employ several versions of headlocks to end his matches, including standing headlocks and bulldogging headlocks in the style of Gorilla Parker, it is difficult to tell precisely when he began to use his defining submission hold, the hip headlock. It was also a challenge for many people to discern exactly what was meant by the term "hip headlock" until the maneuver was provided with another name several years later.

To apply the hip headlock, the Panther would trap his opponent's left leg with his own left leg, thereby pinning his adversary's left foot to the mat. Then he would wrap his own body behind that of his opponent by locking his opponent's right arm behind his left arm as he reached behind the trapped wrestler's neck. Mitchell would then bring his right arm down across his opponent's chest and neck and interlock his fingers beneath his opponent's chin.

The name of the move would later become standardized as the cobra twist, while a variation of the hold — omitting the interlocking of the fingers — would acquire the name of the abdominal stretch. At the Hollywood Legion Stadium, Mitchell would use the devastating hold to dispose of Don Blackman in a little over eight minutes.

Later that month, *California Eagle* columnist J. Cullen Fentress provided some additional background into Blackman, who was apparently rotating through several different nicknames during his first round of sustained, verifiable appearances inside of a wrestling ring.

A Decided Novelty

"Blackman (who has been known as 'Father' and 'Lion of Judah') claims his holds are obtained and executed different from those of other matmen," wrote Fentress. "In fact, he says they are derived from the extinct Seventh Book of Judah, and he wrestles in the name of 'the great father' (whoever that is)."

Fentress also pointed out that Blackman had been learning to wrestle under the tutelage of a familiar fixture in the Southern California wrestling scene.

"Training Blackman, a former New Yorker who has been wrestling at Hollywood Legion and Olympic Auditorium, is Tiger Jack Nelson, holder of the colored heavyweight wrestling belt for 12 years. We can imagine 'Angel' Blackman pinning an opponent with one of those punishing ancient holds and then saying to him, 'Peace! It's wonderful!' The referee and the fallen wrestler would probably be flabbergasted no end."

Proving the point that the stereotype of Black wrestlers possessing thick skulls had not yet saturated the pro wrestling world, Jim Mitchell lost a match to Jimmy Lott when the White Alabama native used a "Sonnenberg billy goat butt" — a combination of words often used to refer to a common headbutt — to fell the Panther in 27 minutes.

In March, the Panther suffered a loss in a title match to eternal world junior heavyweight champion Leroy McGuirk. Mitchell appeared to have McGuirk in quite a bit of trouble early in the bout, softening him up with a headlock, and then pinning him after a series of flying tackles in 22 minutes, 51 seconds. McGuirk recovered to win the second and third falls, including a disputed third fall, of which *The Bakersfield Californian* began its description by referring to Mitchell in less than flattering terms after he had the champion floored and reeling.

"The inky black grappler backed up and charged in for another tackle but McGuirk ducked and the hurtling Panther crashed into Referee Pat "Popeye" O'Brien, knocking him through the ropes and into the first row of spectators," described *The Californian*. "While O'Brien was struggling to get

A Decided Novelty

back in the ring, the Panther went to work on McGuirk and apparently pinned his shoulders down with a body press, but by the time O'Brien scrambled into the ring, the Oklahoman turned the tables and pinned the Panther for the deciding fall.

The article also included the incidental detail that the Panther "looks like a lost Ubangi tribe member." The Ubangi name was introduced to the United States in spring 1930 when Ringling Bros. and Barnum & Bailey Circus introduced a sideshow exhibit of "Ubangi Savages" from the French Congo. In reality, the Ubangi name had been taken from the name of the region's Ubangi River, and never referred to any specific African tribe.

April would see the Panther interacting with King Kong Clayton for the first time. The year had opened with Oregon's wrestling promoters saying that they were trying to keep Clayton — unflatteringly described as a "gorilla-like Negro" in *The Evening Herald* — from leaving the state. In the meantime, a match proclaimed to be tantamount to a Madison Square Garden main event was arranged between Clayton and world light heavyweight champion "Dangerous" Danny McShain.

It would be Clayton's last truly major match in Oregon, and he opened it by scoring the first fall on McShain with a hammerlock submission hold. That's when McShain began to fight a more conservative bout, biding his time until he could outmaneuver Clayton and smash his head into the canvas with a devastating piledriver.

"The seconds dragged Clayton to his corner, but it took the two of them, plus Referee Earl Yoakley and Clayton's handler, to keep the groggy negro from trying to tear Danny to shreds during the rest period," said *The Klamath News*. "When the bell rang, Danny quickly piled on top of Clayton to win the match. It took Clayton until after the crowd had left to get out of the ring."

After conclusively losing this high-profile bout to McShain, Clayton's final order of business in Oregon was to finish his feud with Bob Kenneston. Things got off to a rocky start in Klamath when Kenneston dropkicked Clayton off the ring apron "and squarely into the lap of an Indian woman sitting in the front row."

"King Kong clambered slowly back into the arena, and when Referee Bob Cummings offered him the winning fall on a foul, he refused," reported *The News*. "The wild-eyed marine cuffed him to the mat and fell on him to win the match."

Clayton got his revenge on Kenneston by wrestling a textbook Rufus Jones-style bout. With one foot definitely out of the territory's proverbial door, Clayton secured both of his falls on Kenneston by repeatedly bashing the ex-marine with headbutts until he could no longer stand. *The News* reported that an overzealous fan assaulted Clayton during his walk back to the dressing room, whacking the unsuspecting wrestler in the back of the head with a chair. No details were given as to the fate of the fan following the unscripted attack.

In Medford, Clayton bested Kenneston yet again with a dropkick in the first fall, and "a noggin cracker and chin lift" to win the second. Emerging victorious in his feud with Kenneston, Clayton then bid adieu to Oregon by engaging in a farewell brawl with Pete Belcastro, which Clayton won by disqualification. Two policemen and the referee broke up the altercation, and the last time the Klamath Falls fans laid eyes on Clayton, he was being physically carried back to the dressing room by the officers.

Clayton may have departed from the border of Montana and Alberta, but newspapers in the region continued to circulate tales of his activities from when he was active there. In spring 1940, when reporting for *The Edmonton Journal*, writer Joseph C. Dwyer decided to tell stories about some of the wrestlers who had worked in the province. When he got around to telling stories about Speedy Franks, Dwyer elected to include an anecdote that unfolded when Franks got under the skin of King Kong Clayton, and characterized the "negro champion" as someone who wasn't to be trifled with.

"Once when he was riding in the back seat of a car with the prodigiously strong King Kong Clayton, Speedy

A Decided Novelty

persisted in annoying the big colored boy," wrote Dwyer. "Finally, he applied a match to the paper Clayton was reading. Expressionless, Kong opened the car door, picked up Speedy, and hurled him into a snowdrift swiftly passing. It was just another fall for Speedy. Unabashed, he brushed himself off and thumbed his way into town."

With Clayton and Mitchell united for the first time in California, the writer of *The Long Beach Press-Telegram* apparently failed to realize the novelty of what the tandem presented to audiences. Clayton and Mitchell were paired together at the Wilmington Bowl for a tag team tournament, and *The Press-Telegram* identified the Panther — "the colored boy of the team" — as the tandem's captain, seemingly not realizing that *both* of the team's members were Black.

The two wrestlers — who grew up remarkably close to each other in light of the very different paths of their wrestling careers — defeated Mike Nazarian and Bob Montgomery to advance to the final round of the tournament. They maintained their momentum into the start of the finals by winning the first fall over Yukon Jake and Johnny Swenski, but then lost two consecutive falls when their opponents resorted to illegal tactics, and Mitchell absorbed the final pinfall.

"The Panther refused to leave the ring, where several energetic sympathizers joined him," observed *The Long Beach Morning Sun*. "King Kong was finally hauled away, but a flock of fans remained on the scene, sore as a covey of boiled owls. After many of the customers who stuck around for a long time afterward threatened to walk away from the establishment forever and ever unless a rematch was lined up immediately, Promoter Byron Carpenter said he would try to do so, although the card for next week had already been arranged."

The rematch was scheduled and advertised, but never occurred. On the night of the show, Clayton was absent, and Tony Morelli appeared in his place as Mitchell achieved a measure of revenge over Jake and Swenski.

Following a summer tour of Oregon, Mitchell returned to Ohio in July, where he began to wreak havoc on everyone in sight with his headlock variations, which had now replaced the familiar collection of leg locks as his submission holds of choice. With this series of head-based grips in his repertoire, the Panther was being heavily sold on the basis of his technical ability and "sensational hold making," as *The Akron Journal* defined it.

Lacking a tidy title for one of his headlocks, *The Lima News* referred to it as a "waltzing" headlock, presumably on the basis of the box-step and spin the Panther used once he trapped his opponent, or conceivably because he would use pain compliance to walk his helpless foes around the ring.

By fall 1940, Mitchell had done well enough financially to open his own barbecue restaurant in Toledo. *The Fremont News-Messenger* insisted that the Panther had earned the new nickname of "Spare-ribs" as a result of his new venture, due to the fact that he "serves ribs and well-done chicken while wearing an apron" as opposed to the pain he served up while clad in wrestling tights.

With Mitchell now absent from Los Angeles, Clayton picked up "Dark Angel" Don Blackman as his new tag team partner. When the two faced Ramon Sevilla and Manuel Rodriguez at El Rio Stadium, *The Ventura County Star* declared that the bout would set a very specific sort of history for the building, boasting that it would "mark the first time in the grappling history of El Rio that two Mexicans have been pitted against two Negroes."

Clayton also extended his activity into Arizona, where he was touted as the South African heavyweight champion. In what was proclaimed by *The Arizona Republic* to represent the first time in many years that "a colored grappler was presented," Clayton defeated Myron Cox with what was referred to as "a King Kong special," and described as a variation of a step-over toe hold.

Back in Southern California, Clayton and Blackman continued their pairing, but they were seldom presented as a team that any of the experienced squads had much difficulty defeating. Their union was broken up when Blackman returned

A Decided Novelty

to the East Coast, where he had presumably reenlisted in the U.S. Army based on events that were soon to come.

As World War II continued to escalate throughout Europe, enterprising wrestling promoters in several states off the beaten path would soon make efforts to expose spectators in their towns to bouts requiring Black heavyweight to compete against one another. This desire would cause two Black grappling stars who got their career starts on opposite coasts to engage in a memorable series of heavyweight main events throughout the heart of the United States.

16 – Luck and Godspeed

With Seelie Samara now active in Wisconsin, the former world champion's reputation continued to be centered around his technical wrestling prowess and sportsmanship despite his great strength. *The Sheboygan Press* highlighted him as "one of the cleanest wrestlers" to ever feature in the area as he wrestled his way through the Badger State.

Depending upon where it was that Samara wrestled in Wisconsin, his place of origin might be advertised as anywhere from Chicago to South Africa or Afghanistan. His weight was also given a range of just over 200 pounds to as high as 240 pounds. All the while, Samara sustained his distinction as a technical submission master, as displayed in his match with Jack Moore in Wisconsin Rapids.

The Wisconsin Rapids Daily Tribune described how Samara "worked on the extremities of his opponent almost all the way," winning the first fall with "a combined leg and toe clamp," and then capturing the second fall just a short two-and-a-half minutes later with "a double toe hold."

Against legendary world champion Gus Sonnenberg — who is generally accepted as the inventor of the intentional headbutt — Samara also unveiled another maneuver that had become standard in his arsenal. *The Two Rivers Reporter* illustrated how Samara, even while suffering a loss, reportedly "gave the fans a treat" by showcasing his handstand head spins, which allowed him to escape from "the vice-like head grips of Sonnenberg."

Furthermore, Samara was finally able to pay off the rumor that he had been responsible for the amputation of Gorilla Grubmeyer's middle finger by facing him in the ring. However, the account of the injury that sparked the feud provided by *The Sheboygan Press* was different from the version originally reported by the International News Service, and far less gruesome.

A Decided Novelty

Declining to repeat the tale that it was an intentional bite from Samara that deeply penetrated Grubmeyer's finger and inflicted an infection, *The Press* explained that Grubmeyer "hit Samara in the mouth and smashed his knuckle, and also obtained a badly cut and bruised hand." Also, rather than the amputation of the finger taking place six weeks after the laceration, it was now said to have occurred two days later at the hands of Dr. O.H. Schulze.

"Grubmeyer has not forgotten the fight that cost him a finger and also a great deal of money in doctor's bills," added *The Press*.

The match itself supplied Grubmeyer with a measure of storyline revenge, as he brutalized Samara after the opening bell and scored an early pinfall. Samara leveled the match by catching Grubmeyer with his slingshot tackle from the ring apron back to the center of the ring, but Grubmeyer returned to the use of illegal tactics and then clamped on a "double foot lock" for the third-fall win.

In the summer, Samara could be found wrestling in what had primarily been the home territory of King Kong Clayton when he traveled out to Wyoming. For the occasion, the promoter in Casper dusted off a nearly two-decade-old origin tale, and identified Samara as Senegalese in the tradition of Reginald Siki.

Samara promptly got over with the region's wrestling fans with flying headscissors and thunderous body slams, along with theatrical displays of his immense strength. This included a 10-man tug-of-war in which Samara was required to resist 10 men — five on each side — as they pulled ropes in opposite directions that were fastened to Samara's neck. Presumably the physics involved in the proceedings — specifically that the force of five men pulling on each side of Samara would cancel each other out and enable Seelie to stand in the middle of the fray unbothered — went unrecognized by the Wyoming crowd.

When fall came around, Samara got down to the business of wrestling in Nebraska and Minnesota, and in those

A Decided Novelty

two places he went by the name "Ras Samara." In Omaha, he was described as an Ethiopian Giant who had been a literal "slave rassler" for Ethiopian emperor Haile Selassie.

Ras Samara

Many miles away a wrestler going by the name of Gorilla Parker had been booked to face Art O'Mahoney at the City Auditorium of Birmingham, Alabama in May. Parker, who was billed as a newcomer from Texas, lost his bout to O'Mahoney, and made only one other advertised appearance in

A Decided Novelty

Birmingham before disappearing from Alabama, and not wrestling again in 1940.

Parker was arguably one of the five most famous Black wrestling stars in the world prior to the outbreak of World War II, whose match results and identity were frequently syndicated and distributed throughout the United States, along with his racial identity. The idea that he could be billed on a show in the Deep South without any allusion being made to his race, let alone his fame in the Midwest and along the East Coast, is unfathomable. For this reason, it is totally implausible that the Gorilla Parker who appeared in Alabama was played by the originator of the role, Henry Daniels.

Still residing in Milwaukee, Alex Kaffner was captured in the 1940 U.S. Census as "Alex Kaffnar," with France listed as his place of birth. He was living at the apartment complex on 1450 N. 7th Street with his wife at the time, Lillian, who was said to have been born in Chicago. Lillian had a job as a seamstress, while Kaffner was listed as a stevedore, loading and unloading boats at the nearby docks.

Kaffner's listed birth year of 1901 — if accurate — confirms that he was up to a decade older than most of his wrestling contemporaries, placing him closer in age to Reginald Siki and Jack Nelson than to Jim Mitchell or Jack Claybourne.

The fact that Kaffner had an authentic connection to France can't be dismissed out of hand. Assuming for a moment that the Senegalese origin story of Kaffner is legitimate — far-fetched though this may be — several theories exist for why Kaffner would consider himself French even if he wasn't born there. At a minimum, Senegal was provided unprecedented representation in the French government prior to the fall of the Third Republic, including a parliamentary seat.

Moreover, this would also make the promotional statements that Kaffner had seen combat during the First World War all the more plausible, as there are documented cases of teenage Senegalese soldiers enlisting in the French military during the conflict. Kaffner was the rare Black wrestler

A Decided Novelty

working in the U.S. at the time about whom such claims were made on multiple occasions.

In New England, Jack Claybourne found himself in the familiar role of being the most entertaining and electric wrestler in the country, while losing to seemingly every holder of a championship belt in the region, including Johnny Iovanna and Salvatore Bobo.

Making his debut in Biddeford, Maine, for promoter Gerard Campobasso, Claybourne was named as "the most colorful junior heavyweight wrestler in the world," and "the holder of the junior heavyweight title." However, this was apparently a reference to the fake European championship Jack was advertised to possess upon entering the territory rather than any of the sanctioned light heavyweight or junior heavyweight titles being regularly defended in the area.

Along with referencing the backstory that Claybourne was of South African descent, and was educated at Oxford, the story supplied in *The Biddeford Daily Journal* furthered Claybourne's origin tale for the fans, including how the wrestler was purported to have taken up the sport while attending Oxford, and had then won several tournaments, culminating in his acquisition of the European junior heavyweight championship.

"War conditions drove Jack to this country, and he tells of a funny incident while coming to our shores three months ago," added the article. "It seems the Danish ship he came over on was stopped by a German sub a day out from the port. The sub commander with several sailors came aboard to look the contents of the ship over, and to see if they were carrying any contraband of war. The German commander spied Claybourne, and with outstretched hands greeted him and recalled when they had wrestled as opponents in an amateur tournament staged in Berlin. Though Claybourne is a British subject, the German officer wished him luck and Godspeed, and stated he hoped they would meet when this war is ended."

It's unlikely that many wrestlers, including Claybourne, had the time to keep up with the ludicrous stories that were

A Decided Novelty

being submitted about them to the press through wrestling promoters operating in different cities. They were often caught completely off guard when asked about the details of their lives by fans on the streets.

Evidently, when Harvey Southward of *The Daily Evening Item* attempted to confirm some of the details of Claybourne's childhood in the jungles of South Africa, Southward reported, "Jack Claybourne, the grappler, claims he never was in the African jungle, and that furthermore even though he was a wrestler, he never ate a man, or even had what is known as missionary soup."

Once he left New England, Claybourne spent the bulk of his traceable time during the remainder of 1940 in the Canadian province of Quebec, where he once again wowed fans with his sharp wrestling ability and high-flying athleticism. By this point, Seelie Samara had already twice won and lost the world junior heavyweight championship defended in Montreal, and Samara's title success caused Claybourne to be viewed as an emergent threat in the area, and one of the reasons for this was seemingly because of his race.

"Claybourne is an ace, one of the most spectacular wrestlers to ever come to Montreal," stated *Le Devoir* of Montreal. "He is a man of color, an athlete of the breed of men who inflicted the most scathing failures on [Harry] Madison. We only have to remember the terrible fights fought here by the wrestlers Tiger Flowers and Zelis Amhara. Claybourne is undoubtedly as good as them, and probably surpasses them in classic wrestling science. But Madison is still considered by many experts to be the best 200-pound wrestler in the world. He is the one who currently holds the title, and if there is a black man who has any chance of taking it from him currently it is probably Jack Claybourne."

Unfortunately for Claybourne, he would not be as fortunate in world junior heavyweight title matches contested in Montreal as Samara had been. While the bout played out in a fashion that swayed every onlooker to the point of view that Claybourne deserved to be the world champion, the end result still left Claybourne leaving the Marche Saint-Jacques Gymnasium as the defeated challenger.

Jack Claybourne in his physical prime

"After the two men had fought with equal chances, having each taken a fall, the referee [Saxon] received an accidental blow from Claybourne, and the official was momentarily placed out of action," reported *Le Devoir*. "While Saxon was regaining his senses, Claybourne had pinned Madison's shoulders to the mat, but without the knowledge of the referee. While the Irishman was holding the Negro to the mat, Saxon was able to realize what was happening, and he awarded victory to the champion."

In 1941, Jim Mitchell continued to delight Michigan audiences with his headlock mastery. The *Kalamazoo Gazette* described how the Panther clamped a headlock on Gorilla Poji during a tag team match, and continued "bull-dozing Poji around the ring so viciously that he collapsed," and then did the same thing to Nick Billins before turning Billins over to his partner Billy Rayborn to administer the coup de grâce.

The Gazette followed up on the hold the following week, referring to it as "a new kind of headlock," when Mitchell used it to submit Martino Angelo, and by the time it was used for a third time in four weeks to victimize Walter Miller, the publication was referring to it as the Black Panther's "famous hip headlock."

It was then and there that the frequent pairings of Jim Mitchell and Rufus Jones kicked into high gear. Before crossing paths with Mitchell, Jones headbutted his way through Wisconsin early in the year and then found himself sharing a card with Jack Claybourne in New Jersey. Claybourne was atypically labeled "The African Thunderfoot," while Jones was randomly supplied with a Caribbean origin when he was temporarily dubbed "The Jamaican Tiger." The two then met up in Bristol, Pennsylvania for a match that *The Bristol Courier* advertised as "the first time that a pair of colored grapplers have faced each other on the local canvas."

Jones returned to his familiar haunt of Windsor in the spring, where *The Windsor Star* picked up on Jones' increased fondness for headbutts, which he supplied in abundance against Walter Miller during the opening fall, and continued to administer throughout the match.

"In the opening set-to, Rufus had profited at times by an unorthodox but neat trick that consisted of him bumping his ebony noggin on his foe's more brittle brow," noted *The Star*. "He'd used it again in the mid-session. In the final canto, he really brought it into play."

A Decided Novelty

The only catch was that Rufus *also* dispensed an alarming number of headbutts upon the forehead of referee Joe Lauzon, usually after trapping Miller's neck in the ropes, and then assaulting Lauzon whenever he tried to prevent Miller from being strangled.

"Two or three setbacks like this and Joseph decided enough was enough," continued *The Star*. "He awarded the fall, and bout, to Miller. Rufus, of course, didn't like that. He slugged the chunky arbiter a couple of times. Joe, a bit of a flier-off-the-handle himself, chased Rufe to the corner. Here, a fan butted in and hit Rufus in the face. At that, Rufe wanted to take on the fan, but abandoned the idea when several other fans ran up to the ring to the support of their fellow."

Jones soon returned to the wrestling rings of Ohio to duel with Jim Mitchell, except this time Jones was fully immersed in his routine as wrestling's most prolific headbutter. *The Marion Star* promoted the pair as arch enemies, seemingly based solely on the fact that the "sepia-hued matmen" shared a racial group.

"Until Jones stepped onto the local stage, the Panther had the field all to himself, being the only colored warrior to get more than passing attention," insisted *The Star*. "Jones' arrival, although no words have passed between the pair, creates a situation which had the Panther ready to jealously defend his prestige. He might well feel, who is this upstart, this usurper, who has come to invade his domain? And he'll be out for a clean-cut victory over Jones."

Heaven forbid that two Black wrestlers attempted to coexist in the same wrestling industry at the same time, let alone in the same state. However, before concluding the feature article, *The Star* elaborated on the stylistic differences between Rough Rufus and the Black Panther.

"Jones is a ruffian of the first water; his favorite 'nut cracker' is a tactic that could have been developed only by a tough ringster," the article continued. "It consists of cracking his foes' craniums with his own tough knob, something none have been able to take and survive. If the duel were to be

A Decided Novelty

confined to scientific grappling, the Panther would hold a long edge. Jones hasn't shown any inclination to put up that kind of a battle in any of his appearances, but prefers to resort to those attacks, which despite being illegal, result in victory more often than not."

Absurd origins notwithstanding, Mitchell was the winner of the bout with Jones at the Marion Armory, befuddling his opponent with an assortment of holds and then forcing him to submit to a headlock. From there, Jones upped the ante with aggressive tactics, and rained a barrage of blows down upon Mitchell. Just as Mitchell began to fight back, the sea of fans that had been churning in the ringside area began to bubble over, requiring the intervention of the police to calm the waters.

"They crowded to ringside, and no less than three clambered through the strands to see justice done," reported *The Star*. "None of them got mixed up in the melee, however, to the credit of Patrolman Smith. He unceremoniously conducted Jones on a one-way tour to his dressing room, bringing the mix-up to a close. Jones left nothing undone to earn the disqualification, but hollered long and loud that he had been robbed by the decision."

Technically, if the match had been real, Rufus would have had a point. The referee threw the match out only after ringside fans had inserted themselves into the fray to interfere by attacking Jones on Mitchell's behalf.

In a display of booking that would come to typify the unique partnership arrangements adopted by pre-1960s Black wrestlers as they toured select regions of North America, Jones and Mitchell were cast as the best of friends in Windsor, only to spontaneously develop a deep hatred for one another the instant they traveled back across the Ambassador Bridge and drove to the central part of Ohio.

While the mid-May match between Jones and the Panther in Lima was advertised as "the first time two colored grapplers have appeared against each other on the Lima mat," the two were regularly teaming up to dominate their opponents

A Decided Novelty

in Northern Ohio, with *The Sandusky-Register-Star-News* suggesting that the calming presence of Mitchell as a partner "discouraged rough tactics" on the part of Jones.

According to the report from *The Register-Star-News*, Jones secured two pinfall wins for his team by using the cleanest tactics he had employed in a long time, relying on armlocks to score two eliminations, while Mitchell contributed a backbreaker and a bodybreaker to the winning effort.

Sandusky was the site where Jones put another of the finishing touches on his standard wrestling formula. In a main-event match at Fisher's Hall, Jones absorbed the discomfort caused by Gorilla Pogi's hair-pulling attack and finally "began slugging and then bumping heads." Rufus succeeded in putting Pogi down for the first fall with headbutts, and then he concluded the match by putting Pogi away with what would soon become his signature submission hold.

"Promoter Fishbaugh, in the role of referee for the main event, was instrumental in paving the way for Jones' victory," observed *The Register-Star-News*. "Pogi again began hair-pulling. He socked Fishbaugh when the latter demanded that he refrain from such tactics. Unable to gain attention, Fishbaugh slammed Pogi to the mat. Jones then took over the situation and succeeded in adjusting a crab hold to win in seven minutes."

The Boston crab — perhaps not so coincidentally adopted by a native of the Greater Boston area — would become nearly as synonymous with Rufus as his headbutts.

From this point forward, just as Jones' reach was extending into Indiana during summer 1941, Jones would rarely win matches through any means other than headbutts and crab holds.

Now operating throughout a large stretch of the contiguous Rust Belt states, Jones continued to weave himself into the fabric of the historical development of wrestling in the region. Within the same week, he became one of the first Black wrestlers to engage in sustained participation in Indiana pro wrestling matches since Mitchell had wrestled there years

A Decided Novelty

earlier, while also participating in only the second tag team wrestling match in the history of Detroit.

The stylistic differences between Jones and the Panther came into sharper focus when they each won their respective bouts in Marion. Jones won his bout with Joe Ferona "with a headlock and body press, accompanied by signature headbutts." The two then traded additional punches after the bout. Panther dispensed with Nick Billins by taking him down with a bulldogging headlock, and then forcing him to submit to a hip headlock.

The by-the-numbers approaches to wrestling adopted by Mitchell and Jones may have been very different, with one being more brutal and the other being more technical, yet they managed to set a bizarre precedent when they both competed in Fremont's Christmas battle royal.

"Jones set out to soften up all his opponents, butting them with his head, and then [Joe] Ferona thought he could do the same thing, but he picked the wrong fellow to try it on," explained *The News-Messenger*. "When he bumped noggins with the Panther, he knocked himself out. When the others saw Ferona on the floor, they all jumped on him, and he was through for the evening."

A segment of a match that was clearly intended as a harmless bit of fun managed to communicate a clear message. The Black Panther — who had discarded his regular headbutts years ago and was not a truly prolific headbutter as far as Midwest fans were aware — naturally possessed a cranium that was suggested to be of equivalent thickness to that of Rufus Jones. This cranial thickness was a trait that now seemed to be universally shared by Black wrestlers, suggesting that Blacks in general had thicker skulls than Whites.

The assertion that Blacks had thicker skulls than Whites had persisted for at least a century despite repeated attempts by medical experts to debunk the claim. In 1893, an unnamed surgeon provided an interview that eventually wound up in syndicated reports, stating that Africans' skulls were actually thinner on average than those of Europeans, but that other common Black phenotypic features had contributed to the development of the stereotype.

"The negro's head is covered with coarse, curly wool, which being matted closely over the skull, forms a cushion and proves a constant shield or protector of the cranium, and thus deadens the force of a blow upon the head," the expert was quoted as saying. "Hence the negro is given credit for a skull of abnormal thickness, capable of withstanding the crack of a policeman's club, or even a blow with an ax."

As retroactively preposterous as such claims appear, the skulls of Blacks were credited with supernatural levels of invulnerability in early 20th-century news reports. In 1901, *The St. Louis Republic* devoted considerable space to the story of Dan Oates, a Black man whose life was spared when his thick skull managed to flatten a .38-caliber bullet, resulting in him only suffering a bruise.

"The bullet disarranged a few kinks in the wool at the back of Oates' head, knocked off his hat, and fell to the floor flattened out," reported *The Republic*. "It is perhaps needless to say that Oates is a negro."

More than a decade later, in 1913, another syndicated story circulated of George Wern, who was allegedly shot during an altercation that occurred on July 4. Wern was supposedly fired upon at point-blank range by an unidentified assailant; the bullet deflected off of his skull and struck Mrs. Edward T. Smith, who was passing in a streetcar. Mrs. Smith was taken to a city hospital for treatment.

"Wern, after mopping his brow, went about his business of celebrating the Fourth," concluded the article. "The negro who fired the shot escaped."

Unsurprisingly, the stereotype also thrived when placed in an athletic context. In 1914, it was reported that boxer "Battling" Jim Johnson — who wasn't a particularly successful fighter — was assaulted by fellow fighter Kid Hawkins while seated in a Parisian cafe. Hawkins hurled a water bottle in Johnson's direction, and it shattered against the heavyweight fighter's forehead.

A Decided Novelty

"Jim Johnson suffered no injury save a scarcely noticeable swelling where he was struck," informed *The Ottawa Journal*. "He was annoyed at the incident, however, and has sent a message to Hawkins intimating that if the manners of the latter do not improve, he will decline his acquaintance."

The Journal published the piece under the title "Negro's skull able to defy most anything," and included a statement that "the thickness of the negro skull was practically demonstrated" by the incident.

With stereotypes of such magnitude being delineated as fact in the early 20th-century press, it is altogether unsurprising that the public was so quick to believe that Black wrestlers would have an innate physical advantage when it came to head-oriented offense.

In August, a bout between Jim Mitchell and Seelie Samara took place on the Panther's home turf, with *The Courier-Journal* referring to Mitchell as "a Louisville lad who went away seven years ago and made good in the wrestling world. In reality, it had been more than 10 years since Mitchell had first departed Kentucky for Indiana.

"The Louisvillian is the 'Black Panther,' the dapperly dressed one-time Savoy Theater preliminary boy who has worked his way up from the 15-minute preliminary tilts to one of the contenders for the Negro world's heavyweight wrestling championship," boasted *The Courier-Journal*, which also added that Mitchell had been a former bellhop at a local hotel.

The paper's commendation would have carried more weight if there were more than six Black wrestlers working in America's mainstream wrestling territories, all of whom made regular claims to being the world champions of their race even when there were no similarly complexioned competitors around to contest the claims.

With all of the promotion for the bout centered around Mitchell's Cinderella-like climb to prominence, it seemed like the stage was set for the Panther to win the championship in front of his hometown fans. Instead, Samara defeated him, and then turned his attention to King Kong Clayton.

A Decided Novelty

As for Mitchell, he continued to linger in Ohio, and by December he was praised as a "Toledo businessman" on the basis of his restaurant ownership, granting him an air of respectability that many of the other wrestlers in the region lacked, irrespective of race.

King Kong Clayton was advertised to appear in Bellingham, Washington very late in 1940 only for the event to be abruptly canceled by promoter R.C. Hennig, who cited Clayton's inability to appear as the reason for the cancellation. Instead, Clayton returned to Greeley, Colorado, where he began to wrestle under a rather confusing name combination.

Ditching his surname of Clayton, he instead opted to be presented under the somewhat puzzling name of "King Kong, The Black Leopard."

"King Kong is said to be the perfect athlete — lithe, supple, and catlike," glowed *The Greeley Daily Tribune*. "He is rated as the most sensational and popular wrestler to come out of the west, and he has thrilled Hollywood — which you must admit is a man-sized job of thrilling."

Clayton's name change also carried over to Wyoming, where the publications provided some elaboration as to the meaning behind his altered title.

"King Kong is known as the Black Leopard," stated *The Casper Tribune-Herald*. "He has been setting Hollywood, San Francisco, Portland, and other west coast wrestling centers on fire. Lithe, supple, cat-like in his movements, he is reputed to be the perfect athlete, completely outclassing and baffling his opponents. He recently defeated Pete Belcastro for the junior heavyweight title of the Pacific Coast."

This latter portion was an exaggeration; while Clayton had defeated Belcastro, there had been no championship on the line.

The Tribune-Herald laid it on even thicker in later installments, marketing Clayton as a combination of three different star wrestlers, including Seelie Samara, and then adding "King Kong comes from Hollywood and has appeared in 11 pictures during the past year and a half. The demand for

A Decided Novelty

King Kong has been so great because of his beautiful build and athletic prowess."

Grand claims aside, no records have emerged to confirm that Clayton appeared in any Hollywood films, although it's entirely possible that he made one or more appearances as an uncredited extra.

This comparison to Samara had been by design, as the wrestler who had inherited Reginald Siki's mantle of being frequently booked as a foreign heavyweight had been making first appearances in the area. While matches between competitive Black wrestlers had been becoming more frequent, they were essentially unheard of in the Mountain West region.

"We feel lucky to be getting the Samara-Clayton match," Colorado matchmaker Hank Lauer told *The Fort Collins Press-Courier*. "Other matchmakers in the region are attempting to sign the two Negroes as soon as possible. Never before have these two sensational athletes met. As far as can be learned, never before have two colored heavyweight wrestlers met. New York, Chicago, Philadelphia have never had such a match."

In reality, there had been instances when two Black heavyweight wrestlers had met, most notably the match between George Godfrey and Reginald Siki. However, it is true that Clayton and Samara were the two full-time Black wrestlers in the U.S. at the time who were most consistently billed as heavyweights.

While teasing the showdown between Clayton and Samara in Greeley, *The Greeley Daily Tribune* vastly underrated the number of active Black pro wrestlers in the United States.

"King Kong and Samara are the half of the colored pro mat performers of the U.S.," stated *The Daily Tribune*, employing math that undercounted the number of active Black wrestlers in the United States by at least triple. "The only other two who rate among the pro performers are Rufus Jones and Gorilla Parker."

This article also named five of the films that Clayton was alleged to have appeared in: "East of Java," "Showboat," "Came the Dawn," "King Kong," and "The Ape Walks." Of

A Decided Novelty

those titles, Clayton is only confirmed to have been anywhere near the vicinity of Hollywood for the filming of "East of Java" and "Show Boat," with no way of knowing whether or not he made background appearances in either of those films.

The initial clash between the two Black heavyweights ended in a draw, with Samara taking the first fall in 27 minutes following "a series of 'backflips,'" while Clayton replicated the routine he had borrowed from Jack Claybourne and leveled Samara with several dropkicks to score the second fall three minutes later.

When the venue then shifted to Casper, Wyoming, no time was wasted in anointing the bout as a match to determine the champion of all Black wrestlers, even if such a title would be mythical.

"It is the claim of both Samara and King Kong that there isn't a colored man alive that can beat them, including each other, and claim that this match will be for the colored heavyweight championship of the world," posited *The Casper Tribune-Herald*. "Even though the winner of this match could not claim the championship within the boundaries of the state (Wyoming doesn't belong to the National Wrestling Association) it will be a match in the caliber of that category."

The resulting match was described in *The Tribune-Herald* as "a clean, hard match from the start to the finish with the fighters relying on their wide repertoire of wrestling holds to carry them through."

"King Kong annexed the first fall after about 40 minutes of grueling wrestling with a series of dropkicks and a body smother. Samara won the second fall with an arm lock in 15 minutes," reported *The Tribune Herald*. "The crowd cheered the two colored men for their sportsmanship in the ring and their cleverness in breaking from holds. Each seemed to know a thousand and one ways to break from a hold, and they didn't spare the horses."

Once again, the outcome was a draw, but the pair still had several other towns to wrestle in. During April, in Lincoln Park, Colorado, Samara defeated Clayton in 44 minutes to win the match, and reaffirm his claim to "the world's negro heavyweight wrestling title." *The Daily Sentinel* described a match in which Samara plainly played the role of heel, and won despite the crowd booing his actions and voicing their nearly unanimous support for Clayton.

"Most of the holds in the book were used by one or the other, but they seemed to specialize in variations of torture holds," reported William Nelson for *The Daily Sentinel*. "Kong said little, but Samara almost regularly argued with Referee Ebright or warned Kong against some tactic. Scissors were frequent, and Samara delighted the fans with a top-like spin on his head to break loose. Both men were agile as well as powerful, and they were evenly matched."

Leaving Colorado behind, Clayton and Samara wandered into western Nebraska and faced separate opponents. *The Scottsbluff Daily Star-Herald* offered up the statement that "the negro wrestlers have to be good in order to get matches with white opponents is what men close to the game all insist."

At the event that followed, Samara lost to Jack Conley while Clayton toppled the 265-pound Indian Mayes McLain with two consecutive dropkicks.

Samara was maintaining a very aggressive travel schedule throughout this time. Still going by Ras Samara in the Central States region, he spent much of the year traveling between Nebraska, Minnesota, and Iowa, while also wrestling in some of the less populated areas of Missouri.

When he returned to Michigan late in the summer, Samara proudly sported a keffiyeh head scarf, and was publicly identified as Algerian. While this was in accordance with the increasing newsworthiness of Algeria following the German invasion of the country's colonial nerve center in France, assigning that title to Samara ignored the fact that there are scant few ethnic Algerians of Sub-Saharan ancestry.

Either the wrestling promoters were unaware of the differences in skin shades across different regions of Africa, or

A Decided Novelty

they were banking on the fact that wrestling fans would either not know, or wouldn't care.

In the long run, none of this mattered; Samara's return to Michigan was quickly aborted within a month's time, possibly owing to scheduling conflicts in Illinois rather than what Benton Harbor's local newspapers suggested. To explain the wrestler's sudden departure, *The News-Palladium* reported that Samara had been suspended by the Michigan State Athletic Commission, but neglected to identify what infraction of the rules he had committed.

Instead of continuing to wrestle in Michigan, Samara rematerialized in Indiana, where his Ethiopian origin was restored, and he was briefly reunited with Jack Claybourne.

It wouldn't be until September that Samara and Clayton reunite and wrestle each other for the first time in Nebraska. Both men went into the bout still claiming to be "world's Negro rassling champion" according to *The Morning World Herald* of Omaha. The match was further stated to be "Omaha's first all-Negro rassle."

The Omaha bout was ruled a draw, but the details the two provided to *The Omaha Star* through interviews were far more interesting than the bout itself. Samara asserted that he had started wrestling in 1930 after five or six years of professional boxing activity. He also claimed to have been "the only Negro to rassle for the World's Rassling title" by virtue of his 1936 bout with Crusher Casey at the Boston Gardens.

Likewise, Clayton professed to have started wrestling 12 years prior *after* campaigning as a middleweight boxer for eight-and-a-half years. There was clearly a misunderstanding, as Clayton was only 30 years old, and taking the timeline at face value would suggest that Clayton began boxing seriously at the age of nine-and-a-half before kicking off his wrestling career at age 18. Regardless, Clayton clearly had not begun his wrestling career until the first wave of his boxing career had stalled in 1936 when he was 25 years old.

In addition, Clayton claimed an amateur wrestling background, owing to his time spent at Wilberforce University in Ohio, and also claimed the title of "The Globetrotter" resulting from the time he allegedly spent wrestling in Europe, Asia, South America, and South Africa.

Perhaps the most significant piece of information that either Samara or Clayton provided to their interviewer, Charles Washington, was regarding the status of the wrestling championship acknowledged by Black wrestlers.

"The Negro champion belt is held by Jack Nelson," wrote Washington. "Nelson quit four years ago, but refuses to give up the belt. A tourney is being planned in St. Louis for the near future to decide who really is Negro champ. There are about six Negro rasslers."

Despite the general mediocrity of his career, it's touching to think that Tiger Jack Nelson was esteemed so highly be his Black peers that his championship reign was afforded as much respect as any Negro championship could be shown, at least amongst the Black wrestlers who mattered most.

Breaking from Clayton for a time, Samara had several dealings with Jack Claybourne. Along the East Coast, Claybourne was presented as the "African Streamline" — a comparison to a sleek modern railway train — and was described as "one of the most sensational wrestlers in the country" within the sports section of *The Bayonne Times*. Then the publication went further than any other in providing New Jersey's latest Black wrestling star with an elaborate and preposterous backstory.

"[Claybourne] has the tread of a man accustomed to the jungle, which is natural enough as he spent his early years in the Tanganyika country, a paradise of big game as he acted as a spotter for hunters," began *The Times*, as its writer relocated Claybourne's point of origin more than 2,000 miles from South Africa and into modern Tanzania. "Dangerous work for a lad, but it developed his body, made him quick to react to imminent danger, and in every way prepared him for the mat game, which at the time was far from his mind."

A Decided Novelty

The Times pressed on, describing how Claybourne "the lion boy" was wrestling in bouts in Tanganyika, and became such a legend amongst the locals that he was plucked out of the region and ferried off to the United States to compete in U.S. rings.

The stories got even wilder when Claybourne visited New York, and in February, Buster Miller of *The New York Age* savagely mocked Claybourne's proposed origin while divulging how promoter Jack Pfefer was taking credit for the discovery of Claybourne.

"In accents strongly reminiscent of fried chicken and cornbread country, Jack (Claybourne, not Pfefer) curls your hair with tales of how he used to hunt lions with his father in the old country," explained Miller. "He is a bit hazy on how he learned to grapple, preferring to ascribe his success to lessons received at the hands of an anonymous sailor. Jack avers that his favorite 'holt' is an 'African bear hug,' whatever that may be. At any rate, this will be surprising news to zoologists who have searched Africa in vain for signs of a bear. And won't they be startled to find out that Jack's 'lions' are called 'possums' in their native habitat."

Fables about an African origin aside, Claybourne's tactics impressed everyone who watched him perform. *The Bayonne Times* added that Jack had "tricks of his own on the mat which are unique," and was "remarkably elusive," which served as a fine complement to his unmatched speed.

This same period of time saw Claybourne returning to Louisville, Kentucky for a proper feud with Seelie Samara over the Negro world heavyweight wrestling championship, which Claybourne was said to be bringing with him.

Now nearly a decade into his wrestling career, Claybourne was being described as a 228-pound heavyweight, and while the weights of wrestlers are listed at whatever figures the promoters desired to announce to the fans, photographs of Claybourne from the era do suggest that he was considerably heavier in 1941 than when he debuted as a 170-pound light heavyweight.

A Decided Novelty

Jack's opponent Samara had opted to go by "Haile Samara" to strengthen his claim to Ethiopian status. *The Courier-Journal* went so far as to say that even though Claybourne "whipped Joe Louis" in an unsanctioned boxing match, he had never beaten Samara due to the Ethiopian giant's "unorthodox style," and positioned Gentleman Jack as an underdog against an opponent "who can't read or write, or speak more than a few words of English."

It's possible that everything about this sentence was a lie, as Claybourne had certainly never outboxed Joe Louis, George "Seelie Samara" Hardison could presumably read and write perfectly well, and Claybourne had not only defeated Samara before, but had done so in that same city just one year prior.

This encounter between the two would yield an identical result, as Claybourne won their best-of-three-falls contest. In the rematch, Samara evened their summer series and relieved Claybourne of what was arguably the most credible Negro world heavyweight title defended anywhere on the continent at the time, fictional or otherwise.

"The 'champion' took the first fall in 24:28 with a flying body pin, then Samara retaliated to take the second in 12:10 with a whip hold, and made short work of the third, which he took in 4:56 with a reverse body pin," recorded *The Courier Journal*.

Samara's time as Negro world champion in that setting was short-lived, as Claybourne regained the title at the Allen Sports Arena in the early days of September. *The Courier-Journal* suggested that Samara had been riding high after the British infantry had successfully booted Benito Mussolini's Italian forces from Ethiopia, liberating his homeland, and that the Negro championship had briefly made Samara the champion of a free land before Claybourne had rendered him crestfallen.

"Samara used a flying tackle and a body pin to score at 15:21, but the 'Gentleman' rallied to win the second with a rolling headlock in 12:08, and then secured the deciding fall with a body kick and slam in 22:32," explained *The Courier-Journal*.

Heading north, Claybourne was scheduled to rekindle his feud from eight years earlier with Alex Kaffner at the Hammond Civic Center in Hammond, Indiana, only for *The Times* to announce that Kaffner had injured his foot in Omaha, and would be replaced by Seelie Samara.

Once again donning his Black Panther pseudonym, Claybourne repeated his victory over Samara by bodyslamming him in 20 minutes to settle the feud for the time being.

Somehow, in the midst of this Midwestern tour by Claybourne, wrestling promoter Larry Gall snuck a story into *The Sheboygan Press* that Claybourne was a "former Olympic sprint champion *and* intercollegiate wrestling champ."

As America was preparing for what seemed like its inevitable involvement in the growing global conflict, Claybourne returned to Ohio with the local newspapers stating that he was resuming his pursuit of a regional championship, and specifically the Midwest Wrestling Association's version of the world junior heavyweight championship owned by Speed LaRance of Canada. The hint was also dropped that it would be an incredible milestone for a Black wrestler like Claybourne to win a world wrestling title.

"Unlike the fight game, there are few colored athletes competing in the wrestling game," explained *The Dayton Daily News*. "During the past 15 years, only four men of the race have appeared in the local ring. But all of them were outstanding stars. First to come here was Reginald Siki, the heavyweight star of 12 years ago. Then came Gorilla Parker of Louisville, Ky., and after him was Jimmie Mitchell of Louisville, Ky., known to the game as the 'Black Panther.'"

The Dayton Journal added gravity to the occasion, stating that if Claybourne managed to dethrone Speed LaRance, "Not only would the accomplishment give [Claybourne] championship prestige, but it would allot him the additional honor of being the first Negro to ever garner a major mat title."

A Decided Novelty

After Speed repeatedly wriggled his way out of losing his championship to Claybourne by hook or by crook, the Gentleman appealed to MWA officials in order to get special referees assigned to oversee their matches. The MWA reportedly acceded to Jack's wishes, and designated three different referees to officiate a title bout — one for each fall that would presumably take place.

"This will mark the first time in local wrestling history that such a plan has been used in assigning referees," stated *The Dayton Sunday Journal-Herald*. "Both Claybourne and LaRance have agreed to the plan, and indications point to their battle being the highlight of the current indoor season."

The resulting match between the two concluded with a classic instance of fans having their joy retroactively crushed after believing they had just witnessed wrestling history. The match began with Claybourne achieving the first fall with his usual flurry of dropkicks, only for LaRance to square the tally with three flying headscissors and a pinfall. This set the stage for the final exchange of the match.

"Speed took an impromptu trip over the ropes on an attempted flying headscissors," remarked *The Dayton Journal*. "He regained the mat before he was counted out, but was in no condition to cope with the tiger-like Claybourne, who promptly flipped him to the canvas and tallied the fall on a body smother."

Momentarily jubilant, it was only at this point that the fans in attendance at Dayton's Memorial Hall were made aware of what Claybourne had presumably already known. The announcer informed the audience that Claybourne had weighed in that evening at 203 pounds — three pounds over the 200-pound weight limit — and was therefore ineligible to win the championship. Therefore, Claybourne had physically vanquished Speed LaRance, but by way of a technicality he would be denied the opportunity to make his case as what the fans believed to have been the first Black holder of an American pro wrestling championship.

A Decided Novelty

Centered primarily in the Midwest, the activities of Mitchell, Claybourne, Jones, Clayton, and Samara had elevated the in-ring encounters between Black wrestlers into must-see entertainment. It was a golden era that wouldn't last, as two of the five men were about to be snatched away to serve their country overseas. At the same time, America was about to receive the shocking revelation that the most iconic Black grappler of the previous era had been literally snatched away by the Nazis as the war destabilized the lives of pro wrestlers on multiple continents.

17 – A Large Negro Audience

Conspicuously absent from early 1940s wrestling activity, Zimba Parker's only worthwhile mention of 1941 involved an article written about him in April by syndicated Associated Negro Press columnist Al White, who was based in Washington, D.C. In his brief editorial, White mentioned that Parker had acquired significant fame in Harlem, but also suffered through the misfortune to be racially mislabeled.

"He is the first colored wrestler to show in this burg, and he is doing pretty well for himself — only they persist in calling Zimba a Hindu," penned White. "If he's Hindu, then Father Divine is a Chinaman. Ran into Zimba last night, and he said he had taken my advice and gone in for the sport again, making his own contacts here and getting several bouts. He's a regular attraction, only the colored folk don't know about it yet!"

There is much about this story that strains credulity, beginning with the fact that Parker was always unmistakably promoted as either Negro or colored, since that was often the main impetus for interest in him. Further, nothing about the surname Parker suggests an origin in India, or anywhere in Southeast Asia.

White is clearly committing the faux pas of using Hindu — a religious designation — as a synonym for Indian, and suggesting that Parker went frustratingly unrecognized as a result of the confusion; there is zero evidence of this ever being a problem that Parker was forced to contend with.

In addition, the idea that this encounter with Parker unfolded exactly as it was portrayed in 1941, when the once prolific Black wrestling star had probably been inactive for nearly three full years, suggests that the interaction between the two had transpired several years prior, *if* it actually happened at all. However, time would soon show that it was probable that Parker had relocated to the D.C. area as White suggested.

A Decided Novelty

Far more active was Don Blackman, who moved on to Michigan in 1941, and was wrestling there when U.S. involvement in World War II was officially kicked off by the Japanese bombing of Pearl Harbor.

At the end of that same month, Blackman made his debut in the city where Parker had supposedly been hanging out — Washington, D.C. — with an appearance at Uline Arena, where he was touted as "the Negro wrestling champion of the world" by *The Washington Daily News*.

"Blackman is an ex-Army man and even now is awaiting a second call to the colors," added *The Daily News*. "His clean-cut tactics are expected to prevail over the more spectacular but less polished methods of his Redskin rival (Chief Bamba Tabu 'The Mad Indian')."

Even after the American war effort commenced in earnest and Blackman resumed his service to the U.S. Army, he continued to wrestle when granted leave. As early as January 1942, *The Philadelphia Inquirer* was already referring to Blackman as a 195-pound soldier from Fort Dix. That same month, he was also identified for the first time by an all-too-familiar moniker: "The Black Panther" Don Blackman.

Under his new name, Blackman immediately garnered attention from the local press, including the Black publications.

"Continuing the impressive string of victories he has built up since he recently began appearing for Philadelphia mat followers, Don Blackman, the Black Panther, tossed Ivan Kamaroff of Russia, in 9:17 of a scheduled 30-minute wrestling bout, Thursday, at the Broadwood," printed *The Washington Afro American*.

Blackman continued to wrestle sporadically when he was granted leave time from Fort Dix, and as the months passed, his listed weight gradually decreased. This could be a byproduct of the promoter's preference, but a weight decrease would also be expected from someone on a regular schedule of military rations and conditioning exercises. By October, his

A Decided Novelty

advertised weight had dipped to 190 pounds from its prior peak of 210.

After an absence of several years, Zimba Parker finally did resurface to wrestle on the same cards as Blackman, with Parker labeled as a Washington resident. Labeled as a 200-pounder for the first time in his wrestling career, Parker appeared in D.C. and Pennsylvania for a three-month period before heading off for a few matches in New England.

It became apparent in the spring that some of wrestling's other Black stars besides Blackman might soon become casualties of the Second World War, at least when it came to their ability to continue to entertain audiences in the ring.

Seelie Samara made a full-fledged return to Southwest Michigan at the beginning of 1942, where an interesting wrinkle was added to his backstory. Arriving alongside King Kong Clayton as they brought their feud from the Rocky Mountains and Central Midwest to the Rust Belt, Samara was described as "a 32-year-old grappler who prefers to stick to a clean style of wrestling." *The Herald Press* of St. Joseph then delved into the fictional paternity of Samara, explaining that his father "Ras Samara" had "gained a reputation in Europe as a strong man."

By this point, Samara had been going by the forename Ras in other parts of the Midwest for two full years.

As had become their custom, the pair warred to multiple draws, and *The Herald Press* commended Samara for his histrionics, observing that he "turned out to be as good a comedian as he is a wrestler, much to the fans' delight."

The Berrien County wrestling promoters gleefully rematched Clayton and Samara, who *The Herald Press* added was "often called the Black Panther." This made Samara at least the third Black wrestler to appear in the area under that nickname in a 10-year period.

Surprisingly, the most eventful meeting between Clayton and Samara during 1942 would take place 370 miles away in St. Louis, Missouri during late March. That's where

A Decided Novelty

Sam Muchnick was hosting one of his All-Star wrestling cards, and as one of the selling points, he was promoting Samara vs. Clayton as "the first colored heavyweight professional wrestling bout ever staged in St. Louis."

Samara punches a downed opponent

    Muchnick added that Samara had made a name for himself in Boston years ago by wrestling Crusher Casey to a draw at the Boston Garden in front of 18,000 fans — a figure which assumed the venue had been packed to the rafters for the event, while somehow managing to inflate the maximum seating capacity of the venue by at least 3,000.

    The St. Louis Argus — the city's established Black newspaper — was excited by the prospect of an all-Black wrestling match, but due to their evident and understandable lack of familiarity with the grapplers, the people handling the layout of the paper inadvertently transposed the names of

A Decided Novelty

Samara and Clayton when placing their photos. This resulted in Samara being labeled as Clayton and vice versa.

In the end, Samara won the history-making encounter by downing Clayton in 36 minutes, 6 seconds. *The St. Louis Dispatch*, which earlier in its report noted that Sam Muchnick's show had received the disparaging designation of an "alleged wrestling exhibition" from the Missouri State Athletic Commission, pointed out the hypocrisy of rival promoter Tom Pack's championships being sanctioned by the same governing body. It then critiqued the realism of Samara's performance, noting that he demonstrated "more realistic scissors and footlocks than ordinarily seen in wrestling shows these days."

Samara entered the bout as the advertised "colored champion" and won the match with a bodyslam. The result was disseminated through newspapers all around the U.S., but according to *Argus* reporter C.M. Patrick, the real drama occurred behind the scenes, as "most of the highly publicized white wrestlers decided at the last minute to desert [Sam Muchnick's] card," which was stated to be the very first show Muchnick promoted in St. Louis.

"Much conniving and skullduggery took place behind the scenes, but judging from the way the fans took to the show, and judging from the applause Seelie Samara and King Kong Clayton received during and after their bout, Sam Muchnick's first show was quite a success," wrote Patrick.

It was reported by *The St. Louis Star-Times* that the event was so successful that Muchnick planned to bring Samara back immediately "against another Negro opponent." In spite of this trumpeted success, *The Argus* — a newspaper focusing primarily on Black issues — drew attention to the striking absence of a certain type of wrestling fan from the bout between Samara and Clayton.

"The colored fans were conspicuous by their absence," wrote Richard A. Jackson of *The Argus*. "This was plainly due to the rarity of a member of their race to get an opportunity to participate in wrestling programs."

A Decided Novelty

Jackson closed the piece by saying, "Whether colored wrestlers will take here... depends on how Negro fans turn out for the next card on which they appear. We holler for these chances, and when we get them we should act. Talk is cheap, but it takes money to buy the goods, and at 45 cents for a seat to help put a colored wrestler on big time, we should see at least 5,000 Negroes of St. Louis responding, even if they don't know what wrestling is all about."

Just two weeks later, while a defense of Samara's Negro heavyweight title against Clayton was being advertised for the Armory in Louisville, Kentucky, four hours away in St. Louis, Sam Muchnick announced his next Black heavyweight battle between Jack Claybourne and Rufus Jones.

"Muchnick introduced Negro wrestling to St. Louis at his last show in March when Seelie Samara won from 'King Kong' Clayton," explained *The St. Louis Star-Times*. "They have been rematched for a bout in Louisville on Derby Eve, and the winner is expected to meet the winner of the Claybourne-Jones go at a later date here."

For what it's worth, this certainly makes it sound like there was some merit behind the information that Samara and Clayton provided to Charles Washington of *The Omaha Star* just one year prior. Specifically, Washington wrote that a world's Negro championship tournament was being planned for St. Louis; apparently the bout between Clayton and Samara had been a first-round matchup — and potentially a semifinal-round matchup — in that tournament. The fact that Muchnick was openly acknowledging the rematch between Clayton and Samara lends further credence to this belief.

In the meantime, wrestling fans in Louisville were told that Clayton had earned his local title shot against Samara because he had "decisively whalloped" Jack Claybourne in straight falls just one week prior, which is not true. Claybourne had been busy contending for the light heavyweight title of Ohio, and was nowhere near Clayton during that time frame.

A Decided Novelty

Louisville wrestling fans who were familiar with Samara and had likely never heard of King Kong Clayton were probably quite surprised by the outcome of their title tussle.

"The unexpected happened in the final match when 'King Kong' Clayton hog-tied Hailie Samara, Negro champion, and took over the title," reported *The Courier-Journal* of Louisville. "After Samara, who won the recognition here last summer, had taken the first fall, Clayton came back to win the final two tugs, consuming just nine minutes in the process."

With that, Clayton had added his name to the list of Black stars who had acquired arguably the most credible of the active Negro heavyweight titles at that point. Outside of Kentucky, either this title change amounted to very little, or it simply didn't warrant any disruptions to existing advertising. At events held in both Colorado and Wyoming that featured both of the combatants from Louisville, Samara was advertised as "claimant of the world's colored heavyweight title" in spite of his loss to Clayton.

Both wrestlers were brought back to St. Louis for another special Muchnick event, with Muchnick proposing to place the winner of the bout against the victor between Jack Claybourne and another wrestler in what would amount to a miniature Negro title tournament. This pivot by Muchnick suggests that the availability of Rufus Jones for such a match had become less certain. Either way, the second St. Louis bout between Clayton and Samara concluded in one of their customary half-hour draws.

Clayton then briefly departed for the Rocky Mountain region once again, resuming the use of his Black Leopard name, and claiming the world's Negro heavyweight championship that he had captured at the expense of Samara. Then, both Samara and Clayton seemingly capitalized on the publicity they had generated for themselves in Missouri during Muchnick's shows, as they each made their first appearances in Kansas City.

Likely because he had achieved the lone conclusive victory in matches between the two in Missouri, Samara was booked as the Negro champion instead of Clayton whenever the two appeared together within the state. The two were also recruited for what may have been the first show designed to cater specifically to the Black wrestling fans of Kansas City.

The Call of Kansas City, a Black newspaper, devoted considerable coverage to a July event held at the Scott's Theater Restaurant located at 1701 E. 18th Street, which was a historic jazz venue that had previously been named the Boone Theater in honor of notable Black musical prodigy Jack "Blind" Boone.

The use of Boone Theater as the venue played a huge factor in setting the tone for the night's events. The theater's owner, Emmett "Little Giant" Scott, offered his facility specifically to permit Samara and Clayton to display their skills in what amounted to a home field setting against White opponents. Intentionally heightening the racial tension of the evening was a printed statement from Samara's opponent Jack Conley, who taunted the fans by saying that he insisted that the event be held in a "Negro neighborhood" so that "a large Negro audience can see me tear Samara apart, one limb at a time."

Before Conley and Samara entered the ring, Clayton got the action started by downing Al Getz in 45 minutes with a well-placed dropkick to the face. Afterward, Samara defeated Conley in two straight falls over the course of a long match, finally ending the contest with an airplane spin and a body slam after one hour and 20 minutes of action.

While ostensibly successful, the event was not repeated. King Kong Clayton was drafted into service with the U.S. Army and received his enlistment orders, and a rematch between Clayton and Samara for the world Negro heavyweight championship was quickly booked in Louisville. It would serve as Clayton's farewell match, at least for the time being.

"Haile Samara took over King Kong Clayton's claim to the Negro championship by beating the Chicagoan in the co-feature," reported *The Courier-Journal*. "Samara won the second fall in 19:24 with a head end shake, and the clincher in 11:55

with a body pin after Clayton had copped the opening fall in 24:01 with a kangaroo kick body pin."

Now that Clayton was out of action for the foreseeable future, Samara spent the rest of 1942 appearing elsewhere in Missouri and throughout Nebraska as Ras Samara. Toward the end of the year, he was placed in many supposed boxing matches against other wrestlers, and amplified tales of his alleged past life as a prizefighter to promote his appearances.

Other casualties of the draft were on the horizon. A March edition of *The Kalamazoo Gazette* informed fans that Jim Mitchell had been unable to make a recent appearance and required Joe Ferona to perform in his place because the Panther had also recently been drafted. As if on cue, just one month later residents of Kalamazoo were treated to an appearance from "Alex Kaffner, a new Black Panther from Alabama," strongly implying that local matchmaker Farmer Nick had gone out of his way to replace the most famous Black Panther in the Midwest with the second most popular.

Mitchell had continued to work with Rufus Jones a considerable amount in 1942 prior to his departure. In Sandusky, it was implied by *The Register* that the frequent interactions with Jones had been transforming Mitchell into a rougher wrestler, albeit still not a dirty one. The publication observed that during prior engagements, Mitchell "seemed to absorb punishment from a rougher opponent without slapping him in return," but that he was now "showing 'em in other cities that he, too, can dish out the rough stuff if rivals begin slugging."

In order to compete against the duo of Billy Rayburn and Steve Nenoff, Jones and Panther resurrected their tag team combination in Marion, Ohio, albeit with a twist. The pair had never teamed together in Marion before, and in that city they continued to sit on opposite sides of the heel-babyface dynamic even though they were now a team, with Jones being the unquestioned rulebreaker of the pair.

"Of the quartet, Rayburn and Nenoff are by far the most popular, while the Panther also is regarded by local fight

A Decided Novelty

followers as an excellent scrapper," opined *The Star*. "He has been fighting in Marion rings under the management of Promoter Les Fishbaugh and others for more than seven years. Jones is the not-so-popular scrapper of the four men, resorting to unorthodox procedure when the going gets tough."

Rufus Jones

Working as a heel-babyface pair, Jim and Rufus downed the previously undefeated team of Rayburn and Nenoff, but *The Star* illustrated how a matchup between Jones and Panther appeared to be in the offing considering the contentious interactions between the two as they pursued victory.

The Black team fell behind quickly when Rayburn forced Jones to submit to a crab hold, and then Mitchell was dropkicked and pinned. In the second fall, Mitchell evened the score just as single-handedly, immobilizing first Rayburn and then Nenoff with his favorite hold, the hip-headlock. That's when Jones ambushed his opponents to put them at a marked disadvantage during the third stanza.

"Just after returning for the third and deciding fall, Rayburn was jarred from the ring twice by the highly unorthodox Jones," recounted *The Star*. "The second drop from the four-foot ring put Rayburn out of commission. He was jolted hard on the first fall, but the second, even harder, kayoed him. Fighting alone with one half of the third fall already charged against him, Nenoff buckled down and pinned the Black Panther. With all the vengeance of a prehistoric beast, Jones came to the Panther's rescue, and made quick work of Nenoff with a body press accomplished on a spring from the ropes."

When Jones finally arrived in St. Louis to participate in Sam Muchnick's tournament, his appearance coincided with the debut of infamous wrestling promoter Jack Pfefer in the same city. *The St. Louis Star-Times* touted Pfefer as wrestling's "trust buster" from New York, who "operated a booking office that supplies pachyderms for promoters who desire his wares."

Even in the local newspapers, Pfefer's appearance was viewed as an unmistakable sign that he was taking sides in a wrestling war between Muchnick and Tom Packs, who Muchnick had broken away from to end Packs' local monopoly and start his own wrestling promotion.

It may just be a coincidence that the debut of Rufus Jones in St. Louis was perfectly synchronized with the participation of the promoter who had a heavy hand in amplifying the Tiger Flowers wrestling identity, but this is unlikely.

A Decided Novelty

As far as Muchnick was concerned, Samara had already advanced to the finals of his Negro-title tournament, with Jones and Claybourne filling out the other side of the bracket. On May 1, 1942, Claybourne defeated Jones at the St. Louis Municipal Auditorium with a dropkick and a cradle hold to satisfactorily advance to the finals of the tournament.

Of the bouts on the card, the match between Claybourne and Jones was said to have stood out "for good wrestling" by Ray Gillespie of *The St. Louis Star-Times*, who noted that the show was held "under the protection of a restraining injunction against interference by the police or the state athletic commission," which was apparently a realistic threat during interpromotional wrestling wars of the times.

"The boys spent no idle moments in their tasks and even added a little comedy to their skit with their quick recoveries after hard thrusts to the mat," Gillespie wrote of Rufus and Jack.

Unfortunately, no final bout between Samara and Claybourne — at least not one that can be definitively linked to Muchnick's tournament — appears to have taken place.

With the Black Panther having been drafted into military service, the two wrestlers whose public relationship situationally vacillated between that of best friends and arch enemies depending on time, place, and location would be required to have their final interactions for the foreseeable future.

Seemingly in an effort to make their final feud memorable, Jim and Rufus engaged in an exchange at the tail end of a battle royal at the Marion Armory that *The Star* referred to as "a back-alley fight" that didn't conclude until after both wrestlers reached the locker room.

"The Panther, officially the winner of the regulation ring tiff, but loser in the eyes of more than a few of last night's house, came out on the short end of a locker room climax," the article elaborated. "Jones, whose unorthodox tactics have brought about a strong sense of disapproval among the local fans, battered the Panther's head with a dress shoe, knocking

A Decided Novelty

the Panther senseless, and ultimately resulting in the intervention of Patrolman Smith."

The publication continued to delve into how Jones had been harboring "bitter hatred" toward the Panther for having deserted him during a prior tag team bout after Rufus engaged in disreputable tactics that caused Mitchell to walk out on him in disgust.

In response to the brawl, promoter Les Fishbaugh arranged for a no-holds-barred match with a two-hour time limit to be held at his late-June show. What materialized was a brutal match that lasted just under an hour, including the 10-minute intermissions between falls.

"The low-built Rufus, whose one ambition is to gain the support of the ring gathering, however, couldn't play fair when almost every shady practice was allowed," wrote *The Star*. "He indulged in a session of eye-gouging or low hitting whenever he was placed in a tight spot. Rufus gained the first fall with a devastating series of head punches, climaxed by a body press after a rough and eventful 31-minute tussle."

The Panther evened the match very quickly by coaxing Jones into submitting to his vaunted hip-headlock, and then battered Jones' ribs with a barrage of punches during the final fall until Jones collapsed and was pinned.

As physical, dramatic, and seemingly conclusive as the climactic bout between the former partners was, the wrestling fans of Marion, Ohio would have been absolutely astonished to learn that the two men teamed together just four nights later in Detroit. The experienced partners handily defeated Martini Angelo and Nick Billings in the main event of the Arena Gardens show.

Three nights after *that*, the two were back in Marion competing again in a boxing match, which concluded with a 10-round decision won by Mitchell.

When the Panther received a classic wrestling sendoff, losing his departure bout to Ivan Kalimikoff so that he could report for induction into the U.S. Army on July 24, his absence further thinned the number of Black stars in circulation, causing the value of the remaining Black wrestlers to rise by default.

Back in Dayton, Jack Claybourne defeated Speed LaRance in a best-of-three-falls match after the Canadian had lost his world title in Claybourne's absence. The two junior heavyweights then competed in a series of five matches, which Claybourne won 3-2, but it was a hollow victory as all of these wins against LaRance were stockpiled only after the title was no longer there for the taking.

In October, LaRance regained the title, inviting yet another challenge from Claybourne. As usual, with the world title on the line, Claybourne returned to his habit of losing when it mattered most. Then, when Martini Angelo managed to defeat LaRance for the junior heavyweight title, Claybourne challenged Angelo for the championship and lost to him as well.

Rufus Jones also made his way over to Dayton, finding a new partner in Claybourne now that Mitchell was no longer available. The two partnered on what was advertised as "the first all-Negro team" to compete in Dayton, and it was a losing effort against Bill Venable and Whitey Walberg.

Temporarily breaking off his pursuit of the MWA World Junior Heavyweight Championship, Claybourne traveled to Buffalo, New York at the end of 1942. There, Claybourne was referred to as "the Black Phantom," and *The Buffalo Evening News* praised him as "the best colored grappler since Regis Siki used to draw large crowds at Broadway Auditorium."

The Buffalo area had been starved for Black wrestlers to such an extent that it convincingly identified Claybourne to local patrons as "the only Negro wrestler in the pro ranks today," while attributing to Claybourne the statement that Black athletes "never took to wrestling because it lacked the spectacular" as an explanation for why there were so few Black wrestlers available.

In actual combat against Al Dunlop, Claybourne proved to be impressive as 1943 opened. Cy Kritzer of *The Buffalo News* described how Claybourne "sailed over (referee)

A Decided Novelty

Goodrich's shoulders in a flying dropkick and floored Al Dunlop for victory in 19:28." That's when the shenanigans began.

"Dunlop claimed Claybourne bit him when he had his fingers pulling the Negro's mouth apart," wrote Kritzer. "It was a roaring encounter and continued after the bell. Dunlop offered to shake hands; instead he smacked Claybourne with a right-hand punch. There was a towel around Dunlop's neck and the Negro grabbed it and pitched the Toronto huskie all over the ring until Goodrich stopped it."

Following the bout, local promoter Jack Herman was quoted as saying that the 32-year-old Claybourne was "the best prospect I've seen in the last five years," while comparing him to Scottish wrestler George "Dazzler" Clark. Clark's popularity had peaked in the region several years earlier, and he was known for his size, strength, speed, and well-rounded attack.

Jack was quickly promoted into the main events of Buffalo's wrestling events, with *The Evening News* promptly reminding fans that this marked "the first time a Negro grappler has been on top since the days of Regis Siki."

A short time later, Claybourne offered reporter C. Kritzer of *The Evening News* an exclusive interview, the contents of which appear to have been entirely made up. In the article, Claybourne is quoted as saying that he began wrestling in 1939 after wrestling promoter Al Haft spotted him sparring in a Columbus, Ohio gym and told him he had the physique and athleticism to be an outstanding wrestler. Claybourne added that Haft paid him the ludicrous sum of $2,500 just to undergo the training process.

"Imagine getting $2,500 for just training and working out!" exclaimed Claybourne to Kritzer. "Why, I said, 'yes sir,' before he could change his mind. Mr. Haft hired two professional wrestlers, and for the next ten months, I wrestled every day, sometimes for four or five hours. Then he called me into the office again and said, 'you're ready.' He also said that he was guaranteeing me $3,000 for my first year of wrestling. I never had hopes of making $3,000 a year."

A Decided Novelty

Adjusted for inflation, Claybourne was suggesting that he was paid the 2020s equivalent of nearly $60,000 just to train for 10 months, with a first-year guarantee of nearly $70,000. Of course, the story is complete nonsense anyway, as Claybourne debuted in the states immediately surrounding his home state of Missouri a full seven years before the date he proposed to Kritzer.

The plain truth is that Claybourne was never coaxed into wrestling by Al Haft, nor did he claim anything to that effect in the most genuine interview he ever provided. In his retrospective interview with *The Afro American*, which took place one decade later, Claybourne credited Kansas-Missouri promoter Gus Karras with offering him the opportunity to wrestle.

"I started as a fighter in Kansas City, Missouri, but I quit after a few months to wrestle," revealed Claybourne during his interview with *The Afro American*'s Joseph A. Owens. "I envisioned more money in wrestling."

Late in 1942, Claybourne displayed his willingness to get rough with his opponents, and he did so in a manner that bore an alarmingly striking resemblance to the style of combat favored by Rufus Jones. *The Courier-Express* declared that "the agile Negro… made badman tactics pay off" when he "butted skulls with (Joe) Christy several times, and evidently Jack's noggin was the harder, for Joe sank to the canvas."

Claybourne then twisted Christy's head in a manner similar to Jim Mitchell's famed hip-headlock, causing Christy to submit.

In the aftermath of this aberrant display of headbutting from Claybourne, he was described as a wrestler who "uses his head as a battering ram" by *The Buffalo Evening News*, and even followed up on why his newest trick was "to butt skulls with his opponent and knock him out."

"I have the toughest skull in wrestling," bragged Claybourne.

Fittingly, Claybourne only seemed to break out the headbutts during the rare occasions when he was playing the role of heel, as if seasoning his high-flying style with the head-cracking flavor of Rufus Jones was the easiest way to communicate to the crowd that he was engaging in villainous behavior.

By the close of 1942, there had finally been a tangible revelation as to the unique toll that World War II was taking on Reginald Siki, who had been effectively absent from U.S. wrestling rings for nine years. Even in his absence, every Black star was still being compared to him, as Siki represented the most mainstream example of a Black wrestling star that most sportswriters could grasp for the sake of making comparisons.

"Not since Reginald Siki, the West Indian Negro of more than a decade ago who threw the great Stanislaus Zbyszko, long world's champion, has there been a Negro wrestler of any consequence," stated Richard A. Jackson of *The St. Louis Argus* in 1940. "This has been mainly in the first place because few if any have been interested in the grunt and groan industry; and, in the second place, because they receive little or no encouragement."

Because professional wrestling is such an out-of-sight, out-of-mind business, and because pro wrestling activity during World War II was drastically reduced from its pre-war peak, it's not surprising that very little ink was devoted to Siki or how his life might have been affected by the outbreak of war. Any wrestling fans who were curious of Siki's fate probably responded with panic in December 1942 when *The Kansas City Call* published a card postmarked October 24, 1942, from Tittmoning, Ober-Baycon, Germany.

"I, Reginald Siki Berry, professional wrestler, and seven other race boys are interned here," began the message. "We'd appreciate it beyond words if you'd scatter a few rays of sunshine and cheer by sending each of us a sweater-coat, a sweat shirt, three extra large sizes plus five medium sizes, respectively, shoes and overshoes to match in the following sizes: 11EE, 10 ½ EE, 10EE, 9D, 8 ½ D, 8 ½ D.

A Decided Novelty

"Also, one piece of canvas 12 feet by 12 feet for a wrestling mat, one stop watch and any other gift that you may choose to send.

"A friend in need is a friend indeed. Help us!

"Yours sincerely,

"Reginald Siki Berry."

The Call added that the card had reached Kansas City after passing through the hands of German censors. The article also included a message from Siki's one-time Lincoln High School principal H.O. Cook who "remembers Siki as a young wrestler in Kansas City."

While the revelation that Siki had fallen into the hands of Nazi Germany and was being held captive was certainly terrifying, some preemptive clarification is in order. Because of the horrors that were later revealed with respect to Nazi concentration camps, it is essential to note that the Nazis operated several prisons outside of the concentration camp system where foreign non-combatants received overwhelmingly better treatment than those housed at concentration camps.

Furthermore, the German prison camps for non-combatants usually did allow the exchange of correspondence and care packages — managed by the Red Cross — for the majority of the war, so correspondence like Siki's was not uncommon. Still, Siki's message was one of the first public revelations of the fact that Black Americans were being housed at the Tittmoning castle.

Siki's extreme distress notwithstanding, his message to *The Call* also confirmed several important facts about his background, specifically that he was a young wrestler in Kansas City who attended the exclusively Black Lincoln High School, and who therefore almost certainly played the role of "The Snake" Leonard Rabinette, who participated in the show held in Kansas City more than two decades prior in 1921.

While Siki's safety remained very much in doubt, Ras Samara continued his tear through the heart of the Midwest in 1943, regularly wrestling in Missouri, Iowa, Minnesota, and especially Nebraska. Continuing to be featured as something of a hybrid between a boxer and a wrestler, Samara was also seen receiving occasional assistance from some of the most active prizefighters in the state.

For one of his March 'boxing matches,' Samara enlisted local Black boxer Edward "Bearcat" Wright to work in his corner. A one-time challenger for the Negro boxing championship once held by George Godfrey, Bearcat Wright had been involved in well over 100 matches by this point in his career, with the results of many of those bouts no longer being logged.

This period of time saw Samara engaged in some of the most high-profile bouts of his career. These included a loss in Lincoln by way of a crushing bear hug — known as "The Sunday Hug" — to "The French Angel" Maurice Tillet, a major box-office attraction whose face had been enlarged and disfigured by acromegaly. Samara also lost to former National Wrestling Association world champion Ray Steele in Minneapolis after getting trapped by Steele's "upside down and stepover hold."

In September, Samara wrestled against Ed "Strangler" Lewis, the legendary former world heavyweight champion who was now wrestling well into his 50s. Despite his age and the vast disparity in muscularity between the two, Lewis still bested Samara in two short falls at the Hastings City Auditorium, ending the entire affair in 21 minutes.

"Ras, the muscular Omaha dusky, put up a game battle but found the Strangler too hefty and able," reported *The Hastings Daily Tribune*. "Lewis, always a fast man despite his size, has retained his agility. He was in some tight spots during the first round, but worked out. The Strangler wound up both falls by a series of slams, locking his arms about Samara's head, then banging the dusky to the mat."

Losses piled up, but Samara continued to be promoted as a viable contender for the recognized world heavyweight championships of the era. This included statements from the local press questioning why Black achievements in wrestling seemed to pale in comparison to the successes that Black athletes had achieved through competitive boxing.

"At one time or another, almost every division in professional boxing has been topped by a Negro, with Jack Johnson and Joe Louis holding the heavyweight title," elaborated *The News-Press* of St. Joseph, Missouri. "American track and field, horse racing, football, basketball, and baseball have all had great Negro performers. Samara is one of the few colored stars ever to turn his serious attention to the mat sport. He brought to the game a world of talent backed up by a powerful physique that makes him one of the most feared men operating today. His refusal to go all out as a rougher has probably been his biggest handicap."

The article opened with an accusation that wrestling was "the only sport that hasn't developed a Negro champion," and then positioned Samara as the man who might earn the distinction as the first Black champion in wrestling.

Coincidentally, if Samara's full resume had been disclosed to the public at that point, several readers of the article might have been satisfied that Samara had in fact already been one of the first recognizable Black world champions in wrestling history.

Again, to the extent that it was required that a wrestler needed to be promoted as the nominal holder of a world championship that bore some sort of recognition by an active wrestling organization, Clarence Bouldin and Frank Crozier should be the first two wrestlers that come to mind chronologically. The difference is that Bouldin's Sub Saharan African heritage was hidden from the public, and Crozier's world championship was won in a tournament, and was technically only capable of being defended once annually.

Joe Godfrey's middleweight title reign in Boston certainly qualified as a world title that was won in the ring, while Samara is likely the first Black heavyweight to be acknowledged as a world heavyweight champion even if he was not seen to win the title during active competition. Regardless, his multiple world junior heavyweight championship reigns in

A Decided Novelty

Montreal meet that threshold, but individuals are welcome to apply their own criteria when debating such matters.

Back in St. Joseph, Missouri, *The St. Joseph Gazette* offered a perfect description of the conclusion to a standard Samara bout during the era, highlighting the features that tended to make these endings more exciting than those involving many other wrestlers. The sequence of events began when Jay Meeker knocked Samara out of the ring and onto the arena floor 11 minutes into the third fall of their match, and then went out of his way to make it difficult for Samara to re-enter.

"Referee Billy Atkins forced Meeker to the far side of the ring, and Samara grabbed the top rope and was set for Meeker's next lunge," described the article. "Using perfect timing Samara leaped over the top rope and crashed into the Canadian, knocking him down. Samara fell on Meeker for the fall."

Aside from using this sort of outside-in slingshot maneuver to pounce on his opponents with shoulder tackles and crossbody takedowns, Samara would also leap and swing his legs over the top strand of the ropes, trapping his opponents' heads between his legs, and whipping them to the canvas with flying headscissor takedowns.

Samara's matches offered clear entertainment value, and his widespread popularity in Nebraska, Missouri, and other Midwestern states was undeniable. Still, Samara continued to come up short against wrestling's true feature attractions and acknowledged race-neutral champions. This included further losses to Maurice Tillet, and also setbacks at the hands of dominant Midwestern world champion Orville Brown.

For those who knew what they were looking for, details connecting Rufus Jones with his time as Ed Flowers in New England began to leak out when he began wrestling in Cincinnati. While promoting a bout between Jones and junior heavyweight champion Frankie Talaber at Cincinnati's Music Hall Sports Arena, *The Cincinnati Enquirer* described Jones as "a former champion, having held the middleweight title for several years, increasing weight forcing him to give it up."

Jones would lose his match to Talaber, but the insistence that "the New England Cobra" was a former long-term champion became embellished even further within the pages of *The Cincinnati Post*. The claim appeared in an article explaining how Boston native Jones was trained to wrestle by former world middleweight champion Ted Germaine.

"How well Germaine taught Jones is shown by the fact that after several years of tutelage, Rufus took the middleweight crown away from him," continued *The Post*. "With the championship under his belt, Jones toured the country until too much fine living started to show in his weight, and he had to relinquish the title. Jones misses the acclaim he received when champion and will shoot the works in order to have another crown on his head after Friday's bout."

As preposterous as the longevity granted to this title claim is, it does offer the best hint available as to how Rufus Jones had been taught to wrestle. Aside from being a frequent opponent of Godfrey's when he wrestled as Ed Flowers in the earliest stages of his career, Germaine probably trained with Godfrey behind the scenes to help him achieve his mastery of the wrestling craft.

Just as important, Germaine was well known for his ability to transition seamlessly between straight grappling and wild brawling antics. A career-retrospective article about Germaine printed by *The Boston Globe* in 1964 explained how Germaine's bouts "nearly always ended up outside the ropes, with ring-side patrons scattering and the police moving into action."

More to the point, since there is no record of Ted Germaine ever wrestling in Ohio, his name would have meant next to nothing to the wrestling fans of Cincinnati, meaning that there would have been no reason to invoke his name if there hadn't been at least a kernel of truth to the tale.

A Decided Novelty

The Cincinnati Enquirer later added that Jones was also a former Hollywood extra, but "he couldn't eat regularly waiting for assignments." While there is no clear evidence that Jones ever made an appearance on the silver screen, it's possible that there is some connection between this reference and the past statement that Tiger Flowers was in high demand as a model in New York City.

As far as the wrestling world was concerned, the real Tiger Flowers had disappeared several years earlier, never to be heard from again. In reality, he had been hiding in plain sight the entire time, and a change of scenery for Joe Godfrey would lead to the reappearance of a former champion that New Englanders had believed to be long gone.

18 – Plenty of Color

Predictably, Rufus Jones was called up for his U.S. Army medical inspection in fall 1943, missing a scheduled bout in Hamilton in the process, while *The Hamilton Spectator* lamented on November 3 that Jones "might be lost to the wrestling realm for the duration."

Any fears that Jones would be called up for military service were immediately dispelled. Three days later, *The Spectator* served up the seemingly incongruent announcement that Jones had "failed to pass the U.S. Army test," and would therefore be free to resume violent exchanges with foes in the ring on a nightly basis.

In Dayton, Rufus was pulled aside by *Dayton Herald* reporter Marj Heyduck, and provided what was ostensibly the most direct and honest interview of his wrestling career, with all quotes directly attributed to him, and with the reporter's name fully on the record.

Heyduck opened the piece by saying that Jones, "the grinning 205 pounds of jumping jive on a 5-foot-7-and-a-half-inch frame, is not the Baron of Beall Street, as he has been called," and then included Jones' admission that he had never traveled further south than Louisville, Kentucky in his life. He then proceeded to ask Jones what he liked.

"Nothing but wrestlin', eatin', dancin', and Lena Horne," Jones answered.

Jones added that his favorite meals were chicken and steak, "but mostly steak," that his favorite musicians were Duke Ellington, Fats Waller, and Hazel Scott, and that he did attend Boston University for two years before turning to wrestling, even though that claim contrasts with Jones' own reports to the census takers. As for injuries, Jones stated that he had "only got one broken leg, a broken collarbone, and a couple broken ribs in the last 10 years. Yeah, man."

Certainly, the accumulation of that many injuries would have gone a long way toward disqualifying Jones from military service. Also, based on Heyduck's writing, Jones appeared to have had a distinct habit of punctuating his sentences with "Yeah, man" at the end.

In the summer, Jones briefly reunited with Jim Mitchell. The Panther returned to Ohio and Ontario as "Sergeant Jimmy Mitchell" and made a few appearances during his furlough from the U.S. Army to face Rufus Jones and Gil Lacrosse, and to partner with Rene LaBell in tag team competition.

Jack Claybourne spent his most productive part of 1943 dueling with "Whipper" Billy Watson, who was being hailed in Buffalo as "the best young wrestler" in the business, who had already captured the British Empire heavyweight championship. Clearly, Claybourne's role was to make Watson appear even more impressive, as he lost nearly every bout he had with the regional favorite, while only occasionally managing to secure draws with the master of the Irish whip.

In addition to losing his opportunities at the British Empire title held by Watson, Claybourne also lost to the other prominent holder of that championship, Yvon Robert, when Robert caught Jack in mid-air during a third-fall dropkick attempt and dropped him on his head for the win.

Of far more significance was when Claybourne was offered a title shot at National Wrestling Association world heavyweight champion Bill Longson in Hamilton, Ontario during October 1943. Of the world championships in existence at the time, those of the National Wrestling Association were among the most prized. The organization had the benefit of being established by the National Boxing Association, and its titles were widely recognized throughout the wrestling world.

"The match is pregnant with possibilities, for if Gentleman Jack beats the Salt Lake City slasher, he will be the first negro to enter the heavyweight throne room," observed *The Hamilton Spectator*, once again teasing the cultural and historical ramifications of a potential Claybourne title win. "Coloured athletes have won the topmost crown in many different fields of athletic endeavour, but it remains for

A Decided Novelty

Claybourne to reach the top in wrestling. And right now his chances loom up as plenty strong."

As in prior cases, despite the illusion of hope that saturated the promotion of the match, Claybourne was defeated by Longson in 34 minutes with a piledriver.

Don Blackman seated to the left of Joe Louis

Photos taken during fall 1943 made it clear to everyone that Don Blackman was rolling in celebrity circles even while performing his military duties. That's when the Bureau of Public Relations circulated a photo to all news outlets of Joe Louis driving a U.S. Army Jeep. Seated right next to the reigning world heavyweight boxing champion was Blackman.

Identified across the country as "Sergeant Don Blackman of the Fort Dix Military Police, former wrestling star" while riding next to arguably the most famous Black athlete in American history up until that point, that photo had the potential to do more for Blackman's credibility as a wrestler than hundreds of in-ring victories. Of course, Blackman would still need to survive the war, and hopefully resume a full-time wrestling career while he could still capitalize on the exposure.

Out of nowhere, Lee Umbles emerged from a six-year hiatus in 1943 to wrestle at a show in Chicago organized by promoter J.R. Rolewicz. Umbles was still being advertised as the colored welterweight champion even after years of inactivity, and was booked to compete against Swedish wrestler Ed Vanhereck. Rolewicz vowed to run future shows on Chicago's South Side every two weeks if fans came out to support the events; there are no clear signs that any subsequent events were held.

Starting out 1944 in New England, Jack Claybourne's performances elicited comparisons to "Count" Nicholas Zarnyoff of Russia, who was a frequent main-event wrestler during the 1920s and 1930s, competing against the likes of Gus Sonnenberg and Hans Schroeder.

From a stylistic standpoint, Zarnyoff was known to regularly take to the air during matches, attempting flying headscissors, rapid sunset-flip takedowns, acrobatic rolls from his back to his feet, and most impressively, full front-flip counters to flying mare takedown attempts. To so favorably compare Claybourne with Zarnyoff — or in the case of *The Springfield Union*, to flat-out call him "the colored Count Zarnyoff" — was to equate Claybourne with one of the elite mat showmen of the prior era.

"Jack Claybourne, Lawrence heavyweight mat ace with a million tricks, fastest and speediest of the wrestlers today, has taken the place left vacant by Count Zarnyoff, Russian nobleman-matman," insisted *The Union*. "Count Zarnyoff retired several years ago, and despite the imitative ways of some heavyweights, none of them came close to duplicating his mat trickery until Claybourne moved into the heavyweight ranks. The Negro speedster has showed the same qualities that made the Count in a class by himself. His speed, his lithesomeness, his score of tricks and his ability to give and take make him one of the outstanding performers of the mat."

The Fitchburg Sentinel also pitched in with praise. The publication stated that the "colored bolt of lightning" was the fastest wrestler to ever appear in the local ring, and added that "to see him sailing over the referee's head and landing on his opponent's shoulders is worth the price of admission."

A Decided Novelty

In January, Claybourne engaged in his first bout that actually involved the presence of world heavyweight boxing champion Joe Louis, albeit with Louis playing the role of arbiter rather than opponent. In Portland, Maine, Claybourne faced off with Manuel Cortez, while Louis served as the referee.

As a condition of his military service, Louis had been making almost daily public appearances to rally support for the U.S. war effort. These engagements often bestowed refereeing duties at boxing and wrestling events upon the world boxing champion. Although Claybourne and several other Black wrestlers had been referred to as associates of Louis for nine straight years, not to mention being assessed to be his pro wrestling equivalents, this would be the first time that Claybourne was confirmed to have been within arm's reach of the famed Brown Bomber.

"Cortez took advantage of Louis' obvious unfamiliarity with the mat rules to give Claybourne a beating in the first fall, and won it in 13:32 on a lift and slam," reported Frank Curran of *The Portland Press Herald*. "Claybourne wasn't doing much better in the second till he landed a drop kick and ended things at 6:36, but he went to town in the finale. Here, Cortez egged Louis on with every trick in the book, but Louis evidently didn't see any enjoyment out of punching a mere wrestler, so Claybourne captured the melee in 12:21 with a double-arm press."

Claybourne's match against Cortez with Louis serving in the role of referee turned out to be a mere dress rehearsal for the feature event in Boston, which was a bout for the "duration world's heavyweight wrestling crown" between Jack Claybourne and the massive, 379-pound masked champion known as the Golden Terror.

"After taking the first fall in the match which Louis refereed, Claybourne dove for the Terror, missed, catapulted off the ropes, and landed on his back," reported *The Springfield Daily News*. "He was carried away unconscious and taken to a hospital, where attaches said today he was resting comfortably."

The authenticity of Claybourne's injuries notwithstanding, the night was additionally memorable due to the riot that ensued at the arena. Attracted by an opportunity to see the reigning world heavyweight boxing champion in person, 7,200 spectators showed up, overwhelming the capacity constraints of a building that was never intended to hold more than 5,000 persons.

When rioting fans broke down the doors to the venue in their attempts to gain entry, mounted police had to be summoned to restore order.

Freed from the mandates of military service, Jim Mitchell returned to action early in January 1944, and apparently suffered from some semblance of "ring rust" due to his inactivity. Joe Burns of *The Windsor Star* wrote a scathing critique of Mitchell's performance — and more so his physique — and surmised that it was a lack of conditioning that led to the Panther's release from the U.S. Army.

"Certainly, he got no Ranger training, otherwise he wouldn't have gone down to defeat so unimpressively as he did, if at all, and as for his appearance, evident fleshiness made him look like anything but the sleek Panther of old," scolded Burns. "About the only resemblance the Panther bore to the streak of brown, greased lightning who used to do his stuff here a decade ago was in the matter of sportsmanship. Oh, yes, and maybe when he was using his bulldogging tactics."

Mitchell's bulldogging methods were actually described by people in the crowd sitting within earshot of Burns, with one of the spectators preparing his companions for what was to come by saying "Watch him, now, when he puts on that headlock, runs him forward, and lets him fall on his face."

Other than the fall he achieved on Angelo Savoldi, which came by way of a bulldogging headlock that set up the Panther's regular headlock submission hold, Mitchell lost two falls to Savoldi in 12 minutes, 10 seconds and 2 minutes, 10 seconds, respectively.

A Decided Novelty

Mitchell quickly began to operate within the orbit of Rufus Jones once again, which led to a few occasions when both wrestlers used headbutts in the same matches, deepening the growing stereotype that Black wrestlers used headbutts due to their genetically hard heads.

The heavier "Black Panther" Jim Mitchell

In Adrian, Michigan, *The Daily Telegram* described both Jones and Mitchell as "head-bunters," and promoter Al Ross suggested that the result of the match would hinge on "their respective abilities to crack the opponent's skull." It apparently never occurred to Ross that if both wrestlers' heads were

A Decided Novelty

impervious to pain, they would negate one another's advantage, and have to win their matches with other methods. While Ross may have teased an evenly matched headbutting war on this occasion, the match results between the two wrestlers betray a pattern in which Jones tended to get the better of Mitchell whenever head-to-head exchanges were brought to the fore, whereas the Panther had the edge when the action tended toward straight wrestling.

The frequent adversaries brought their act to Benton Harbor in the spring, where Jones was forced to contend with language from *The St. Joseph Herald Press* that stretched the boundaries of racial sensitivity.

In one article, the writer proposed that "Rufe, with all due respect to his ancestors, looks not unlike an ape," and suggested that his match would therefore "have all the aspects of a visit to the zoo." In describing how Rufus preferred to deliver his headbutt, the article further elaborated that Jones would stand upright "with the backs of his hands all but touching the mat," as if he dealt with postural struggles caused by arms of primate-like length.

If anything, the thickly muscled arms of the 5'7" Jones skewed toward the shorter end of the spectrum, but the writer from *The Herald Press* certainly wasn't going to allow something like the truth to interfere with a creative racist analogy.

A description of Jones' match against Tiger Jack Moore showed that *The News-Palladium* of nearby Benton Harbor had also gotten in on the act, saying of Jones that "he bit, he kicked, and he slugged his foe… and he did it with all the grace displayed by 'Cheeta,' the chimpanzee in Tarzan films."

After the bout ended with Jones suffering a loss, *The News-Palladium* continued to describe how referee Sammy Price had to shove around "the happy savage," and then the writer inexplicably expressed surprise when Jones "seemed to resent one fan who kept asking him if he wanted a banana."

That fan is lucky that Jones never got within arm's reach of him. After a match against the Panther in Hamilton,

Ontario the following month, a fan got much too close to Jones once the show was presumed to have ended.

"When Rufus was on the way to the dressing room, after hostilities ceased, an irate spectator made a pass at him to his sorrow, for Rufus retaliated with a stiff right to the face which left the man with a souvenir to carry around for a few days," reported *The Spectator*.

Outside of Michigan, Jones and the Panther resumed their pattern of wrestling as a team in Ohio while competing against each other in Ontario. When their reunited tag team returned to Marion, Ohio, Jones and Mitchell both collected falls with headbutts, proving the superior and universal thickness of Black men's skulls once again.

During their next team-up in Marion, Jones apparently leaned on Mitchell to do the bulk of the dirty work, as the Panther disposed of both Angelo Martinelli and Irish McGee with headbutts while Jones watched from the apron of the ring.

As the summer unfolded, Jones made a few appearances in Montreal under the name of Tiger Flowers for the first time in years, and with the Black Panther right there by his side. Soon thereafter, Jones appeared in New Brunswick under the guise of Tiger Flowers, just as he'd done in Canada's other eastern provinces in the past.

On August 24, *The Moncton Daily Times* announced that "a bit of color" would be added to one of their bouts, and that it would be owed to the presence of Tiger Flowers, "one of the best known colored grapplers in the game today," who possessed "a wide knowledge of wrestling holds through extensive campaigning in the United States."

To ensure that the wrestling fans of New Brunswick were suitably prepared for Flowers' debut, *The Daily Times* provided them with a fair warning of what they should expect to see in the ring on the occasion of the veteran wrestler's arrival.

"Flowers is another of those wrestlers who raises the ire of the fans the minute the going gets underway, and when the going gets tough he leans back and butts his opponent's noggin with his own dome," explained *The Daily Times*. "His head butt is distinctly different; the fact is he has just the kind of head to butt with. At times he amuses the fans with his comical gestures."

In the wake of Flowers' debut, the sports page of *The Moncton Transcript* was critical of the grappler's performance in a way that was atypical to what he was accustomed to hearing in the Midwest. The report from *The Transcript* outright declared that Flowers' performance during his bout with Mike Demetre had "failed to live up to expectations."

"Flowers came here with a big reputation, but aside from some tricky tactics, he displayed little in the way of real wrestling," complained the reviewer. "The bout reached a climax when it showed both wrestlers 'bowlegged,' presumably punched that way by the pseudo heavy gong."

Flowers lost the match when he was disqualified in the final fall. Even if the show hadn't been a critical success in the eyes of *The Transcript*'s sportswriter, the publication's editor Bill Hutchinson said that the show featuring Flowers had drawn one of the largest crowds ever to the Moncton Arena, but then added that the presence of wrestling star Yvon Robert at the next show would be "needed to atone for the show put on by Tiger Flowers, the colored gripper," which had clearly left him feeling underwhelmed.

The writer from *The Daily Times* was of an altogether different opinion, declaring that the match between Flowers and Demetre was "easily the best performance presented here in a long, long time." *The Daily Times*' report included the observation that Flowers was also "one of the fastest wrestlers to appear in the local ring," and also regarded the first use of Flowers' famed headbutt as a major unveiling.

"For the first time in Moncton, fans were treated to the head butt, a novelty which Flowers uses extensively, in which he holds his opponent's head in his hands and then butts it with his own. This drew a big laugh from the fans," added the article.

A Decided Novelty

Clearly, Joe Godfrey was making absolutely no effort to mask the fact that Rufus Jones and Tiger Flowers were one and the same.

One week later, in early September, *The Daily Times* announced the presence of "plenty of color" at the next show, when Flowers' faithful comrade Jim Mitchell arrived in New Brunswick. As for his opponent, Flowers was granted an opportunity to wrestle against world junior heavyweight champion Paul Lortie. Flowers took the first fall "with a series of punishing holds, most of which were on the illegal side, followed by the Boston crab."

Lortie won both the second and third falls of the match, even resorting to illegal tactics to win the third fall, "pinning the Negro with the ropes," which *The Transcript* interpreted as the champion repaying Flowers for his foul play.

From there, the original Tiger Flowers returned to the New England area for the first time in more than five years, and took up residence in the wrestling rings of Vermont, continuing the longest absence of the name Rufus Jones from the wrestling scene in seven years.

However, the images of Rufus Jones circulating in the press certainly didn't disappear, as the promotional photos used to advertise the appearances of Tiger Flowers were totally identical to the promotional photos used to market Jones in other states.

By no means were fans of Rufus Jones kept in the dark about where he was and what he was doing, or at least the wrestling fans in Hamilton, Ontario weren't. A mid-November edition of *The Hamilton Spectator* informed fans that Jones was "plying his trade in the Maritimes where he travels under the name Tiger Flowers."

If Ontario's wrestling fans had missed Rufus Jones, the first line of the first article announcing his return to Canada would have suggested otherwise. In what was probably the most racially insensitive introduction to an article announcing the return of a Black wrestler ever written, *The Windsor Star* opened its December 14, 1944 edition with the line, "Get out

A Decided Novelty

your lynching ropes, boys. Rough Rufus Jones is going to be in town."

As alarming as it was that a Black professional wrestler had fallen into Nazi hands, nothing of significance regarding Reginald Siki or his fate reached the press until it was revealed that he had returned home. Siki was brought back to the U.S. along with several other former Tittmoning prisoners aboard the MS *Gripsholm*, a Swedish ship chartered by the U.S. State Department from 1942-1946 for prisoner exchanges. Operating under the International Red Cross with a Swedish crew, it made 12 round trips carrying over 27,000 repatriates.

Late in March 1944, Max Lieberman of *The Hartford Daily Courant* described how a Black wrestler named Kemal Abdul Rahman walked to the ring in Hartford, Connecticut and dispensed with Art Legrand in a shade over 15 minutes. After the bout, Rahman revealed that he was the wrestler formerly known as Reginald Siki, who had returned to the U.S. from a German internment camp just one month ago. Rahman expressed that the care packages supplied by the Red Cross had dramatically eased the hardship experienced by himself and others while they were imprisoned.

"Those at home cannot do enough to help the Red Cross for what they are doing in the way of service overseas," said Rahman.

Rahman soon found his way to his old haunt in Springfield, and appeared on the same cards as Jack Claybourne, a standard bearer of the generation of Black wrestling stars who had emerged to take Rahman's place. *The Springfield Daily Republican* described Rahman as a "bearded Mohammedan," and gave an abbreviated account of what happened to Siki, saying that he had been on a European wrestling tour when the Gestapo arrested him.

In at least one of his Springfield bouts, Rahman was still claiming to be the world's colored wrestling champion, which was just as well. To the extent that he had ever defended or even truly competed for such a title — with his only confirmed bout with a race-based title on the line being his loss

A Decided Novelty

to George Godfrey in Belgium nine years prior — no one in America had ever even heard about the match, let alone recalled the outcome or cared one way or another.

While Siki had physically returned, in some respects, his name had never left. Elsewhere in 1944, Gorilla Parker was engaged with a Black wrestler who went by the name Young Siki, who was absolutely *not* Reginald Siki. The pairing of the two resembled that of Jones and Mitchell, as they interacted as friendly teammates on one night, and then turned around and wrestled each other as bitter adversaries on the next night.

The bout between the two in July 1944 was declared by *The Wilmington Morning News* to have been the first bout between Black competitors in the history of Delaware.

In spring 1944, Seelie Samara finally made a long overdue trip to Los Angeles, California. *The Los Angeles Citizen-News* positioned Samara as an aspirant to accomplish in wrestling what other Black sports heroes of the era had managed to pull off and capture a championship. Presumably, it would have been less enticing to inform fans that by some measure, Samara was already a multi-time world champion in the sport of wrestling, and was simply hoping to add to his tally.

True to the pattern typically employed to introduce newcomers to wrestling territories, Samara methodically piled up victories during his early days in Los Angeles. As the local newspapers maintained a record of his winning streak at the Olympic Auditorium, Samara also traveled to Phoenix, where *The Arizona Republic* informed local wrestling fans that Seelie had been active in the ring for only six years.

This was likely an attempt to conceal Samara's true age from the paying customers, who would probably have assumed that such a muscular specimen was still in his youthful prime, as opposed to being a 38-year-old ring veteran who had nearly completed his fourth decade of life.

Very quickly, Samara became a smash hit across the entire state of California, and he was soon traveling the length of the state to also make appearances in Sacramento and

A Decided Novelty

Oakland, along with his engagements in the southern portion of the state.

Samara's first major loss in the Los Angeles area would occur at the hands of Jim Casey in May, but that wouldn't prevent news outlets in the San Francisco Bay area from continuing to advertise him as a wrestler who was undefeated on the Pacific Coast.

During his time appearing in the wrestling rings of Northern California, Samara was portrayed as an unrelenting force for good. In the pages of *The Press Democrat* of Santa Rosa, it was reported that "The Joe Louis of the mat is doing more to rid the game of 'villains' than all the rules and regulations of the State Athletic Commission."

Just when Samara appeared to be invincible, he absorbed a series of losses. This included defeats at the hands of the masked wrestler Achilles, regional title match losses at the hands of Dean Detton, and multiple losses to Steve "Crusher" Casey — the same wrestler who had terminated any claims Samara may have held to world heavyweight title status six years earlier in Boston.

Adding insult to the injury of Samara's frustrations in bouts with race-neutral championships on the line, *The Arizona Daily Star* of Tucson seemed to strike a mocking tone when acknowledging Samara's participation in a match in late June, referring to him as a claimant to the "colored wrestling championship of the universe."

Samara's media exposure in September was either favorable or unfavorable depending on individual perspective. Ed Orman of *The Fresno Bee* reported how Samara was surprisingly handcuffed and taken to a Modesto jail after a match with King Kong Ted Cox. The legitimacy of the fight is questionable, as it reportedly took place in the locker room following a show. However, the intervention of the police in the squabble between Cox and Samara, perhaps not realizing the audible locker room altercation was probably part of the evening's entertainment, was apparently genuine.

"It seems the two engaged in an exchange of blows in the dressing room after their match in the ring," stated *The Bee*. "Fans tried to crowd into the dressing quarters to see the extra curricular affair, but police intervened; one was injured, and the result was John Law took both parties responsible for the melee to the jail — charged with disturbing the police. Billy Hunefeld, the former Fresno promoter now promoting in Modesto and Stockton, tried to get them off the hook but could not turn the trick. Finally, they paid $50 bail each and were released, but chances are that is what the rumpus will cost in the end, because they no doubt will not fight the charge."

Promoter Hunefeld, in an effort to capitalize on the incident, issued a statement to *The Stockton Record* that included an alleged quote from Seelie Samara that was definitely phony. In the submitted quote, Samara adopts the pandering posture that Blacks were too often seen to assume in the era's entertainment, referring to his territorial employer Billy Hunefeld as "Mr. Billy" while begging him for a bout with Cox to settle the score. It was not the sort of statement that one would expect to emanate from a muscular, self-respecting man who was nearly 40 years of age, regardless of race.

"Mr. Billy, please match me with that screwy Cox in Stockton so I can make him ashamed of what he done to my reputation in Modesto," Samara was quoted. "All I ask you to do is to get special police guards to make Cox stay in the ring Thursday night, and I'll guarantee you he'll be sorry he ever caused this baby such embarrassment and humiliation as goin' to jail. Cox may like jails, but I don't. Please, Mr. Billy, get me Cox."

Worse than the servile manner in which he was depicted as he begged for the rematch with Cox is the fact that Samara lost the subsequent encounter with Cox at the Stockton Civic Auditorium, dropping the one-fall match in 15 minutes, 30 seconds.

To defeat Samara, Cox countered the Negro champion's slingshot leap from the ring apron, which had become a common method by which Samara would suffer

A Decided Novelty

defeat on the Pacific Coast. Given the inherently high-risk nature of the maneuver, there was an abundance of ways that Samara's leap could backfire, resulting in him receiving the worse end of the exchange.

This tendency played out almost identically when Samara wrestled George Coverly in the fall, and the Orange County Athletic Club watched as Coverly ducked underneath Samara's leaping tackle attempt, and then successfully covered Seelie after he crashed to the mat.

November 1944 would see the return of Jack Claybourne to Southern California after an absence of nearly a decade, resulting in the familiar ploy of pitting one Black wrestler against the other for racial supremacy. By this point, Samara's sterling reputation in the region has risen to the point where promoters in Los Angeles County were comfortable promoting him as "without a doubt, the greatest Negro wrestler of the age," who was "considered by many the best Negro grappler in history."

Based on his resume — which included past reigns as a world champion in multiple wrestling territories — Samara was certainly a reasonable candidate for that honor at this stage of his career. Then again, it would certainly have strengthened his argument if he could have acquired a victory against an opponent of the caliber of Jim Londos, and Samara would be granted several opportunities to do so.

"Samara is the first wrestler of his race ever considered in the same class as Londos," praised *The Los Angeles Times*. "The powerful Negro, who formerly was a heavyweight fighter in New England rings, boxing under the name Young Wolcott, has been wrestling for almost 10 years — during the past year he has toppled the best wrestlers on the Coast, and he has many followers who are convinced that he will win the championship tonight."

Presumably, Samara was claiming to have been the boxer "Young Joe Wolcott of Greenfield," who boxed almost exclusively in Massachusetts, and should *not* be confused with a different Black fighter from New Orleans who fought under

A Decided Novelty

the name Young Joe Wolcott in Philadelphia, and who was accused of murdering a woman by strangulation in that very city.

Either way, Young Wolcott of Greenfield was a 147-pound welterweight fighter, meaning that if George Hardison had indeed been both Young Wolcott the boxer and the wrestling Black Demon before ultimately being renamed to Seelie Samara, then he gained well over 50 pounds of solid muscle in less than three years in order to convincingly alter his identity.

Pre-match hype aside, Samara was not presented as Londos' peer in any practical sense. At the Olympic Auditorium, where Samara had previously been depicted as a dominant combatant, Londos defeated Samara in straight falls. *The Los Angeles Times* described how Samara submitted to a Londos arm twist after 33 minutes, and the effects of the hold were so devastating that Samara could only hold out for 33 seconds of the second fall before submitting yet again.

Many miles away in Wisconsin, Alex Kaffner had awakened from another perceived round of inactivity and materialized in Madison once again to battle his old foe Jim Demetral.

"Kaffner, the Black Panther, hasn't shown here for several years, but he is a savage fighter and well versed in ring savvy," said *The Capital Times*. "The Negro battler will give Demetral plenty of trouble in the headline bout which goes on a two-out-of-three-fall basis, with a 60-minute time limit."

As demonstrated that fall, Kaffner was still being used as a special attraction in areas of the region where certain color barriers had not yet been broken. In Moline, Illinois, Kaffner was introduced as "something new" being offered up to the local wrestling fans at Swedish Olive Hall by promoter Bill Broderick.

In October, Kaffner made his second round of appearances in Michigan, playing the role of heel against Al Sabbath in a losing effort on the undercard of a show headlined by Maurice Tillet. Kaffner was described in *The*

A Decided Novelty

Herald-Press of St. Joseph as "a hard-working villain" that local referee Alex Karpenski "was really no match for."

Later in October, Kaffner also appeared in Kenosha, Wisconsin, and the reporters took his feline persona quite literally when hyping his arrival.

"A treat for all wrestling fans will be the appearance of Alex Kaffner, known throughout the world as the Black Panther," stated *The Kenosha Evening News*. "He derives his name from the sleekness and coordination of his long and sinewy muscles, and his actions are like those of a cat when wrestling on the mat. He is also a master of the art of Jiu Jitsu, and uses his feline tactics to beat his opponents."

As expected, Kaffner was as unsuccessful in his bouts against Tillet as Seelie Samara had been, usually falling prey to Tillet's vaunted backbreaker, or a series of thunderous body slams.

Still operating on the East Coast, Don Blackman had even fewer matches in 1944 than he had in 1943, but the Associated Press still provided the nation with an update as to his status, and informed more U.S. citizens than had ever heard his name before that he was a professional wrestler.

"Don Blackman, a wrestler who masqueraded as the Black Panther, is an MP sergeant at Fort Dix, NJ," printed the AP.

Between the photo with Blackman positioned alongside Joe Louis and this syndicated report, Blackman likely received greater notoriety under the Black Panther alias than wrestlers like Jim Mitchell and Alex Kaffner ever had, even though both had been consistently performing in that role for over a decade.

Throughout the early part of 1945, Rufus Jones continued with his usual act, and even appeared in new towns within his familiar states, including Muskegon, Michigan. As had become their custom, Jones and the Panther appeared on cards together, as both friends and foes.

Unfortunately, there were occasional interruptions to their schedule. In March, *The Hamilton Spectator* wrote about how easily Rufus healed from injuries. This wasn't in reference to an in-ring injury, but instead came in response to an unfortunate incident that occurred during travel.

"The coloured wrestler, who was badly injured in an automobile accident in Windsor one week ago last Thursday night, saw action in Windsor last night, and may be available for a bout here shortly," said *The Hamilton Spectator*.

The pattern of Jim Mitchell and Rufus Jones being inseparable both inside and outside of the ring — whether working as friends or foes — resulted in an awkward situation that was nearly catastrophic, as it turned out that the two had been riding in the same car together when they were scheduled to face one another in Kalamazoo, Michigan on March 1, 1945.

"Rufus Jones, who was to have met The Black Panther in the other half of the double windup, showed up about this time to report the accident," reported *The Kalamazoo Gazette*. "He was cut about the head and face and his teeth had been knocked loose. Jones reported The Panther had been taken to the hospital after the accident."

It's unclear based on the report whether or not Jones addressed the crowd at the Kalamazoo Armory directly. What was stated is that Jones delivered his report of the accident around the time that Gil Lacross and Maurice LaChapelle were concluding their match, and the announcement from Jones necessitated a reworking of the main event into a tag match featuring all of the wrestlers who had previously performed in the ring on that night.

Only the Panther's injuries warranted an overnight stay at a Windsor hospital. Luckily, Mitchell's hospitalization was brief, and he went straight back to work the following week.

It was fortunate that the car accident in which Jones and the Panther were found to be traveling together occurred in Canada, where they were now partnering regularly, and not in either Indiana or Ohio, or devoted wrestling fans would have wondered why such bitter rivals could bear to ride with one another in between their vicious brawls.

A Decided Novelty

By the summer, the two men were facing each other everywhere, battering one another and exchanging victories at all points between Marion, Ohio and Kokomo, Indiana. In Canada, the two men were not only positioned as best friends, but also as ruthless heels, as Jones had finally succeeded in swaying Mitchell over to the dark side.

While authentic wrestling championships had been collected by Black wrestlers in earlier years, those coronations had been primarily isolated to the eastern half of the continent. On the West Coast, one Black wrestler was about to give the concept of a Black world championship greater credibility than it had ever received before. Meanwhile, the loser of that exchange would go on the sort of title run in the Northwest that would exceed any exhibition of sustained dominance that a Black wrestler had ever been allowed to display in a wrestling territory before.

19 – The Gold Dust Twins

Out in Los Angeles, Seelie Samara had failed in his efforts to defeat Jim Londos, as he lost two consecutive bouts to the 48-year-old world champion in front of the Olympic Auditorium crowd. From there, things were only going to get more uncomfortable for him as Jack Claybourne gained his bearings in Southern California.

The local press frequently compared Claybourne and Samara. In their efforts to elevate the newest Black wrestling star, *The Los Angeles Times* went so far as to report that Claybourne had defeated Samara "and all the other Negro grapplers" in one-on-one matches.

While this was true inasmuch as Claybourne had defeated every Black star he had wrestled against at least one time, he had never wrestled against Reginald Siki, Gorilla Parker, or King Kong Clayton even though he had appeared at events with the first two, and was said to have lost a fictitious bout to the third in order to boost Clayton's appeal in Louisville.

All the comparisons between Claybourne and Samara were by design, as a match was finally signed for the pair to square off at the Pasadena Arena in front of a California crowd for the first time in January 1945. However, on a scary night in Culver City, it appeared that an injury might prevent a bout between the two wrestlers from happening.

Claybourne performed his regular stunt of leaping over the referee to attack his opponent Sandor Szabo, but the spacing between the grapplers in this instance was apparently not what it should have been. Claybourne clipped Szabo awkwardly and landed on his head, putting him out of commission, and leading many of the fans in attendance to believe that the impact with the mat had broken Claybourne's neck.

"Santa Monica police told us this morning that all that happened was that Claybourne misplaced a vertebrae in his neck," reported a relieved Bob Needham from *The Evening Star-News*.

With his loose vertebrae apparently snapped back into place, Claybourne was cleared to wrestle against Samara. This time, a physical trophy would be up for grabs, as a belt that Samara had allegedly won in New York City would be at stake.

"It is the first time that Promoter Morrie Cohan has ever matched the two leaders of the big fellows in a showdown," offered *The Monrovia Daily News-Post*. "This bout was the apple of the eye for every big club in the country. Pasadena got it because it is the testing place of the heavies. Both Samara and Claybourne have headlined in the Crown City spot. Fans figure they are a toss-up as to which is the real champion of the Negro race."

At the conclusion of a match that was knotted at one fall apiece, Claybourne dropkicked Samara clear over the top rope, out of the ring, and into the audience. Samara failed to return to the ring prior to being counted out, and Claybourne was awarded "the New York belt" and the title of colored world heavyweight champion along with it. By all appearances, it was the most sophisticated handling of a colored championship match ever conducted on U.S. soil up until that time.

In some respects, the match also served as the long-delayed conclusion to Sam Muchnick's tournament to crown a Negro world heavyweight champion, since Claybourne and Samara had been the wrestlers who had advanced to the finals of the event. The tournament's conclusion had simply been delayed by nearly three years, and its venue had been shifted westward by more than 1,800 miles.

Just days later, in early February, Claybourne and Samara participated in a rematch in San Bernardino that essentially served as a replay of the championship match that had occurred in Pasadena. Samara once again entered the match as champion despite the title change that had taken place just days earlier.

A Decided Novelty

"Jack Claybourne of South Boston won the world colored heavyweight championship last night, defeating Seelie Samara of Kansas City in two straight falls at the San Bernardino Club," reported *The San Bernardino Daily Sun*. "Claybourne won the first fall after 25 minutes of clean and fast grappling with a dropkick and body press, and repeated in 11 minutes."

Jack Claybourne as the Negro World Heavyweight Champion

In other California matches outside of his feud with Seelie Samara, Jack Claybourne continued to be mostly competitive. In April, he got a measure of revenge on the Golden Terror for his lack of championship success against the masked wrestler throughout New England by permanently unmasking him after defeating him in Pasadena. Then, at the

A Decided Novelty

Wilmington Bowl in San Pedro, Claybourne won a one-night, eight-man tournament to determine the number one contender for the state wrestling championship by defeating Myron Cox, Craig Jaras, and Hardy Kruskamp in three separate matches.

Seemingly displaced by Claybourne as the best Black wrestler in Southern California, Samara traveled to the Pacific Northwest and Western Canada. In Edmonton, Samara provided an entertaining interview to Hal Dean of *The Edmonton Bulletin*, insisting that he had previously had a prolific boxing career consisting of 150 fights, during which he was supposedly "never knocked down and never knocked out."

Samara also insisted that the original Joe Walcott was a great friend of his father's, resulting in Samara fighting under the name "Young Walcott," with the spelling used by *The Bulletin* deviating from that used by other publications, and also differing from the spelling used by the fighter from Greenfield, Massachusetts who went by Young Wolcott.

Bizarrely, Samara claimed to have been a common opponent of the boxers Tiger Flowers, Joe Delaney, and Ernie Schaaf, which would make him an opponent of three fighters across three drastically disparate weight divisions who all fought during roughly the same era; there is no record of a fighter known by any version of the name Young Wolcott competing against any of the aforementioned fighters.

Finally, Samara claimed to have fought on the undercard of the major 1923 fight between Jack Dempsey and Luis Firpo in September 1923. While this didn't happen, Samara was betraying his age simply by suggesting that it *could* have happened. Since George Hardison was born in December 1905, he would still have been a few months shy of his 18th birthday when the Dempsey-Firpo fight occurred. No matter what aspects of Samara's story fans chose to believe, this anecdote alone would have tipped off discerning fans that the Northwest's latest Black wrestling import was either 40 years old, or perilously close to it.

Also concerning is the way Dean chose to print Samara's prose, visually rendering it in a stereotypical Southern manner. When asked how he got started as a boxer, Samara supposedly answered, "Ah got ten dollahs fo' mah fust fight, and when Ah got a hundred, Ah stayed up all night jus' countin' it ovah and ovah." As charitable as newsmen often were when adjusting the sentence structures of White Southerners for print to make them more intelligible, Samara's speech was not extended the same courtesy.

For a few months, Samara continued to make appearances in Southern California, where he and Claybourne were briefly partnered together in a tag team as "The Gold Dust Twins." The history of the name of the short-lived team is surprisingly complex due to the time and location of when it was used.

The original Gold Dust Twins were the pitch-black mascots of the Gold Dust washing powder brand. While the original caricature of Black children had been clearly racist, the term Gold Dust Twins had grown to allude to certain business partners, sports figures, or politicians who were known to work closely together, regardless of race. In fact, most of the popular combinations of "Gold Dust Twins" in popular culture were White.

Particularly in Southern California, the most famous reference to a Gold Dust combination during that era had been The Gold Dust Gang — the grouping of Jackie Robinson, Kenny Washington, and Woody Strode in the backfield of the University of California, Los Angeles.

While partnering with Claybourne in California, Samara was simultaneously experiencing the familiar pattern of success enjoyed by many Black wrestlers when he spent several of his evenings wrestling in a fresh territory further north.

In Portland, Samara piled up victories, and soon found himself in the ring against Pacific Northwest heavyweight champion Jack Forsgren. Once again, Samara succeeded where it seemed all of his peers typically failed, and he defeated Forsgren to win the championship.

Samara's first reign as the champion of the Pacific Northwest would not be long-lived. Thirteen days after

A Decided Novelty

defeating Forsgren for the title, he would lose it to Ted Christy in one of the most objectionable miscarriages of ring justice.

Christy took the first fall of the match with a series of body slams, and Samara evened the bout with his flying toehold. As the match reached its conclusion, Samara appeared to be solidly in control when his title was unfairly snatched away from him.

"The Boston Negro ace was disqualified by Referee Buzz Freeman after he had leaped from outside the ring over the ropes to pin Christy," reported *The Oregonian*. "Freeman, who was also knocked flat by Samara's swan dive, ruled the Negro had illegally entered the ring."

The end result was a rare case of a wrestler being relieved of his championship stemming from a disqualification, whereas most title changes occurred by way of pinfalls and submissions. *Oregon Journal* writer Marlowe Branagan chose to describe the outcome unflatteringly as Christy having "outmaneuvered Seelie Samara to remove the Northwest heavyweight crown from Seelie's kinky dome."

Samara's recovery of the championship one week later seemed like poetic justice. Christy took the first fall with a double wristlock, but was then disqualified in the second fall for rubbing soap in Samara's eyes. Samara then recovered his vision, and convincingly defeated Christy with "a series of flying tackles and dropkicks."

Now a two-time heavyweight champion in the Pacific Northwest, Samara settled into the role and quickly asserted his dominance by spending the remainder of April defeating Forsgren and Christy in return bouts.

Being the champion of the Pacific Northwest changed the handling of Samara's outings against big-name opponents in an obvious way. In May, Samara was booked as "the 230 pound 'Black Panther'" who defended his title multiple times against former world heavyweight champion and major pro wrestling star Lou Thesz.

In previous years and territories, these bouts would have been walk-through victories for Thesz, as it was common

A Decided Novelty

for Thesz to tally straight-fall victories against most of his rivals, let alone his Black opponents. This time would be different, and Thesz would have to content himself with one-hour draws with Samara in Tacoma and Portland, while Samara recorded a fall against Thesz on at least one occasion.

Against most opponents, Samara fell into a pattern of surrendering the first fall, and then heroically battling back to score two consecutive victories, with the final fall usually coming by way of his slingshot shoulder tackle.

July would culminate in a career-defining encounter for Samara when he faced "The Angel" Maurice Tillet once again. Still a feature attraction in the pro wrestling world, Tillet entered the ring with Samara after recording a clean victory over Lou Thesz with his vaunted bear hug.

Samara held his own against Tillet during their first confrontation in Portland; each grappler had recorded a fall with their preferred submission hold before Samara's unnamed manager entered the ring illegally and Samara was disqualified. This set the stage for a rematch in Seattle, which would result in the signature victory of Samara's entire wrestling career.

"Maurice Tillet, famed as 'The Angel' from Paris, met his master last night in Seelie Samara, claimant to the Negro heavyweight championship of the world, in the main event of the State Athletic Club mat card at the Civic Auditorium," reported *The Seattle Star*.

After Tillet won the first fall with his bear hug, Samara once again utilized his "rollover leglock" to tie the bout at one fall apiece. During the final fall, Samara once again found himself on the mat, trapped in Tillet's bear hug, but managed to reverse it and pin Tillet's shoulders for the three-count victory.

Samara immediately lost the non-title rematch to Tillet in Portland, succumbing to the bear hug in consecutive falls, but the fact that he had ever registered a clean victory over a box office attraction on the level of the Angel became his calling card.

Tillet played into the hype in other regions of the Pacific Northwest; an article from *The Vancouver Sun* observed that Tillet "spent the entire evening" following his arrival in British Columbia pointing out how "his only loss in two years was to negro Samara in Seattle last month."

Seelie Samara crouches over

Samara's entry to Vancouver was accompanied by promotional language that harkened back to the earliest portrayals of Reginald Siki. In what was either a tongue-in-cheek reference to contradictory geographies or simply a bizarrely constructed backstory, *The Vancouver Daily Province* identified Samara as "a Senegalese from the wilds of darkest Alabama."

Proving that his victory over Tillet hadn't been a one-time aberration, Samara repeated the feat more emphatically in front of 3,500 fans at Vancouver's outdoor Capilano Stadium. *Vancouver Sun* reporter Duke McLeod described how Samara had left his toe holds in Seattle, and instead "body-slammed

Mons. Tillet about until ringsiders begged him to harpoon the docile Frenchman."

By bodyslamming the Angel into oblivion, Samara captured a statement win that cemented him as a true champion who was also every bit as capable as the specialty attractions with greater name recognition.

Samara continued to be booked as a dominant champion in August and September. Finally, after spending more than five months as the belt-holder of the Pacific Northwest across two separate title reigns, Samara was dethroned by Dean Detton on October 3 at the Portland Auditorium.

After Samara succeeded in winning the first fall with his drop toehold submission, he was forced to relent to the pressure of Detton's own stop-over toehold, and the resulting injury made Samara easy pickings for Detton during the third fall. The rematch between the two in Coos Bay, Oregon played out in a similar fashion, with Samara winning the first fall, but surrendering the final pair.

The rarity of Samara's achievement in the Northwest underscored the prevailing belief that placing championships around the waists of Black wrestlers wasn't considered smart business, and it was a fact that was publicly discussed even within Black news publications.

In 1941, *The Atlanta Daily World* answered a question posed by a Cleveland reader as to "why the two or three top-flight Negro wrestlers" who appeared regularly in other parts of the country were never offered opportunities to appear on major wrestling cards in New York City.

"There is scarcely any box-office appeal in the city for Negro grapplers," answered the editor. "Even when Regis Siki and George Godfrey were headliners, they still didn't possess the all-important drawing power or the gate appeal."

Theoretically, this was an answer supplied by the editor of a newspaper who had a vested interest in Black success in the field of professional wrestling. Presuming that his opinion was widely shared even among Black Americans, then the Black wrestlers of the era were still being handicapped by impressions generated during the U.S. phase of Reginald Siki's early wrestling career, which had truly come to a halt back in 1933.

Speaking of Reginald Siki, he resumed the use of his widely recognized ring name when he returned to wrestling in March 1945 in Troy, New York. *The Troy Record* insisted that "old-time wrestling fans" of New York's capital district would recognize Siki due to his prominence during "the boom days of the sport."

While most of the announcements for Siki's appearances made a reference to his time spent as a Nazi prisoner, they barely mentioned any details except that he had "spent two years in a concentration camp in Germany."

By now, the first concentration camps had been discovered — with the Soviets famously liberating the Auschwitz concentration camp in January 1945 — but there was little being done in the press at the time to distinguish these extermination camps from ordinary Nazi prison camps. This probably led some people to question how Siki managed to survive for two years inside of what was essentially a death camp, and especially as a Black man.

Once Siki arrived in New Jersey, *The Bayonne Times* sought to elaborate on the circumstances of his imprisonment, and it would be the first of several different versions of the tale that would eventually be told. In the account supplied by *The Bayonne Times*, "Siki was so well liked that he was allowed to go on wrestling for some time after the outbreak of World War II," stated *The Bayonne Times*. "He eventually was placed in a concentration camp in the Rhineland, and eight months later, was repatriated."

Again, Siki was not placed in a concentration camp, but was presumably imprisoned for around two years based on the date on the card he sent to *The Kansas City Call*. Furthermore,

A Decided Novelty

while *The Bayonne Times*' article suggests that Siki's popularity in Germany in particular was such that he was permitted to continue to wrestle there, this is unlikely.

The haste with which Julius Streicher personally shut down appearances by Jim Wango prior to the war based on what he deemed to be the impropriety of White Germans cheering for Black wrestlers makes it implausible that the Nazis would have made any special concessions to Siki while the war was in progress.

On another card in Asbury Park, Siki participated in what could easily be considered an early all-star evening of Black wrestling, with Zimba Parker, Ardell Kindred and Don Blackman also making appearances at the event. It was one of the earliest instances of Siki encountering his legacy, as he was able to share the ring with three other prominent Black wrestlers on the same night. Parker had developed into a star while Siki was in Europe, and Blackman and Kindred would eventually become stars in their own right.

In promoting that same show, *The Daily Record* of Long Branch, New Jersey made a rather tasteless remark, stating that when Siki's opponent Hans Kampfer was finished with him, Siki "will probably wish he were back in the prison camp."

The Daily Record also mischaracterized the nature of Siki's release, stating that he had been freed from a prison camp that had been liberated after the Allies had beaten the Germans back. Siki was returned to the U.S. as part of a prisoner exchange in February 1944, which took place more than a year before Allied forces entered Germany, which occurred in March 1945.

Ardell Leroy "Don" Kindred's entrance into the pro wrestling world appears to have been fraught with domestic difficulty. Living in Philadelphia, Kindred got married in June 1943 to Lois Veal. At this point, Kindred's military career was already in progress, as his image ran in the *Atlantic City Press* in July of that same year for the purpose of heaping praise on Sgt. Ardell Kindred for passing the examinations required for entry into officer candidate school.

A Decided Novelty

This was certainly a proud period for Sgt. Kindred, who was a member of the 372nd Infantry, Company B, and entered the U.S. Army when World War II commenced.

Just one year later, *The Paterson Evening News* carried the unfortunate report that Kindred had been officially charged with non-support and neglect of a minor by his wife. Judge Schamach, who managed the proceedings, accepted Kindred's promise to pay $12 per week, along with any unpaid bills, and also reserved a decision on an accompanying assault-and-battery charge.

Domestic affairs aside, the first time the world learned about Kindred in a wrestling capacity was in February 1945, when *The Bayonne Times* reported how the new Black grappler had been "flattened" by Frank Bronowicz in 18 minutes and 21 seconds.

Subsequent reports did their part to build Kindred as a military hero who had rendered admirable service to the United States and the war effort.

"Ardell Kindred, Negro wrestler, who served with the Army overseas, will display his wares in one of three preliminary tussles rounding out the grip and groan program," reported *The Times*. "Kindred, a discharged officer, faces Gus Raap of Camden, a popular grappler who has appeared in Hudson County on many occasions."

The Times doubled down the next day, stating that Kindred "saw service in both the Pacific and European theaters with the Army."

At the show in Asbury Park featuring the all-star collection of Black wrestling talent, Kindred's military background was eschewed from coverage in favor of the story that he was "straight from Harlem." *The Asbury Park Evening Press* joked that Kindred should have gone "straight back" after his quick defeat via bodyslam, which was once again administered by Frank Bronowicz.

Given his station as a wrestler in the early stages of his career, Kindred amassed losses rapidly, regardless of his size and strength or where he performed. New York was soon added to the growing list of locations where he wrestled, and lost, while performing curtain-jerking duties at the beginnings of shows.

As for Gorilla Parker's participation in the Asbury Park event, a description of the wrestler from March 1945 — if accurate — may provide an explanation for the intermittent nature of Parker's in-ring activity over the prior three years. The report from *The Bayonne Times*, which described Parker as a "chunky colored grappler" in a stark contrast from the way his chiseled physique was gushed over 10 years prior, noted that Parker worked as the captain of a river barge during his time away from the ring. Multi-week excursions on major waterways would certainly have a way of taking their toll on a wrestler's conditioning.

As Reginald Siki returned to ring action, his country of origin once again became a mixture of Senegal and Ethiopia depending on where he was wrestling. Also, if there was any sympathy felt toward Siki for the time he spent in a Nazi prison, it wasn't reflected in the match results. Throughout 1945, he lost the overwhelming majority of his matches on the East Coast, and usually rather soundly.

The story behind Siki's imprisonment became more fleshed out as he traveled to the Midwest. *The Journal Herald* of Dayton, Ohio told the untrue story of how Siki was "taken into custody when the Germans invaded France," and was held in an internment camp for three years only to be released when the U.S. liberated France.

"Those three years took their toll so far as physical makeup is concerned," added *The Journal Herald*. "Siki lost more than 45 pounds, and at the time of his release, he scaled under 190 pounds. Back in the United States less than three months, Siki had built himself up to the 200 pound mark."

A few days after *The Journal Herald* published this account of Siki's capture, Marj Heyduck of *The Dayton Herald* printed a totally different and far more detailed account of what led to Siki's arrest on the paper's editorial page, presumably after speaking with Siki directly.

A Decided Novelty

According to Heyduck's report, Siki was imprisoned for 21 months "for turning his back on the Nazi flag." According to Siki, he had been on a wrestling tour of Europe that stopped in Berlin, which resulted in Siki being a target of several incidents involving the Gestapo.

A post-war photo of Reginald Siki

"Because he refused to 'Heil Hitler,' Siki was reprimanded by the Gestapo in several German cities," explained Heyduck. "Then, on Aug. 8, 1942, at a Munich parade, Siki turned his back on a Nazi flag and woke up in Elag 7-Z in Tittmoning in Upper Bavaria, where he spent 20 months before being transferred to Elag 7 for a month before his liberation."

A Decided Novelty

"Without the American Red Cross, I would have starved, and without the YMCA, I would have gone crazy," Siki is quoted as saying. "The Red Cross parcels augmented the moldy bread, and watery rutabaga soup diet, and the YMCA's gifts of books and music kept the prisoners from going crazy."

Heyduck then noted Siki's linguistic mastery, which conspicuously omitted Amharic — the language of Ethiopia — but now included Czech, Arabic, and "a little Hebrew." Siki claimed to have taught 30 prisoners to wrestle while confined to Tittmoning, which would explain his original request for a 12x12-foot piece of canvas.

Most interesting was the alleged state of Siki's married life at the time, as he claimed to have had two wives and one son — Omar Ibn Abdur Rahman. No reference was made to the status of his daughter Margellen, who was born in January 1933.

"This country does not recognize religious marriages; only state marriages," began Siki. "I had to divorce my English wife, Sue, so my Czech wife, Fatima, and my son could enter the United States under the Mohammedan quota. Sue, with American citizenship by reason of her marriage to me, was permitted to stay here only one year. She doesn't want to leave and she will have to unless I marry her again. And Fatima and Omar want to stay here but the country says I am not married to her, either. At the moment, I am a single man, but I don't know what to do about my two wives."

Elsewhere in the Midwest, *The Sheboygan Press* declared Wisconsin mainstay Alex Kaffner to be "the most popular performer to appear here." Even if hyperbolic, Kaffner's popularity in Sheboygan was impressive given that only one of the city's 40,000 residents was Black in the 1940 census.

However, Kaffner would soon be on the move. In March, he traveled to Cleveland for the first time, and once again appeared on the undercard of a show headlined by Maurice Tillet. He then ventured into Detroit for his inaugural Motor City appearance, where he was billed as the "Boer Champion" in a match against Bert Ruby for the Mid-Western

A Decided Novelty

Wrestling Association's vacant junior heavyweight championship belt. Ruby won the match and the belt in two straight falls.

Even if it was intended to elevate him, referring to Kaffner as the Boer champion was an obvious misapplication of the term. While it was likely intended to characterize Kaffner as the wrestling champion of South Africa, the term Boer was typically used to identify a specific group of White, Dutch-speaking residents of South Africa who resisted the British presence there. As such, it would have been very odd for a Black wrestler of any nationality to have represented the Boer people.

When the summer ended, Rufus Jones disappeared from the Midwest once again, but instead of retreating to his hometown on the East Coast, he instead traveled to the opposite side of the country, as announcements in Oregon heralded the arrival of one of the greatest superstars in the wrestling world. However, the Oregon promoters inflated Jones' accomplishments well beyond being "one of the finest showmen and all-around matmen in the business."

"Jones, who hails from Birmingham, Alabama, is an all-around athlete, and a former professional football player, baseball player, and boxer," stated *The Eugene Register-Guard*.

Yes, it would have been possible for Jones to have been a professional boxer, or even a professional baseball player; organized Black professional baseball leagues had been in existence since 1920. However, there was no organized Black football league, and the color lines of the major professional football leagues had not yet been broken as of 1945. Therefore, anyone possessing any familiarity with football who reviewed *The Register-Guard*'s statement would have quickly spotted the lie.

The Oregon Statesman was far more accurate with its take that "the negro meanie is said to be the hottest piece of torso twister to come out of the Detroit-Chicago-Cleveland area in some time." Yet Jones couldn't debut the headbutt-heavy style throughout the Pacific Northwest, as he had been beaten to the punch by the Grey Mask, a masked wrestler who had first performed in Oregon just one year earlier.

The newspapers in the region immediately teased an eventual showdown between the two prolific butters of heads, one of whom clearly came about the sturdiness of his head honestly, and the other who was rumored to conceal objects beneath his mask to amplify the damage of his blows.

Jones was similarly positioned as a threat to surpass the dastardliest heels of the region, including Danny McShain, Bulldog Jackson, Sailor Moran, and "Gorgeous" George Wagner, with *The Register-Guard* noting that Jones was arriving in Oregon "with a reputation that surpasses the villainy of anyone in the grappling business."

The Register-Guard also heaped nicknames on Jones — like "Pinky," "The Birmingham Bomber," "The Alabama Assassin," and most topically, "The Black Atom Bomb" — and included that most of the interest stemmed from the fact that Jones was "the first Negro villain ever to show here."

"Jack Claybourne, the last dusky matman to appear here, was a great favorite of the local fans, but Jones is apparently as different as day and night," added the article. But, unlike Gentleman Jack, who relied on uncanny athleticism accompanied by a bright smile, Jones met his opponents with "battering-ram headbutts, accompanied by foaming at the mouth."

The segmentation of Oregon into several cities managed by different promoters created the opportunity for each location to develop separate origin tales for their wrestlers. As such, even though Jones had received as many as four separate nicknames reliant on the premise that he was born in Alabama, the fans in Portland received a steady diet of articles stating that he was from Detroit.

In comparison to the relatively playful match descriptions provided for Jones in many of the cities of the Midwestern United States, as well as Ontario, the writings of the newspapers in Oregon placed greater focus on the sheer

A Decided Novelty

violence of his actions. This much was clear when he defeated Jack Kiser during one of his early matches in September.

"Kiser made good use of his limber tricks to avoid any powerful approach, and it enabled him to stay on even terms with the 'Alabama Assassin,'" reported *The Register Guard*. "After 21 minutes of hectic action, Kiser fell victim to deadly headbutts, and was easy prey for a body press, losing in the first fall. In five minutes' time, the Birmingham Bomber easily overpowered his groggy opponent with a brutal onslaught, leaving Kiser limp on the mat to give Jones a straight-fall award by Referee Walk Achiu. The arena crowd stormed around the ring in zealous hatred for the mat meanie."

Afterwards, *The Herald and News* alleged to have intercepted a message from Jones to promoter Mack Lillard expressing his refusal to participate in any more wrestling bouts unless he received top billing. The paper also stated that Rufus' headbutt "overshadows any similar attack ever seen in the local ring," and reminded fans that he "cold-cocked Kiser," resulting in the grappler being unable to leave the building under his own power.

Jones was also the recipient of the same derogatory nickname that was applied to Claybourne during his earliest visit to the Pacific Coast, and was dubbed "Snowball Jones" by a writer from *The Oregon Statesman*.

Against crowd favorite Buck Davidson at the Roseburg Armory, Rufus was ambushed at the outset of the bout, absorbing a pair of dropkicks, a series of punches, a bodyslam, and a Boston crab to lose the opening fall in only 45 seconds. From there, Rufus turned the bout into the first of many blood-soaked wars he would eventually engage in throughout the Pacific Northwest.

"Buck paid heavily in the second round when the Negro stunned him with head butts, twice kicked him out of the ring, and subdued him with a toe hold at the end of 14-and-a-half minutes," said *The News-Review*. "Bleeding badly from the area of his left eye, which had suffered previous injury, Buck was in bad shape, but he spurned urgings to retire from the battle and gamely reappeared for the third stanza. Jones displayed no mercy, centering all of his efforts with head and fist on the injured optic until Buck lay in the ropes almost helpless. At that juncture, referee Owen, who had repeatedly wanted Jones to cease headbutting, halted the match and raised Buck's hand in victory at the end of five minutes."

Apparently, Owen — who was both referee and promoter — had not counted on the fans fully understanding the rules of wrestling when he scripted that finish to the match. Because there was no rule in professional wrestling that prohibited the use of headbutts, that also meant that there was no reason for Owen to disqualify Jones simply because he had headbutted his opponent. This resulted in the unanticipated protests of the fans, who felt like the heel wrestler Rufus Jones had been cheated out of a legitimate victory over Buck Davidson.

"To a group of ringsiders who protested, Owen explained that Jones was less interested in defeating Davidson by 'legitimate' wrestling than in dealing injury to his eye that might blind it for life, and that he was justified in halting the bout both on that account and because Jones ignored warnings to change his style of attack," concluded the article.

Perhaps realizing that this decision was still without grounds according to the articulated rules of wrestling, Owen refrained from ever using this particular finish in a Rufus Jones match ever again.

Seemingly fearful of Jones, champion Jack Lipscomb refused to defend his title against the latest Black grappling threat. However, if Lipscomb's refusal to put his championship up for grabs against Jones had been questionable and eroded his favorability with Oregon's wrestling fans, the reason publicly offered for his decision only caused his stock to plummet further.

"Lipscomb, the hated Indianan, had been guarding his belt zealously for the past few weeks, using every means including refusing to put his belt up," reported *The Register Guard*. "He has refused to wrestle Jones for obscure reasons of racial prejudice, but has been forced to defend the title by the city wrestling commission."

Subsequent articles in *The Register Guard* depicted Lipscomb as doubling down on the reasons behind his refusal, stating that he had "drawn the color line" and was "refusing to put up the belt because of Jones' race."

Perhaps even more stunning than Lipscomb invoking the I'm-a-racist defense to duck a title challenge was the fact that this act of cowardice did not result in Lipscomb being universally disliked or cast as the unmistakable villain of the match. In this climate of the 1940s, being a racist did not automatically turn a wrestler into a heel, and the press made sure to stress how equally unpopular Jones remained with the wrestling fans of Eugene.

In fact, Jones was so unpopular that he was attacked at a Klamath Falls dining establishment by a fan of Lipscomb's who spotted Jones peacefully eating his dinner.

"Rough Rufus Jones has a split skull, rendered that way by a Jack Lipscomb booster as the dusky boy was consuming a plate of ham and eggs in a Sixth Street Cafe after the fights last Friday night," reported *The Herald and News*. "The embittered Lipscomb fan entered the cafe, saw Rufus at the counter, and promptly bounced a chair off the Detroiter's dome. The railbird was taken to the city lockup, and five stitches were taken in Jones' pate."

For the few Jones' fans in attendance at the Roseburg Armory, the ending of the bout between Jones and Lipscomb was bitterly disappointing, especially if they were hoping that Jones would punish the brash racism of Lipscomb by relieving him of his Pacific Coast title. Instead, Lipscomb slipped lead into his shoes, and relied on a loaded boot to punt Jones in the head and pin his shoulders to the mat.

Even more inflammatory than the levels to which Lipscomb stooped to retain his championship was the quote he was reported to have uttered by *The Register Guard* in response to the request that he defend his title against Jones a second time.

"I've already beaten that nigger once for the belt and see no reason why I should give him another chance," insisted Lipscomb.

Although LeRoy Clayton had been shipped off to Europe in service of the American war effort, his name was still suffused throughout the Montana area in his absence. In January 1945, the bulk of the "High and Inside" editorial section of *The Great Falls Tribune* was allocated to a retelling of a telephone conversation that wrestling promoter Bill Root had allegedly had with the absent Clayton.

While it's far more likely that the message was originally conveyed via postcard, or was relayed to Root indirectly through Clayton's wife Mattie, the information was presented as if it came directly from Clayton's mouth in the unmistakable speech pattern of an antebellum plantation worker.

"I'se jest goin' through the Falls, Boss, in a flying machine," Clayton was reported to have said. "Was wounded twice in the laig while in France. Couldn't keep mah big mouf shut so I got nicked there too. Now I'se on my way to a hospital."

Much later in the year, a wrestler appeared in Casper, Wyoming performing under the name King Kong Clayton for a single show on November 8, but *The Casper Tribune-Herald* offered no physical description of Clayton, and described the show-opening bout as consisting of "16 minutes of rather uninteresting wrestling."

Since Clayton had almost always been described by his race, and "uninteresting" was a word that was never used to characterize his bouts, it is a safe bet that the King Kong Clayton appearing in this one-night stand in Casper was not the authentic King Kong Clayton.

Without a doubt, 1946 was one of the most eventful years for the collective Black stars of pro wrestling, and it all began with the increased activity of Reginald Siki within the squared circle. Siki got back to serious business in 1946, defeating Ali Aliba with what *The Mansfield News-Journal* referred to as "the Abyssinian Crowbar," presumably a colorful name

A Decided Novelty

for his famed cravat headlock. Then Siki continued on to Minneapolis, where he provided yet another colorful account of what happened to him in Europe to *The Minneapolis Spokesman*.

In this version, Siki was initially imprisoned in Laufen for one month before he was moved to Tittmoning, where the prisoners were provided with several distractions that were sent to them by the YMCA. These items included books, musical instruments, game boards, poker chips, a gramophone, and 18 records. Siki also confirmed that he requested a wrestling mat, but the scarcity of the material resulted in it never being provided.

Siki then added a story that he was living in Prague at the time of his internment, which apparently occurred well after he had supposedly struck a member of the Gestapo who questioned him about the authenticity of his passport. Siki said he was jailed after that incident, but was released. He also reinforced his previous statement that the root cause of his imprisonment was his refusal to salute the flag of Nazi Germany.

In a similar account printed by *The Minneapolis Morning Tribune* one month later, Siki changed a few details, but kept the essence of the story the same. This time, he not only refused to salute the Nazi flag, but he turned his back on it altogether during a Nazi ceremony in Prague, resulting in a 10-day imprisonment. He further committed to the story that he had struck a Gestapo member who insisted his passport was fraudulent, and was released, but wound up arrested and housed in Tittmoning regardless.

Interestingly, Siki makes no mention of multiple wives in this account — only one wife and son who were allowed to join him in the United States in early 1945.

Realistically, Siki was imprisoned precisely because he was a U.S. citizen in German-occupied territory, and no inflammatory incident would have been necessary to justify his internment. Hundreds of Americans and other non-Germans were preemptively taken captive so that they could be used as collateral to exchange for German nationals and diplomats detained in the U.S.

Curiously, Siki stated that Blacks living in Germany who were native Germans held the same rights as White Germans both before the war and after it began. The reality is that Black Germans were banned from marrying White Germans, prohibited from pursuing higher education, and denied employment, not to mention the fact that many were forcibly sterilized and murdered.

Approaching the age of 50, Siki probably thought that he had concluded his tenure as a full-time American wrestler more than a decade earlier when he had departed for Europe. Now wrestling at a stage of life when most wrestlers had long since retired from action, Siki was about to endure the full brunt of what life was like as a wrestler in the U.S. territorial system of the 1940s. Simultaneous to this, two of the nation's top Black stars of the generation that succeeded Siki's were primed to discover how much more appealing life could be as a Black wrestler in an international market.

A Decided Novelty

20 – For Goodness' Sake

Shortly after he resumed his wrestling career in earnest, Reginald Siki was in Nebraska being hailed as the Negro heavyweight wrestling champion, and the local publications teased a showdown between Siki and the local incumbent Black champion Ras Samara.

Samara had returned to the Midwest after a major victory in the Pacific Northwest over Jack Claybourne. Gentleman Jack had struggled to find victories after his early successes in California, and after failing to take the Pacific Coast title from Dean Detton, Claybourne found himself in the Pacific Northwest, where he was once again greeted as "the St. Louis Black Panther" to connect him with his earliest appearances in the region.

This reattachment of the feline appellation to Claybourne's name was completed in spite of the fact that the Oregon publications had done everything but dismiss Claybourne as a fraud when it was time to introduce Jim Mitchell as the *real* Black Panther in Claybourne's absence.

In a showdown with Samara, Claybourne was caught in midair, slammed and pinned during one of his dropkick attempts, at which point Samara "filed a claim with the National Wrestling Association for the 'Negro Championship of the World,'" according to *The Seattle Star*.

The Morning World-Herald of Omaha made the outrageous assertion that Siki considered his claim to the world's colored wrestling championship "frozen during his absence from the rings." In truth, the only match of record that Siki ever had with a world's colored wrestling title on the line was a loss he suffered at the hands of George Godfrey. Even so, *The World-Herald* insisted that Siki had defended his colored title a further 48 times since his release from prison when there is no evidence that he had ever faced a Black wrestler in the U.S. before aside from his earliest matches in Kansas City in 1921.

A Decided Novelty

Therefore, in what was potentially Siki's first match against a Black wrestler on U.S. soil since adopting his famous ring name, he lost to Ras Samara in front of 3,800 fans at the Omaha City Auditorium. Siki actually won the first fall in 16 minutes "with a headlock and press," but *Evening World Herald* writer Wayne Livingston observed that Siki "didn't look too much like a champion" even during his most outwardly successful moments of the match.

"Ras came back to win a quick fall in the second session," wrote Livingston. "After preliminary sparring, Samara caught Siki in an off-the-ropes flip. He followed with a body slam and press to win in 7:30. The action was the hottest — and the shortest — in the third fall. There wasn't any trademarked dirty work, but both rasslers were working hard. Samara won the third fall in 4:30. He slammed Siki into the ropes, then caught him in a 'roll-around' toe hold to triumph."

If the bout could be said to have represented a passing of the torch, it was a fitting transition; Siki was referred to as an Ethiopian native for the majority of his career, while Samara adopted an Ethiopian name and persona two years after his debut, and 15 years after the debut of Siki. Also, as Samara was possibly the first true Black heavyweight wrestler to make a major splash in the business after Siki, he was the closest thing to a symbolic successor that Siki had in the wrestling business.

After years of claiming to be the Negro heavyweight champion of the world, Samara now had a series of impressive victories he could cite to back his claim. That claim would become even more credible when Jim Mitchell arrived in Omaha, and Samara scored two straight falls against him in under 32 minutes.

Still, Samara's Midwestern title claims would remain exclusive to his race; he was turned back multiple times by world heavyweight champion Ed Virag early in the summer. During a brief return to the Pacific Northwest, where he was introduced to Idaho residents by *The Coeur d'Alene Press* as "one of the few wrestlers in the business today that has thrown the famous 'Angel,'" he also lost to star wrestler and football player Bronko Nagurski in Vancouver.

After dropping the mythical colored title to Samara, Siki went back to the Upper Midwest. In Wisconsin, he was billed as 6'7" even though most papers had accurately listed him as 6'2". He also repeated the now familiar story of his imprisonment to the *Eau Claire Leader*, adding that he was able to stay in shape during his imprisonment primarily by teaching his fellow prisoners how to wrestle.

"I got as many of the younger men together as possible who wanted to wrestle and taught them by classes," explained Siki. "It kept me busy, and some of them turned out to be excellent athletes."

In Chippewa Falls, Siki was touted as "the greatest of all colored grapplers" by *The Chippewa Herald-Telegram*, with his most recent accomplishment being that he had defeated Jim Londos in Cairo, Egypt in 1937.

Then, in Minneapolis, Siki's name made it into the news for two unfortunate events that happened concurrently. On March 15, *The Minneapolis Spokesman* reported that Siki was riding back from a show in Duluth with Wally Karbo and Bill Gillette when the car they were riding in skidded off the road and crashed into a bridge. Karbo and Gillette were thrown from the vehicle onto the ice-covered creek below and knocked unconscious. As the only wrestler wearing a seatbelt, Siki suffered a cut over his eye but was only temporarily stunned.

Upon returning to his dwelling place in Minneapolis, Siki was met by a letter from the U.S. Department of Immigration "informing him that his wife Jarmila Fatima and son Omar, who have been living in New York City, are to be deported back to Czechoslovakia." Siki informed *The Spokesman* that he intended to follow his family to Czechoslovakia in the near future.

In May, Siki reunited with Seelie Samara in Tacoma, Washington where they once again competed for the world colored championship, with Samara correctly listed as the reigning champion for the sake of consistency. No mention was made of the fact that Samara had supposedly captured the world colored title or legitimized his claim to it by defeating Siki in Omaha a few months earlier. Their rematch in the Pacific Northwest concluded in a one-hour draw.

Siki remained in the area for a while, and was able to one-up Samara by claiming to be the African champion "by virtue of a victory over Jim Londos in Cairo, Egypt." Siki and Samara were then paired together as a tag team to face Abe "King Kong" Kashey and Cliff Thiede.

As historical as the Siki-Samara pairing was, the bout ended in defeat for the Black stars, as it seems that Siki missed a body splash and remained on the canvas, and "Samara proceeded to get roughed up as he attempted to fray alone," according to *The Tacoma News Tribune*. The crowd at the Midway Arena was apparently unable to hide its great displeasure when Siki and Samara lost.

The Black dream team didn't fare much better when they competed on the same cards in separate matches. Two weeks after they lost as a team, Samara and Siki were split off in singles bouts, with Samara facing Kashey and Siki exchanging holds with Pierre Lasarettes.

Samara lost both of the falls in his match when he submitted to crab holds. Siki — described as "a superbly built Negro with a 'foreign' goatee" by *The Spokesman Review* — also lost two falls to Lasarettes, but managed to elicit some laughter from the fans during his bout.

"Among the grunts and groans, Siki uttered the remark of the season in wrestling parlance, 'for goodness' sake,' when Referee Hank Vogt insisted he break a number of strangleholds," added *The Review*.

Samara had grown accustomed to receiving his fair share of star treatment during more than a decade of wrestling engagements in the United States and Canada, but that would pale in comparison to what awaited him in Australia.

In mid-July, *The Sydney Morning Herald* announced that "'Tiger' Seelie Samara, coloured American wrestler," would

A Decided Novelty

soon be debuting. He was also identified as "the first coloured wrestler to come here, and the first wrestler to fly from America" when he arrived via Skymaster.

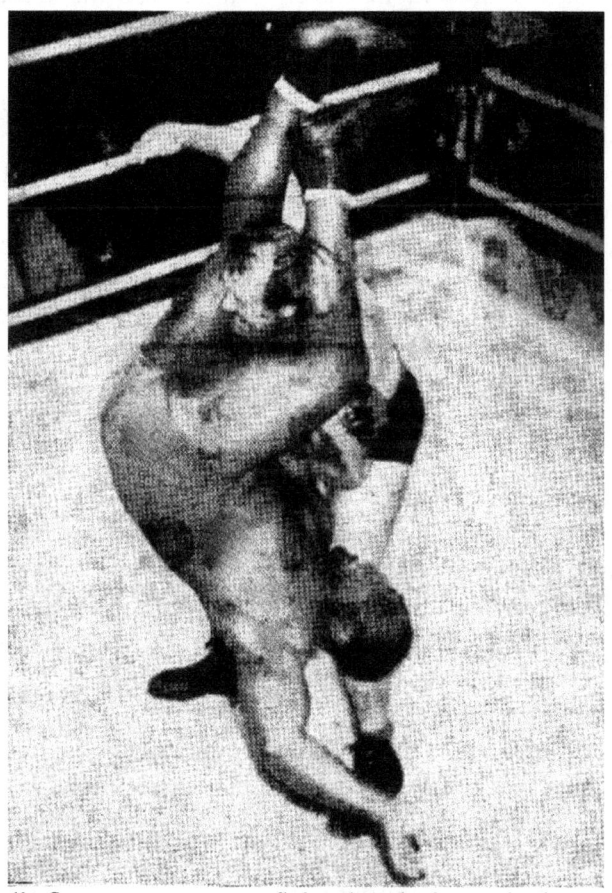

Seelie Samara executes a flying headscissors in Australia

Reginald Siki briefly wrestled in Australia alongside Stanislaus Zbyszko in fall 1925, but wrestling's popularity was so much greater in Australia 20 years after Siki's first appearances there. Therefore, it's possible that *The Morning Herald's* staff may have truly believed their claim that Samara was the first Black professional wrestler to compete in Australia.

A Decided Novelty

Samara was apparently in a jocular mood when his plane landed, as he was quoted by *The Sunday Sun* as insisting that his security screening upon arriving at the Sydney Airport in Mascot was the "toughest ever." Samara also added that had he not had his chewing gum tightly clamped between his teeth, "they would have grabbed that, too."

The American newcomer quickly captured headlines when he wowed a crowd of 6,000 fans at Sydney Stadium and defeated Australian Fred Atkins with a toehold. Tactics that wrestling fans in the Midwest and Pacific Northwest of the United States had grown accustomed to over nearly a decade of exposure were completely novel in the Australian market.

"Launching himself from the outside of the ring where Atkins had thrown him, he catapulted from the top rope," illustrated *The Morning Herald*. "Atkins, three or four feet inside of the ring, met the force of Samara's flying shoulder with his chest."

Samara's trademark submission move was quickly christened "The V2 Flying Toehold," and he further impressed the audience by performing one of his headstand escapes when Atkins had him locked in a headscissors. He successfully scored a fall with this counter method during his next bout against Babe Smolinski, when he "spun like a top on his head and came out to secure a body press."

Soon, Samara had amassed a multi-month winning streak that stretched across several Australian states. During that time, he garnered a great deal of press attention, and it seemed as though his every move was covered, with an outsized but expected amount of focus being placed on his race.

Several Australian writers clearly enjoyed making analogies related to Samara's "smoky" appearance. One of the standout comments came from W.F. Corbett of *The Sun*, who described Samara as being "as black as a velvet night on the African veldt."

On another occasion, *Daily Telegraph* writer Jack O'Brien posed the question, "Have you ever seen a coloured man turn white?" and then described the scene that unfolded when Seelie Samara received his first paycheck after several appearances in front of packed arenas.

"Samara slumped into a nearby chair," wrote O'Brien. "It was some minutes before the color started to trickle back into his cheeks. Seelie wanted to know why his 'chop' was so light. He was told that the tax had been taken out. Seelie let out a couple of grunts, just like he does in the ring. But this time, he really was in pain."

With all due respect to Samara, it would be quite difficult for any writer to surmount the creativity he displayed when submitting his interview answers to Hugh Dash of *The Daily Telegraph*. First, he claimed to have auditioned for the bass role of the famous singing quartet The Ink Spots when founding member Orville Jones died in New York City in 1944 after suffering through multiple cerebral hemorrhages.

The Ink Spots filled the hole in their lineup with two close friends, and it was never so much as hinted that they had auditioned a mammoth-sized professional wrestler who was busy performing in Omaha at the time. Regardless, Samara apparently maintained that he would have been added to the lineup of The Ink Spots had it not been for the demanding schedule of being a singer, which would have required him "to do three shows a day, rehearse, make recordings, and sign autographs."

This gave Dash of *The Daily Telegraph* an opportunity to categorize Samara as "incorrigibly lazy," adding that he played the saxophone and tenor horn during "jive sessions" with Duke Ellington, Count Basie, Cab Calloway, and Lionel Hampton. Samara purportedly stated that he "never progressed farther than 'jump music'" because he couldn't be bothered to take the time to master the instruments. He apparently also "turned down" appearances in Hollywood films while wrestling in Los Angeles.

From there, Samara professed to be personal friends with dancer Bill Robinson, comedian Stepin Fetchit, and blues singer Lena Horne. He also added that he played two seasons

A Decided Novelty

of pro baseball in Kansas City before becoming a pro wrestler and even competed against Babe Ruth in an exhibition game.

Finally, Samara claimed to have spent his final night before leaving for Australia hanging out with baseball player Satchel Paige and boxer Henry Armstrong, and said he was "a constant visitor to Joe Louis' home in Detroit."

The interview concluded with Samara allegedly adding to the image being painted of him as a lazy Black man by offering that he was going to sleep for 18 straight hours after completing his upcoming series of matches, while maintaining that his personal record for consecutive hours of sleep was 26.

Given the timeline of Samara's career and the locations where his activities were concentrated, the most plausible statement attributed to him amongst this batch of claims is that he *may* have been on friendly terms with ace pitcher Satchel Paige, who spent the majority of his time between 1940 and 1946 playing for the Kansas City Monarchs of the Negro American League.

As might be expected, it was the professed Joe Louis relationship that was discussed with the greatest regularity. In an article by R.W. Reid of *The Brisbane Telegraph*, Samara supposedly said that he began boxing in the same gymnasium as Joe Louis, which would have required Samara to have been living in Detroit rather than Western Massachusetts during key periods of his life.

In addition, it was explained to Reid that Samara learned his famous flying toe hold from a young man at Father Flanagan's Boys Town in Omaha, Nebraska. In reality, Samara was utilizing leg locks long before he ever relocated to Omaha.

In an interview with *The Sunday Mail*, Samara then claimed to have been in the dressing room of Joe Louis on the June night that Louis defended his world heavyweight boxing championship against Billy Conn. This is an absolute impossibility considering that Samara had a title match of his own that night — a world championship match against Roy Dunn in Kansas City.

A Decided Novelty

Impressive winning streak notwithstanding, Samara was apparently still subjected to some of the stereotypical presumptions about Black wrestlers and their expected roles within the pro wrestling hierarchy. Jack O'Brien of *The Daily Telegraph* — the same writer who so vividly described Samara's reaction to receiving less of a payoff than expected — observed that Samara had opened the wrestling seasons in Sydney, Brisbane, and Newcastle, and then added, "Because Seelie is a coloured boy, he is considered the right type for an 'opener.'"

In early September, *The Newcastle Morning Herald and Miners Advocate* ran a brief article suggesting that White wrestlers on the tour had opted to "draw the color line," and refused to wrestle against Samara. At least that was the story being told by Newcastle Stadium manager Harry Mack.

"We have approached four wrestlers, and each has refused to meet him," Mack elaborated. "They claim that in America, where there are 3,000 wrestlers and only six are coloured, they are not forced to meet them."

Mack concluded his statement by painting himself in somewhat of a heroic light, and insisting that he was "not going to change the programme to suit certain wrestlers."

It's worth taking a moment to address Mack's estimates on the number of American professional wrestlers active in the business in 1946. The actual number of active pro wrestlers in the U.S. at the time was probably far closer to 300 than to 3,000, with a similar roster of talent often being shared across several states at a time, and with competent bookers often being capable of holding lengthy shows with no more than six wrestlers appearing.

As to the claim that there were only six Black wrestlers working in the entire U.S. wrestling business in 1946, that is clearly an undercount by at least one-third if you only included accepted stars on the list. By that time, Reginald Siki, Jack Claybourne, LeRoy Clayton, Alex Kaffner, Jim Mitchell, Don Blackman, Don Kindred, Gorilla Parker, and Rufus Jones were all quite active, which is to say nothing of the many Black wrestlers who briefly stuck their toes in the wrestling waters.

As Samara's winning streak in Australia came to an abrupt end owing to a series of losses to John Katan, attention was once again drawn by some of Samara's colorful interviews, and the distinct difference in the way Samara was quoted by each publication makes it very difficult to know which depiction is the truest reflection of the wrestler's actual speech pattern.

For example, when Samara allegedly lodged a complaint about the lack of heat emanating from the Newcastle Stadium's showers, his argument was presented in the most articulate of manners within the pages of *The Morning Herald and Miners Advocate*.

"Every other stadium in the state has hot showers. It is a shame that athletes should be denied a hot shower in a city like Newcastle," scolded Samara. "A fortnight ago, I caught a cold at Newcastle and cannot shake it off. I think more of my health than wrestling. It is necessary to wash off all possible infection from one's body and face after struggling on a wrestling mat for about an hour."

That eloquent affirmation about the importance of cleanliness bears no resemblance to the inarticulate series of statements attributed to Samara by *Daily Telegraph* writer Bob Slessor one month later, when Samara supposedly voiced his belief that he should open a chain of shoe-shine parlors — of all things — in Australia. And as if that statement alone didn't reinforce the stereotypes as Black Americans being a bunch of "shine boys" who needn't aspire to higher stations in life, he cemented the stereotype when he identified who he expected to be staffing his shoe-shining establishments.

"Ah'd have a few darkie kiddies doin' the polishin'," Samara was quoted as uttering. "Ah laike any place where Ah can make the dough. Ah live bush if Ah could make dough there. Ah kinda reckon on a sooper shoe-shayne parlor in every capital city. Australians became shayne-minded when Yanks were home through the war. Wal, Aussie, bring along yuh shoes."

Aside from the unflattering representation, Samara's purported statement that he would have "a few darkie kiddies" doing the shoe polishing clearly implied that his establishments would be staffed by indigenous Australians, who accounted for less than two percent of the nation's population in the 1940s. Of course, even this interpretation generously presumes that Samara didn't intend to import dozens of young Black Americans to Australia for the sole purpose of shining shoes.

Even though the losses piled up for Samara as he made his exit from Australia, he still managed to accumulate enough wins overall to qualify for a November title match against the visiting Jim Londos at Sydney Stadium. Predictably, Samara lost the bout when he submitted away the first fall to Londos' Boston crab, and then failed to return for the second fall. The Associated Press reporter, apparently not familiar with Samara, detailed how Londos had defeated an "Aussie matman" by putting Samara out of commission.

When Samara departed from Australia, the Australian newspapers assured their readers that a brand new Black American wrestler was inbound, except that Jack Claybourne was the rightful world champion of his race even though he had lost his most recent bout with Samara.

"This laughing negro, with a tremendous width of chest, has arrived from New Zealand, where he was sensational," glowed *The Age* of Melbourne. "For a man of such weight, he moves with the litheness of a panther, and is the greatest specialist of the 'Drop kick.' In his execution of the feat, he leaps six feet from the ground to apply the 'knockout,' which was a specialty of 'Jumping Joe' Savoldi and Paul Boesch when they were here."

The Age included that Claybourne would be arriving in Australia after accumulating a stellar record of 26 wins, two draws, and two losses during his time in New Zealand, and added that he had competed in more than 1,200 total contests to date. This was probably a fairly accurate match estimate for

A Decided Novelty

a full-time wrestler of Claybourne's stature with nearly one-and-a-half decades of full-time activity under his belt.

The Sunday Mail of Brisbane described Claybourne as "an entirely different animal" from the recently departed Samara, noting that Claybourne's forte was blinding speed that was best displayed through the use of dropkicks and flying tackles.

Jack Claybourne dropkicks that hat of promoter Bern Potts

Just as in the United States, the Australian press explored the links between Black American wrestlers and boxers. As *The Mail* drew a physical comparison between Claybourne and former Black American world heavyweight boxing champion Jack Johnson, *Sydney Morning Herald* reporter Ken Hardy asked Claybourne what Joe Louis was like in real life.

Claybourne is recorded as describing Louis as a "nice, quiet fellow," which may simply indicate that the world heavyweight champion didn't have much to say to Claybourne either before or after the riotous evening they shared together inside of Boston Arena's wrestling ring.

Prior to his Brisbane appearance, Claybourne demonstrated his leaping ability to the press by dropkicking the hat of stadium manager Bern Potts as flashbulbs exploded all around him. Claybourne then sat for an interview, and supplied the Australian press with a personal origin story unlike any that Claybourne had told in the U.S. Although Jack admitted that he grew up on a Missouri farm, he professed that he had also been both a professional baseball player and — of all things — an ice skater.

It just so happens that Jackie Robinson had already signed a contract to play baseball for the Brooklyn Dodgers of the National League, and the first stage of the experiment required that Robinson play a season for the Dodgers' affiliate in Montreal.

Robinson had just completed a season in which he batted .349 and was voted the Most Valuable Player of the International League. As such, the sudden attestations from both Samara and Claybourne that they had been professional baseball players were likely provoked by Robinson's success, and the anticipation that his big-league debut would open new frontiers for Black athletic achievement.

In comparison to the baseball reference, Claybourne's ice skating comment seems to come totally out of left field unless you realize that 1946 was one of the peak years of popularity for Mabel Fairbanks, the first Black figure skater to achieve significant fame. Apparently, no members of the Australian press offered to take Claybourne to an ice rink to test his abilities.

In a *Brisbane Telegraph* article from the middle of October, Claybourne repeated the story that he had won "the coloured championship of the world" from Rufus Jones in New York at some point in 1943. In fact, Claybourne and

A Decided Novelty

Jones hadn't sparred with one another since their St. Louis match for Sam Muchnick in 1942, which had no titles on the line, and which was part of a Negro title tournament that never arrived at an official conclusion.

The coverage of Claybourne's Australian travels included a lengthy story about steady thumping sounds emanating from the wrestler's hotel room, the cause of which was initially implied to have been far more provocative than its actual source.

"The first time it happened, the manager thought Elmer had a wrestling partner in his room practising back slams," reported *The Daily Telegraph*. "When he put his head to the door to say 'shush,' Elmer was standing in front of the mirror peacefully shaving himself. There was no other person in the room."

The housemaid apparently discovered "strange chalked hieroglyphics" on the wall, some of which were six feet from the ground. The marks were first attributed to an African religious ritual that Claybourne was suspected of engaging in.

"Elmer is partly to blame himself for this legend," continued *The Telegraph*. "On the third finger of his left hand, he wears an enormous ring. It weighs six ounces. It is made of silver and gold with sacred symbols engraved on the stone. Elmer told the staff that it had been in his family for more than 200 years. He had got it from his grandfather, 'Toby' Claybourne, who was a direct descendant of the famous Zulu tribe of warriors."

As for the marks on the hotel room's walls, *The Telegraph*'s sports reporters surmised that the presence of the smudge marks on the wall was either due to Claybourne's habit of rehearsing his dropkicks indoors, or attempting to practice his boomerang throwing form by using a walking stick.

"He goes down to Rushcutters Bay each day with a veteran boomerang coach, and practises throws out over the water," added *The Telegraph*. "After a fortnight, he is now able to make the boomerang return, and has caught it a number of times. He uses an outsize boomerang with his picture stenciled on it between the images of a kangaroo and an emu."

Then, as if the story hadn't been bizarre enough, *The Telegraph* got down to the topic of Claybourne's broad smile and bright teeth. The wrestler attributed both qualities to eating apples, and especially to drinking milk, the favorite source of which was his Jersey cow, Rebecca.

"During his travels, [Claybourne] carries a picture of Rebecca in his wallet to remind him of home," concluded the story.

Presumably Rebecca remained on the Claybourne family property in Mexico, Missouri, as there wouldn't have been much room for a cow in Roxbury, the neighborhood Claybourne had relocated to within the borders of Boston that was heavily populated by Blacks.

Fresh from his experiences down under, Claybourne stepped off of an Australian Skymaster airliner on Sea Island, British Columbia in late October 1946 absolutely gushing about the favorable treatment he received from the Australians, while wrestling in front of crowds of 11,000 fans.

"I won myself a big wad of dough," Claybourne told the reporter from *The Vancouver Sun*. "Don't ask me how much, fella!"

Adding that he had won 30 of his 35 matches, Claybourne "pointed happily to his Aussie-style blue shoes and dapper purple serge suit." Jack said that the Australians had "treated him royally," and that he hadn't been forced to suffer through anything approximating Jim Crow racism. This is to broadly say that there was no codified system of segregation that restricted his access to facilities or amenities, or enabled him to be legally denied access to rights afforded to others on the basis of skin color.

Making his way to New England, Claybourne wrestled in Hartford, Connecticut, and made one of the first East Coast unveilings of "the diamond-studded belt which rates him as champion among the Negro heavyweight wrestlers."

A Decided Novelty

While in Hartford, Claybourne participated in yet another match against his Murderers' Row peer Jim Mitchell, which matchmaker Frank Perry advertised as the first time that the two well-traveled Black wrestling stars had ever faced one another. Obviously, this was false, since Mitchell had beaten Claybourne in his hometown of Louisville more than seven years prior.

For the sake of long-term recordkeeping, it could be said that Claybourne evened the score between them in Hartford, taking two falls out of three from Louisville's Black Panther. After surrendering the first fall to a "head-over-shoulder headlock" — which was yet another awkward way of describing the Panther's cobra twist — Claybourne won the second fall with a dropkick, and the third with a backdrop.

By the time this meeting took place, Jim Mitchell was putting a cap on what had truly been a bizarre year in every respect. Mitchell arrived in New England in July, and because it had been a full decade since Mitchell had wrestled in Maine as the Black Panther, perhaps it was assumed that fans of that era would have completely forgotten the specific characteristics of the Black grappler who had performed there under that name 10 years earlier.

Even with this in mind, it is startling that the decision was made to take Jim Mitchell — whose features were clearly those of an American of Sub-Saharan African descent — and place a black mask over his head while declaring him to be a native of India.

Making this decision all the more bizarre was the idea for the now hooded Mitchell to continue to be known as the Black Panther in Connecticut while he simultaneously wrestled unmasked only two hours away in Massachusetts under the same name.

In the midst of this peculiar scenario, Mitchell underwent a stylistic reimagining of his wrestling approach that would reshape the way he worked the majority of his matches going forward.

A Decided Novelty

If fans suspected that Mitchell was the Panther whose visage was concealed beneath that black mask, his earliest matches in Maine during 1946 would have appeared to be business as usual. When the masked Panther used his hip headlock to subdue Jack Larue, the writer from *The Portland Evening Express* formally identified it as a "cobra hold."

Things took a sharp methodological turn for Mitchell the next month. Following the pattern now employed by several masked wrestlers — but most popularly employed by his erstwhile companion Rufus Jones — Mitchell transformed into yet another aggressive headhunter who relied upon his own head as the tool for hunting.

"The Black Panther, who carries a steel-noggin under his mask, butted Lew Laird of Texas so strenuously in the semi-final that Lew must have thought he was bull-dogging steers... and missing," observed *The Portland Evening Express*. "Laird, softened up, succumbed to a perfect flying mare in 26 minutes."

The Evening Express included the news that the Panther would be facing Ivan Braun of Bucksport the following week, but added that Braun's New England championship would not be on the line since "the Panther is from India, and India is not part of New England." Apparently, this residency requirement was a device that could be exploited to allow champions to suffer losses without the fear that they might lose their titles.

Later that same month, the "Indian" Panther battled to an impressive draw with Ted Germaine, the man credited with training Rufus Jones, while battering him in a fashion not unlike what would have been expected of Rufus if he had been present in the Portland Expo's ring instead of the Panther.

Germaine took the first fall with a forearm smash, but the Panther came right back to pin Ted "after butting Germaine groggy and running him to the mat with a headlock." That's when both wrestlers began to trade illegal holds and blows, prompting referee Brooks to throw the match out. The disqualification only served to further stoke Mitchell's ire, and the referee "fell victim to four butts by the enraged Panther."

In the rematch one week later at the same Portland venue, which was said to have prompted "cheering on the campuses of dear old India," Mitchell destroyed Germaine in two straight falls. In the first frame, the Panther countered Germaine's full nelson with an underneath wristlock and ankle press to gain the pinfall. Then the Panther transformed into a completely different animal when the second fall began.

"If Ted thought he was coming back in the second fall, he was disillusioned," averred *The Evening Express*. "The Panther, scenting victory, leaped to the kill with head butts, and the first one caught Germaine more interested in whacking Referee Meixner, who was interfering with his pre-bell rush. In 30 seconds, Germaine was down again and the fans were wending their respective ways homeward."

If Mitchell's wrestling approach in Maine had shifted sharply from what was ordinarily a squeaky-clean style that was light on head-based offense, his techniques outside of Maine were reminiscent of the majority of his work throughout his career. There is no mention of any headbutts being administered during Mitchell's work as an unmasked wrestler in Massachusetts.

Ted Germaine won the New England junior heavyweight championship in October, which was also right around the time when it was revealed that the Black Panther he had been wrestling against was from Toledo, Ohio — as opposed to Toledo, Spain, as *The Evening Express* was quick to differentiate — and certainly *not* from India.

The following month, the publication even joked that if the Panther was from India, it was "via East St. Louis" — a city in Illinois directly across the Mississippi River from St. Louis, Missouri with a sizable Black population. The city had been famously plagued by racial strife in decades prior, including a race riot with a Black death toll so severe that its aftermath was personally investigated by NAACP president W.E.B. Du Bois.

A Decided Novelty

Even with Mitchell now squarely established as a U.S. citizen, his lack of New England residency was still brandished against him after he defeated Germaine, and the crowd was reminded that "the Black Panther comes from Ohio and isn't eligible to remove the lid." Mitchell had forced Germaine to submit to the cobra hold, and then ambushed Germaine with a surprising pounce in the third fall after the Panther had appeared to be comatose.

While two of his peers spent large stretches of 1946 overseas, and his constant companion was being booked as a masked Indian in New England, Rufus Jones spent his year wrestling in familiar Midwest locations.

Overlapping with Jones' activities from late May through early July were matches involving a wrestler going by the name "Tiger Jack Flowers" in Oregon and Washington. This particular Flowers — referred to as "a speedy Negro wristlock artist" — arrived in the Pacific Northwest alongside promoter Jack Pfefer.

According to *The Oregon Daily Journal*, Pfefer was being brought in by Don Owen to resurrect wrestling in the Northwest — and in Portland in particular — while incumbent promoter Ted Thye was taking a hiatus.

Marking the debut of the Tiger Flowers name on the West Coast, at least as far as wrestling was concerned, this particular version of Flowers won none of his matches in just over one month of activity, and was never heard from again. While neither photos nor substantive descriptions of this Tiger Flowers exist, there is ample reason to believe that the wrestler portraying him was not the original Tiger Flowers, and certainly not Joe Godfrey, especially since he appeared in environs where Rufus Jones had already made a name for himself and was quite recognizable.

Also worth noting is that intentionally misleading devices like soundalike names were regularly utilized by Pfefer during his career as a wrestling promoter. Some of the most blatant instances of this practice occurred in later decades, when Pfefer promoted events with advertised appearances

A Decided Novelty

from Bruno Sanmartino and Haystacks Muldoon as stand-ins for popular wrestling attractions like Bruno Sammartino and Haystacks Calhoun.

Reginald Siki ultimately arrived in Los Angeles in July, where *The Los Angeles Times* positioned the man who had "just returned from 37 months in a Nazi concentration camp" as a "welcomed change of scenery" since there hadn't been a steady Black performer in the wrestling rings of Southern California since Seelie Samara, who had departed several months prior.

One of Siki's first victims in Los Angeles was the Swedish Angel, who Siki crushed in front of 8,000 fans at the Olympic Auditorium with his cravat "head twister." In a late July bout between the two, *The Daily News* reported that Siki applied his specialty headlock to his adversary so tightly that it "made the Swedish Angel say Uncle in every language, including Scandinavian." This supposedly represented the Angel's first defeat in two years, and the Associated Press offered a very detailed account of the bout.

"Siki demonstrated tremendous strength as he applied the clincher, and lifted his opponent bodily off the canvas to shake him like a terrier and slam him to the canvas three times before he pinned his shoulders," wrote the Associated Press. "It took the referee, seconds, and the assistance of the victor several minutes before they could bring the Angel back from the land of nod following the fall."

What proceeded from there was one of the most favorable booking periods of Siki's career, as he scored a respectable number of wins. Even if he was misidentified as a "barefoot Egyptian" — which was possibly owed to his profession of faith in Islam and his stated desire to relocate to Egypt — Siki racked up several victories with his creative collection of headlocks.

When Siki did lose matches, it was usually to wrestlers with substantial fame. Such was the case when he lost a 13-minute bout to former undisputed world heavyweight boxing champion Primo Carnera in front of 9,400 fans at Olympic Auditorium.

A Decided Novelty

In Porterville, Siki joined the company of several other Black wrestlers when he was compared to reigning world heavyweight boxing champion Joe Louis. In Siki's case, the comparison did not fit as seamlessly, as the now 46-year-old ring veteran was more than 14 years older than the Brown Bomber. The most era-appropriate comparison for Siki would have been his one-time associate and contemporary George Godfrey, who had fought his final fight before World War II had even started.

Arriving in Winnipeg, Siki offered yet another account of his career and his internment at the hands of the Nazis. When interviewed by Gorde Hunter of *The Winnipeg Tribune*, Siki said that he received his formal education at Ohio State University, and that's where he took up wrestling. This is obviously untrue, as Siki took up wrestling a full decade before his two short months of attendance at Ohio State.

While in other interviews Siki mentioned that the Nazis enjoyed wrestling and allowed him to carry on as usual, this time he told Hunter that wrestling was "one of the first things Hitler put a ban on," which left Siki and several other touring wrestlers stranded and out of work. He then retold his story of being forced into prison for turning his back on the Nazi swastika "during a military parade."

"I was just sick and tired of having to give the Heil Hitler wherever I went, and was fed up with the slander that was being thrown at the United States," said Siki.

Siki capped the interview by estimating that he had participated in more than 3,000 matches in his career, and that he had been the victor in more than 75 percent of them. In order for this estimate to be even close to true, Siki would have needed to have won roughly 100 percent of his overseas matches, as the clear majority of his U.S. matches ended in losses and draws.

As for his actual match in Winnipeg, Siki was felled by the dreaded suplex of Sandor Szabo — recognized world champion of the Northwestern Wrestling Association — in 26 minutes, 10 seconds.

A Decided Novelty

Although Siki had never been the sort of wrestler who benefitted from major winning streaks in North America, the accelerated rate with which his losses first mounted after he returned to wrestling had served to tarnish whatever mystique his name still carried as he completed what was likely his 23rd year as a wrestler, taking into account the time he lost due to wartime imprisonment.

Siki probably never thought he would live to see American wrestling gold around his waist, nor would he see Black wrestlers being viewed as featured attractions in the heart of the old Confederacy. In a short time, both events would come to pass.

A Decided Novelty

21 – **The So-Called Hero**

As momentous as 1946 had been for so many of the top Black American wrestlers, it is difficult to argue against the fact that Don Blackman and Don Kindred had the most important year from a historical standpoint.

With his military service well and truly behind him, Blackman began to wrestle far more frequently. In April, he formed what would become a defining partnership with Kindred, and the two kicked off their alliance by teaming up to face tag teams in Blackman's familiar stomping grounds of New Jersey and Pennsylvania, like the pairing of Lou Farino and Alex Alexinis.

Things became truly interesting for the duo when they made the relatively short drive across the border from Pennsylvania to the Southern state of Virginia in May 1946, and were pitted against one another in a series of singles matches. In Norfolk, the notion of two Black wrestlers facing each other in a formal wrestling match had apparently been unfathomable, and the newspaper went out of its way to advertise the novelty of the encounter.

"Norfolk has seen just about everything the wrestling game has to offer in the way of unusual attractions except Negro grapplers, but that exception will be wiped off the books next week when Professor Bill Lewis will bring a pair of ebony groaners here to battle in a special 30-minute match," printed *The Norfolk Ledger-Dispatch*.

Kola Kwariani and Jimmy Cofield may have been advertised as the participants in that evening's main event, but the history-making encounter between Blackman and Kindred was undeniably the most alluring element of the show.

"I have matched Don Blackman of New Hope, Pennsylvania against Ardell Don Kindred of Kansas City, and I feel perfectly safe in offering this match to the fans," said Bill Lewis to a writer from *The Portsmouth Star*. "The Negro bout will be a novelty, but I have seen these boys operate, and they are up there with the best in the game. They are feature attractions in the North. From what I know of the Negro wrestlers, I can go on record as predicting that they will be two of the best conditioned matmen ever to show at Norfolk. Mark my word about this."

Don Blackman

If the reports from the evening accurately reflect reality, the Blackman-Kindred bout was so wildly successful that *The Norfolk Ledger-Dispatch* referred to it as "a 14-karat attraction" that drew one of the largest crowds of the season.

A Decided Novelty

"There were 1,500 Negro spectators in the arena, and 500 more were turned away for lack of additional seats," revealed *The Ledger-Dispatch*.

The 1,500 Black wrestling fans supplemented 2,000 paying White customers, resulting in a sellout crowd of 3,500 total fans.

"The colored men, Don Blackman of New Hope, Pa., and Ardell Kindred of Kansas City, lived up to their billing and gave the customers a fast, action-packed 30-minute match that ended in a draw. It was one of the most pleasing exhibitions of straight wrestling seen here in a long while," continued the reporter's account.

Blackman was such a hit with the audience that the *Ledger-Dispatch* followed up on his background, and discovered that he operated a gym in his home city of New Hope, "which explains why he is always in top condition."

The Blackman-Kindred bout was repeated in Richmond. Once again, the pair were promoted as the first Black heavyweights "to appear on a card in Richmond," and they once again wrestled to a draw. Then, after attracting a turn-away crowd in Norfolk with the Black pair, Bill Lewis immediately booked a return bout between the men and guaranteed that the match would conclude satisfactorily.

"This will be the second and last bout for the Negro wrestlers at Norfolk," Lewis told *The Portsmouth Star*. "I brought them in as a novelty. They certainly made the grade with their sizzling draw, and I have booked them to a finish for next week. But after that, they're gone from Tidewater. They are in great demand in the North and cannot return anytime soon."

Blackman won the bout, and when they repeated the affair in Richmond — with an additional $100 promised to the winner no less — Blackman emerged victorious in that match as well.

Returning home to New Hope, Pennsylvania, Blackman's grappling accomplishments were exaggerated to a remarkable degree. At the New Hope Street Fair, Don hosted a strongman sideshow — likely as an advertisement for his gym — and was touted as the "undefeated heavyweight world wrestling champion."

Up until this point, Blackman had seldom even been referred to as a "Negro wrestling champion of the world." Yet, as far as his friends and neighbors were concerned, he was an undefeated world champion with no racial qualifiers added to the achievement.

Blackman then made his way to New York City for some summer appearances before returning to the cities within driving distance of his Pennsylvania home for the fall. He then returned to Virginia in November to capitalize on his popularity there.

The Norfolk Ledger-Dispatch assured its readers that "additional seating in the balcony will be set aside for Negro fans at the USO Arena" before Blackman's bout with fellow Black wrestler Frank Harris of Baltimore.

"Those who saw Blackman rated him easily on par with many of the best grapplers appearing in Norfolk," concluded *The Ledger-Dispatch* article.

Unsurprisingly, Blackman got his hand raised at the conclusion of the bout.

Blackman soon began to appear in areas of his home state that he still hadn't visited in a professional capacity. In Lancaster, the promoter came up with a backstory for Blackman — one that made him a resident of Detroit, Michigan — which deviated sharply from his established origin, despite the fact that Blackman lived less than two hours from Lancaster, and had made a huge name for himself in nearby Harrisburg.

"Blackman is a husky 220 pounder who has a select assortment of holds," stated *The Daily Intelligence Journal* of Lancaster. "He is a great showman and is highly popular because of his clever style of grappling. He hasn't been in circulation very long because he's just a young fellow. He handles wrestling at a Negro boys' club in Detroit, which also happens to be the hometown of Joe Louis."

A Decided Novelty

Someone must have informed the promoter of how ludicrous this alternative origin tale was, because Blackman's hometown reverted to its usual location by the time *The Intelligencer Journal* reported that Blackman had defeated opponent Stu Smith with an airplane spin and a body press.

Kindred may have been the clear loser in his series of Virginia bouts with Blackman, but the feud established that Kindred could at least be an attraction if he was showcased in the proper setting, and paired with the right opponent.

Fresh from his series with Blackman, Kindred explored the Detroit territory during early summer 1946 and began to amass wins for the first time in his career, as he dropped Stanley Buresh during his first matches in the Motor City.

By fall, when Kindred began touring some of the outlying areas surrounding Detroit, including portions of Ohio, he was given the now-familiar label of world's Negro heavyweight titlist.

Eventually Kindred made his way west to Benton Harbor, where he received a slight demotion in weight class to nominally become the "world's Negro junior heavyweight champion." Far more significant than a fake championship is the fact that the reporters covering wrestling, like those who worked for *The News Palladium* of Benton Harbor, were taking note of Kindred's "unusual strength and skill."

The exaggerations of Kindred's backstory grew along with his winning streak. In the midst of that string of victories, *The News Palladium* not only reiterated Kindred's claim to world title status of a sort, but bestowed world-class amateur credentials upon him as well.

"[Kindred] was an Olympic finalist in the 1936 games, and he possesses unusual strength to go with his acquired skill," stated *The News Palladium*.

The idea that a Black wrestler could have traveled to the 1936 Olympic Games in Berlin, which took place in the epicenter of Nazi dominance, and advanced to the gold-medal match of a wrestling division without it being global news is laughable.

A Decided Novelty

In fact, the timing of Kindred's supposed achievement was off by three to four decades. No Black American wrestlers would compete at the Olympics until the 1964 Olympic Games in Tokyo. That's when Bobby Douglas, Charles Tribble, and Robert Pickens achieved that milestone. It would be a further 12 years before Lloyd Keaser became the first Black American wrestler to medal in wrestling at the Olympics, which occurred at the 1976 Olympic Games in Montreal.

Perhaps recognizing the absurdity of heaping fictional Olympic credentials upon Kindred, subsequent coverage of the Negro heavyweight champion backed away from establishing him as an Olympic medalist, and supplemented his background with exaggerations of his very real military service.

"Kindred is a former amateur champion who was released from the Army as a first lieutenant after six years and five months of service all around the world," stated *The New Palladium*. "He was very popular in pinning Al Laclerc in the short space of seven minutes last week."

Across the Ambassador Bridge in Ontario, *The Windsor Star* stopped short of calling Kindred a Black world champion, instead declaring him to be "Negro champ of the Middle West."

Regarding military service, while it remains debatable whether or not the King Kong Clayton who appeared for one November night in Casper, Wyoming was the genuine article, the version advertised to appear inside the ring in Grand Junction, Colorado in January 1946 was the real deal. Touted as a Negro world heavyweight champion who had "tossed the boys around a bit in matches here early in the war," Clayton was said to be a wrestler who fans remembered as "supple, agile, and quick" even though was now described as 20 pounds heavier than before he had been shipped overseas.

Although advertised, Clayton never made it to the ring in Colorado, as Joe Parelli was summoned to substitute for him. Instead, Clayton's official homecoming bouts occurred in the familiar rings of Montana, where fans were informed that Clayton's weight had swelled to 235 pounds. For a wrestler who promoters only ever dared to advertise as standing 5'8" at most when he was likely closer to 5'6", the addition of 40 pounds to his once lean boxer's frame would have been impossible to miss.

The newspapers of Montana also continued to disseminate the story that Clayton had served in the African and Sicilian campaigns during the war, "receiving the purple heart for wounds sustained in combat." *The Independent Record* added that Clayton had served with the U.S. Army Corps of Engineers, and the precise details surrounding the returning grappler's alleged injuries would change several times over the coming months and years, ultimately causing their veracity to fall into question.

In Great Falls, fans were told that Clayton had been "injured on the Anzio beachhead," and told by army doctors that he would never walk again, but "expert care and continuous exercise" had helped him to work his way back into ring shape. In Edmonton, it was explained that the city's once-favorite boxer-wrestler had been "shot in the jaw and in the leg during U.S. Army landings in Sicily, but had completely recovered."

Inside the ring, the heavier-than-usual Clayton was still strong and agile enough to wrestle competently. In Great Falls, he outclassed Tom Bradley with a Boston crab and bodyscissors transitioned into a headstand. Still, Clayton may have had some difficulty effectively wielding his new bulk, as his famed dropkick was atypically absent from the match's description.

In Lewistown, Clayton apparently remained a target of prejudice from *The Democrat-News* sportswriter. After Clayton had dispatched Tom Zaharias, the writer acknowledged that Clayton was "the so-called hero" of the main-event match, but contended that "no villain could take a more villainous picture than King Kong, with his ebony bullet head."

Clayton may have been the unfortunate victim of a promotional stunt gone wrong in March, when he followed his match against Zaharias with a display of his immense neck strength. Using a strongman tactic that both he and Seelie Samara had employed to tremendous effect on more than one occasion, Clayton was set to struggle against the combined might of 20 men as they pulled a bull rope that was tied around his neck.

The description of the incident offered by *The Independent-Record* implies that an accident took place with the rope, resulting in Clayton being rendered unconscious, with emergency personnel "requiring several minutes to revive the daring negro." In the aftermath of this incident, Clayton disappeared from action for one month, and when he returned, he was very vocal about his desire to retire and open a nightclub. LeRoy also admitted that the decision to retire was a concession to his wife, who implored him "to give up the hazards of the ring."

Days later, Clayton opened "The Sportsmen's Club" on top of the Exchange Tavern at 101 ½ S. Main Street in Helena, but he remained active in the ring throughout the remainder of the year. Perhaps owing to his stated desire to get out of the wrestling business entirely, Clayton spent the remainder of the year losing the overwhelming majority of his matches to up-and-coming talent in both Montana and Alberta, since promoters had reason to believe that there was no compelling need to preserve the reputation of a wrestler who was permanently exiting the business.

Included in those losses was a handicap bout against the masked Phantom at the Fox Theater in Butte, Montana. After the Phantom had flattened Jack Turner in just 30 seconds with a backbreaker, Clayton, now advertised at a portly 247 pounds, climbed into the ring and traded holds and punches with the Phantom for 10 minutes until the action spilled out of the ring and into the orchestra pit.

"The Phantom lost balance as he landed a stiff kick to the face. Both giants fell on the piano, which was crushed to the floor of the pit," illustrated *The Montana Standard*. "As they returned to the ring, the Phantom was hit with a club tossed by a fan, then promptly used the club for a devastating head attack

A Decided Novelty

that knocked Clayton cold. Police eventually dispersed the excited mob which wanted at the Phantom."

Comically, among the many photos used to advertise Clayton's appearances during this period, one of them was a 10-year-old photo of Rufus Jones that had been in use since 1937.

When 1947 opened, Jim Mitchell was still getting slighted in New England. Now working without his identity concealed beneath a thin layer of cloth, the "butting Black Panther" was still headbutting his opponents into unconsciousness without the effectiveness of the move being attributable to any illegal objects stored within a mask.

Mitchell's series of mid-January matches against Jackie Nichols proves multiple points about the norms of wrestling in New England at the time. First, although he was a White New Englander, Nichols was quite the headbutter in his own right, as if he was filling the void left by the death of Gus Sonnenberg, who had originally popularized the headbutt in that very region.

This much was made evident when the recently crowned New England junior heavyweight champion battered Mitchell with "a series of successful headbutts that had the Black Panther reeling dizzily," in the words of *The Portland Press Herald*.

Made equally clear was the fact that, even without a mask on his head, the Panther's refusal to relocate to New England was still being wielded against him as far as the territory's wrestling storylines were concerned. When Nichols missed a third-fall flying tackle "and landed flush against the middle ring-post strand and fell an easy victim to a press by the still-dazed Panther," Mitchell was awarded the victory, but not the championship due to the previously cited residency requirement for champions.

At 41 years of age, Ras Samara also got straight to the business of challenging the holders of the top championships in the Midwest, and this included Orville Brown, holder of the world heavyweight championship of the Midwest Wrestling

A Decided Novelty

Association. On the last day of February, Brown won a straight-falls victory over Samara at the St. Joseph Auditorium.

In April, Samara lost a more hotly contested bout to Brown in Kansas City, with Samara taking the first fall by "leaping off the ropes with a flying body tackle and follow-through press."

"Brown had dropkicked Samara into the ringside pits four straight times, then on the fifth attack, the Negro climbed back in and bounded off the ropes with a giant leap to catch Brown off guard," reported *The Kansas City Star*. "Brown really went on the offensive to tie up the bout with a rolling head lock and press in 6:27, setting up a second fall with a series of forearm smashes and body blows. Brown continued his attack in the third fall and was complete master of the situation, flooring Samara with a barrage of slams and backdrops to win the decisive marker."

In Iowa, Samara faced Brown again, except this time the bout was contested for "the National Wrestling Alliance's belt," and with *The Des Moines Register* identifying Samara as "one of the few Negroes in history to get a shot at a world wrestling heavyweight title."

This version of the National Wrestling Alliance had been a regional organization founded in Kansas in 1941, with its championship moving to Iowa with Ed Virag in 1943. For the time being, its influence had been effectively isolated to the Hawkeye State, and the specific world championship defended by Brown was dependent upon the location he found himself wrestling in from one night to the next.

On this occasion, Samara once again scored a first-fall victory, but Brown knotted the score by "drawing liberally from his store of illegal tactics," and was cautioned by the referee throughout the match when he "continued to grapple in a manner unbecoming a champion," according to *The Register*. The bout ended in a time-limit draw.

Like Samara, Jack Claybourne had received star treatment in Australia during fall 1946, but he would continue to be shut out of the North American. title picture even though he drew rave reviews everywhere he went.

In Boston, in the middle of January, it was reported that Claybourne attended a women's basketball game between the Boston Giants and the West Medford Vets to open the local winter basketball season, and grabbed the spotlight by tossing up the ceremonial jump ball at the beginning of the game. It was included in the report that he then went "dashing to the arena to tangle with the Black Panther."

The problem with this description is that Claybourne and the Panther weren't booked to wrestle one another for another month. Since Claybourne lived in the Roxbury neighborhood of Boston in an apartment building he owned and rented to tenants, it's quite possible that he was speeding home to tangle with the Panther over a home-cooked meal.

At the St. John Forum, Claybourne was dueling with the rugged George Calza, with the fall tally between the two knotted at one apiece. Both men slid outside of the ring and out to the floor, and then Calza bolted into the audience with Claybourne hot on his heels.

"While the customers were spilled right and left, and police and others tried to separate the participants, the fans first scattered, and then, bolstered by rush seat holders who leaped over barriers, closed in on the ringmen, pushed them back into the squared circle, and cheered wildly as Claybourne pounded his opponent into submission for the deciding fall of three," described sports editor Doug Costello.

The Evening Times-Globe of St. John would capture another important detail from the bout when it described exactly how the final fall was recorded. Calza was the first to reenter the ring, and when Claybourne tried to make his way through the ropes, "Calza tried to kick him in the face but only succeeded in getting a head butt that put himself out of business."

This amounts to the first clearly recorded instance in five years of Claybourne concluding a match with the sort of thunderous headbutt that Rufus Jones would have endorsed.

A Decided Novelty

In the meantime, on the other side of the world, *The Melbourne Age* was apparently queried as to why there were no Black wrestlers present for that year's summer wrestling tour. The dumbfounding explanation went as follows:

"Although the colored black wrestler Jack Claybourne desired to visit Australia again, the white wrestlers here this season drew the color line and refused to meet him or Seelie Samara."

It's hard to imagine a more puzzling explanation for the absence of Black grapplers than to accuse nearly an entire roster of wrestlers — both heels and babyfaces — of racism while expecting that answer to satisfy the fans.

When Claybourne moved on to Niagara Falls, *The Evening Review* proposed that Claybourne would be making some interesting modifications to his repertoire of offensive maneuvers, while also adding further details to his backstory.

It was stated that Niagara Falls promoter Sammy Sobel "only recently discovered" that Claybourne had been awarded the honor of being named "the world's Negro wrestling champion" by the New York Wrestling Association in 1941. The two major issues with that statement were that Claybourne made no claims to being a world champion when wrestling in New York in 1941, and more importantly, the New York Wrestling Association was a completely phony wrestling organization.

The article said that Claybourne had been married to his wife Lillian Smalls for eight years, when they had actually tied the knot only five years earlier in Minneapolis. Lillian had grown up in Roxbury, Massachusetts, and met her famous husband once he moved into her neighborhood.

Claybourne apparently also announced that he was originally from South Africa, and had first been a major star on YMCA wrestling teams before turning professional 10 years earlier.

This may mark one of the first attempts to conceal Claybourne's true age; he had been wrestling professionally for

15 years at this point, and had just turned 37 years old that summer.

It's possible that Claybourne's rising age was a contributing factor to the set of statements that followed, which described Claybourne's favorite in-ring holds and tactics.

"Claybourne, like most grapplers, has pet holds," the article continued. "One is the standing leg split, and the other is 'the Koko bump,'" said *The Evening Review*. "The latter scarcely can be described as a hold as it only calls for Jack to bump his head against his opponent's head, and as Jack's noggin is an unusually hard one, this weapon can prove a very handy one in a close bout."

Overlooking for a moment the fact that this is the first extensive article written about Claybourne in more than a decade that failed to mention his penchant for leapfrogging over referees and dropkicking his opponents' faces, the description of his supposed love for headbutting and the proffered reason for its effectiveness — thus far almost totally absent from Claybourne's recent match reports — reads like a carbon copy of every analytical piece written about Rufus Jones after 1938.

The suspicion is that some combination of age, injuries, declining athleticism, and the desire to add variety to his arsenal had prompted Claybourne to at least strongly consider utilizing a less demanding wrestling style that more closely resembled the headbutting style popularized by his Malden-born contemporary.

Regardless, the piece made very little sense in the context of what had transpired in the location where it was written. Claybourne's documented matches in Niagara Falls had been won with dropkicks up until that point, with no mentions of headbutts included in the reports. Instead, the advertisements for his appearances stressed Jack's "kangaroo legs" and acrobatic proclivities.

Even more curiously, Claybourne never got the chance to unveil his proposed brawler-inspired persona to the audience for whom it was advertised.

A Decided Novelty

Reginald Siki returned to Minneapolis early in 1947, complaining to *The St. Paul Recorder* that the housing shortage in California was "the worst in the country." Given the way Siki was set to be treated, one must wonder if he had some prior business to attend to and decided to earn some money during the trip. Otherwise, it's difficult to fathom that he would have subjected himself to the sort of booking that awaited him.

Throughout the first three months of 1947, Siki lost almost every match he appeared in, and pro wrestling must have seemed like a completely foreign business to a man who had regularly wrestled in multi-fall matches with the Zbyszkos that lasted well over an hour, and who was now losing single-fall bouts to Hans Kaempfer in less than 10 minutes.

A mid-March edition of *The Minneapolis Star* provides some insight into what Siki was doing during his downtime in between matches. The paper revealed that Siki had been volunteering extensively for the Red Cross of Hennepin County — of which Minneapolis is the county seat — in the organization's effort to raise $300,000.

"The Red Cross saved my life when I was interned by the Germans as a prisoner for 20 months during the war," Siki told *The Star*. "My fellow prisoners and I absolutely would not have lived on the meager rations provided by the Nazis had they not been supplemented by American Red Cross prisoner of war food packages."

Siki added that — in a fashion identical to Gorilla Parker — he had worked as a barge captain in New York harbor following his repatriation, and before he returned to the ring on a full-time basis.

In April, Siki went straight back to Southern California. That's when his booking fortunes did a 180-degree turn, and Siki finally embarked upon a winning streak commensurate with his legendary status. He quickly stockpiled victories against Jules Strongbow, Al Billings, Otto Von Bussing and Dutch Schultz throughout April and early May. Then in mid-May, he defeated Maurice La Chapelle in a best-of-three- falls match at the Pasadena Arena to capture the California State Heavyweight Championship.

Since Siki's career likely began in 1921 under a different name, it took 26 years for him to finally capture his first authentic race-neutral championship on American soil.

From there, Siki dominated all comers throughout summer 1947, turning back every challenger to his championship. He wasn't relieved of his title until October, and even then, the loss had the appearance of a fluke.

"Vincent Lopez tossed Reginald Siki out of the ring last night at the Olympic Auditorium, and when Siki couldn't continue because of an injured back, Lopez was awarded the state heavyweight wrestling championship," reported *The Valley Times* of North Hollywood. "The two heavies grappled for 20m. 4s before Siki was tossed out of the squared circle."

On the opposite coast, Don Blackman found himself at the center of the most significant series of events in Black professional wrestling that year. This occurred when he served as the headliner of a traveling all-Black wrestling extravaganza that toured multiple states south of the Mason-Dixon Line, including Tennessee and Alabama.

It was in early May when Blackman met "The Boston Tiger" Frank James in the main event of the inaugural show, with Blackman heralded as a former holder of "the National Negro Wrestling Association world's light-heavyweight championship." As such, Blackman became the ex-champion of an organization that had never existed.

Blackman's physical characteristics also began to draw media attention outside of his bodily dimensions. *The Sunday Call-Chronicle* of Allentown referred to him as a "bearded, barefoot Negro sensation."

An advertisement for the show noted that there was a special seating section reserved for White fans. With other wrestlers like "The Black Panther" Alex Kaffner and Buddy Jackson on the card, the "All-Negro Wrestling Show" featured several wrestlers who had either played a prominent role in the development of Black American wrestling, or were about to.

A Decided Novelty

After the Negro wrestling cards of Blackman concluded their swing through the Southern states, Buddy Jackson's name was thrown into the mix by Indiana wrestling promoter Leon Balking, who informed *The Courier and Press* of Evansville in October that he was "dickering" with Jackson to see if he could get him to appear, and "add a Negro match on the program."

When Jackson did reemerge, it was in the Midwest, but not in Indiana. Instead, he popped up in Wisconsin and Illinois— billed as the "Junior negro heavyweight champion" — to wrestle against opponents like Jim Pappas and Stan Karolyi.

In November, Jackson worked his way down to Kentucky, where he joined Alex Kaffner on a card that they co-headlined with Lou Thesz and Mike Mazurki. Clearly reversing the wrestlers' intended hometowns, *The Courier Journal* of Louisville listed Kaffner's city of residence as Columbus, while declaring Jackson was from Harlem, New York.

The Courier Journal also observed that this was the first appearance of "Negro wrestlers" in Louisville in three years, which is remarkable considering the frequency with which wrestlers like Seelie Samara, Jack Claybourne, and Jim Mitchell had headlined shows in that very city.

It was during this show in Louisville that the first major elements were added to Jackson's backstory.

"[Jackson] is the son of a Columbus, Ohio pharmacist, and a fugitive himself now from pharmacy classes at Ohio State," offered *The Journal*.

The Journal played up the pharmacological angle, joking that Jackson would be a "bitter pill" for Kaffner to swallow, before continuing to supplement the rookie wrestler's origin with impressive details.

"Unable to pay his way at Ohio State on the G.I. allotment, Jackson dropped out until he can build up a cash reserve from wrestling," *The Journal* added. "He had turned pro before going into the service with the 92nd Infantry Division. He whipped all comers in the Army. So far, he hasn't lost a

A Decided Novelty

decision in 141 matches. He has won 63 since returning from an 18-month tour of duty in France, Germany and England."

Aside from the obvious fabrication regarding Jackson's win-loss record, anecdotes about his supposed military service, pharmaceutical background, and Ohio State attendance would remain consistent throughout his career.

For once, a tale of higher education achievement by a Black wrestler was true, although it skipped a generation. Buddy Jackson actually was the son of practicing pharmacists in Columbus, Ohio. Jackson's real name was Ernest P. Jackson Jr. — the son of Ernest Jackson and Viola Walker, of Alabama and Arizona respectively. He was born in Ohio on June 21, 1921, and his parents had been employed as pharmacists for several years before he began wrestling.

Despite the achievements of Jackson's parents, the registrar's office of Ohio State University was able to confirm that Ernest "Buddy" Jackson never enrolled at the school.

Jackson defeated Kaffner in Kentucky, and then toured other Midwestern states with him in what amounted to a passing of the torch from the incumbent Black junior heavyweight in the Midwest to the newcomer. Kaffner shed his Black Panther title for these appearances, and was instead billed as "The Great Kaffner," and then as Alex "The Panther" Kaffner.

Continuing to be labeled as the Negro junior heavyweight titlist, Jackson defeated Kaffner in Kentucky, Indiana, and Missouri in rapid succession. Afterwards, Jackson faced Frank James of Baltimore in St. Louis. James was one of the other newcomers to the wrestling business who was featured prominently during Don Blackman's all-Negro tour, but he was previously introduced to fans as an opponent of Blackman's in Virginia under the name Frank Harris well before the tour had taken place.

"As early as the first bout, in which Frankie James, a bearded Negro, took a trimming from Buddy Jackson, and also had his chin whiskers yanked by the referee, the patrons began to throw objects into the ring," reported *The St. Louis Star*

Times. "James was simply too rough, the customers thought, and refused to break holds when ordered to do so."

Frank James

Sam Muchnick brought James and Jackson back for a rematch, and teased that the winner of the match would be in line for some future bouts. It's conceivable that Muchnick was attempting to revisit his plan of a definitive Negro world title tournament, which was disrupted by the onset of World War II.

While his erstwhile touring partner Don Blackman had been actively developing more Black wrestling stars, Don

A Decided Novelty

Kindred remained in Michigan into the early part of 1947, and newspapers like *The News Palladium* continued to rave about the popularity of the "Negro claimant to heavyweight honors who impressed local fans recently with his unusual strength and skill."

In the Benton Harbor region, Kindred was so popular, in fact, that the sight of him getting cheated by his colorfully attired and masked opponent the Red Ace nearly started a riot.

"With the match squared at a fall apiece, the Ace had Kindred tied like a pretzel in the ring ropes," recounted *The News Palladium*. "Referee Evans made a feeble attempt to break it up, but the Ace stepped in right behind him and tossed the Negro champ for a quick fall before he had a chance to get untangled. Kindred protested even to the point of throwing Evans all around the ring, and fans kept up the heckling all the way to the dressing room."

Kindred spent the middle of the 1947 summer in Vermont, and then moved to Ottawa in the fall. Subsequent events would suggest that Kindred may have been attempting to ingratiate himself with the coaching staffs of Canadian Football League teams during both stints.

Very late in the summer, Jim Mitchell traveled to the opposite side of the country from Maine, and returned to Los Angeles, where he served to accelerate the spread of a racial stereotype. Now carrying the same Rufus Jones style of wrestling into Southern California that he had replicated to great effect in New England, Mitchell aggressively headbutted his way to dozens of victories.

Interestingly, the main figure standing in the way of hastening the pace at which the stereotype spread was Reginald Siki, and in distinguishing between the styles of the two Black wrestling stars now active in the Los Angeles area, *The Whittier News* provided the most rational explanation to date as to why Mitchell could be compared to the most famous professional fighter of the era, and conversely, why Siki could not be.

"Only recently have Negro athletes turned to the wrestling game, and Mitchell and Siki are two of the outstanding contributions of the colored race now performing in local circles," began *The News*, blatantly ignoring that Siki had debuted more than 25 years earlier. "Mitchell has been tabbed the 'Joe Louis of wrestling' due to his hard socking, rugged style, while Siki relies more on his science to combat his opponent's rough tactics."

The irony is that the Panther had been introduced to wrestling fans very early in the 1930s as a much lighter version of Siki, right down to his scientific approach to wrestling and his supposed mastery of several European languages. Now, he was being positioned as the rugged counterpoint to Siki's clean, tactical grappling approach.

By the end of the month, *The Sun-Telegram* of San Bernardino was hailing Mitchell, "a wrestling protege of the late Jack Reynolds," as being "rated as the greatest Negro grappler." This bit of common hyperbole comes across as being rather insulting to Siki in this instance, as the Black wrestling pioneer had just concluded a multi-month reign as the California state champion, which had been an unprecedented success for a Black wrestler in that state.

Unsurprisingly, a bout for the metaphorical colored heavyweight championship was quickly signed between Siki and Mitchell.

"Leading claim to the colored heavyweight wrestling championship of the world is expected to be settled here tomorrow night when Jim Mitchell, 'called the Joe Louis of wrestling,' faces Reginald Siki, former California state title claimant, in a three-fall to a finish special attraction at Municipal Auditorium," reported *The Long Beach Press-Telegram*. "Mitchell is favored to win over the veteran Siki, despite the latter's experience."

Unsurprisingly, Mitchell won the match and the symbolic championship that Siki had already lost twice, and to two separate opponents. In fact, although Siki's claim to the world colored heavyweight championship was cited quite often throughout his career, there are no documented cases of him being successful in *any* matches where any championship bearing that title was supposedly up for grabs.

In the three confirmed instances in which Siki wrestled another Black wrestler of note with the championship of the race up for grabs, he lost to George Godfrey, Seelie Samara, and Jim Mitchell. In fact, there are no identifiable cases of Siki defeating another Black wrestler in head-to-head competition, at least not on U.S. soil.

Siki bounced back from his loss to Mitchell and continued to be competitive in Southern California wrestling rings, but he would be put back in his proverbial place in December when he faced "Gorgeous" George Wagner less than a month after the national television appearance that made Gorgeous George a bona fide celebrity and a household name. In that match, Siki was selected as the figurative tomato can used for George to showcase his dominance; George quickly dropkicked and pinned Siki immediately after the opening bell sounded, resulting in Siki suffering a humiliating defeat in only 12 seconds.

As the victorious Black Panther continued to tour through California, "Ironhead Mitchell" made regular use of his "cranium cracker," which was seen as a very novel form of wrestling, and which served as a stark contrast from the sort of wrestling that had been showcased by the Panther in his prior visits to the Golden State.

"Jim Mitchell, the Black Panther, gave local fans a demonstration of a style of wrestling that they hitherto had not seen in the local ring," observed *The Porterville Recorder*. "Mitchell pounded his way to victory over his hulking 300-pound opponent with his famous 'cranium cracker' — where he bumps heads with his opponent."

Relying on what had almost always been perceived as heel tactics in the Midwest, Mitchell's drastic departure from his fundamentally clean wrestling style was still perceived to be justified as long as he was meting out vengeance upon the vilest ring villains of California.

A Decided Novelty

    Thanks to the contagious nature of Rufus Jones' dynamic headbutting displays, the aggressive, head-first approach to wrestling was seemingly becoming the norm amongst Black wrestlers, including those within his longstanding personal peer group.

    That stereotype was only going to strengthen when the most natural athlete of the group decided to blend his style with that of Jones, resulting in that wrestler gaining a vise grip on one of the most iconic championship belts of the early 20th century.

A Decided Novelty

22 – **Bad for the Box Office**

In early 1947 in Sandusky, Ohio, Rufus Jones was booked in a boxing match against Sandusky's own former world light heavyweight boxing champion George "Johnny" Nichols. By this point, it had been 15 years since Nichols had won the championship and then lost it by failing to defend it within the mandatory eight-month period. It had also been eight years since Nichols had officially retired from competitive fighting altogether.

To add an air of legitimacy to Jones' skirmish with Nichols, the veteran grappler was provided with a backstory as an "ex-big-time pugilist" who "had a colorful boxing career behind him, having battled many of the top eastern boxers during his heyday."

"Sure sign that the Link's Hall fight will be filled with action is Jones' determination to stop the Sandusky leather-pusher in order to settle a long-standing dispute between the two performers," continued *The Sandusky Register-Star-News*. "The husky grappler switched to wrestling after being barred from boxing because of rough tactics in the Boston area. Jimmy 'Black Panther' Mitchell figured prominently in Jones' change to the mat game."

Even if Jones had been a boxer at one point — a claim lacking clear evidence — he was unlikely to possess skills matching those of a former world champion, albeit one 15 years past his prime. Fittingly, Jones lost his predetermined fight with Nichols by way of a third-round TKO after a flurry of punches from Nichols sent Jones to his knees and the referee called a halt to the action.

Jones had undoubtedly gained a great deal of weight over the course of his wrestling career, which different publications took note of along the way. However, in describing one of Jones' bouts with Alex Kasaboski during July 1947, the word selection of *Windsor Star* reporter Jack Dulmage suggests that weight, age, injuries, or some combination of the three had slowed Jones considerably over time, and that certain

A Decided Novelty

moves that had once been commonplace in his repertoire were becoming increasingly rare.

"There was gasping and eye-popping as ol' Rufe erupted with a speed that compared favorably with his licks of yesteryear when he was hailed as the swifty of the circuit," described Dulmage. "At one stage, he even launched a flying drop kick. Matchmaker Bill Thornton was flabbergasted. It was a wonderful sight to behold…"

With Jones apparently losing mobility and having exhausted every feasible wrestling role during his 10-year regional run, he continued participating in numerous boxing matches, which required far less creativity or challenging movement than his wrestling bouts.

At the Memorial Hall of Lima, Ohio, Jones competed in yet another simulated boxing match, this time against his familiar opponent Gil LaCross. *The Lima News* described how LaCross finally "knocked Jones cold" in the sixth round of a fight scheduled for 10 rounds, continuing Jones' career-long losing streak in boxing matches.

Returning to Sandusky, Jones was knocked out by Billy Fox in the seventh round of yet another boxing match, with *The Register-Star-News* stating that Fox "jarred the headbutting Jones to the Links Hall canvas."

Finally, Jones returned to New England late in fall 1947, this time making his first appearance in Maine. *The Portland Evening Express* described Jones as "a newcomer from Detroit, who is reported by the powers that be as something bordering on hysteria for the fans."

In Portland, Jones treated the fans to the sort of bloody spectacle that Midwestern wrestling fans had grown accustomed to from viewing a decade of his work. On the undercard of a show headlined by a women's world title defense from Mildred Burke, Jones brutalized Jack Kelly and rearranged his face.

"Jones forced Kelly to succumb from the pressure of a reverse arm lock in 2:30, then shifted his attack to Kelly's head, butting him repeatedly with his own skull until Referee Fred

A Decided Novelty

Moran stepped in at the eight-minute mark to stop the affair," wrote *The Portland Press Herald*. "Kelly was bleeding freely from a gash over the eyebrows."

This New England tour reunited Jones on cards with his early opponent and credited mentor, Boston legend Ted Germaine. The descriptions of the matches seem to indicate that Jones still remained capable of delivering the same level of action as he did in the Midwest, like the summary of his bout with Johnny "Moochy" Muccaccario at the Hartford Auditorium that was supplied by *The Hartford Daily Courant*.

"The squatty Negro was the fans' choice, and he came through to take the first fall in 14 minutes and 10 seconds with a headbutt and leg hold," wrote Max Liberman for *The Daily Courant*. "Moochy seemed fully qualified to even the score, but Jones stopped whatever ambitions Moochy had with a series of butts. Both struggled through the remaining 26 minutes without success as the gong ended their 45-minute time limit bout. It was a lively set-to."

Jones also subjected Hartford fans to one of his signature Detroit-style brawls, battling the equally bellicose Bull Curry all over the Hartford Auditorium.

"Curry took the first fall in 10:45 with a series of smashes and a top body press," wrote Liberman. "In this set-to as well as in the following two frays, both plunged in the hard wooden aisles in a blur of flailing, flying fists and arms to culminate a steady procession of heave-hos by one or the other combatants. In the second affair, which Jones took to even the score, he headbutted Curry into defeat, needing but a top body press to win. In the final fall, which Curry took in 8:30 with a series of elbow smashes and a crab hold, action went sky high requiring the assistance of the attending policemen to keep things in order."

Rufus also had his first hometown match under his most frequent stage name in November, finally wrestling under the name Rufus Jones in Boston Arena, and dueling Chuck Montana to a draw. This means Joe Godfrey wrestled in his

A Decided Novelty

home state of Massachusetts under all three of the identities he would adopt during his career.

In the Rocky Mountain region, King Kong Clayton continued wrestling a busy schedule in 1947, though he took off the first few months of the year. When he returned, he resumed his habit of wrestling in Montana, Idaho, and Alberta, and continued to lose most of his matches.

As Clayton traveled, the exaggerated legend of his feats in battle continued to spread. *The Edmonton Journal* told the tale of how Clayton had served in "the All-Colored division of the U.S. Army," and was "one of eight men who miraculously survived a Nazi trap which caught Clayton's group in a deadly cross-fire in the Sicilian fighting." Clayton was said to have received a purple heart for his troubles.

Not to be outdone, *The Edmonton Bulletin* added the detail that Clayton had crawled six miles on his hands and knees — presumably with bullets lodged in his jaw and leg if *all* the stories were true — to reach safety.

One Black wrestling legend who would not reach the end of 1947 safely was George Godfrey. In 1943, Russ Newland's gossip column from *The Fresno Bee* included the tidbit that Godfrey had gotten a new job "as a day time spieler" in front of a Southern California boxing gym.

"[Godfrey] coaxes spectators inside at so much a head, and also is a bouncer in a Long Beach night club," added Newland.

It was a steep fall from grace for a man who had once held a disputed claim to a world heavyweight boxing championship, and who served as an accelerant to increase opportunities for Black pro wrestlers.

On August 14th of 1947, the sad report was issued by the Associated Press that George Godfrey "died in poverty in his dingy little room yesterday with only his large black dog by his side." Godfrey's doctor and friend Darrington Weaver said that Godfrey had been under treatment for heart inflammation that had been complicated by kidney trouble.

A Decided Novelty

According to Darrington, Godfrey had called him to complain about the symptoms of his illness, only for Darrington to find the 50-year-old former fighter dead in his room a few hours later. It was an inauspicious end for a boxer who had not only earned a substantial income for many of his biggest fights, but also for someone who made the best of an unfortunate professional setback, thereby proving the point that Black wrestlers could attract fans when presented favorably.

Don Kindred spent the early portion of 1948 touring the large East Coast cities of Philadelphia and New York. From there, he moved to Baltimore where he was introduced to wrestling fans under Don Blackman's former name "The Dark Angel." He was also presented as a rival of fellow Black wrestler Frank James, who was touted as a Baltimore native in a match that was said to be historic.

"Marking the first local showing of Negro grapplers, the opening bout will pit Frank James, local boy, against Don Kindred, New York grunter, in a one-fall, half-hour time limit encounter," stated *The Baltimore Sun*.

It was a contest that Kindred won in 18 minutes with a kangaroo kick, little realizing that he had just defeated a man he would make history with a few years later, and thousands of miles away.

In New Jersey, Kindred began to be painted as a former collegiate athlete. When he made his first appearance in Asbury Park, *The Red Bank Register* described him as "a muscular man of proportions who won his spurs at the University of Michigan."

Ironically, just two days after *The Asbury Park Evening Press* made its spurious reference to Kindred's athletic exploits at the University of Michigan, *The Daily Record* of Long Branch, New Jersey described Kindred as a "former Ohio State University athlete." In short, depending on who you asked within the Garden State, you might have been told that Kindred had been a student-athlete at either Michigan or their detested archrivals to the south.

A Decided Novelty

Eventually, some papers gave up on specifics and simply called Kindred a former Big Ten wrestling champion — another claim that was off by more than a decade. Simon Roberts of Iowa didn't become the first Black wrestler to win an individual Big 10 wrestling championship until 1958.

Don Kindred demonstrates a piledriver for the press

Kindred's time in the East was coterminous with that of his familiar foe Don Blackman. This time, rather than working in opposition with one another, the pair formed a semi-regular tag team to contend with tandems like the pairing of Herby Freeman and Pat Welsh.

A Decided Novelty

In March, Blackman headlined a mixed wrestling and boxing event in Perkasie, Pennsylvania, midway between Philadelphia and Allentown. *The Central News-Herald* of Perkasie printed some downright ludicrous claims about Blackman's wrestling accomplishments while advertising the show. The paper referred to Blackman as "a willowy Negro, and only one of his race to ever hold a wrestling title." As if that wasn't already incorrect, the newspaper wandered even further into the realm of fiction.

"Blackman was light-heavyweight champion for seven years, and retired unbeaten when he became too heavy and had to enter the heavier division," continued *The News-Herald*, perhaps unintentionally echoing a lie that had also been told years earlier about Rufus Jones.

Beyond the fact that Blackman certainly *wasn't* the only Black wrestler to hold any title, no evidence existed that he had *ever* held an official championship.

Blackman returned to Norfolk and Richmond to defeat the Harlem Angel in summer 1948, and then he made his first official appearances in Detroit. Despite getting pinned in his debut, Blackman's attire became more colorful in the Motor City, and his animal-print attire became the focus of the spectators and the local press.

The Windsor Daily Star identified Blackman as "the bewhiskered colored star who wears a leopard skin in place of a robe when he enters the ring."

As for Kindred, in March 1948, it was reported that he had failed to show up for his scheduled match with Canadian Stu Hart, and was appraised with a harsh reprimand.

"Kindred was suspended immediately from wrestling in New Jersey by Dave Spence, state inspector, who was attending the bouts," reported *The Asbury Park Evening Press*.

The next day, a follow-up story in *The Evening Press* updated fans on Kindred's situation: Abe J. Greene, the commissioner of the New Jersey State Athletic Commission, had decided to suspend Kindred for 30 days.

A Decided Novelty

Whether the suspension was legitimate, covered for an undisclosed injury, or masked Kindred's pursuit of other opportunities remains unknown. What is known is that the next time Kindred appeared in a North American wrestling ring, it was in the state of Vermont in July. Simultaneous to that, *The Montreal Star* listed "Don Kindred, 200-pound negro lineman" as a standby player for the Montreal Alouettes of the Canadian Football League, located just one hour north of St. Alban's, Vermont.

Instead of taking to the gridiron as a full-time contributor to the Alouettes, Kindred found himself splitting time between wrestling in Vermont, and wrestling in North Bay, Ontario, where he was introduced to fans as a junior heavyweight champion.

The early portion of 1948 for Seelie Samara was marked by high-profile losses to Orville Brown, as well as Maurice Tillet, and former world heavyweight boxing champion Primo Carnera. Then Samara made a brief stop in the Pacific Northwest in the summer before returning to Australia. This time, he had Jack Claybourne with him.

When Dutch Hefner arrived in Australia in July, *The Truth* of Brisbane reported that "the most popular wrestler ever to work here" had caused booking plans to be altered by refusing to wrestle Samara because of his race.

That same week, a detailed, anonymous account from someone who had allegedly shared a plane ride with Samara over to Australia was printed in *Smith's Weekly* under the inflammatory title "Plane Talk Turned Negro Villain Into Uncle Tom."

Over the course of 48 hours of travel, Samara had supposedly leaked to the passenger in the adjoining seat a host of details about his life. This included that his father "Alfred Samara" was a preacher in Georgia, and that his mother was a teacher at a Black Sunday school.

"Seelie confided to his fellow passenger how he had shocked his devout family by becoming first a professional boxer, then a wrestler," continued the article. "His father preached a special sermon about it as a warning to the parents of other colored boys. Seelie later completed his disgrace in his family's eyes by buying an interest in a Kansas City beer tavern, acting as a crooner, barman, and bouncer. Special prayers were read for his salvation. His mother actually went into mourning for a week."

The punchline to the article was that Samara was now wrestling as a "goodie," and *Smith's Weekly* suspected that the process of Samara unburdening himself of his sins throughout his conversation on the plane might have had something to do with his unexpectedly wholesome behavior after he landed in Sydney. This was reported in spite of the fact that none of the reports from Samara's bouts from his previous Australian tour described him as an unrepentant rulebreaker.

"He has insisted on the hero role in his four matches to date, and hasn't pulled one really naughty trick, even in reprisal," concluded the article. "He has been transformed from a Simon Legree to a kindly old Uncle Tom. He has given up smoking and swearing, and has signed up to play baseball with Canterbury-Bankstown... Some of his rival wrestlers are complaining. Besides, it's bad for the box office."

In the context of the article and the location in which it was written, the "Uncle Tom" reference is likely intended as a positive comparison in keeping with the original intent of Harriet Beecher Stowe in her novel *Uncle Tom's Cabin*. In the original novel, Tom is a devoutly religious preacher who would rather be beaten to death than betray two fellow slaves who had successfully escaped from the plantation.

With time, the shifting dynamics of racial relations, and the reinterpretation of the Uncle Tom character for stage plays, the term "Uncle Tom" became a derisive term used against Blacks who were perceived to have accepted their subordinate position to Whites, and then undermined efforts to uplift their fellow Blacks.

Another interview was recorded while Samara was allegedly at the Burlington Hotel in Sydney recuperating from biting off the tip of his tongue. The grappler fielded the

A Decided Novelty

questions of a reporter from *The Sun*, and during one portion of the interview, Samara let slip his real name, but then paired it with an absurd story involving the death of a fellow wrestler.

"You know, my name Seelie Samara is a phony. It's really George Hardison," he disclosed. "I took the name as a sort of gesture. It belonged to a good wrestler I beat once in Costa Rica. Well I beat this guy and afterwards he died, so I took over his name. The only difference was that he spelled Seelie with a Z."

Unless this tragic match in Costa Rica occurred between July 14 and July 17 — the night of George Hoddison's final match in Massachusetts as the Black Demon and his first appearance in Montreal as Zelis Amhara — then it was a product of his lively imagination.

What was apparently not a source of fiction was Samara's fondness for baseball. He was photographed playing baseball in a nearby park, and insisted to reporters that there was no better sport for remaining in ring shape than baseball.

Before joining Samara in Australia, Jack Claybourne began the year wrestling in the Pacific Northwest before making his first appearance in Hawaii on March 30, 1948. He was advertised as "the world's greatest Negro wrestler" who "should make a big hit here," but it's unlikely that the person who wrote those words had any idea just how prescient they would turn out to be.

Claybourne drew rave reviews in his few Hawaii bouts prior to his departure for Australia, but Ted Thye, who helped promoter Al Karasick with the booking of qualified talent, quickly assured *The Star-Bulletin* that Gentleman Jack would be returning to the Hawaiian Islands as soon as his stint in Australia reached its end.

Even with Claybourne appearing in only two Hawaiian matches, his fame there was already worth reporting about on the U.S. mainland, at least within Black news circles. While Claybourne had already moved on to Australia, an Associated Negro Press writer based in Hawaii — Hubert H. White — published a syndicated article informing the ANP's readership

A Decided Novelty

about the popularity that Gentleman Jack had rapidly achieved in the heart of the Pacific.

"Jack Claybourne, world famous wrestler, arrived here from California two weeks ago and has become the greatest drawing card of wrestling events, given every Sunday night at the Civic Auditorium," wrote White. "He is one of the cleverest and fastest mat men ever to appear here. When he made his debut two weeks ago with Maurice Chapelle, junior heavyweight champion of California, he demonstrated unquestioned ability to use holds and tactics far superior to many of the wrestlers seen here."

Now back in Australia after a two-year absence, Claybourne went straight back to headlining shows in what had clearly become one of his favorite places to wrestle. This time, the presence of a companion by his side was rather conspicuous, and became an immediate topic of interest to the Australian press.

"World champion negro heavyweight wrestler, Elmer (call me 'Jack') Claybourne, would rather talk about his wife's prowess at bowls than what he does in the ring," printed *The Sun* of Sydney. "'Yes, I've got the champion's belt — but, listen, you ought to see my Lillian operating in the bowling alley. She's mighty good,' [Claybourne] said today when he arrived in Sydney from the U.S. by ANA Skymaster. Mrs. Claybourne beamed broadly."

Lillian Claybourne humored the members of the press who asked her how much she weighed after confirming the weight of her husband at 17 stone; *The Sun* actually printed Lillian's weight of 13 stone, or a little over 180 pounds.

Expectedly, some members of the Australian press got around to discussing the tremendous popularity that Black American wrestlers had achieved in Australia in recent years — Claybourne and Samara in particular — and racked their brains searching for explanations. *The Newcastle Sun* bluntly opined that the frequent rivals, who had yet to face one another in Australia, were the two most popular wrestlers to have appeared in Australia, excepting no one.

A Decided Novelty

"Reasons for this favoritism are not hard to find," offered *The Sun*. "The negroes are non-stop matmen, very agile, and able to use all the recognized holds. Good showmen, they keep their temper in the face of the greatest provocation."

Claybourne and Samara headlined a show in Sydney as Claybourne was making his exit from the country, and Samara gained the victory in what can be presumed to have been a non-title match, since Claybourne was still repeatedly referred to as the Negro world heavyweight champion in the aftermath of the contest.

"Coloured wrestlers Seelie Samara and Jack Claybourne staged one of the most scientific and clever bouts seen at the stadium in a long time, Samara winning by two falls to one in the sixth round," stated *The Newcastle Morning Herald and Miners' Advocate*. "Samara gained a submission fall in the third. Claybourne equalised in the fifth with a series of dropkicks and a body press. Samara clinched the match with a crotch hold and press in the sixth round."

Leaving Samara to continue headlining in his absence, Claybourne once again departed from Australia after what was presumably another prosperous tour and returned to Hawaii. Without question, Jack wouldn't have flown back to Hawaii if he didn't think he would make money. He probably had no idea that he was about to make history.

With Claybourne due to reappear in the wrestling rings of Hawaii, *The Honolulu Star-Bulletin* made the announcement on October 4 that the "colored mat artist" was set to arrive from Australia, where he had been touring for the prior six weeks.

When Claybourne's plane landed, the red carpet was rolled out for both him and his wife Lillian, while the pair posed for photos while wearing Hawaiian leis. *The Honolulu Advertiser* referred to Claybourne as the "undefeated Negro heavyweight wrestling champion of the world," which was a false commendation no matter how creatively a promoter might have attempted to manipulate the words in that sentence.

A Decided Novelty

At that moment, Claybourne's Hawaiian record stood at no wins, one draw, and one loss in a Hawaiian title bout. In Australia, he had not only lost on more than one occasion, but he had dropped his final bout in the country to Seelie Samara.

In addition to landing in Hawaii with his wife and an exaggerated claim to being undefeated, Claybourne also arrived in Hawaii in the possession of something else that was of equal interest to the press.

"A veteran of 10 years in professional wrestling, Claybourne said he won the Negro heavyweight title in 1943, and is the proud owner of a jewel studded gold belt presented to him by the New York Boxing and Wrestling Commission," reported *The Advertiser*. "Only two others wore that belt before Claybourne. They were Tiger Nelson in 1941 and Rufus Jones in 1943. Claybourne has turned back all challengers since he won the title in 1943."

Claybourne blasted through his first three October matches, leapfrogging Oki Shikina as the top contender to the Hawaiian title. It became a foregone conclusion that the main event of the final wrestling show of the month would have Hisao Tanaka defending the *Ring Magazine* belt against Jack Claybourne.

Outside of Hawaii, wrestling fans would have been hard pressed to find a wrestler with a worse record in title matches than Claybourne up until that point, simply looking at the raw numbers. Setting aside two dozen or so matches Claybourne had participated in with a theoretical Black wrestling championship on the line — very few of which were represented by a physical belt or trophy — Claybourne had competed for championships in many of the territories he had visited, and had *never* emerged from any of those matches wearing a title belt.

Ironically, Hawaiian newspapers published no articles noting how historically significant a Claybourne title victory over Tanaka would be for racial breakthroughs in wrestling generally, and in Hawaii particularly.

A Decided Novelty

This time, in his 17th year as a professional wrestler, Claybourne would indeed reach the summit, defeating Tanaka on Sunday, October 31, and becoming Hawaiian junior heavyweight champion and *Ring Magazine* title belt holder before the largest Civic Auditorium crowd of the year.

"The agile and clever Claybourne, who also holds the world's Negro heavyweight title, proved too strong and quick for Tanaka, one of the outstanding wrestlers to show in Honolulu this year," observed *The Advertiser*. "Tanaka, unable to keep any of his powerful holds on Claybourne, attempted to rough up the challenger, but only succeeded in spurring his opponent to greater heights."

Claybourne's victory was also a dominant one, as he scored two consecutive falls on the vanquished Japanese titleholder without surrendering a fall in return. Fittingly, both of the falls would come by way of dropkicks set up by tried-and-true tactics in Claybourne's arsenal.

"Claybourne applied the first fall in 16 min. 33 seconds with a flying dropkick and a body press. He leapfrogged over the referee and caught Tanaka by surprise with his dropkick," continued *The Advertiser*. "Another dropkick gave Claybourne the clincher at 5 min. and 13 seconds later. As Tanaka attempted to kick him out, Claybourne cut loose with a flying tackle from the apron of the ring, then dropkicked Tanaka clear across the ring to set up the body press."

Gracious in defeat, Tanaka personally supervised the coronation of the man who supplanted him as champion by placing the *Ring Magazine* title belt around Gentleman Jack's waist.

After defending his title against Chief Little Wolf, Claybourne turned his attention to Brother Frank. Prior to the bout, the Hawaiian newspapers predicted that the bout would be decided by the wrestler whose style dictated the action — the speed and agility of Claybourne, or the aggressive roughhousing tactics of Frank.

What ultimately transpired during that bout was a shocking turn of events, and while it may have been intended

A Decided Novelty

to represent a one-time ironic twist for the sake of keeping a match entertaining and unpredictable, it marked the critical moment that Gentleman Jack dramatically altered his approach to professional wrestling.

"The match was a torrid tussle, with Claybourne pitting his speed and skill against the Utah grappler's rough tactics," reported *The Advertiser*. "Brother Frank gained the first fall in 17:50 with a corner piledriver, followed by body slams and a press."

From this moment on, *The Advertiser*'s account of the match reads *identically* to the description of a match headlined by Rufus Jones in 1942.

"Infuriated by his opponent's wild tactics, Claybourne began butting Brother Frank with his head and opened a cut over the left eye," continued *The Advertiser*. "Claybourne kept up his butting tactics until Brother Frank began reeling dizzily and virtually helplessly. The referee then intervened and stopped the match, awarding the fall to Claybourne. Frank was unable to continue, so Claybourne was given the match on a medical disqualification."

Every element of the third fall reads as if it was lifted straight from the playbook of the most influential Black heel wrestler in history. It was Jones' custom to drop an early fall to an opponent who was well versed at the technical aspects of wrestling, only for Jones to become angry and bludgeon his adversary with repeated headbutts. The fact that a babyface aerialist like Claybourne would replicate Jones' match-ending sequence beat for beat was undoubtedly shocking.

This was far from an isolated incident: Claybourne used high-flying dropkicks, cartwheels and leaping headbutts in nearly all subsequent matches, setting a precedent that would become an expectation for young, athletic Black babyface wrestlers for decades to come.

Before the end of the autumn, Seelie Samara was announced as a new arrival to Hawaii who was being brought in to face Leo Wallick on the undercard of Claybourne's title defense against Little Wolf.

A Decided Novelty

Expectations were immediately established that Claybourne and Samara would be on a collision course regardless as to the outcome of the Claybourne-Little Wolf match. *The Star-Bulletin* quickly brought readers up to speed about the sort of regional wrestling history they were witnessing, stating that for the first time ever at a Hawaiian wrestling event, "two outstanding Negro stars are appearing on one show."

"Claybourne holds a gold belt presented to him in New York when he won the 'Negro heavyweight mat title,'" *The Star-Bulletin* reminded its readers. "Samara says he is after the belt."

More accurately, Samara was attempting to recover the same physical belt that he had lost to Claybourne in Pasadena, California, but which was the personal property of Claybourne, and would therefore never leave his side for very long.

Al Karasick later held an interview alongside Samara, and as the promoter explained the significance of landing a star of Samara's caliber to the press, he also doubled down on his intention of getting Claybourne and Samara in the ring for the first bout in the history of Hawaii featuring two Black competitors.

"I know the fans will see a great wrestler in Samara, who came to Hawaii with the special intention of challenging Jack Claybourne to a match for the world's Negro wrestling championship," Karasick explained to *The Advertiser*. "Both claim the title. Claybourne has a belt presented to him by the New York commission. The mix-up will be cleared if these two sign for a match."

With his title bout against Chief Little Wolf nearly being overshadowed by the promise of a future bout between himself and Samara, Claybourne still managed to score a decisive victory over his faux Native American opponent. This occurred despite Claybourne falling victim to Little Wolf's Indian deathlock and surrendering the opening fall.

"The colored mat star evened matters after 4 minutes 38 seconds with a flying drop kick and a body press," reported

A Decided Novelty

The Star-Bulletin. "After breaking the chief's Indian death lock twice, once by grabbing the ropes and the second by butting, Claybourne won the deciding fall in 8 minutes 45 seconds."

In the featured undercard match, Samara flattened Brother Frank, ending matters in a little over 17 minutes with a "flying bear hug and body press."

"The Gold Dust Twins" – Jack Claybourne and Seelie Samara

To no one's surprise, Samara and Claybourne were booked to share the ring during the next Civic Auditorium event on December 12th. The unanticipated twist was caused by the revelation that the two would be paired together as members of the same team.

A Decided Novelty

Before they would make Hawaii history as the first Black wrestlers to compete against one another — and in a main-event title match no less — the two Murderers' Row members would make history of a different kind as teammates on the first Black tag team in the history of the territory.

"We're not rough and we prefer wrestling, but we won't be pushed around," Samara warned the pair's opponents, Dick Raines and Brother Frank. "We can rough it up if we have to."

The reunited Gold Dust Twins drew with Raines and Frank, with Claybourne absorbing the pinfall loss for his team after a series of backbreakers from Raines. The two Black stars then double-teamed Frank to score the equalizing fall before the time limit expired.

Back on the American mainland, Jim Mitchell returned to the New England area early in 1948, and he accomplished what can rightly be construed as a major milestone for Black wrestlers, although the scope of the achievement becomes somewhat condensed the more it is analyzed.

On June 18, Mitchell teamed with Jim Kelly to capture the regional tag team championship from Ted Germaine and Tiger Tasker in straight falls. Just one month earlier, *The Transcript Telegram* of Holyoke stated that Germaine and Tasker had held the tag team championship of the Boston-based American Wrestling Association for years and "still retain the crown."

This was presumably news to Germaine and Tasker, who had not been mentioned as being the tag team champions of the AWA for *five* full years up until that point. Furthermore, even during the period in which those titles had been active in the early 1940s, the rank of those championships vacillated between national and world championship status, and was seldom reported with any consistency.

The Panther and Kelly continued their title reign for two months, with several regional newspapers teasing that Germaine and Tasker would eventually get another opportunity to wrest the championship from them. No

A Decided Novelty

recorded title-change ever occurred, and the next time the area's tag team championship was mentioned after summer 1947, it was early in 1948, with Tasker and Germaine in possession of the championship as if they had never lost it.

In the meantime, Mitchell and Kelly surprisingly began wrestling one another in several New England cities without any mention of the fact that they were either the reigning tag team title holders of the region, or even that they had once been former partners and champions.

Regardless, Mitchell can be credited as one of the first Black wrestlers to hold half of a territory's top tag team championship, if not the very first to do so.

After making history in New England, the Black Panther returned to California once again, and although papers like *The San Bernardino Sun* praised him as a wrestler who possessed "great strength and versatility," he was becoming increasingly known as a wrestler "whose chief weapon is his hard head."

A common promotional tactic of the era was to inflate the credentials of wrestlers through race-exclusive championships, or alternatively to talk about the scarcity of certain types of wrestlers. Both of these tactics were often used in the marketing of Black wrestlers. However, combining the two tactics merely served to diminish the significance of the wrestlers.

As a case in point, when *The Sun-Star* anointed Mitchell as "the colored world's light-heavyweight wrestling champion and one of three colored grapplers in the game," fans probably wondered why there was value in selecting champions among Black wrestlers — let alone within separate weight divisions — if there were only three Black wrestlers in existence.

Rufus Jones followed his friend the Black Panther straight into California, and *The Santa Barbara News-Press* announced the California debut of Jones in March by offering a description of Jones' in-ring demeanor that would have left fans familiar with the antics of Rufus wondering if *The News-*

A Decided Novelty

Press staff had gotten the nearly 35-year-old Jones confused with someone much younger.

"Rufus Jones, one of the few Negro wrestlers in the United States, will make his Pacific Coast debut at the Mission Athletic Club Arena Thursday night according to Don Sebastian, promoter," declared *The News-Press*. "Jones has been wrestling for about seven years, and has built up a large following in the East, where he has become somewhat of a sensation among grunt and groan fans."

In a separate article on the same page, *The News-Press* stated that Jones would be making the first Santa Barbara appearance by a Negro wrestler, and that he was "considered by his people as the uncrowned mat champ." They also listed him as weighing 210 pounds, and standing 5'10", while also laughably describing him as "a rugged but clean fighter."

In truth, Jones was now a 15-year mat veteran who stood barely 5'7". Not to mention, by telling wrestling fans that Jones was essentially a clean fighter, the promoter must have been setting them up for a startling turn of events once the headbutts and blood began to fly.

Simultaneous to the advertisement that Jones would be debuting in Santa Barbara, *The Ventura Weekly Post* announced that Rufus Jones and the Black Panther would be forming a partnership to take on Gino Garibaldi and Bulldog Clements. Clearly, the intention was for Jones and Mitchell to resurrect their tag team and batter all of the other teams in Southern California with headbutts.

Unfortunately, the closest Jones would get to wrestling in California was a visit to the ringside seats. *The News-Press* explained that when Jones appeared in Santa Barbara, his presence was announced to the fans, who were then told that Jones would be unable to wrestle until he got his license cleared by the California State Athletic Commission. Instead, the Black Panther substituted for Jones, and promptly lost his match to Martino Angelo.

Apparently unable to get himself cleared by the Athletic Commission of California under any circumstances, Jones

A Decided Novelty

instead found himself booked in a few shows at Phoenix's Madison Square Garden. Introduced first as a claimant to "the Boston championship" — a claim that was quickly amended to that of "Boston Negro champion" — Jones faced Jose Lopez of Mexico, and in the words of *The Arizona Republic*, "used his hard head to knock Lopez into Tamale Land."

The short-term limbo Jones found himself occupying after his anticlimactic exit from California didn't last long. As soon as Jones could get himself booked in Oregon, it appears that he hustled back to the West Coast to wrestle for Don Owen. *The Coos Bay Times* informed fans that hadn't seen Jones during his initial tour of the state that he was "the head-buttinest Negro" in these parts, who combined "unusual tactics" with a "red-hot wrestling style."

Jones' first major bout in his return to Oregon was a textbook dismantling of George Dusette in Salem. Jones dropped Dusette with headbutts and applied a Boston crab to win the first fall, lost the second fall to a full nelson, and then pinned Dusette to conclude the match after repeatedly butting his head. According to *The Statesman*, Jones then "took leave of the crowded premises in the escort of city cops, as he had the customers ready to help, as usual."

The Coos Bay Times described Jones' actions against the masked Phantom at the North Bend Community Building as "an exhibition of animal brutality." During the bout, the two men "spent most of their minutes in the ring slugging, gouging, kicking, and head-butting, with the Phantom ending up with a badly split forehead that streamed blood over wrestlers, referees and fans."

"The bout ended outside the ring, where Jones ran the Phantom's head into a heavy ringside bench, finishing the job he started with head-butts," added *The Times*. "[Referee] Williams managed to get between the men long enough to pull the bloody and almost unconscious Phantom and award him the match on fouls. As he and spectators were carrying the Phantom to the dressing room, Jones attacked him from behind again, trying to head-butt him further."

Losses aside, the consistent message being sent in these matches was that if Jones could simply manage to restrain himself at critical moments, he would avoid losing falls by disqualification, and potentially never lose a multi-fall match.

The fans also sent a consistent message to Jones: "We don't like you." It was a message that was delivered loud and clear when a fan attempted to snipe Jones with a hunting knife in the middle of a late-July show in Salem.

"His aim was poor, and no damage was done, but someone threw a long-bladed pocket knife at wrestler Rufus Jones Tuesday night during the wrestling program at the Salem armory," reported *The Oregon Statesman*, providing a wrestler with rare front-page coverage. "Jones was just leaving the ring after taking a fall over an opponent when the knife, believed by the police to have been thrown from the balcony, sailed toward Jones and missed him by a few inches. Although city police went into action immediately, they did not apprehend whoever threw the dangerous missile. Jones has wrestled in Salem many times, and is extremely unpopular with the armory fans."

The flinging of edged weapons in Jones' direction wasn't the only close call he was forced to contend with. In Salem, Jones had to deal with a different type of ringside distraction from the hostile crowd.

The Capital Journal reported that while Jones was in the midst of combat with Jack Lipscomb as the two were standing close to the audience, Jones was "hit in the head by an outsider while a firecracker exploded." Despite initially fearing that someone had fired a gun at him, Jones still completed the match by headbutting and pinning Lipscomb.

When a late-September match between Rufus and Farmer Jones was being advertised in *The Register-Guard*, the utterance attributed to Farmer Jones was that he'd have "nothing to do with the Nigger," but later decided that he'd "like nothing better than to toss Rufus around for a bit."

This was the second consecutive tour that resulted in Jones being called a nigger in the Oregon press. While the second use of the racial epithet had been credited to a supposed pig farmer from Arkansas, the first had been assigned to a straightforward grappler from Indiana.

In his daily life, Farmer Jones was Cecil Murdoch of Waxahachie, Texas, the brother of wrestler Frank Murdoch, and the uncle of future wrestler Dick Murdoch. For what it's worth, the younger Murdoch had several accusations of racist behavior leveled against him throughout his career and following his death, including tales that he drove fellow wrestlers to KKK rallies, and proudly displayed his Klan membership card.

Because of his family ties that actually point to a racist legacy, the idea that the N-word could have actually come out of Cecil Murdoch's mouth during an interview isn't particularly far-fetched.

In Pasco, Washington, Jones adopted the pre-show ritual of permitting boards and boxes to be smashed over his head to demonstrate its sturdiness, and to reinforce its reputation as the deadliest weapon in wrestling. With Jack Claybourne and Jim Mitchell also both adopting headbutting to lethal effect, it was now evident that the frequent use of one's head as an instrument of destruction was becoming an expectation of Black wrestling performance.

With Black thickheadedness becoming a stereotype that seemed to be taking on a life of its own, it would take the refusal of some wrestlers to indulge in the maneuver to slow the stereotype's spread. However, the unexpected death of the wrestler who had set a standard for Black wrestlers based on crisp technical work would seemingly eliminate the only restraining influence that could have prevented the essence of the Black American wrestling style from trending further in a conformist and reputationally harmful direction.

A Decided Novelty

23 – Mildred, I...

After his California partnership with Rufus Jones failed to pan out, Jim Mitchell returned to New England for the summer, where the local fans were told that the Black Panther had returned from a worldwide campaign. He lost a main-event match to former world champion Steve Casey despite unleashing his headbutt upon him, and then returned to California in the summer.

Mitchell was now being advertised as a 210-pound wrestler, and photos of him clearly reveal that he had packed on a great deal of weight compared with the thin figure he cut during the early stages of a wrestling career that was now in at least its 18th year.

Just one year earlier, Mitchell was described in California as a strategic wrestler who had "developed a method of butting heads with his foes" that left them vulnerable. Now, the language used to describe him was beginning to shift toward characterizing the Panther's weaponized head as the product of a genetic mutation.

The Whittier News described Mitchell as "the hard-hitting negro with the thick skull," while *The San Pedro News-Pilot* presented him as the beneficiary of "a concrete-hard head." The Panther wielded that superhumanly thick skull to advance to the finals of the Olympic Auditorium's 1948 club wrestling championship against Bobby Managoff.

Managoff wrenched his knee during the final bout of the December tournament, which prevented him from finishing his bout with Mitchell. In front of 5,200 fans, the Panther performed a gesture in alignment with the holiday spirit and refused to accept the default victory. Instead, he and Managoff shared the annual club title.

While Mitchell and others in his peer group were still hanging on, others were saying their final goodbyes. Between 1946 and 1948, Gorilla Parker appeared in a handful of matches for a portion of each year, generally in Pennsylvania, New Jersey, and New York. His final match on record occurred in the summer of 1948, with Parker altogether disappearing from wrestling afterwards. Still, his name would be fondly recalled by members of the press on a few occasions, and imposters would emerge to wrestle under his name a full 15 years after his retirement.

During Parker's wrestling prime, *The Chillicothe Gazette* unequivocally stated that "Parker is undoubtedly one of the greatest colored wrestlers ever to set foot on a padded mat, and at present is one of the most persistent challengers for the light heavyweight title." This could have served as the epitaph for Parker's entire career. The fact is that Parker was one of the wrestlers most consistently positioned as a first-rate challenger to established light heavyweight champions without ever capturing a championship.

Years later, when Don Kindred appeared in Australia, he claimed to *The Courier-Mail* of Brisbane that he had been taught to wrestle at age 11 "under the able instruction of his uncle, Zimba Parker, himself a noted wrestler."

While a genetic link between the two wrestlers is unlikely, the idea of Parker and Kindred being placed within the fictional bloodline of a prominent Black wrestling family is intriguing. If nothing else, it certainly signifies the influence of Parker and the respect that the next generation of Black wrestlers had for him that his name would be introduced by Kindred out of nowhere simply for the sake of forging a non-essential attachment between the two.

Given that Australia is 9,000 miles away from Parker's stomping grounds, and there is no record of Parker ever wrestling in Australia, Parker's reputation gained more from Kindred's reference than Kindred could ever have benefitted from mentioning him.

While Don Kindred forged a fictional genetic relationship with Parker, Don Blackman could be considered Parker's stylistic successor. In the aftermath of Parker's retirement, Blackman inherited the practice of wearing animal skins and prints in lieu of wrestling tights just like Parker.

A Decided Novelty

In early 1948, Alex Kaffner made his first recorded visit to Atlanta, Georgia. The match was originally supposed to be another bout between Kaffner and Jackson for the latter's Negro junior world title, but Jackson was replaced on the show by "The Chicago Demon" Mike Whatley.

That same month, Kaffner was advertised for what was one of very few matches he ever had with a fellow Black wrestler in his typical stomping grounds, as he was booked to wrestle Buddy Jackson in Iowa. Some papers declared the bout was for the Negro wrestling championship of the United States.

However, Jackson didn't appear for the match, and *The Rock Island Argus* reported that he had suffered a broken leg. Instead, Kaffner dispatched Pete Walker in consecutive falls with a standing body scissors and a full nelson. Kaffner had also been booked for a bout in Atlanta against Jackson, but a replacement was found for that match as well.

When 1948 opened, big things had appeared to be headed Buddy Jackson's way. Jackson was scheduled to tour the upper Midwest as the Negro heavyweight champion of the U.S. before heading down to Macon, Georgia, to wrestle for Dick Lever as his "world heavyweight Negro wrestling champion." The first stop along that tour was intended to be a title defense against another Black wrestler, Henry Jones.

"This bout will mark the first time a Negro claimant to a wrestling title has ever appeared here," stated *The Macon Telegraph and News*. "Jackson is fast, aggressive, and features the dropkick and hammerlock. His foe, a rugged type grappler, features the step-over toe-hold."

While the legitimacy of Jackson's reported leg injury is unknown, he clearly disappeared from ring activity for nine months before returning in fall 1948. When he finally returned, it was in Ontario, Canada, where he was hailed as a Las Vegas product, and yet another symbol of Black athletic dominance that was manifesting itself in other sports besides boxing and baseball, as he prepared to face Maurice Roberre in Brantford.

A Decided Novelty

"Just to give the Frenchman a fierce battle, Joe (Maich) secured Buddy Jackson, a Negro battler who seems set to put his race into the same athletic contention as his brothers have in big league baseball," wrote *The Expositor*. "The Nevada champion should carry a great fight to Roberre who is still Maich's hope that he will eventually be the title holder of his weight division in Canada. The Negro flash cannot afford to be defeated if he wishes to make good in this part of North America."

Buddy Jackson

Descriptions of Jackson's in-ring demeanor during this stage of his career suggest that he had not yet achieved a state of total comfort in the ring. When a reporter from *The Expositor* attempted to characterize the mannerisms of "Dusty" Buddy Jackson, the "Nevada Negro," as he headed into a bout against Joe Maich, he said, "Jackson was stated to have acted more like a human being in his bout with Roberre last week."

A Decided Novelty

In Windsor, the migrations of Jackson once again intersected with those of Don Blackman, who had provided Jackson with his first serious taste of wrestling during the all-Negro tour of the South the year prior.

King Kong Clayton's in-ring activity would be drastically scaled back in 1948 as he seemed to ready himself for retirement from the ring. In markets like Boise, Idaho, he was still praised as the Negro heavyweight champion who "recently threw Seelie Samara" even though the majority of the matches in their famous series had occurred in 1941, and the most recent bout between them had been a full six years earlier.

In both Montana and Alberta, the 37-year-old Clayton wrestled in several matches against 33-year-old Stu Hart, with Clayton dutifully doing his part to improve the standing of the Canadian grappler in the eyes of his fellow countrymen.

"Stu Hart and King Kong Clayton had a stretch and pull session with clean breaks and a varied display of wrestling," reported *The Calgary Herald* after a February bout between the duo. "Hart came up with the decision when he followed a series of flying tackles with a flying cross that missed, but he was able to turn it into what he called a southern cross to pin his opponent's shoulders to the mat."

Following a handful of matches wrestled mostly in Regina, Saskatchewan in 1949, Clayton would bow out of the wrestling profession altogether, save for occasional appearances in Montana as a special guest referee in later years.

In a career retrospective interview supplied by Clayton to *The Park County News* of Livingston, Montana in 1958, Clayton shed some light upon the true nature of his wartime activities, as well as some of his other accomplishments that had been embellished to promote him while he had been a wrestler.

In his interview with John Mackay, Clayton effectively confessed that he had suffered a head injury while serving with the U.S. Army Combat Engineers in Italy, but made no insistence that the injury had been the result of a gunshot

A Decided Novelty

wound suffered in combat. As for his ring name, Clayton would only go so far as to claim that he had played the role of a villager in the film "King Kong," but made no claims about subsequent appearances in any other Hollywood films.

Regarding his retirement from wrestling before age 40, Clayton explained that U.S. government insurance premiums covering his head injury would be revoked if he continued wrestling, colorfully summarizing his decision: "$10,000 in the hand is better than a few dollars in the bush league."

Sadly, the fact that Clayton was only 47 years old at the time of the interview and working as a porter at the Northern Pacific Depot in Billings, Montana indicates his plan to retire as a successful nightclub owner probably hadn't panned out.

With that being said, at least Clayton had been able to dictate some of the terms of his departure from professional wrestling. That stands in stark contrast to Reginald Siki, who had continued wrestling into 1948 despite his crushing loss to Gorgeous George, and who was still booked rather favorably in the Los Angeles region following that defeat, all things considered. Siki had even teamed with Jim Mitchell in March during a bout against Chris and Babe Zaharias, which the two lost.

Then, during the first week of June, Reginald Siki dueled to a draw against Vic Holbrook, and promptly disappeared from the ring without any updates or statements about what had caused his extended absence. The answer would be revealed during the Christmas holiday, and it would arrive in devastating fashion.

On December 30, *The California Eagle* offered the first report about the death of a man whose name they anglicized as Kemal Abd-Ur-Rahman, but who wrestling fans recognized as Reginald Siki. According to the account provided to *The Eagle*, Siki dropped dead at the feet of his wife Mildred.

"Rahman, who was 48, and who once held the California State wrestling championship, had gone to the Bel Air home of singer Tony Martin by whom his wife is employed for a holiday visit," stated *The Eagle*. "When she opened the door, he said, 'Mildred — I—,' then he gasped and fell to the floor."

The Eagle described Siki as a wrestler who'd enjoyed an excellent career that "ended last June due to an injury he received while wrestling." Siki's wife expressed "disappointment over the neglect shown her husband following his injury."

Reginald Siki with Joe Louis

Calling Siki 48 stretched that age to its fullest extent. He was born December 28, 1899, and died on December 24, 1948, just four days before his 49th birthday.

The Minneapolis Spokesman provided additional details on Siki's life, including confirmation of the fact that Siki had been born Reginald Berry in Kansas City, and had attended Lincoln High School, which is where he first learned to wrestle.

"He found that American Negroes were not allowed to participate in professional wrestling in America," added *The Spokesman*. "He decided to go to Europe. Over there he changed his name and was known as Siki the Senegalese. When he returned to America, he was booked against the biggest wrestlers in the business."

Finally, *The Spokesman* concluded its coverage by stating that Siki met his final wife, Mildred Strader, while wrestling in Minneapolis in 1945, and the two were married after a brief courtship.

Certainly, the details of Siki's life provided to *The Spokesman* were offered by his widow, and don't accurately reflect the progression of his career. However, if the timeline provided by her is even remotely accurate, her relationship with Siki began well before the deportation of his son and prior wife from New York to the Czech Republic, which occurred in 1946.

Siki's funeral was held at Douglas Temple in Los Angeles, and his body was interred at Evergreen Cemetery.

Aside from wrestlers who were famous on the basis of world championship reigns and sustained fame, there were few performers within the professional wrestling business of the 1940s whose feats and accomplishments were preserved for historical celebration. This being the case, the passing of the man who forged the mold for how a mainstream Black wrestler could establish themself as an appreciable draw went unappreciated at the time.

Then again, the features that helped Siki to stand out during his career — possessing above average height with a chiseled physique and a unique appearance, combined with an exotic origin, technical wrestling prowess, remarkable athleticism, and the ability to competently speak half a dozen languages — would almost guarantee a main-event-level push to any wrestler in any era. While Siki obviously happened upon some of these traits by dint of hard work and the company he kept, it seemingly required a can't-miss prospect in order to make the case that Black wrestlers could effectively intrigue a mainstream audience.

Despite the passing of an unmistakable legend, the wrestling industry marched on without any of the promoters Siki had wrestled for pausing to honor him or his accomplishments. While promoting his first show of 1949, Hawaii promoter Al Karasick explained to *The Advertiser* that he sought an opinion about Jack Claybourne's sudden and frequent use of headbutts, from Northern California wrestling promoter Frank Malcewicz.

"The only hold that is universally barred as illegal is the stranglehold," submitted Malcewicz. "Of course, eye gouging, hair pulling and such tactics are not permitted, but shoulder and head butts are rather common practices. They have been practiced here as well as all other parts of the country. The most effective way to discourage headbutting is to butt right back. So far as professional wrestling around here is concerned, it is recognized around here as part of the game."

When this question was posed, it also created a stir in parts of California where Claybourne had been a strong attraction.

"Claybourne's use of the head to butt opponents groggy has divided Honolulu into two camps, one for him, and one against," wrote Russ Newland of the Associated Press. "Professional wrestling is something in which we are decidedly inexpert, but we never heard of the use of the head as a battering ram as one of the finer points of the game. Whether legal or not, the disputed method of attack is filling Honolulu's Civic Auditorium practically every time Claybourne wrestles."

Dave Beronio, sports editor of *The Times Herald* of Solano County, California, was apparently more familiar with Claybourne's established routine, and seemed stunned at the tactics the Gentleman had adopted in Hawaii.

"Claybourne, a wrestler well known to Vallejoans through his many appearances here in recent years, is currently the sensation of the Hawaiian Islands," wrote Beronio. "'Jumping Jack,' as he was known here through his mighty leaps around the ring, and at his opponents, is currently the hit of the Honolulu shows with his latest tactics. Seems as though Jack has quit jumping in favor of using his head as a battering ram."

A Decided Novelty

With Claybourne's change of style sparking intense debates on the mainland, promoter Al Karasick gave wrestling fans in Hawaii what they had been begging for and booked a bout between Claybourne and Samara with Claybourne's Negro world heavyweight championship belt on the line.

Karasick, in his efforts to promote the bout while ostensibly adhering to the rules governing weight classes, stipulated that only Claybourne's Negro heavyweight title would be up for grabs during the bout, as Samara was too heavy to qualify for a shot at the Hawaii junior heavyweight title.

Angered by the ruling, Samara was later quoted in *The Advertiser* saying he would claim the *Ring Magazine* belt regardless of Karasick's edict if he defeated Claybourne.

As Claybourne and Samara prepared to make history as the first two Black wrestlers to face one another in Hawaii — and in a main event title match no less — the press positioned the contest as a duel between the speed, agility, and headbutts of Claybourne and the size and strength of Samara. They also repeated the false claim that Claybourne had defeated Rufus Jones in 1943 for that particular belt.

"Jack has brought along his championship belt for the occasion," wrote Dan McGuire of *The Advertiser*. "It was presented to him after he defeated Rufus Jones at New York in '43. Jones had been the second wearer, the original holder being Tiger Nelson in 1941, the first year the New York Wrestling and Boxing Commission had offered the belt. It is studded with 21 diamonds and is indeed a thing of beauty. No wonder Samara would like to fasten it around his middle."

When the day of the much-anticipated showdown arrived, *The Advertiser* printed a photo of Claybourne and Samara together, along with an explanation as to why Samara had been making prior claims to being the rightful titleholder.

"Samara claims he was recognized as the champion in South Africa, and that he was trying to force a showdown with Claybourne for years," stated *The Advertiser*.

A Decided Novelty

This represents an instance where candor might have been a more effective promotional tactic. Specifically, Claybourne had won the belt from Samara in Pasadena in 1945, and the last time the two wrestled — which had been in a non-title match held only a few months prior in Sydney, Australia — Samara defeated Claybourne cleanly.

This time, the outcome would be reversed, as Claybourne triumphantly defended his championship, and made it clear that he was the most dominant wrestler in Hawaii, irrespective of race, ethnicity, or weight.

"The match went 14 minutes 37 seconds before a fall was registered. After clever exchanges and holds, Claybourne butted Samara against the ropes, and as the challenger reeled backwards, the Boston grappler cut loose with a flying dropkick," detailed *The Advertiser*. "Samara fell hard, hitting his head, and fell victim to a body press."

Nine minutes later, Samara pinned Claybourne with a tactic similar to how he'd defeated him in Oregon, catching Jack in mid-air as the titleholder attempted a leapfrog, and slamming him to the mat to even the fall count at one apiece. This set the stage for a dramatic third fall with the Negro championship hanging in the balance.

"Claybourne came back strong and scored the deciding fall 7 min. 37 sec. later when he came off the ropes with a flying dropkick that landed flush on Samara's jaw," concluded *The Advertiser*. "Samara didn't know what hit him and was pinned easily."

Right after the Claybourne-Samara match ended, Hubert White of the Associated Negro Press tracked down Al Karasick to discuss Claybourne's success as a babyface in the main events of the promoter's cards, which was atypical, if not completely unprecedented.

"Claybourne is one of the greatest wrestlers of modern times," glowed Karasick. "He is as tough as they come. I only regret that at times Claybourne loses his head; when he does this you may rest assured that his opponent will get hurt."

A Decided Novelty

Karasick also acknowledged that he had "yet to see one loved so much by the fans" as Claybourne, while White supplied the detail that the Samara-Claybourne tag bout had helped attract a crowd of 8,000 fans to the Civic Auditorium prior to the dissolution of their tag team and feud over the Negro belt.

Proud Negro world champion Jack Claybourne

When Seelie Samara made his way back to the Pacific Northwest, he was announced by *The Oregonian* as having returned directly from Australia rather than Hawaii. Still a popular figure in the territory where he had enjoyed one of his most significant runs, Samara remained successful, and won a one-night tournament during which he defeated Ted Christy, Henri Lasalle, and Bob Lortie in three consecutive matches.

Just a few days after that victory, Samara was back in the Midwest, and back to using his Ras forename. Once more,

A Decided Novelty

his range of travel extended all the way to the Upper Midwest, where *The Daily Herald* of Austin, Minnesota referred to him as "a dead ringer for Joe Louis," which is a statement that no one with a functioning pair of eyes would have ever had the audacity to make. Along the way, Samara even had a few matches in North Dakota.

That summer in Iowa, Samara again challenged Orville Brown for the world heavyweight championship of the National Wrestling Alliance. This time, the National Wrestling Alliance was a full-fledged national organization, representing territories that extended from the U.S. mainland all the way out to Hawaii.

While the significance of the NWA's most cherished championship had been dramatically upgraded, Samara fared no better against Brown than he had in any of his prior title matches against him, losing to him at the Electric Park Ballroom of Waterloo, Iowa in 42 minutes, 20 seconds.

The fall months brought a significant change in scenery, style, and stated origin for Seelie. Appearing for the first time in Niagara Falls, Ontario, Samara was described as "a full-blooded Negro from South Africa, where he gained wide experience and acclaim."

"Only a generation out of the savage jungles of that dark continent, Samara combines all the speed, agility, and grace of his native jungle with the science and know-how of modern grappling," continued *The Niagara Falls Evening Review*. "Those who have seen him in action claim that he's a picture of smooth and rapid motion, and that he's the top Negro grappler ever to show in this country."

When the scenery shifted to Toronto, wrestling fans of Canada's largest city were forewarned that Samara had altered his standard wrestling style, and had adopted a new signature maneuver.

"[Samara] has a new gimmick, the conk bonk," explained *The Toronto Star*. "He dazes his adversaries by bonking them sharply on the conk with his own conk, which is apparently armor-plated. Then he gives them the head twist,

A Decided Novelty

which is a variation on starting an outboard motor. He uses his arm as the string, and the result is the same. He leaves them spinning, sputtering and coughing."

It's impossible to know if Samara adopted excessive headbutting because he had received a firsthand demonstration from Jack Claybourne of the gimmick's success, or because Ontario promoters suggested to Samara that he should replicate Rufus Jones's provocative wrestling routine. Regardless of the reason, Samara quickly became yet another Black grappler whose principal weapon was his forehead.

In Hamilton, he displayed the use of his "coconut hold," as it was referred to in the pages of *The Hamilton Spectator*, on four different wrestlers. The butting began on Samara's opponent Hi Lee, but was also doled out to referee Bunny Dunlop in a scene that sounds identical to the way countless matches of Rufus Jones concluded.

"Samara and Lee were all even at one fall each when the coloured wrestler, peeved over what he terms 'poor work' by the referee, bumped heads with Dunlop and sent the official to the canvas as flat as a rug," printed *The Spectator*. "He then picked up Hi Lee, and when Dan O'Connor, Jimmy Sims and Tony Leone stepped in, he flattened them all."

Similar to how Jim Mitchell limited his headbutts to Connecticut and refrained from their use in Massachusetts, Samara's headbutting routine seemed to be exclusive to only one side of the Niagara River. When he wrestled in Buffalo, Samara's act consisted of clean wrestling, including his "chin spin," flying toehold, and slingshot tackle. He also treated Buffalonians to an interview in which he complained about the sort of cuisine he consumed in Australia and New Zealand.

"Next time I go back to New Zealand and Australia, I'm taking along a deep freeze loaded with pork chops and hams," Samara told *The Buffalo News*. "In New Zealand you can feast on steak and two eggs for 21 cents. I bought five one-inch T-bone steaks for 32 cents and had the best meals in the best places for 42 cents. But the drawback is that if you don't like lamb and mutton, and I don't, you'll lose your appetite for steak. New Zealand has 1,250,00 people and 42,000,000 sheep. Here in Buffalo the chefs are wonderful. They can serve you up anything you name."

Back in Canada, Samara's use of his "ramrod noggin" was credited with helping him steal the show from Lou Thesz in Toronto. Now described as an "iron-skulled coloured man" in the press, Samara appeared to understand that the use of his head in the manner made famous by Rufus Jones was a villainous tactic, and he was required to answer for his behavior prior to yet another bout with Hi Lee and his partner Fred Atkins.

"If I wanted to, I could go right into action bumping skulls with Lee and Atkins and get the bout over with in a hurry," Samara told *The Buffalo News*. "But — and I agree with Atkins to this extent — it isn't wrestling. But neither are the tricks Atkins and Lee spring. If they will stick to straight wrestling, I'll never crack their heads. It's just up to them."

Using clean tactics in Buffalo that December, Samara wrestled AWA world heavyweight champion Fred Sexton to a draw. Afterward, Sexton reportedly called Samara "the finest defensive wrestler I've met in the last two years," while *The Buffalo News* writer Cy Kritzer stated that Samara was "as elusive as a greased porker."

Just days later, Samara had his brand-new car stolen from in front of 160 Hickory Street in Buffalo by 25-year-old Charles Townes. *The Buffalo News* illustrated how Townes led police on a "wild chase" at 4:00 a.m. until he was finally brought into custody.

The next day, *The Buffalo Courier Express* printed Samara's full real name, George James Hardison, as he explained that he picked up several "friends and admirers" after getting his new car and drove them around town. After eating at a restaurant and visiting with a friend, Samara returned to discover that his car had vanished. Samara told the judge that he really didn't want to prosecute Townes "since I got the car back."

A Decided Novelty

Jim Mitchell spent the early stages of 1949 dishing out headbutts to Lord Jim Blears in an effort to establish himself as a worthy challenger for former world champion Wild Bill Longson and box office attraction Gorgeous George. Mitchell and Blears traded victories during their upper card feud, but against less impressive competition, the Panther was often dominant.

In February, the Panther downed Tony Morelli in nine minutes and Al Billings in three minutes, each with headbutts, before winning the final match of the one-night tournament by forcing Jesse James to submit in 26 minutes.

Mitchell was overpowering in stretches, but his claim to being the best Black wrestler in the area — let alone in the world — was called into serious question by the presence of Woody Strode. Certainly, the Panther was presented as being a wrestler of a caliber that was well above average, but Strode was nigh unbeatable.

A 6'4" professional football player and local hero who towered over almost every wrestler of the era with his chiseled physique, Strode compiled an impressive unbeaten streak that made him appear destined to win whatever championship he pursued if he devoted himself to full-time wrestling.

This was far from Strode's first foray into pro wrestling. The top-tier athlete had briefly wrestled in Los Angeles in 1940 during the period between his college football career and his first stint in professional football in 1941. Since then, Strode has also served in the U.S. Army Air Corps for three years before breaking the color line of the National Football League in 1946, and finally becoming a star with the Canadian Football League's Calgary Stampeders.

Strode's return to serious wrestling in 1949 consisted of a rapid five-minute victory over Al Billings, which *The Los Angeles Evening Citizen News* referred to as Strode's "mat debut," either not knowing or not caring about his brief flirtation with wrestling nine years prior.

As Woody began to mow down the mat competition in Southern California, his off-season activities were relayed back to football fans of Calgary in a positive light that categorized pro wrestling as more of a healthy off-season strength-and-conditioning program than a risky side gig.

"Woody Strode is keeping in shape for next season's football with a spot of wrestling down California way," reported sports editor Bob Mamami of *The Calgary Herald*. "The long striding Calgary Stampeder end appeared on a special event of a mat card at Olympia Auditorium and beat Rocca Toma before a crowd of 7,500. Calgary's football followers realized he knew most of the answers for gentlemanly conduct on the gridiron, but apparently he also knows how to bounce an opponent on his noggin should the occasion arise."

Meanwhile, Strode's image began appearing in many pro wrestling advertisements in the Los Angeles region, identifying him as a top attraction even though his presence usually served to enhance events headlined by wrestlers like Lord Blears, Danny McShain, and Bobby Managoff. A description of Strode's match-ending sequence supplied by *The Visalia Times-Delta* in April 1949 indicated that Strode hadn't altered his wrestling methods despite a one-decade hiatus from the ring.

"Woody Strode, giant Negro football star, put up with Mel Petterson's roughhouse tactics for 20 minutes before reverting to gridiron tactics and putting the blond lumberjack down and out with a series of flying tackles," reported the *Times-Delta*. "The second fall came quickly as Strode bounced Petterson's head on the mat and then flopped him for the three count."

As Strode racked up wins, some folks in Canada seemed to be getting nervous about what wrestling success might mean for Strode's future availability to play football, and how that might prove to be a hindrance to the success of the Stampeders.

"Some people are wondering if Woody Strode, big Negro end with the Dominion champion Calgary Stampeders Football Club, will be on hand for the April 17 roll call when

A Decided Novelty

Coach Les Lear names his candidates for this year's club," wrote Jack Sullivan. "Woody has been wrestling professionally – at a reported $500-a-week price – in California during the winter."

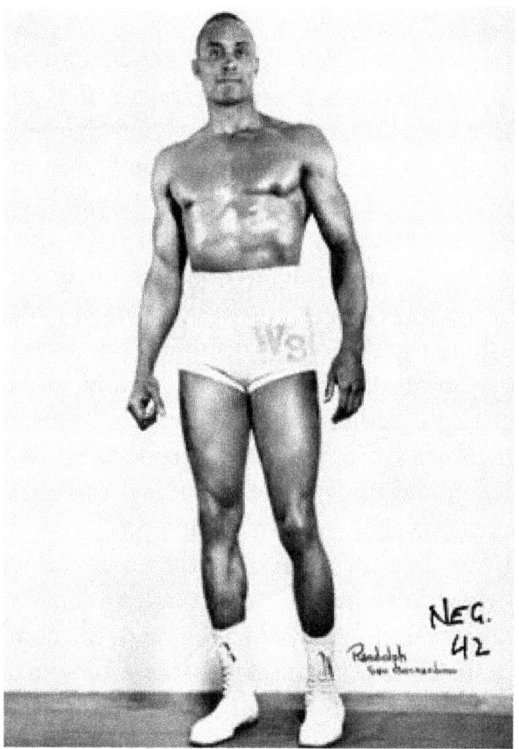

Football player and wrestler Woody Strode

Stampeders fans probably had little to be concerned about, at least at that moment. With top CFL stars earning salaries in the realm of $15,000 per season, Strode would have needed to earn more than $400 every week for each of the 36 remaining weeks of the year that he wasn't committed to the Stampeders simply to earn a sum that could compete with his seasonal football salary.

By the summer, even the non-wrestling fans in Los Angeles had been made keenly aware that Strode — stripped of his pads and uniform — had one of the most impressive muscular physiques in all of wrestling. A July edition of *The Los Angeles Daily News* published a daily workout that had supposedly been supplied by Strode.

"On the days when he isn't competing, Strode does 1,500 push-ups and 1,000 knee-bends," printed *The Daily News*. "Takes him a good seven hours before he's through."

This workout seems rather far-fetched for two reasons. First, in light of what Strode would explicitly declare his workouts to consist of later on, it is unlikely that he performed this many push-ups on a daily basis. Second, even if Strode *had* engaged in this many push-ups and knee-bends, it would certainly not have taken an athlete of his caliber and conditioning level seven hours to complete them all.

Strode's reliance on football-themed shoulder tackles to put the finishing touches on his opponents was frequently reported, but Strode also demonstrated that he was competent in situations that called for classic grappling. In his final Southern California match of 1949, Strode wrestled Sammy Menacker to a draw, in what the reporter described as "the real match of wrestling skill" on that night's card.

"Strode took the first go in 10:28 minutes with an arm lock while Menacker threw the Negro after a series of body slams that left the fans paralyzed along with the courageous colored boy. It was one of the cleanest wrestling matches ever witnessed."

Don Kindred was in California very briefly during the spring, wrestling at an event at the Pico Palace in Whittier just outside of Los Angeles, which was headlined by "The Black Panther" Jim Mitchell competing against the inimitable Gorgeous George. Just one week later, Kindred and Mitchell were wrestling one another on the undercard of shows in Fort Worth, Texas, with Kindred promoted as the "colored junior heavy champion," and labeled as "The Brown Bomber of Wrestling."

The booking of the matches between the two appears to have differed from one city to the next. For example, Kindred defended his negro junior heavyweight championship

A Decided Novelty

against Mitchell in Fort Worth on April 25, while Mitchell defended his negro heavyweight championship against Kindred in Galveston on April 28.

The Galveston Daily News reported how Mitchell defeated Kindred with his "Cranium Sock" headbutt. One month later, *The Long Beach Press-Telegram* reported that Kindred carried the clubs for Mitchell while the wrestlers dueled with sportswriters during a special golf tournament at Recreation Park in Long Beach. Retired wrestler Tiger Nelson was also present, serving as the caddy for wrestling promoter Harry Rubin.

Starting in June, Kindred joined Claybourne in the Hawaiian territory, which had developed an odd tradition of bringing new wrestlers in under masks and having them retain those masks until they lost a match. This had been done most successfully when Ben Sherman was brought in under a red hood as "The Scarlet Pimpernel" until he was defeated by Lee Grable.

In Kindred's case, he was asked to don a white mask and was given the identity of "The Bat." *The Honolulu Star-Bulletin* began to build the expectations for Kindred's clandestine arrival in late May.

"The Bat, who comes here with his identity concealed, makes his debut in the special event against Charley Shiranuhi," said *The Star-Bulletin*. "A masked grappler, The Bat is reported to be a sensational performer."

The Bat made a public appearance ahead of his first bout in Hawaii, and onlookers listened in as a "powerfully built colored grappler" wearing "a shoulder-length golden hood" sat to offer a detailed account of his background.

"[The Bat] gave interviewers a clue by disclosing that he played football here with an Army team during the war," stated *The Honolulu Advertiser*. "He was a first lieutenant and saw action in the South Pacific."

Clad as the Bat, Kindred made the laughable claim that he had kept his identity a secret for 10 years despite the fact that he hadn't yet occupied his Bat persona for 10 full days. Kindred also added that his favorite hold was the piledriver,

A Decided Novelty

along with dropkicks and flying tackles, and he put all of them on display during his first match, which was a sound thrashing of Charley Shiranuhi.

"Wearing a white hood, the newcomer proved to be unusually agile for a grappler of his weight and build," reported *The Advertiser*. "He moved quickly to position Shiranuhi for the piledriver."

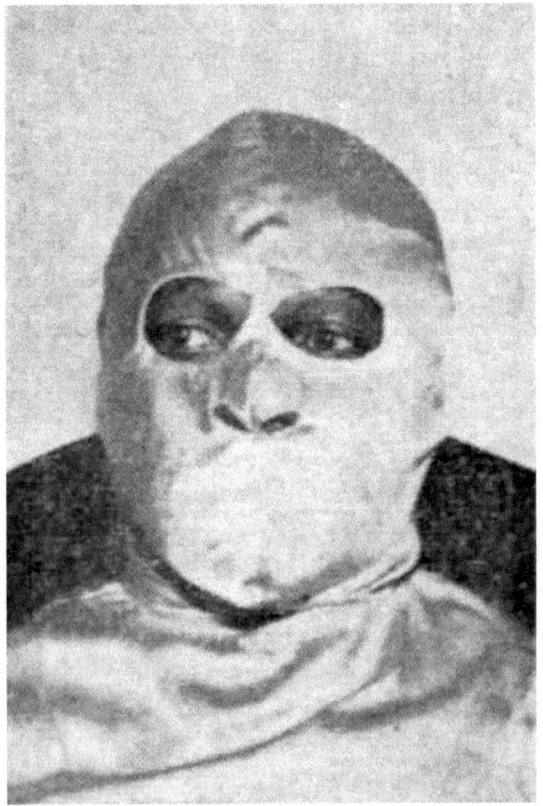

Don Kindred as "The Bat"

Kindred was able to retain his mask and his identity as the Bat by scoring either wins or draws in all of his matches in June, and up until the midway point of July. That's when he finally lost his first match in Hawaii to George Pencheff of Australia via a "reverse bodyslam."

A Decided Novelty

"The Bat congratulated Pencheff, then took off his white hood and announced that he was Don Kindred — Montreal-born grappler who served in the American army for a number of years during the last war," wrote *The Advertiser*.

In subsequent interviews, Kindred made the absurd claim that he opted to wrestle under a mask — presumably for all 10 of the years he claimed to have been wrestling, though he had only been wrestling for little over four years — because his family disapproved of him wrestling professionally.

Kindred also added that he would prefer to be known as pro wrestling's "Brown Bomber" now that his face was no longer concealed beneath a mask. If that was a reflection of Kindred's actual preference, things didn't work out that way. More often than not, he was referred to as Don "Bat" Kindred in nearly all subsequent wrestling advertisements while he remained in Hawaii.

Following a bout in Hawaii during which Jack Claybourne bludgeoned Kay Bell with his head until the referee stopped the bout due to blood loss, Karasick ordered a bout between Bell and his partner Peter Managoff, while Claybourne teamed up with Kindred for the second pairing of Black wrestlers in the history of Hawaii.

The occasion also marked the first time Claybourne teamed with one of the true up-and-coming stars from the succeeding generation of Black ring performers that his generation had inspired, but it would be far from the last.

Despite the novelty of having another all-Black tag team in Hawaii, the Claybourne-Kindred pairing would be even less successful than the Claybourne-Samara tandem. While Claybourne and Samara had at least wrestled their opponents to a draw despite Claybourne absorbing a pinfall loss during the bout, Claybourne and Kindred would lose their match outright, with both members of their team suffering losses.

"Kindred was the first to [lose], yielding to a Boston crab hold applied by the powerful Bell. The fall came in 1 min. 46 sec.," stated *The Advertiser*. "Head butts by Claybourne subdued Bell for the equalizing fall 11 min. 40 sec. later. The

A Decided Novelty

final fall came after an unusually wild session. Body slams and a press by Managoff flattened Claybourne."

In August, Jim Mitchell earned a high-profile match against Gorgeous George by dominating Pat Fraley throughout a Pico Palace bout that was refereed by none other than Joe Louis, the wrestler that Mitchell and his peers were so frequently compared to.

"The Negro champion used his famous hammerhead smash to finish off the groggy Fraley," reported *The Whittier News*. "Four terrific head butts and a body press ended the match. Louis, looking in the best shape he has looked in recent months, turned in a capable job of refereeing and kept both boys in hand."

The resulting match between Gorgeous George and Jim Mitchell would become the most important match of Mitchell's career — for all the wrong reasons. The contest between the two was one of the featured attractions on an August show at the Olympic Auditorium, which featured Lou Thesz, who was now the NWA's world heavyweight champion, and who was stressing that he was the only true heavyweight champion to be found anywhere on the planet.

The match between George and the Panther seemed to be proceeding as usual when George hurled the Panther into the ringside seating area. This apparently served to rile up the fans in the arena, and when George climbed back into the ring and was subsequently awarded the victory, bedlam ensued.

Several fans stormed into the ring, weapons were drawn, and the skirmish quickly spread from the ring and out into the aisles of the venue. The scene instantly became chaotic, and a calamity was narrowly prevented from turning deadly by the timely intervention of a squad of 15 police officers.

"C.M. Bullard, 38, of Azusa, was stabbed in the right shoulder as he struggled to get free of the rioting fans," reported *The Los Angeles Mirror*. "His companion, Lee Howard, 38, of Azusa, received abrasions in the melee. Both men were treated at Georgia St. Receiving Hospital and sent home.

A Decided Novelty

Norma Romero, 31, of 962 Mayo St. was hit in the eye by a 'blackjack' when the fans swarmed around the ring and yelled for Gorgeous George's golden scalp."

In the aftermath of the unfortunate free-for-all, two things happened almost immediately. First, the Black Panther's name was shared in newspapers around the country as word of the riot spread to all corners of the nation. Second, the Panther was quickly whisked far away to the East Coast as lawsuits were hastily filed against Gorgeous George by the fans who had been injured during the melee.

For the first time ever, Mitchell started making appearances in New York, New Jersey, and Pennsylvania, as the nationwide publicity generated by the fallout from a match he lost made him a bankable name in those selective East Coast markets for the first time ever.

The Atlantic City Press went so far as to identify the Panther as a former Olympic champion, although he declined to identify exactly which Olympic sport Mitchell had supposedly earned a gold medal in.

If *The Press* was implying that Mitchell had been an Olympic gold medalist in wrestling, they were only off by four decades. Kenny Monday would become the first Black American to win an Olympic gold medal in wrestling when he won the freestyle championship at 74 kg (163 lbs.) at the Seoul Olympics in 1988.

With Mitchell now absent from California, Kindred made his way to Los Angeles where he was declared to be the "young colored protege of Jim Mitchell" even though he had been clashing with Mitchell for the Black supremacy of Texas just six months earlier.

While Kindred was being introduced as Mitchell's protege back in Los Angeles, the Panther was performing his act in front of brand-new audiences, and against a fresh crop of opponents. This included "One-ton" Elmer Estep, a mammoth-sized 400-pound wrestler. After realizing that he couldn't physically control Elmer to move him around the ring, the Panther relied on a trick that supplied a tried-and-true solution to his enormous problem.

"In the twinkling of an eye, [Mitchell] matched heads with the bearded gent, forehead to 'fo head,'" illustrated *The Journal News*. "Jim won the nod after two butts, the Arkansas good-will ambassador sat heavily on the canvas, taxing the Arena ring to the limit. In a flash, the Panther was on him, and with a body press, the thing was all over. Elmer shook his head for many minutes after the bout."

By the end of October, Mitchell was performing in the heart of New York City, where readers of *The New York Age* were introduced to the Panther as a grappler "who was born in Louisville, Ky., and reared in Massachusetts, started out to be a baseball player, then he switched to football, tennis, basketball, boxing, and finally wrestling." The paper then informed fans that Mitchell could be alternatively known as either "The Black Panther" or "The Cranium Cracker," before humorously appending the brief biography with the sentence, "His holds are real."

Yes, Mitchell made liberal use of his head during his East Coast swing, but he also brought along his other novel maneuvers, some of which had not yet acquired names that were well-circulated in the New York area. This included the Panther's cobra twist, or hip-headlock, which the writer from *The Rockland County Journal-News* struggled to describe as a "neck stretcher" and "a reverse chin lock with his shoulder as the bar."

The Four Kings of Black wrestling were now delivering headbutts to opponents all across a map that was beginning to open up and yield greater opportunities to even more Black wrestlers. As such, it wouldn't be long before the younger generation followed suit, and in Benton Harbor, Michigan, the standout of that inbound crop of talent was about to make his debut.

A Decided Novelty

24 – Unexpected Ability

After headbutting his way to several more months of title victories in Hawaii, Jack Claybourne was finally defeated by Bobby Managoff, halting Claybourne's impressive reign with the *Ring Magazine* belt at 343 days. At nearly a full year, it was far and away the longest single title reign by an identifiably Black pro wrestler in a U.S. or Canadian territory at the time of its ending.

Just prior to the reign's cessation, a photo of Claybourne with his beaming wife Lillian fastening the *Ring Magazine* belt around his waist circulated in several Black news publications, along with an in-depth article about Jack's career written by Frank Marshall Davis of the Associated Negro Press. In the article, Claybourne offered a number of tales from his life in the ring, a surprising number of which were probably true.

The wording of the article essentially revealed that Claybourne's departure from Hawaii was preplanned, as it was disclosed that he would next be appearing in matches in California even though he was still the Hawaiian champion at the time of the interview.

Claybourne said he got his start in the ring at age 16 when he weighed 175 pounds, though all evidence points to him starting at age 21. It's conceivable that Claybourne was attempting to hide his age from the interviewer, who referred to Jack as being "in his 30s" even though he was 39 years old and right at the cusp of turning 40.

The writer credits Claybourne with appearing in 2,000 matches, which is certainly possible, and then states that he "appeared before troops for three years as a wrestler with the USO" even though there's no gap in Jack's wartime activity record that would have afforded him the opportunity to do such a thing.

Claybourne included the true tale of how he wrestled under the name Pablo Hernandez in Cincinnati, but added that he had supposedly been presented with the name while wrestling in Cuba. Allegedly, Claybourne assumed this gimmick to avoid detection as an American Black wrestler, because Cincinnati supposedly had laws in place that prohibited mixed-race matches involving Blacks.

Jack Claybourne with his wife Lillian

By that logic, a Cuban as darkly colored as Claybourne would be permitted to compete against a White wrestler, while a Black American of a slightly lighter shade would have been prohibited from doing so. Regardless, Claybourne went on to say that he was presumed to speak only Spanish, and that a verbal slip-up on his part ultimately forced a change in the law.

"Then one day while training, [Claybourne] spoke several sentences in English," wrote Davis. "When the rest of the gymnasium recovered from the shock, they learned he was from Boston instead of Havana, and the whole story came out. Up to then, mixed bouts had not been allowed in the Ohio city, but officials took a realistic view. After all, Jack had already wrestled a number of opponents. So they let him continue and the ban on mixed matches was lifted."

Fluctuations in the law aside, Black Cincinnatian Chick Harris competed in several mixed-race wrestling matches in his hometown during the earliest years of the 1930s, so unless rules became more restrictive between 1932 and 1938 due to the passing of an anti-George-Godfrey law, no such ban was officially enacted. Moreover, Claybourne had not even wrestled in Massachusetts prior to the end of 1939, let alone did he live in Boston at the time.

Finally, Claybourne closed the piece with a story involving a member of his extended family that presumably took place during the earliest days of his career when he was wrestling in rural Missouri.

"[Claybourne] tangled with an opponent who was plenty tough," continued Davis. "Among the spectators was his sister-in-law, then in high school, who was there with a whole group of teenagers. When it seemed that Jack was getting the worst of it, she couldn't stand it any longer. She leaped up and dashed for the ring, followed by her crowd. Crawling through the ropes, they ganged up on Jack's opponent and got him down on the canvas before the astounded officials could stop them. They had to call the cops to restore order."

Since Claybourne emerged on the scene early in 1932 and appeared to have already been rather adept at wrestling, it is impossible to account for every circumstance he found himself in prior to when he first captured media attention. There is no way to know if Claybourne was describing an event

A Decided Novelty

that happened before he achieved notoriety, if he was embellishing elements of a true story for the sake of entertainment, or if he was making up the incident out of whole cloth.

Upon returning to California, Claybourne was treated like any other wrestler, as if his Hawaiian title reign had never happened. In Wilmington, Claybourne teamed with a Black wrestler known only as the Brown Bomber — likely Don Kindred — in a tag team loss in late October. A few weeks later, he was wrestling against "The Bat" in Visalia, which was also likely to have been Kindred wrestling under the same mask he had worn in Honolulu.

On November 12, *The Wilmington Press Journal* stated that Claybourne possessed "the *Police Gazette*'s world championship belt." *The Police Gazette* was famed for awarding title belts to bare knuckle boxers starting in the 1880s, and had awarded some world championship designations to wrestlers in the late 19th and early 20th centuries. However, the idea that such a distinction fell upon Claybourne in the late 1940s certainly strained credulity, and *The Police Gazette* had not been in the habit of handing out title belts to "colored champions."

The Press Journal quickly amended the statement, referring to Claybourne once again as "holder of the *Ring Magazine*'s championship and belt as the colored champion of the world." With the photo of Claybourne displaying the Hawaiian title belt around his waist now being used for promotional purposes — with his wife conveniently cropped out of the photo — it probably seemed like too good of an image not to capitalize upon.

In the middle of December, Claybourne faced Antonino Rocca for the first time, and was defeated twice by Rocca's "famous Greek simplex hold" according to *The Independent* of Long Beach. This marked yet another occasion where Claybourne was made to appear totally ineffectual against an established White star. The fact that Rocca was said to wrestle in a manner similar to that of a young Jack Claybourne would soon be highlighted by the press.

A Decided Novelty

Within two months of his return to the mainland, Claybourne was back to working in opening matches and semifinal bouts, and occasionally losing in handicap matches despite being on the side with the greater number of wrestlers. Further, there seemed to be an outright refusal to acknowledge his reign as the champion in Hawaii — let alone the impressive length of the title reign — in any of the promotional materials related to his appearances.

This possibly stemmed from promoters not wanting to explain how a Black wrestler who had been such a dominant champion in Hawaii could achieve comparatively little elsewhere.

Much further east, when Rufus Jones returned to wrestling for promoter Jack Carter in Vermont in February 1949, he once again dusted off his persona of Tiger Flowers. *The Sunday News* of Vermont dutifully warned fans that Flowers "has lost none of his zest for the illegal means of gaining the upper hand, and is one of wrestling's public enemies."

Accompanying Flowers on this trip was Don Blackman, whom the newspapers positioned as being a wrestler under the tutelage of Flowers. This being the case, *The Daily News* offered ample warning to the fans about the tactics Blackman might use, adding "not too much is known about Blackman, except that he is highly recommended by Flowers," and was presumably a disreputable character by association.

The Burlington Free Press added that Blackman was "the prized pupil of Flowers, educated in the ring culture that Flowers likes," and also inserted the false detail that Flowers "has been touring the world" and had just returned from Australia "where he won 28 consecutive bouts."

During this return to Vermont, Joe Godfrey eliminated any pretense that the persona of Tiger Flowers was anything other than Rufus Jones wrestling under an alternative alias. *The Burlington Free Press* illustrated how Flowers, during his February 23 bout at the Burlington Auditorium, "stunned both Referee Jacques Trudeau and his opponent by cracking them on the head with his own," thereby earning a disqualification.

A Decided Novelty

After carrying out repeated bludgeonings of his opponents in like manner, the typed descriptions of Flowers' ring tactics continued to read as duplicates of the descriptions for Rufus Jones' matches, except with the name Tiger Flowers offered as a substitute.

"A real cutie in the ring, Flowers gets away with most of his rough stuff, fooling even the referee," submitted *The St. Albans Daily Messenger*. "Flowers' most dangerous weapon is his head butt, which weakens and dazes his opponents so that they are easy to pin. Holding him by the shoulders, he repeatedly cracks his forehead against his opponent, apparently suffering no ill effects himself."

The remainder of 1949 had also been full of interesting developments for Joe Godfrey. After leaving Vermont, Godfrey resurrected his Rufus Jones name and made appearances in areas of Ontario that he had never appeared in before, like Sault Ste. Marie and North Bay.

One of Jones' earliest bouts in Sault Ste. Marie, which was officiated by wrestler-referee-promoter Larry Kasaboski, was apparently used to educate fans in the area that headbutting was now a legal tactic that all wrestlers — and especially Rufus Jones — should be free to use liberally.

As a means of both proving the point and attaining a measure of revenge, Jones' first bout after the clarification of the rules would be against Kasaboski himself in a show advertised as an event featuring "the black boy and the black bear," as Gorgeous Gus the black bear was also booked to make an appearance.

"Jones was dissatisfied with the decision rendered by 'Kas' when he started the headbutting in last week's show," reported *The Sault Star*. "He maintained the headbutt is just as legal as a flying tackle, and forthwith challenged Kasaboski in order to show him a few tricks in the ring. Perusal of the latest guide to wrestling revealed that the headbutt is now legal, so the fast and coming Jones will go all out to show Kasaboski how to use his head without getting bumped."

A Decided Novelty

 The "education" Jones offered to Kasaboski unfolded exactly as expected. *The Star* reported that Jones used his head "in an unorthodox manner" to win the match, and that by "using it in the form of a sledgehammer" he had "literally pounded out a victory."
 Although he accompanied Tiger Flowers during portions of his Northeast tour, clues were already evident that Don Blackman was attempting to ease out of pro wrestling in 1949
 When he participated in a wrestling exhibition sponsored by a Jewish community center's youth group at a high school in Bridgewater, New Jersey, Blackman was already insisting on being referred to as a *"former* national wrestling figure." Still, Blackman was immediately considered a big deal when he made his debut in Atlantic City, New Jersey.
 "Don Blackman, world's colored wrestling champion and physical culture tutor at New Hope, Pa., will make his local debut Tuesday night... At present, Blackman, who formerly campaigned as a light heavyweight in the grappling industry, is recognized as one of the best physical specimens in the world," printed *The Atlantic City Press*. "However, it doesn't stop there. Don is an excellent wrestler and has breezed through his last 17 bouts without any setbacks whatsoever."
 The next time *The Atlantic City Press* wrote about Blackman, the exaggerations were even more absurd.
 "Blackman, a brilliant performer, is undefeated in professional wrestling, having won 32 consecutive bouts," wrote *The Press*.
 Blackman was again billed as "world's Negro champion" on the undercard of an Atlantic City show headlined by Gorgeous George. Even as the staff of *The Atlantic City Press* alluded to the box office and attendance records that George was in the process of setting, the paper also ran a syndicated Associated Press article about how the modern pro wrestling of the late 1940s — typified by Gorgeous George — was a pale impersonation of the pro

wrestling style that predominated during the vaudeville era 30 years prior, in the era of Illa Vincent.

The story then went into detail about the atmosphere of some of the first major wrestling shows to tour the Northeast, headlined by wrestling luminaries like Ed "Strangler" Lewis and "le Colosse" Paul Pons.

"On the bill with the grapplers, who operated under both the staid Greco-Roman and bruising catch-as-catch-can rules, were a troupe of vaudeville performers," elucidated the AP story. "Along with the wrestlers went an orchestra, jugglers, acrobats, and singers. The show was backed early in the first world war by Andres Dippel, manager of the Metropolitan Opera House in New York. It was promoted by Sam Rachman, a German marooned in New York by the war. The wrestling, billed as an international competition, was run along European lines with the vaudeville acts in the background. But before the week was out, the wrestling got so funny they didn't need the vaudeville anymore."

Two of the men that Blackman had gotten started in the business were quite active during the year. Frank James had begun making appearances at East Coast wrestling venues yet again. *The Rockland County Journal-News* said of James that he "sticks to the scientific part of the game," which was ironic considering what was to soon come.

James made his debuts in New York City and Buffalo before heading westward to Evansville, Indiana. There he was matched against Buddy Jackson yet again, and referred to as "the colored Red Devil" of Trenton, New Jersey. *The Evansville Courier* also stated that James bore a resemblance to Joe Louis, although a side-by-side comparison between the two makes it evident that any similarity was attributable to their skin shades and nothing else.

Jackson won the bout two falls to zero, using flying mares and a body block to take the first fall, and a crab hold to win the final fall. Provided with an opportunity to win a fall, James made his first clear use of Rufus Jones' Boston crab

A Decided Novelty

hold, which would become the move most commonly associated with him, right next to Jones' headbutt.

James and Jackson took their act straight from Evansville to Texas where they appeared as the designated "Negro heavyweights," competing against each other in special attraction bouts that Jackson usually won.

After finishing his Texas business, James went to New York and made his Harlem wrestling debut. He was advertised as "one of the top Negro stars" despite having very few victories to his name at that time. *The New York Age* called James "the crack Negro prospect," and revealed that his legitimate stomping grounds back in Baltimore was on Ashland Ave.

In the spring, James ventured further east to the heart of New England. Offered up as a native of New Orleans, Louisiana, James racked up the occasional opening-match victory with his Boston crab hold.

By the time summer rolled around, James was wrestling as an unequivocal heel. The description of his treatment from the crowd during a match against Chris Belkas in Newport, Rhode Island serves as testimony to this fact.

"James, the villain of the piece, received jeers from the crowd, not to mention the barrage of peanuts and rolled pieces of paper for his rough work," described *The Newport News*. "James won the first fall in 22 minutes with a headbutt, and press. Belkas took the second in 10 minutes with a dropkick. The time limit of 45 minutes ran out before either wrestler was able to gain a second fall."

While James might have been "rough and dirty," as described in *The Berkshire Evening Eagle*, there are also accounts that suggest he understood his foremost role was to entertain in the mold of the man who clearly inspired his act, Rufus Jones.

After another bout between James and Belkas, *The Hartford Courant* said about that match, "The affair was pleasing as well as entertaining, especially James, whose exhibitions gave the fans many a chuckle."

A Decided Novelty

Moving to Colorado in November, James was hailed as the "king of colored wrestlers" by *The Greeley Daily Tribune* before having his first match in the Rocky Mountain State. When James actually had his first match, which was against Mr. Boston, it was clear that he intended to make liberal use of the headbutting style that Rufus Jones had popularized.

Ernest "Buddy" Jackson

After parting company with his fellow all-Negro-tour alumnus, Buddy Jackson arrived in Tacoma, Washington at the behest of promoter Nick Zvolis. It was here that he was first publicly mentioned in the same breath as a man who would one day have a massive influence on his career.

"Jackson comes west with the reputation of being one of the fastest men in the junior heavyweight division," printed *The Tacoma News Tribune*. "He claims to be on the trail of Jack Claybourne for a shot at the colored heavyweight title."

Jackson didn't arrive in time for his first scheduled appearance in Washington, but when he did reach the Pacific Northwest, he began wrestling in Vancouver, where Lyall Dagg of *The Vancouver Sun* referred to Jackson as "a displaced African."

When Jackson finally wrestled in Tacoma the following month, the story of his pursuit of Jack Claybourne's championship had been discarded in favor of portraying him as Gentleman Jack's protege, personally trained by the nearly 20-year mat veteran. Regardless of whatever affiliation between the two was being declared, Claybourne was nowhere to be found.

Given the extent and general duration of Alex Kaffner's Midwestern tenure — and in Wisconsin in particular — it is difficult to believe that he disappeared from the region's wrestling scene with so little fanfare in 1948. The Black Panther reemerged in Tacoma, Washington in 1949, and it was only then that Tacoma promoter Nick Zvolis officially took credit for starting Kaffner in the mat game many years prior, confirming once and for all that The Black Panther of Washington, Alexis Kaffir, and Alex Kaffner were all one and the same.

After wrestling for Zvolis for the final two months of 1949, Kaffner appeared to have officially retired from full-time wrestling. Except for a very brief return at the tail end of 1955 — once again in Tacoma — The Black Panther of Washington had officially given up the hunt.

Taking Kaffner's place in Wisconsin had been perhaps the unlikeliest of wrestlers. At the age of 33, Johnny Cobb of Dallas, Texas was drafted into the U.S. Army, signing his name

A Decided Novelty

as "Johnnie Cobb," while his draft card listed him at 6'3" and 220 pounds.

During the war, Cobb — while he was stationed in Benning, Georgia and serving as a mess hall cook — gave an account of his civilian life to a reporter from *The Black Dispatch*. Private first class Johnny Cobb identified himself as professional wrestler "Cyclone Cobb" of Dallas, Texas, and *The Dispatch* offered the following account of how Cobb's life first became interwoven with the world of pro wrestling:

"Back in 1931 while living in Dallas, Cobb took up wrestling and has been at it ever since. When the Cole Brothers' Circus came to town, he was out in the audience. He made his way to the front of the crowd when the fearsome looking 'Big Whitie,' the house wrestler, was introduced. All comers were invited to try and throw this mountain of a man. Young Cobb took him on, throwing him not once but twice in a short while. When the circus moved on to the next town, Cobb stepped into the limelight instead of Big Whitie."

At the war's conclusion, Cobb's service records indicate that he almost immediately re-enlisted in the military on September 25, 1945, and remained in the employ of the U.S. government until September 23, 1948.

His commitment to the U.S. military notwithstanding, Cobb had apparently racked up sufficient leave time to briefly return to professional wrestling during summer 1947. This time, he invaded the wrestling rings of Texas in a heel capacity, competing as Johnnie Cobb "The Colored Detroit Demon" against local Black wrestler "Corn Bread" Brown.

Although Cobb was a Dallas native by all accounts, he was billed as the out-of-state heel and was defeated by the undersized Brown in 14 minutes.

These bouts may have taken place in the Dallas area, but the attention they generated was sufficient to warrant press coverage as far away as Pittsburgh, with *The Pittsburgh Courier* noting that Cobb's bout with Brown had been the first Negro wrestling match to take place in Dallas in six years.

After fulfilling his military commitments and receiving a discharge, Cobb set out for the Midwest in spring 1949, where he was immediately greeted as "one of the greatest colored wrestlers out of the South."

"Cyclone" Johnny Cobb

Although he had been relegated to wrestling almost exclusively against Black wrestlers in his home state of Texas, Cobb squared off against a steady stream of non-Black combatants throughout the Midwest, like Reno Lencioni, Stan Karolyi and Spike Peterson. One of his few Black opponents

A Decided Novelty

was fellow Texas wrestler Tex Brady, with Cobb emerging victorious during their first engagements with one another.

When fall 1949 rolled around, Cobb was already being advertised in the area as the "world's colored wrestling champion," and by the time he faced Wisconsin Heavyweight Champion Mike Blazer in Green Bay, Cobb was credited by the press with having secured 62 victories in a row during his tour of the Midwest.

As the fall progressed, Cobb — whose billed height and weight of 6'4" and 240 pounds were only slight exaggerations in a world where the height of the 6'2" Reginald Siki was boosted to 6'6" — was booked in main-event encounters with the world-famous Maurice Tillet, who by that point had twice held the AWA (Boston) version of the world heavyweight championship.

For his bouts with Tillet, the career-plaguing tendency to treat Black wrestlers as "brand-as-required" commodities once again reared itself, as Cobb was touted as a "giant Arizona Negro" to account for the fact that he towered over the 5'9" Tillet.

The Tex Brady that Cobb wrestled against throughout the Great Lakes region was also a Texas transplant. In the future, he would also wrestle under the name Tex Grady, but his real name was Grady Singletary.

Before becoming a professional wrestler, the 18-year-old Singletary — uncle of future National Football League All-Pro Mike Singletary — worked at the Officer's Club in Dallas, Texas. That was his place of employment when he was drafted into the U.S. Army during the late stages of World War II in December 1944. His draft registration card lists him at 6'2" and 196 pounds.

After concluding his tenure as a U.S. Army private, Singletary commenced his wrestling career in the Upper Midwest during the summer months of 1949, and he was immediately billed as a former wrestling champion from the U.S. Army.

A Decided Novelty

Grady lived with his brother Derwood Singletary in Rockford, Illinois at the time. Accordingly, Singletary was living in Rockford, Illinois when he was captured by the 1950 U.S. Census; he listed his official occupation as "wrestler."

Described in newspapers as weighing anywhere from 215 pounds to 240 pounds, Singletary's first serious ring experience was acquired in those losing efforts against the veteran Cobb as they both toured through Illinois, Wisconsin, and the Upper Peninsula of Michigan.

Even with all of this exciting activity transpiring in the region, there was still a debut of much greater historical relevance that occurred in Michigan during spring 1949. That's when *The Herald Press* of St. Joseph reported that "Huston Harris, 220 pound matman from Benton Harbor" had made his way into the nearby Benton Harbor Naval Armory to accept the challenge of Armond Meyer, a St. Joseph resident, and a student at Benton Harbor Junior College.

The use of the name "Huston" was not a typo; it identified actual Benton Harbor resident Houston Harris. Someone seemed to believe that the omission of an 'O' would be sufficient to obscure the identity of possibly the largest young Black resident of a small city that still had an overwhelmingly White population in the late 1940s.

The bout was advertised as being for the Twin Cities championship, with St. Joseph and Benton Harbor representing the two cities in that equation. Although the contest ended in a draw, *The News-Palladium* of Benton Harbor observed that Harris had displayed "unexpected ability" throughout the contest, and managed to cause substantially more trouble for Meyer than the St. Joseph resident had ever imagined.

Still, in the late spring and early summer months, "the Benton Harbor colored giant" presented little opposition to wrestlers like Rex Sheeley, Eddie Slake, and the Red Devil, who handled him with ease during preliminary contests at the Naval Armory.

A Decided Novelty

Cast in the role of promising newcomer who couldn't quite get the job done, Harris issued a public promise that he would "retire from the mat game forever" if Sheeley was able to defeat him yet again during their June bout. *The Herald-Press* cheerfully reported that Harris would "be around in wrestling circles for a while longer" after he managed to pin Sheeley 23 minutes into his win-or-retire match.

Harris followed that effort by wrestling Sheeley to a 45-minute draw in their August rematch, indicating that he would not be slipping straight back to the bottom of the standings. That same month also saw Huston adopting the familiar sobriquet of "the Black Panther," which had by now adorned at least four different Black wrestlers who had appeared within that very same city.

Later that month, Harris was scheduled for a match with Polish star Al Warshawski, and promoter Joe Savoldi informed the press that if Harris successfully emerged from this best-of-three-falls contest — depicted as his "first big-time mat test" — he would be set on a collision course with the region's other top-notchers.

The Herald-Press reported that the final outcome of the match at Savoldi's Silver Arena was an anticlimactic disqualification victory for Harris, which technically still satisfied the preconditions for him to be tested by stiffer opponents. *The News Palladium* took note of this, and stated that Harris had taken "another step up the ladder" by facing "Strangler" Ed White the following week.

The card was shuffled at the last moment, and Harris and White faced different opponents than advertised. Still, *The Herald-Press* declared that Harris had "climbed another notch up the ladder of matdom" when he held veteran Pierre Le Clair to a draw.

"Houston had Le Clair on 'queer street' in the closing minutes of the match, and had the set-to gone another five minutes, would undoubtedly have pinned the Frenchman," concluded *The Herald-Press*.

A Decided Novelty

Harris maintained his position as a regular contributor to Savoldi's cards, and as 1949 drew to a close, *The Herald-Press* listed Harris in its annual wrap-up segments, naming him first among "local matmen who advanced rapidly during the year," and described Harris as a giant man who stood 6'4" and weighed 225 pounds.

With all of the changes that were afoot in the pro wrestling world as a new decade dawned, the most unlikely appearance in a wrestling ring by a Black wrestling legend in 1950 almost certainly belonged to Lee Umbles. After being absent from pro wrestling for nearly seven years, Umbles materialized in Manchester, England, as a physical education instructor for the Chicago Board of Education seeking ideas about British physical training styles to implement back in Chicago.

The 52-year-old Umbles told *The Manchester Evening News* how he found it intriguing that rope skipping was being taught to English children at a young age, as he had only ever taught rope skipping to adults.

Just five days earlier, *The Manchester Evening News* ran an advertisement for a professional wrestling event headlined by Leo Demetral and Rex Gable. Listed at the bottom of the card and set to compete in a bout against Tony Van Hal was Lee Umbles. One wonders if the staff of *The Evening News* even noticed that the American representative they interviewed just days later shared a name with a pro wrestler advertised in their paper less than a week earlier.

Umbles was not the only Black pro wrestler active in England during his brief time on the British Isles. In fact, since the early 1930s, there had been a regular performer named "The Black Arrow" Phil Siki who had been wrestling there regularly.

In England, the promoters generally eschewed the use of colored or Negro championship titles in favor of referring to Phil Siki as the West Indies champion. As such, Siki was usually advertised as a native of either Trinidad or Jamaica, although promoters also weren't above occasionally listing

A Decided Novelty

Siki's home country as Algeria if they found it to be advantageous, and in keeping with current events.

However, in 1939, Phil Siki engaged in a brief feud over the "world's coloured championship" with a Black wrestler named Robert Adams, who at different times was said to hail from either South America or South Africa. Adams' ring name was — of all things — the Black Panther.

As 1950 progressed, Johnny Cobb continued to be marketed as either the "U.S. colored champ" or the possessor of the "world Negro title," and shared the spotlight with such notables as Jim Londos, and young Reginald Lisowski.

That summer, Cobb returned to Texas and wrestled Tex Grady again, this time in the home state of both men, with Cobb billed as a northern invader from Philadelphia. The 1950 U.S. census captures Cobb here, living with his wife Lenora, along with his daughter and son-in-law. His profession is clearly listed as "wrestler" on the census form. A few months later, Cobb re-enlisted in the U.S. military and remained in their employment until April 30, 1951.

Jim Mitchell began 1950 still wrestling in Pennsylvania, New York, and New Jersey. He even teamed with Don Blackman for a few tag team matches in the area, which was the general area where Blackman had himself been operating under the Black Panther name.

Having a new territory provided several opportunities to craft new narratives about Mitchell's backstory. *The Courier-News* described him as "a former all-star athlete at Toledo University," while *The Daily Argus* of Mount Vernon anointed him "the boy with the college degree."

The Patriot News of Harrisburg provided one of the most colorful accounts, describing Mitchell as a Kentuckian who had moved in with his "Uncle Tom" in Massachusetts during his youth and ultimately took up boxing with plans to make it his profession.

"He won his first two bouts, but boxing did not meet with his uncle's approval," continued *The Patriot News*. "Uncle Tom threatened to throw Nephew Jim right out of the house if

A Decided Novelty

Mitchell didn't stop fighting. Naturally, Jim quit the glove game right then and there and got himself a job. A short time later, however, his uncle died and Young Jim was left on his own. He left Massachusetts and went to Chicago where he became a trainer for six-day bicycle racers. This job took him to all parts of the country. But the pay was poor, so Jim decided to again try his hand at boxing.

"It was while training for a fight that Mitchell met several wrestlers who were conditioning in the same gym. The grapplers convinced Jim that with his marvelous physique he was a 'natural' for the wrestling business. And, when they predicted a bright future for him in the mat game, Mitchell decided to become a gripsmith. After several weeks of training he accepted an offer from Paul Bowser, Boston promoter, to launch his grappling career in Beantown. He won his first match and has been a constant winner ever since."

While the story contained enough detailed elements to sound plausible to some, Mitchell doesn't appear to have been anywhere near Boston during his teens or early 20s, and certainly didn't receive his big break from Paul Bowser.

Even so, *The Patriot News* was far from the only newspaper telling bold fibs while embellishing the Panther's background. *The Lake Shore Visitor* described the 42-year-old Mitchell as "a well-built Negro of 39," who "studies medicine at Ohio State when he is not in the ring."

Funnily enough, *The Bergen Record* provided what may have been one of the most unintentionally truthful statements about the plight of Mitchell and several of his peers in its attempt to explain to fans why the Panther had been essentially unknown in several vital East Coast markets until the prior fall.

"When [Mitchell] first started to wrestle he thought that ability was all that was required for success. Later, however, he found out that skill was of little aid to a gripster unless it was bolstered by one or more tricks that weren't in the book of rules," stated *The Record*. "Accordingly, he proceeded to forge his own weapon, the cranium cracker, with which he bumps or butts opponents into dreamland. Generally, Mitchell doesn't resort to the use of his main weapon, unless an opponent, by his lawless conduct, gives him a right to use it."

Although Mitchell can't be credited with inventing the headbutt, nor revolutionizing its use as Rufus Jones did, Claybourne, Mitchell, and to a lesser extent Seelie Samara certainly enabled its proliferation, along with the stereotype that Black wrestlers wielded this move to capitalize on the racial belief that their skulls were genetically thicker than those of other races.

While the role and significance of each wrestler in helping to spread the stereotype is debatable, the fact that all four of the Murderers' Row wrestlers achieved new levels of success after making the headbutt their principal weapon is not.

After a brief visit to Missouri in early 1950, which ended in a loss to Mike Sharpe, Seelie Samara returned to wrestling rings around the border between New York and Ontario, where he defeated Wally Dusek with "a noggin smash and a well executed swan dive from outside the ropes."

Still playing the role of a "thickheaded Negro" in the words of *The Niagara Falls Review*, Samara then engaged in a lengthy feud with Yukon Eric, and he always seemed to get the worst end of the exchanges between the two.

The Toronto Star singled out Eric as the one wrestler who seemed to be impervious to Samara's headbutts, and added that Samara "was lucky he didn't suffer a fractured skull" when he applied his favorite strike to Eric's own thick head.

The heart of the 1950 summer would see Samara apparently miss a month of in-ring action due to an injury. *The Daily Standard-Freeholder* of Cornwall, Ontario informed fans that a late June show lineup required adjustment because both Samara and Ray Gunkle had been "confined to hospital beds as a result of an automobile accident."

When he returned to action, Samara went straight back to headbutting his opponents, and also had an NWA world heavyweight championship match against Lou Thesz, the man

A Decided Novelty

who had defeated Samara's long-standing opponent Orville Brown.

This time, the outcome of the bout between Samara and Thesz would be far different from their highly competitive draw on the West Coast. Instead, Thesz defeated the 44-year-old Samara in two consecutive falls in front of an audience of 3,000 fans.

With every member of the Murderers' Row fraternity except Rufus Jones now in their 40s, they found themselves encountering the generation of Black wrestlers they had inspired with far greater frequency. They were also becoming acutely aware that they were collectively beginning to lose a step or two in the ring. On top of that would come the painful realization that their acceptance in certain parts of the world may not have been as universal as it had first appeared, even if the positive social outcomes of their career-long efforts had been undeniable.

A Decided Novelty

25 – Oldest Negro in the Business

In 1950, Don Blackman made his debut in Harlem, and just one week after being referred to yet again as the Black Panther during a match in Philadelphia, Blackman dropped the name when he once again shared a card with the wrestler who defeated him during some of his earliest matches, Jim Mitchell.

In all likelihood, the main reason Blackman was in New York was due to his acting aspirations. By now, Blackman was a dedicated thespian who had appeared in several stage plays. In addition to wrestling a few nights per week, he was also actively involved in the shooting of the film *Two Tickets to Broadway*, starring Tony Martin and Janet Leigh.

In the spring, Blackman returned to the Mid-Atlantic to face Buddy Jackson, who had seemingly been anointed by promoters in several territories as the newest Black wrestling sensation worth pushing. Beginning in Richmond, the pair then visited Charlotte, where they appeared at the behest of legendary wrestling promoter Jim Crockett.

When the duo arrived in Charlotte, Jackson's oft-stated background as an Ohio State graduate and a second-generation pharmacist was apparently deemed useless for pro wrestling purposes. Instead, *The Charlotte Observer* relayed the equally untrue backstory that Jackson was a former Ohio State *athlete*, with his sport of choice going unidentified. *The Observer* added that "a large Negro crowd" was expected, and Crockett promised that the entire balcony would be "reserved for colored fans."

Speaking with *The Charlotte News*, Crockett emphasized the significance of the bout. While it was reported that the Blackman-Jackson match was the first time "a pair of colored wrestlers" had ever wrestled on one of his weekly fight cards, Crockett went so far as to suggest something he knew to be untrue, adding that the encounter "may be the first Negro match in the South."

A Decided Novelty

Crockett subsequently backed away from that claim, settling on declaring Blackman and Jackson to be the first Black wrestlers ever brought to Charlotte, at least with respect to a pair of qualified Black wrestlers directly competing against one another.

Either way, the announcement that Black wrestlers would be appearing in Charlotte spiked the advance ticket sales for the show. Based on Crockett's predictions, *The Charlotte Observer* stated, "The balcony will be bulging with Negro spectators when Promoter Jim Crockett trots out a couple of colored boys on the forthcoming wrestling card."

"It will be the first Negro match of this type in the history of the Charlotte ring," added *The Observer*. "The receptions the boys get and the number of patrons will determine how many more will be put on here."

The match was apparently an unqualified success. The next day's edition of *The Charlotte News* reported, "Jim Crockett saw a first pay off handsomely last night."

Based on the execution of the match, Crockett apparently didn't want to give away too much during this historic first encounter between Black wrestlers in Charlotte. Jackson won in only eight minutes after Blackman got himself disqualified for his overreliance on "rough tactics."

The match may have been brief, but *The Charlotte Observer* reported that the fans in attendance — and particularly the Black fans — were pleased with what they saw out of Jackson in particular.

"The two Negro boys — Don Blackman and Buddy Jackson — proved such a tremendous hit on the last wrestling show that Promoter Jim Crockett is bringing 'em back for a repeat performance," stated *The Observer*. "Local colored fans packed the balcony and received a big kick from the antics of Jackson, who reminds them of Johnny Long. The same place at the Armory will be reserved again for Negro spectators."

Back in Richmond, *The Times-Dispatch* revealed Jackson's actual full name for what was potentially the first time it was ever shared in print, noting that "Ernest (Buddy)

Jackson" would soon be making another appearance in Richmond against a yet-to-be-named opponent. Meanwhile, *The News Leader* informed its readers that Jackson had been wrestling since 1940 — when he would have been 18 or 19 years old — even though there is no clear evidence that he wrestled prior to 1947.

Don Blackman

While these details were being released in Charlotte and Richmond, Blackman and Jackson were already being advertised to appear in Columbia, South Carolina. Possibly to separate the identities of the two wrestlers to help fans identify their favorites, Blackman was labeled as "a former Army

A Decided Novelty

sergeant," while Jackson's legitimate military service was ignored in favor of referring to him exclusively as a "former Ohio State star athlete."

Credentials aside, *The State* focused primarily on the ground being broken by the match, stating unequivocally, "It will be the first time in history that Negro wrestlers have appeared on a wrestling card in Columbia." *The Columbia Record* added that the pair would "have to hustle" during their match in order to outshine the true main event contest between Bibber McCoy and Rowdy Reb Russell.

In front of 2,500 fans — 60 percent of whom were Black — Jackson defeated Blackman by disqualification. Blackman dutifully played the role of the colorful heel, and his bald head was described as potentially giving him an unfair advantage in the match.

"[Blackman] entered the ring attired in a leopard skin, a goatee, and a head as smooth as a billiard ball," reported *The State*. "Jackson tried several times to apply headlocks, but it was similar to trying to get a headlock on a banana. Blackman's head would pop out of Jackson's grip like a pea popping out of a pod. Blackman was disqualified after he bounced Jackson out of the ring several times and refused to allow him to return."

Blackman and Jackson were soon booked for Norfolk, Virginia, where *The Portsmouth Star* offered fans what may have been a realistic peek into the private life and background of "Buddy (Doc) Jackson," despite unintentionally making him a graduate of the wrong Ohio university.

"Jackson is a graduate of Ohio University and is a registered pharmacist," disclosed *The Star*. "He operates a drug store in Columbus, Ohio, and wrestles as a side line. Blackman, of New Hope, Pa., is undefeated in three previous appearances in Tidewater."

The Jackson-Blackman match was also described as the first all-Negro bout in the history of Greensboro when it arrived there.

In May, Blackman also reconnected with Don Kindred for what would prove to be the final major tour of his career.

A Decided Novelty

The pair competed in matches all across Texas, with Blackman billed as world's colored wrestling champion in a setting where the title finally carried some meaning, as he could defend it against Kindred on a nightly basis.

Despite being of greater nominal importance, the world's colored championship carried by Blackman was usually contested on the undercards of events like a show in Galveston headlined by Nell Stewart and Carol Cook for the Texas women's championship.

In Fort Worth, the colored title match went on second out of five matches. The bouts positioned higher on the card were a Texas women's title match between Nell Stewart and Beverly Lehmer, a Texas tag team title match pitting Danny McShane and Al Lovelock against Rito Romero and Carlos Moreno, and understandably, a defense of Lou Thesz's world championship against Timmy Geohagen.

In the midst of the Blackman-Kindred tour of Texas, the pair were photographed working out in the ring for the entertainment of children at the Moorland Branch YMCA in Dallas. When asked for details about his wrestling career, the "Negro heavyweight wrestling champ and undisputed light heavyweight champion of the world" Don Blackman — who was somehow able to hold the titles in the two weight divisions simultaneously — made some amusing claims.

"With 20 years of wrestling experience, Blackman says he is the oldest Negro in the business; his matches have taken him to 26 countries," *The Call* reported.

Blackman certainly should have known better than to offer such ludicrous statements, and especially the remark about his age. At 38 years of age, Blackman was easily younger than Seelie Samara, Jack Claybourne, and Jim Mitchell, with Claybourne, Mitchell and even the younger Rufus Jones all having many more years of ring experience than Blackman.

In Austin, Kindred finally defeated Blackman, winning the world colored wrestling title, and signifying a passing of the torch from one to the other as Blackman began phasing himself out of professional wrestling. While Kindred pressed onward, Blackman returned home, and then finished the year wrestling in California while waiting to make his first major splash in a Hollywood film.

Blackman and Kindred spar at the Moorland Branch YMCA

Kindred did not remain in Texas to capitalize on the torch that was symbolically passed to him. Instead, he traveled back to Michigan and Ontario, where he primarily put over other wrestlers, and particularly junior heavyweight champion Lou Klein. In late August, Kindred traveled to Alberta, where he was a rare Black wrestler in the province following LeRoy Clayton's retirement.

"Another newcomer early in the season will be Don Kindred of New York, a negro who is fast and strong," announced *The Edmonton Journal*. "He will be the first colored wrestler to appear in Edmonton under the Oeming regime with the exception of Woody Strode, who was here for a one night stand."

Promoter Al Oeming soon followed up through *The Edmonton Bulletin* by stating that he "hopes to sign Kindred, a husky Negro from New York, and Woody Strode as a tag team pair later."

The Kindred-Strode tandem never materialized, although Kindred would soon end up in potentially the most prolific all-Black tag team partnership of the era in just a few short years. In the meantime, Kindred would have to content himself with ordinary singles competition in the Alberta province.

The Calgary Albertan characterized Kindred as a "smooth wrestling colored boy" when he made his debut. The publication also perpetuated the tale that Kindred was a collegiate athlete. They labeled him as a graduate of New York University, and an amateur wrestling champion who had only been wrestling professionally for two years even though he was well into his sixth year as a performer.

During one of Kindred's bouts in Edmonton, he received considerable help from Stu Hart to defeat Bob Lortie. Ironically, it was Hart who Kindred had been scheduled to wrestle two years prior before he skipped town for the border of Vermont and Quebec to try out for the Canadian Football League.

Hart was busy acting in the capacity of referee during the bout between Kindred and Lortie when the latter grew annoyed with Hart's interjections and tossed him out of the ring and out onto the ringside floor.

"But Hart soon vaulted back into the ring and held Lortie in a full nelson while Kindred delivered a timely slap to the Frenchman's chops," stated *The Edmonton Journal*. "Lortie dropped, and it required little effort for Kindred to flop on him for the winning fall."

After a subsequent match against Lortie in Edmonton — a contest Kindred lost when Lortie held his tights for

A Decided Novelty

additional leverage — multiple papers reported that Kindred's back had been dislocated. Consequently, Kindred was admitted to the hospital where he was expected to remain for several days.

There had been no truth to this, of course, as Kindred was involved in action the following night. This time, he would drop his match to Ivan Kamaroff as a consequence of being struck with repeated kicks and punches to the kidneys.

When Buddy Jackson departed from the South, he returned to the Midwest, appearing in Wisconsin, Minnesota, and Ohio. By the middle of the summer, he was being discussed in laudatory terms within the borders of his home state as he prepared to battle Duke Keomuka in Dayton.

"So far Jackson has done everything asked of him," offered *The Journal Herald*. "He's undefeated in 11 matches in the Middle-west, and promoters are inclined to believe he is more than a flash in the pan."

More significantly, *The Journal Herald* attempted to establish a clear — and likely untrue — connection between Jackson and a wrestler who had come to epitomize clean Black wrestling throughout much of the United States.

"[Jackson] was a great admirer of 'Gentleman' Jack Claybourne, another top Negro star of recent years, and it was Claybourne who took Jackson to Chicago where he studied wrestling at the YMCA under Lou Talaber, who retired as undefeated middleweight champion," said *The Journal Herald*.

Several advertisements placed in Ohio newspapers singled Jackson out as a "colored television star" who had appeared on black-and-white TV sets in different markets throughout the country.

This was not true in Jackson's case, and would seldom be the reality for most Black wrestlers. As Jack Claybourne would later divulge during a candid interview, agreements between television networks and Southern states prohibited matches involving Black wrestlers from airing in the South, thereby limiting their exposure to national TV audiences.

A Decided Novelty

When wrestling in Detroit and Windsor, Jackson linked up with "The Black Panther" Jim Mitchell. Together, the pair headed south to Tennessee and Kentucky, where *The Park City Daily News* introduced the younger Jackson as the "ruler of the Negro junior heavyweight division" who would be defending his title against the veteran Mitchell. Almost everywhere they wrestled, the papers were courteous enough to note that a special seating section was being reserved for "colored fans."

"The colored boys are sure to bring some of the most rapid-fire action ever seen at the Arena," proclaimed *The Leaf-Chronicle* of Clarksville, Tennessee. "Both are highly regarded in the business and have ample experience behind them. Jackson has done most of his wrestling along the eastern seaboard and in the Midwest. Weighing 210, he has shown the ability to rise to the top and stay there. The Panther, who isn't a masked man, has 12 years of ring warfare to his credit and an eye on Jackson's title."

Jackson escaped with his title at every stop, although the outcomes of the matches were of secondary importance to their originality, since their intent was to spread the novelty of Black wrestling matches to locations where they had never been held before.

"This will be the first time two Negroes have clashed in the ring here, and fans, mindful of how well colored talent has done in the boxing field, are anxious to see if they wrestle as well as they box," *The Park City Daily News* stated. "Buddy Jackson and the Black Panther, two ring vets, will give mat followers the best possible chance to find the answer, because both are ranked right at the top of their race in the wrestling field."

By the time February 1950 rolled around, allegations were being lobbed that Woody Strode might opt not to return to football due to a shoulder injury that he had suffered during the 1949 season.

However, the very next month, contradictory news reports confirmed that Strode had undergone a successful surgery and was about to make his return to the wrestling rings of California. This was true, as Strode reemerged in the ring in April, and was soon competing in tag team action alongside another returnee, "The Black Panther" Jim Mitchell. The press contended that the two were collectively "two of the Negro race's most popular contributions to the mat profession."

Woody Strode

The next month, promoters Cal Eaton and Aileen Labell hosted "Woody Strode Night" at the Olympic Auditorium in Los Angeles, and presented a special trophy to "the tall, well-shaped bronze giant" who "took to wrestling like a duck to water, and in no time at all was easily one of the best-liked wrestlers performing."

It's true that Strode had a habit of flattening his opponents with football-themed moves like flying shoulder tackles, but there were also occasions when he displayed a

A Decided Novelty

surprising level of technical know-how. In several matches that took place both before and after Woody Strode Night — when a reported 12,000 Los Angeles residents came out to honor the football-player-turned-wrestler — Strode made use of a stepover toehold to secure submission victories over his surprised opponents.

Further east, Rufus Jones left the Midwest and returned to North Bay, and a new word was introduced into the professional wrestling lexicon. In an effort to describe the chaos of Jones' match with Dick Marshall of Quebec City, the sportswriter for *The North Bay Nugget* typed out the sentence, "The clean-cut Mr. Marshall was unable to stand up against burly Rufus' coco-butts, and finally succumbed to one of Jones backbreaking Boston crabs."

Thus, a word that would frequently refer to headbutts administered by Black wrestlers — and by *one* very famous Black wrestler in particular — came into existence. According to a quote published by the paper, Jones even took ownership of the new name for his favorite move, as he name-checked it during his stated defense of why the violent use of his head should remain legal.

"Just because I have a harder head than the rest does not mean that my coco-butt is illegal," said Jones. "In fact, because there's so much fuss about it, I'll be out tonight to show the boys I've really never started to get rough."

While fans were introduced to a colorful new term for a headbutt in that article from *The Nugget*, they were also introduced to something else, or *someone* else to be specific. The writer from the paper made sure to include that one of the angry spectators "went so far as pushing Mrs. Rufus Jones on the way out, but found out to his displeasure that Mrs. Rufus also packs a solid wallop, as he had a handbag cracked over his head."

The real name of Mrs. Rufus Jones was Gertrude Clements Godfrey, who Joseph Godfrey had married in Montreal on November 13, 1944. While it's downright probable that she had ventured out on the road with her

A Decided Novelty

husband before and watched his matches in person, this was the first reported case of her being caught up in any post-match shenanigans. This report also suggests that Godfrey's marriage to his previous wife Ursaline had been dissolved at some point between the middle of 1940 and the end of 1944.

Gertrude Godfrey also reportedly brawled with a lady fan who attempted to assault her husband at a separate North Bay event.

The precise technique Jones implemented to butt his opponents was described in detail in the pages of *The Olympian* after Rufus headed westward and prepared to make his debut in Olympia, Washington against Gordon Hessel. This technical breakdown was offered in conjunction with an authentic correction, as the paper decided to inform fans that Jones was a northerner rather than a native of the American South as originally stated.

"Jones, who makes his Olympia debut Tuesday night, is from Boston, not from Mississippi as erroneously stated on the program, and has a ruthless style that wrecks most opponents in short order," stated the article. "The 'head butt' for which he is famous, although in appearance it is as though he were making a short, quick nod, is as generally lethal as a hefty slug from a hammer, and it will take all of Hessel's agility to not be there when he 'butts.'"

As it often happened, Jones had a victory stripped from him when the referee retroactively disqualified him for using headbutts, reversed the stoppage victory for Jones, and awarded the bout to Hessel, leaving the "infuriated" Jones protesting the decision.

These proceedings once again allowed the issue to be raised as to the legality of headbutts in the areas of Washington where wrestling was gradually being introduced. *The Daily Herald* of Everett even cited an alleged ruling by the Washington State Athletic Commission, establishing with respect to headbutts that "there is nothing illegal about them."

Jack Claybourne began 1950 where Jones ended it — in Oregon and Washington — before returning to Hawaii once

A Decided Novelty

again. Back in the islands, Jack was justifiably touted as a serious threat to reclaim the *Ring Magazine* title belt that he had worn for nearly a year. In the four months since Claybourne had departed from the island of Oahu, the Hawaii junior heavyweight title had changed hands multiple times, and now adorned the waist of Sandor Szabo, who Claybourne had wrestled regularly in California.

Claybourne was still booked favorably, but was ultimately served up as fodder for former world heavyweight boxing champion Primo Carnera. He then began a six-month tour of Australia that would stretch through several major Australian cities.

Once Claybourne touched down in Australia, he worked in nothing short of a main-event capacity, and immediately attracted 5,000 fans to Sydney Stadium to watch him wrestle Ted Christy to a draw.

Claybourne then made enough use of his head in a draw with Karl Davis in Brisbane that the Australian writers took note of it.

"Throughout the bout, Claybourne had made his target a bald patch on Davis's head, and this eventually led to Davis's roughhouse tactics at the finish," stated *The Brisbane Telegraph*. "Claybourne repeatedly brought his head down on his rival's crown! And, after all, a man can only take so much."

Over the course of his time in Australia, Claybourne seemed to have endeared himself to the nation's Aboriginal community on multiple occasions. In early June, he was on hand to bounce the ball to open a match for the Lake Tyers Aboriginal rugby team. On at least one other occasion, Jack mingled with Aboriginal Australians in their place of worship in Fitzroy, just outside of Melbourne, and was blamed for the inattentiveness of the congregation's children.

"Seated in their midst was American coloured wrestler Jack Claybourne, idol of the aboriginal kiddies of Fitzroy, and 'Uncle Jack' to a lot of them," wrote *The Argus*. "Claybourne, accompanied by American negro boxer Freddy Dawson, and his manager Mr. H.D. Rudolph, was the guest of Mr. Nicholls, who has conducted the mission in Gore St., under the auspices of the Church of Christ, for the last seven years. Welcoming the visitors, Mr. Nicholls said that the people of his church felt that they belonged to them."

The kinship between Claybourne and Aboriginal Australians may have stemmed partly from their similar complexions, coupled with Claybourne's increased experience with racial discrimination that had been absent during previous trips to the country.

Under the title "Racial discrimination practised against coloured visitors," the August 10 edition of *The Labor Call* devoted considerable space to the discriminatory treatment experienced by Claybourne upon his arrival in Broken Hill, along the western edge of New South Wales.

The writer noted that most Australians were quick to denounce mistreatment of the Aboriginal population and would have said Australia had no color problem comparable to other countries.

"The stigma of the color bar is being applied mainly to visitors to this country who come out, or are brought out, under contract, because of their talents, and to demonstrate their prowess," stated *The Labor Call*. "These people come to Australia in good faith and are snubbed when they arrive. They are being denied accommodation and banned from hotels."

The writer then went on to say that continuing to discriminate against others on the basis of race would result in bad publicity for Australia, which had the potential to do irreparable damage to the nation's reputation.

"Australians themselves are doing something they have so often criticised," continued the article. "In Broken Hill last week, several of the city's leading hotels refused accommodation to visiting American wrestler Jack Claybourne."

The writer from *The Labor Call* then contacted the hotels to confirm that "a ban existed, and that it applied not to any particular person or type of person, but to all colored people."

A Decided Novelty

"Such a ban means that no matter who the colored visitor is; no matter how well educated, behaved, popular, or otherwise acknowledged, he or she is unable to stay at the leading hotels," concluded *The Labor Call*. "Mention of Jack Claybourne was only an instance, as was the information that Chief Little Wolf's reception would be cold, and that he would be downright unwelcome. It is pleasing, at least, that such discrimination is not carried out in other parts of Australia. It would indeed be a sorry day for Australia if racial discrimination were allowed to develop."

Claybourne's race was also factored into at least one of his Australian feuds in a fashion that was seldom utilized in the United States. For multiple months of the tour, race-based animosity between Claybourne and Ernie "Dutch" Hefner was played up for the sake of raising interest in their eventual clashes.

"A question now intriguing followers is whether Hefner and the negro champion, Jack Claybourne, will meet," pondered *The Argus*. "Hefner is a Texan, and with the southerner's deep-rooted prejudice against coloured people, has resolutely declined on previous visits to go into the ring with negro wrestlers. One thing certain is that if Hefner and Claybourne meet, it will be a real 'blood' match."

It is true that Hefner had been on a tour of Australia with Seelie Samara in 1948 and a brief mention was made that racial prejudice prevented a bout between the two men from occurring. Even so, it's unclear whether or not this was an authentic outcome of true prejudice or was being played up for dramatic effect.

Regardless as to whether Hefner's lack of prior Black opponents resulted from authentic racism or merely coincidental scheduling, the Claybourne-Hefner pairing reportedly resulted from threats against Hefner's future career prospects.

"Hefner, who comes from the 'deep South' of USA — his home is in Houston, Texas — has repeatedly refused matches with negroes and objected strongly when his bout

A Decided Novelty

with Claybourne was suggested," stated *The Herald*. "However, Stadiums Ltd. enforced the clause in Hefner's contract which specifies that it has the right to select Hefner's opponents in Australia."

Perhaps as a means of playing up his racial hatred toward wrestlers of a different complexion, the press suggested that Hefner seemed to adopt a rougher style when facing wrestlers of different races, whether they were Black, presumably Native American Indian in the case of Chief Little Wolf, or East Indian like Joginder Singh.

"Hefner accepted the ultimatum, but insisted that he is wrestling under protest," said *The Telegraph*. "Matched with these wrestlers, Hefner completely changed from straight wrestling to a rough, rugged style."

Some of the bouts between Claybourne and Hefner were filled with such acrimonious tension that the passion emitted by the two even prompted altercations amongst the spectators, which *The Age* pointed out in one of its reports from Sydney Stadium.

"With the Stadium in uproar as Hefner crashed the negro to the canvas with punches and kicks, a brawl developed in the bleachers, and three men were ejected by attendants," reported *The Age*.

Most of the confrontations between the two grapplers ended in draws, but even when Hefner won, he was presented as a pitiable figure for allowing his racial animosity to get the best of him. Noting that Hefner had won a match against Claybourne one fall to nil, *The Courier-Mail* reported that Hefner "finished without a friend at the Brisbane Stadium last night."

"There was a revival of the age-old war between American whites and negroes in the wrestling bout between Dutch Hefner and Jack Claybourne at Brisbane Stadium last night, and the white man, Hefner, did not show to advantage," reported *The Telegraph*. "Without any provocation, Hefner indulged in an orgy of punching, jolting, and eye gouging, while

A Decided Novelty

Claybourne, obviously trying hard to keep his temper, concentrated on wrestling."

When Hefner won, he was booed mercilessly by the fans, and yet "Claybourne forgot and forgave at the end of the bout, went over to Hefner's corner, and shook his hand."

Surprisingly, Claybourne's most far-reaching U.S. publicity — at least as far as his image is concerned — resulted from one of his matches in Australia. In the middle of a bout against Frank Valois in Melbourne, Claybourne leapt over the back of referee Bonny Muir and planted both of his feet squarely into the face of his French-Canadian opponent.

The photographer for *The Argus* snapped a picture-perfect photo of the moment, which was soon shared in sports sections across the United States, including in places like Atlanta, Georgia, where Claybourne had never wrestled before.

Claybourne left Australia and went straight back to work in Southern California. What awaited him was the use of an advertising slogan that probably made sense in the minds of the promoters who introduced it, but begged further analysis.

The title applied to Claybourne in fall 1950 was "The Negro Argentina Rocca." This comparison was clearly intended to position Claybourne favorably alongside Antonino Rocca of Argentina, who was rapidly becoming a wrestling superstar by virtue of his acrobatic presentation, chiseled physique, and handsome face.

The comparison was inherently insulting: Claybourne was 11 years older than Rocca, had debuted at least 10 years earlier, and had established his style's foundations long before Rocca entered wrestling. To apply a boxing analogy, it would have been like Joe Louis being described as "The Negro Rocky Marciano" right when Louis was on the brink of retirement, and the much younger Italian American champion was entering his prime.

Just as Claybourne was preparing for a match against the newly crowned holder of the version of the world heavyweight championship recognized in the Los Angeles market — Baron Michele Leone — a sportswriter from *The*

A Decided Novelty

Wilmington Press-Journal actually had the sense to point out this anachronism.

Jack Claybourne dropkicks Frank Valois

"The Baron opposes 'Jumping Jack' Claybourne, Boston tar baby, who was performing ring acrobatics and spectacular jumping tactics before Argentina Rocca knew what the inside of a wrestling ring looked like," stated *The Press-Journal*. "The Amazing South American only capitalized on what 'Jumping Jack' has been doing for years without more than passing mention. Now they heralded Claybourne as the 'Negro Argentina Rocca.'"

A Decided Novelty

From there, the approach of the publicists changed, with Claybourne receiving a larger and more appropriate share of the credit for helping to innovate — or at least propagate — the wrestling style that Rocca had so effectively monetized. In effect, they attempted to rebrand Antonino Rocca as "The White Jack Claybourne."

The Independent of Long Beach acknowledged Claybourne as "the original mat acrobat." *The Progress-Bulletin* of Pomona went one step further, hailing Claybourne as "the originator of the ring acrobatics that have since made Argentina Rocca famous."

During this time, Claybourne did something that was atypical in his career; he won a one-on-one match against a former world champion, and in straight falls no less. While the version of the world title Babe Sharkey wore in Maryland wasn't necessarily the most prestigious of the bunch, it still permitted him to lay claim to the status of being a former world titlist even when he wrestled in California. By proxy, the victory finally enabled the 40-year-old Claybourne to look like a man capable of being a true world champion.

Back in Southwest Michigan, 1950 began for Huston Harris with a continuation of his feud with Rex Sheeley, but then Harris was quickly rerouted into a showdown with the inexperienced Charley Murray. With Murray being praised as "one of the best colored matmen in the world" by *The Herald-Press*, this somehow translated into Harris being supplied with "a taste of his own medicine."

Harris had supposedly been clamoring for a shot at "the colored heavyweight championship," although there was no champion even superficially holding that title who was active in the area at the time. Regardless, Harris defeated Murray with ease to supposedly strengthen his own claim to being the best Black wrestler in the area, despite scant evidence that Murray had ever wrestled in a single match prior to that night.

Harris then began to reel off victories one right after the other. His mid-February defeat of Bill Demetrios marked

A Decided Novelty

his fourth win in a row, and he continued knocking off the majority of his opponents in single-fall matches that usually lasted less than 10 minutes.

While Harris' career in the ring appeared ready to soar, not everything in his life was proceeding as smoothly. In March, *The Herald Press* reported that the 27-year-old Harris had been arrested for non-support, and was booked into the Berrien County Jail.

After getting bailed out of jail, Harris had his winning streak halted by a disqualification loss to Pierre Lasalle. *The Herald Press* illustrated how Harris went berserk and refused to break an illegal hold, leading to his disqualification at the hands of referee James Austin. Promoter Ray Kruger stipulated that Harris would not be permitted to wrestle again until he learned to compete with a gentler style, and the article concluded by informing readers that Harris had been "getting rougher with each match, and was at his most villainous Saturday night."

This marked an abrupt transition of Harris into the role of heel, and when he returned from his suspension and eventually allied himself with "Bad Boy" Brown, the pair caused quite a stir. This is adequately exemplified by their late-May interaction with the team of "Farmer" Don Marlin and Jack Carter.

"The Brown-Harris combo, using all the favorite tactics of back-alley brawlers, had scored the third and deciding fall when their eagerness to inflict more punishment on their foes led to their final disqualification," reported *The News-Palladium*. "Harvey Totzke then reversed his decision and awarded the match to Marlin and Carter."

The paper added that the intervention of the police was required to protect Harris and Brown from the fans. All of this was especially risky considering that Harris was not only wrestling in his hometown under his real name, but his actual address of 266 Cornelia Street had been printed in the newspaper for all to see during the reporting of his arrest for non-support.

A Decided Novelty

In June, Harris was able to appear on a card in South Bend, Indiana, marking the first time that he would appear on the same show as world champion Lou Thesz, who was claiming the status of world champion "in the 41 states controlled by the National Wrestling Alliance," according to *The South Bend Tribune*. Harris then returned to the Benton Armory and lost a match in straight falls to Jim Spencer, after which the local giant turned to a *Herald-Press* reporter and "blamed his defeat on the fact that he had tried to change his style and wrestle 'clean.'"

As the summer stretched into its late months and Harris began splitting his time between Michigan and Ohio, he became known by another name — Bobo Brazil. Coincidentally, the colorful name was first used by a 135-pound Golden Gloves fighter in New Jersey earlier that year.

Since the first-ever use of the name predates Harris' utilization of the identical name by approximately six months, it's likely that there was some sort of inspiration drawn from the fighter's use of the Bobo Brazil pseudonym and whomever it was that recommended it to Harris.

There was an overlapping period when the names of Huston Harris and Bobo Brazil both appeared in advertisements for wrestling events. However, the use of the Harris name was completely phased out by the time the grappler made his September appearances in Wisconsin. Moving forward, Huston Harris was completely erased in favor of "Bobo Brazil, 240-pound native of the South American nation from which he has taken his name," according to *The Green Bay Press-Gazette*.

Under his new guise, Brazil achieved far greater notoriety, particularly as he ventured further away from his hometown, where Benton Harbor's residents had grown accustomed to his presence. By the close of the year, *The Herald-Press* had informed residents of Michigan's Twin Cities that Harris, "who showed to such good advantage against first class opposition" had been "lured away to Chicago, New York, and other large cities, where under the name 'Bobo' Brazil he has scored some outstanding successes."

Houston "Bobo Brazil" Harris

That statement was only true inasmuch as Brazil had managed to appear in the wrestling rings of Chicago. Aside from that, he had been primarily confined to the wrestling rings of small cities in Wisconsin and Minnesota, and papers like *The Evening Tribune* of Albert Lea gleefully reported when "the towering Negro from Brazil" was left "begging for mercy" by his predominantly White opponents.

Unbeknownst to anyone, as the 1950s continued to unfold, Brazil would achieve every bit of the success that his hometown news reporters had dreamed up for him, and then some.

EPILOGUE

The tragic death of Joseph Alvin Godfrey on November 17, 1951, in Ogden, Utah seemed to signal a seismic shift in the professional wrestling world. Not only would it seemingly mark the beginning of the end of the Murderer's Row era of Black professional wrestling, but it would also set events in motion for the inheritors of Godfrey's most famous gimmick to thrive in his absence.

At 8:34 a.m. on that bitterly cold morning, Godfrey was killed in an automobile collision on Highway 84, one mile north of the forebodingly named "Death Curve" in Ogden, Utah. He was only 38 years old, and was in the midst of a solid 18-year tenure as a wrestler that showed no signs of slowing at the time of his death.

Witnesses suspected that Jones had fallen asleep behind the wheel of his car. The coroner reported that Godfrey sustained a crushed chest as a result of the collision. *The Standard-Examiner* of Ogden would add the further detail that Godfrey had "suffered a skull fracture" among his other injuries; a cruel irony if true given the celebrated invulnerability of the wrestler's head.

The other vehicle involved in the wreck plunged 60 feet from the overpass following the collision, but its occupant — 27-year-old Joseph Arrave — fortunately survived the ordeal.

With the demand for wrestling in the style of Rufus Jones still high in the Rocky Mountain and Northwestern regions of the United States, Don Kindred and Frank James — both of whom had already independently adopted excessive headbutting into their arsenals — were paired together as "The Brown Bombers," although some newspapers in the region fairly appraised them as a pair of Rufus Jones clones.

As an unstoppable heel tandem, the Bombers ran roughshod over every team in the two regions during 1952 and 1953, simultaneously capturing the Rocky Mountain and Pacific Northwest tag team championships, and becoming the first Black unit to win the tag team championship of a major wrestling territory in the process.

The very next year, 44-year-old Jack Claybourne would make up one half of the first Black babyface tag team to accomplish the same feat, when he teamed with newcomer Luther Lindsay to win the Canadian tag team championship.

"The Brown Bombers" — Don Kindred and Frank James

At the same time, Claybourne's victory with Lindsay also heralded a changing of the guard along the pro wrestling landscape. Within months, the increasingly immobile Claybourne, whose fading athleticism had left him all the more reliant on the use of his headbutt, was phased out of his pairing

A Decided Novelty

with Lindsay in favor of the much taller and younger Ed "Bearcat" Wright Jr., whose boxing father had frequently stood by Seelie Samara's side in Nebraska, and who also had a penchant for leading with his head.

In the meantime, Houston "Bobo Brazil" Harris, at the suggestion of "Black Panther" Jim Mitchell, would adopt the cocobutt as his signature maneuver. With his combination of size, strength, and charisma, and aided by a promotional climate that was growing inexorably more accepting of Black wrestlers in main-event positions, Bobo Brazil would surge past Jack Claybourne, Seelie Samara, Jim Mitchell, and every other Black star that preceded him in terms of bankability and mainstream acceptance.

Brazil wouldn't be alone, as the younger Bearcat Wright and Luther Lindsay would also benefit from the groundwork that had been laid over the decades that preceded them and amass numerous title reigns across several territories.

As icing on the cake — or insult to injury — a young Texan by the name of Elkin James would adopt the name of Reginald "Sweet Daddy" Siki, and blend flashy, high-flying wrestling with a healthy dose of headbutts in a fashion identical to that of Jack Claybourne, who began wrestling one year before James was even born. In what amounted to a dual tribute act that borrowed its name and repertoire from two separate Black wrestling legends, Sweet Daddy Siki completed the quartet of wrestlers that would supplant Claybourne, Samara, Mitchell, and Jones as the top Black stars in wrestling heading into the 1960s.

Unfortunately, Jack Claybourne would not live to see the events that would unfold beyond this point, and when his body was found lying lifeless on the bathroom floor of his Los Angeles home just before 6:00 p.m. on January 7th, 1960, it wasn't a surprise to many of his closest friends. Apparently, he had told anyone who would listen that he would take his own life if he wasn't given an opportunity to extend a wrestling career that had lasted nearly 30 years.

A Decided Novelty

Clearly, Claybourne's threat of suicide had not been idle. Sometime after arguing with his adopted daughter and then calling his wife Lillian at work to inform her of the altercation, Claybourne had loaded a 12-gauge shotgun, pressed the working end of the weapon against his head, and pulled the trigger.

The Los Angeles County coroner would encapsulate the ghastliness of the scene by summarizing Claybourne's cause of death as such: "Shotgun wound of head with multiple skull fractures and almost complete evisceration of the brain."

The description provided by the Associated Negro Press was equally graphic. After setting the stage by correctly stating that Claybourne "had to fight an unwritten racial ban in professional wrestling for 20 years," the ANP described Claybourne's suicide by saying that the wrestler turned the shotgun on himself, and "blew the top of his head off above the lower lip."

"Portions of his body were scattered over the walls and ceiling of the bathroom of his home where he ended his life," added the ANP's grisly report.

Symbolically, Jack Claybourne's suicide in 1960 concluded the pre-civil rights era of Black professional wrestling in the most tragically fitting manner possible. It was heartbreakingly appropriate that the period's most gifted and athletic performer — having watched others capitalize on the foundation he and his peers had laid — would take his own life while heartbroken.

Presumably, the knowledge that each turn of the world would cause collective amnesia with respect to his accomplishments to cloud the memories of wrestling fans while subsequent generations reaped greater fame and financial rewards was more than he could bear... especially when he was too old and broken to personally avail himself of them.

By the same token, stepping outside of what the Black pioneers of the era may have been feeling during that time period in terms of their early arrival to the party, the industry they left behind was one of expanding opportunities and

A Decided Novelty

broadening horizons. This was made evident not only by an increase in the opportunities that Black performers received within the wrestling industry itself, but also the opportunities they would enjoy once their wrestling careers concluded.

In the next decade, both Don Blackman and Woody Strode would perform in noteworthy roles in Academy-Award-Winning films, with Blackman appearing as Luke in "On the Waterfront," while Strode's appearance as Draba in "Spartacus" also netted him a Golden Globe nomination for Best Supporting Actor.

Starting from a time when Blacks were effectively absent from pro wrestling's ranks, and when a match featuring Black grapplers could be classified as a decided novelty, they had advanced the business to a point where the presence of Black wrestlers could no longer be dismissed as a novelty, and had instead blossomed into a necessity.

A Decided Novelty

AFTERWORD

"This is the first time two black men went for the number one contendership for the AEW World Championship. I have no problem saying that over and over again, and saying it louder. I'm proud of that as well."

The words came from Swerve Strickland following his successful March 2025 bout with Ricochet at the All Elite Wrestling (AEW) per-per-view *Revolution*. I remember watching live and having my interest aroused. The show had sold more than 11,000 tickets at the Crypto.com Arena in Los Angeles and, while the match was not the main event, it was certainly one of the marquee attractions and served to further solidify Strickland's standing as one of the most marketable acts on the current professional wrestling landscape.

I was intrigued by both the content and context of what he said. Was this really the first time in that promotion's history that two black men were in that position to vie for a chance to wrestle against the world champion? Surely by now, we had made enough progress in the industry that a statement like that could not possibly be true – particularly in a company that prides itself on being forward-thinking. But the more thought I gave to Swerve's comment, the more I understood the significance of acknowledging the success and struggle that black wrestlers had been facing for more than a century.

In many ways, I have always viewed professional wrestling in North America as micro culture that reflects our larger macro culture. It's both pageantry and sport that brings in its audience by capitalizing on the prevailing attitudes of the time. On the mat and behind the curtain professional wrestling mirrors the many facets of society's cultural, economic, and racial elements.

A Decided Novelty

When Ian asked me to write this foreword, he was doing it to honor my older brother, Brian Jean-Joseph, his best friend at the University of Michigan, who died in a drowning accident at age 23 in 2002. Ian and Brian bonded over both their love of pro wrestling and shared heritage and even portrayed themselves around campus as a tag team, labeling themselves the "Caribbean Connection" when they worked together in the East Quad Dining Hall. Brian was a one of kind individual. There is not a day that goes by that I don't think about his humor, his integrity, and everything that made him special.

At home, pro wrestling was also a vital part of our lives. When no one else was around, Brian and I were tag team partners, battling our Mega Powers stuffed toys and usually winning. But when my cousin Michael Ange came over, the dynamics changed, with both practicing their wrestling moves on me.

Since I was five years younger and smaller than each of them, I would usually howl in pain, prompting my father to punish my brother and cousin. Fortunately for the older kids, the penalty was never severe. Usually, they would be asked to stand in a corner.

You see, my father was also a wrestling fan and would never fathom a decree banning wrestling viewing in our home. Like the World Wrestling Federation's rhetoric said, pro wrestling was family entertainment in our house and everyone watched together.

I can remember one time when my family went to stay at my grandmother's home in South Caicos, a quiet fishing island that was part of the Turks and Caicos Islands. Despite the beauty of the scenery, there was not much for Brian and I to do. Luckily, we had a VHS tape of *WrestleMania VI,* the 1990 spectacular that can now be viewed as an end cap of the '80s wrestling boom in North America.

Billed as "The Ultimate Challenge," the main event pitted Hulk Hogan vs The Ultimate Warrior. It never disappointed, and we probably watched it more than two dozen times during that vacation. But there was another match that, for reasons we didn't fully understand, made us feel less exuberant: Roddy Piper vs Bad News Brown.

Brown's real name was Allen James Coage, and he'd won a bronze medal for the U.S. in judo at the 1976 Olympics. While the roster at time was filled with over-the-top and in some cases, cartoonish, wrestlers, there was always something different about Bad News Brown, even though he was still outlandish at times. Though we hadn't yet heard of Bobo Brazil, the original Rufus Jones or Clarence Bouldin, we sensed that Bad News was upholding a proud tradition. There was something legitimate about him that was different from everyone else, especially the other black wrestlers.

Even at that young age, we yearned to see black people in North America receive representation that was authentic and multilayered. So you can imagine our disappointment when Piper, a fan favorite at the time, came out to the ring with half his body painted black. Although he may have been trying to send a message of unity and brotherhood, it felt disturbingly like some type of minstrel show.

Was he doing it for us or doing it for *them?* Looking back at it now, it's even more dumbfounding to imagine Bad News Brown, even with all his credible wrestling and judo accolades, put in that sort of situation as late as the 1990s. But as mentioned earlier, the match was very much a reflection of the daily plight of black American athletes and performers struggling against being othered and portrayed as something less than equal to their contemporaries in society.

That's why Swerve's words from that 2025 press conference ring so important today. For so long, as the title of this book states, black wrestlers were treated as a novelty. And the battle goes on, even among the black wrestlers today.

As adults, most of us have heard of black superstars from the past like Brazil. Ernie "The Cat" Ladd, Ron Simmons and Bearcat Wright. And we know about the white trendsetters in the early 20th Century, including Frank Gotch, George Hackenschmidt, Farmer Burns and Strangler Lewis.

A Decided Novelty

But very few have heard of their black contemporaries, including Viro Small, Jack Claybourne, Jim Wango, the original Reginald Siki and many others. Their journey and contribution performing throughout North America, Europe, and Australia in the 1800s and 1900s is part and parcel to building the foundation that is today's professional wrestling. Despite that, it is sad to realize that many of their exploits have been forgotten.

So we all owe Ian a debt of gratitude for reviving their stories and giving these greats the glory they've long deserved.

Patrick Jean-Joseph
Producer, Film and Documentaries

A Decided Novelty

EDITOR'S NOTE

I've edited hundreds of manuscripts and dissertations in the course of my academic career. Maybe a dozen made me put down my pen and stare at the wall, trying to process what I'd just read. Ian Douglass's latest magnum opus, the ninth in a long and varied career, belongs in a category by itself.

Let's start with Viro Small. The man wrestled professionally with a bullet lodged in his neck, a permanent souvenir from being shot. That detail alone would make him memorable. But Small was only one of dozens whose stories Douglass has rescued from oblivion. Consider King Kong Clayton, who performed strongman stunts with a bull rope around his neck until a mishap rendered him unconscious, requiring several minutes of resuscitation. Or Jack Claybourne, who spent a year as Hawaiian junior heavyweight champion while perfecting the aerial techniques that would later make Antonino Rocca famous — except "Gentleman Jack " was doing it a decade earlier. Together they form a hidden history so vast and intricate that our accepted narratives about wrestling's racial integration collapse entirely.

Fictional gumshoes like Frank Columbo and Philip Marlowe would appreciate some of the detective work on offer. Douglass tracked down Clarence Bouldin, who spent decades passing as Cuban while potentially holding wrestling's first Black world championship. He uncovered Frank Crozier's 1909 victory for Britain's legitimate middleweight title. He documented how George Godfrey's New Jersey appearances drew triple the crowds that white headliners managed at identical venues. The author even solved the mystery of wrestlers using decade-old photographs of completely different

A Decided Novelty

people in their promotional materials — a level of identity fluidity that would make postmodern theorists dizzy.

But raw data tells only part of this story. What Douglass reveals is an entire creative ecosystem born from exclusion. When Jim Crow laws and regional prejudices barred straightforward participation, Black wrestlers invented something far more complex: a fluid performance art where identity itself became negotiable. One night you're billed as Senegalese. Next week, Ethiopian. Cross state lines and suddenly you're Aboriginal Australian. The same performer could be simultaneously advertised as a former Olympic wrestling finalist (impossible given the era's restrictions) and a pharmacist's son (actually true). At least six different men wrestled as "Black Panther" between 1920 and 1950, passing the character between them like folklore. One of them was simultaneously billed as a "Tiger." And the photographic evidence was often of little help when it came to distinguishing one Black wrestler from another: Douglass reveals how King Kong Clayton's promotional photos were actually decade-old images of Rufus Jones

The geography also tells a brutal story. Douglass maps how Lee Umbles could display pure technical wrestling to cheering crowds in Detroit, then drive south into territories where those same skills had to hide behind degrading caricatures. He traces the literal borders where Seelie Samara could headbutt opponents legally in one Canadian province while facing disqualification for the same move just across the river. The stakes were often life-and-death: White Noble's murder by a tenant he was evicting remains one of wrestling's most violent (and essentially unavenged) racial incidents. On the positive side, consider Reginald Siki, whose five-language fluency enabled a European touring career that predated modern globalization by decades, or the Aboriginal Australians who formed kinship bonds with visiting Black American wrestlers facing hotel discrimination in supposedly enlightened democracies.

A Decided Novelty

Every chapter contains revelations that upend conventional wisdom. Fabricated championship tournaments where the "National Wrestling Association" existed only in promotional copy. Fictional sanctioning bodies created specifically for Black titleholders, complete with diamond-studded belts that moved from wrestler to wrestler like mystical artifacts. Drawing strategies that sometimes outperformed mainstream promotions — Don Blackman and Don Kindred's Virginia appearances drew sellout crowds of 3,500 when the novelty of "Negro grapplers" proved irresistible to both Black and white audiences. Technical innovations that wouldn't be foregrounded in white wrestling for decades: the aerial moves perfected by Claybourne, the submission holds developed by Samara, the crowd psychology mastered by Rufus Jones, whose "coco-butt" became Bobo Brazil's signature move and a component of nearly every other Black and Samoan wrestler's moveset for decades to come.

The international scope proves equally stunning. These wrestlers didn't just break barriers at home — they conquered foreign markets that mainstream American performers couldn't crack. Australian newspapers declared Claybourne and Samara the most popular wrestlers ever to appear there, "excepting no one." Their success overseas often dwarfed their domestic recognition, revealing how America's racial prejudices cost the industry genuine international stars.

The photographic evidence alone tells the story of deliberate erasure. Douglass documents how King Kong Clayton's promotional photos were actually decade-old images of Rufus Jones, how wrestlers' wives were cropped from championship celebration photos to eliminate their humanity, how the visual record was manipulated to maintain certain fictions about these performers' lives and backgrounds. Most damning is what this recovery project reveals about historical memory itself. The wrestling press has spent decades celebrating later figures as "firsts" while actual pioneers vanished from record. Not through accident or oversight, but through systematic replacement of complex truths with

A Decided Novelty

simpler, more comfortable fictions. For a lot of supposed wrestling historians, Black history begins in the 1950s with Houston Harris, the king-sized Benton Harbor resident who became known as Bobo Brazil, thereby conveniently erasing three decades of pioneers who paved his path.

Sometimes a book changes how you see its subject. This is one of those books. After reading it, there's no excuse for those lazy wrestling observers who choose to perpetuate incomplete just-so stories about the sport's complicated racial evolution — or for the similarly-situated tastemakers in any other field where convenience has replaced complexity in our collective memory. Now that Douglass has done the hard work of recovery, the rest of us have no excuse for ignorance.

Oliver Lee Bateman
The Ringer

A Decided Novelty

ACKNOWLEDGEMENTS

In your hands you hold a book that I thought would be impossible to write. I always hoped beyond all reason that someone would eventually write it for me, but then I realized how selfish it would be for me to depend on someone else to put the time and effort into its creation, so I decided to do it myself.

Oliver Bateman has been a constant presence and friend who supported this project since the instant I suggested it, and he was always willing to offer suggestions and rate ideas. It makes things much easier when you have such a brilliant friend who is so passionate about the subject matter that you're investigating.

Mike Johnson is someone I have listened to for years, and as a fixture in the field of wrestling news and journalism, he deserves far more respect than he often receives. I am honored to have his foreword included in this book.

Patrick Jean-Joseph is the younger brother of Brian Jean-Joseph — the best friend I ever made during my college years — whose life ended far too early. It is truly remarkable that our mutual friend Keith Elliot Greenberg helped us to connect in adulthood, and in a space where we could both contribute to a work dedicated to the memory of Brian.

Thank you to everyone who encouraged and motivated me throughout this book's writing, including my parents James and Pauline Douglass, my wife Teisha, and our son Isaiah. It's impossible to complete a project requiring this level of research and attention to detail without a great deal of understanding from your family, and from your spouse in particular.

"For the wages of sin is death, but the gift of God is eternal life in Christ Jesus our Lord." – Romans 6:23

Regards,

Ian C. Douglass

A Decided Novelty

CREDITS

Author
Ian C. Douglass

Editor
Oliver Lee Bateman

Cover Art **Foreword** **Afterword**
Marc W. Leitzel Mike Johnson Patrick Jean-Joseph

Additional Aid and Thanks
James Douglass   Ken Bevan
John Cosper   Jon Snowden
Khal Davenport   Emio Tomeoni
David Shoemaker   Phil Lions
Ohio State University   Notre Dame University
Jamie Hemmings   Bradley Craig

Photo Credits
The Broad Ax, The Kitchener-Waterloo Record, The Sunday Oregonian, The Courier-Mail, The Age, The Honolulu Advertiser, The Honolulu Star-Bulletin, The North Bay Nugget, The Brisbane Telegraph, The Newcastle Morning Herald, The Age, The Argus, The Daily Telegraph, The Sunday Mail, The Alabama Tribune, The Kansas City Star, The Hamilton Spectator, The Ogden Standard-Examiner, The Herald and News, The Edmonton Journal, The California Eagle, The Longview Daily News

ABOUT THE AUTHOR

Ian Douglass has been a contributing writer for *Men's Health Magazine*, *The Ringer*, *Splice Today*, *Cracked*, and *MEL Magazine*, and has had his material curated into the New American History project at the University of Richmond. He has also been a content contributor to *Popular Science Magazine*, *Fixed Ops Magazine*, *The Pro Wrestling Post*, *Pro Wrestling Stories*, The International Pro Wrestling Hall of Fame, and The Bahamas Historical Society.

    In addition to writing, Ian was also an on-air reporter for the NBC News affiliate in Flint, Michigan. He is a graduate of the University of Michigan in Ann Arbor, earned a master's degree from Northwestern University's Medill School of Journalism, attended the Specs Howard School of Media Arts, and completed the Executive MBA program at the Quantic School of Business and Technology.

    Between 2016 and 2024, Ian co-authored the autobiographies of professional wrestlers Dan Severn, Dylan "Hornswoggle" Postl (along with Ross Owen Williams), Buggsy McGraw, Brian Blair, and Steve Keirn, with multiple books earning "Best Wrestling Book – Finalist" honors from *The Wrestling Observer* and the "Best of the Best" ranking from *The Pro Wrestling Torch*.

    He is also the author of "Bahamian Rhapsody: The Unofficial History of Pro Wrestling's Unofficial Territory," published in 2022, and "Gentleman Jack and Rough Rufus: The Rise of Black American Wrestling in 2025."

A Decided Novelty

Ian was inducted into the Pro Wrestling Author's Hall of Fame in 2024, and contributed to the 2025 Webby-Award-winning project "Leroy Smith: Michael Jordan's Myth."

www.ingramcontent.com/pod-product-compliance
Lightning Source LLC
Chambersburg PA
CBHW070732170426
43200CB00007B/500